The Economics of Education and the Education of an Economist

The Economics of Education and the Education of an Economist

Mark Blaug

Emeritus Professor of the Economics
of Education, University of London,
Consultant Professor of Economics,
University of Buckingham

NEW YORK UNIVERSITY PRESS
Washington Square, New York

Published in the U.S.A. in 1987 by
NEW YORK UNIVERSITY PRESS
Washington Square
New York, N.Y. 10003

Library of Congress Cataloging-in-Publication Data

Blaug, Mark
    The economics of education and the education of an economist /
Mark Blaug.
        p. cm.
    Bibliography: p.
    Includes index.
    ISBN 0-8147-1101-4 : $45.00
    1. Education—Economic aspects. 2. Education, Higher—Economic
aspects. 3. Education—Economic aspects—Developing countries.
I. Title.
LC65.B557 1987   87-16022
338.4'737—dc19   CIP

Manufactured in Great Britain

Contents

Introduction

I became interested in the economics of education in the early 1960s largely as a result of reading Theodore Schultz's presidential address to the American Economic Association on 'Investment in Human Capital' (1961)[1] and Edward Denison's book on *The Sources of Economic Growth in the US* (1962). Nevertheless, when I applied for the post of lecturer in the economics of education at the University of London Institute of Education in 1963, I still knew relatively little about the subject. Much to my surprise I was appointed to the post, no doubt because my interview panel knew even less than I did about this new specialisation in economics.

The first article in this book, published in 1965, was also one of my first publications in the economics of education. It is obvious from the very first page of that paper that I was then a True Believer in human capital theory and rate-of-return analysis. That point of view was at the time enjoying a considerable vogue in the United States but was not taken seriously in Britain. The British expert of the day, the late John Vaizey, my predecessor at the University of London Institute of Education, had published a book on *The Economics of Education* in 1962, which threw cold water on the notion that the calculated rate of return on educational investment – the estimated earnings differentials of better-educated individuals expressed as a proportion of the cost of acquiring the extra education – had any economic significance either for individuals seeking education or governments contemplating additional spending on education. I saw myself as meeting Vaizey's objections and importing into Britain the American enthusiasm for 'the human investment revolution in economic thought'. The paper was a success, at least as judged by the grapevine – it was said that I made one or two converts even among the civil servants in the Ministry of Education – and yet it strikes me now as a clever but not wholly convincing brief.

The next paper, 'Approaches to Educational Planning' (1967) coupled rate-of-return analysis with the manpower-requirements and social-demand approaches to educational planning and sought, in vain I think, to reconcile them with one another. The contrast that I drew in this essay between the three approaches to educational planning and the respective 'views of the world' that they reflected formed the backbone of my textbook, *Introduction to the Economics of Education* (1970), a book which I dare say marked the apogee of my 'faith' in human capital theory.

The first sign of cracks in the facade appear in the next paper on 'The Correlation Between Education and Earnings' (1972). On the surface, it appeared to be a defence once again of human capital theory and-all-that but its distinction between what I clumsily called the 'economic', 'sociological' and 'psychological' explanations of the correlation between education end earnings – in those days I was convinced that all great truths come in three – marked the beginning of a slide towards my present 'revisionist' position, summed up in the last essay in this section, 'Where Are We Now in the Economics of Education?' (1985).

In retrospect, the acid that corroded my confidence in human capital theory was the so-called 'screening hypothesis', the view that education acts principally not to enchance vocationally useful skills, but merely to select people in accordance with their native abilities. In the 1972 paper on 'The Correlation Between Education and Earnings', I was still trying to suppress the subversive implications of the screening hypothesis but in 'The Empirical Status of Human Capital Theory' (1976), I virtually capitulated to the half-truth of screening and 'credentialism'.

They say that it takes an alternative theory, and not just recalcitrant facts, to kill a theory and there is no doubt that the very formulation of the screening hypothesis by a number of different writers in the early 1970s made me take a fresh look at the empirical track-record of human capital theory: what I found was, not so much refuting evidence, as evidence that simply corroborated human capital theory; it failed to discriminate between it and alternative explanations of the same phenomena. In short, the evidence for human capital theory was such that as would confirm a believer but which would never persuade a sceptic.

So John Vaizey had been right after all fourteen years earlier? No, I do not think so. Apart from the fact that most of his objections were *a priori* and verified only by casual evidence, he also passed categorical judgement on a research programme that had hardly taken off in 1962.[2] It is a great mistake to pass premature judgement on young research programmes; to do so is to demand that all new ideas, if they are to be given any credence at all, must emerge full blown. Besides, even today the evidence for or against human capital theory is inconclusive and as for the screening hypothesis, it remains a tantalising but nevertheless unconfirmed conjecture.[3] In short, the evidence may excuse a 'jaundiced' attitude to human captial theory but it does not justify an outright rejection of it.

The essay on human capital theory is more than a survey of a particular brand of theorising in the economics of education. It is also an excercise in the methodology of economics, that is, an attempt to evaluate the past performance of a scientific theory with the aid of concepts borrowed from the philosphy of science. This is an interest of mine that I have pursued at greater length in my book, *The Methodology of Economics* (1980).

We turn now to contentious problems of educational policy in industrialised countries. The paper on recurrent education, written jointly with John Mace, another colleague at the University of London Institute of Education, takes up one of the great fads that periodically sweep through educatonal circles: the notion that we would all be better off if only secondary and particularly tertiary education were postponed to later life to alternate with stretches of gainful employment. This idea was all the rage in the early 1970s but seems almost to have disappeared from the scene in the late 1980s. The paper is a good example of the continuing relevance of the human capital theory: the idea that proposals to alter people's educational prospects must take account of their likely effects on the private rate of return to education served Mace and I in good stead in successfully predicting the early demise of the recurrent education movement.

Next comes a comprehensive discussion of the perennial issue of subsidies to higher education, co-authored by Maureen Woodhall. It surveys the pattern of government subsidies to higher education around Europe and concludes with recommendations for reforming that pattern consisting of a sharp rise in tuition fees coupled with an income contingent loans scheme (or graduate tax) for both undergraduate and postgraduate students. This paper is as relevant today as when it was written almost ten years ago: nothing has been done to alter the outrageous manner in which virtually all European governments finance higher education to the benefit of a privileged minority. So long as such scandals prevail, the economics of education will continue to have policy relevance!

In 1981 the British Labour Party finally adopted a programme for the abolition of private schools, a policy from which it had always drawn back in previous times. In the essay 'Can Independent Education Be Suppressed?' (1981), I registered my objections to the Labour Party case against private schools but, at the same time, endorsed their proposal to withdraw all indirect subsidies to private schools, thus displaying once again my habitual penchant for making enemies on both the right and the left.

No paper caused me more nail-biting than 'The Distributional Effects of Higher Education Subsidies'. The question it poses – can we equalise lifetime chance by particular educational policies? – is one of the great questions of our times but I am not at all sure that I produced a satisfactory answer to it in this paper. I reworked the argument with reference to Britain on two separate occasions[4] but continue to be troubled by the distributional effects of the British students grants system.

Higher education has been on the retreat throughout the industrialised world in the last decade or so. In 'Declining Subsidies to Higher Education' (1983) I ask in effect whether economic analysis can show that these cutbacks in higher education spending will have deleterious effects on economic growth. My answer in brief is NO, which does not of course imply that the cutbacks are justified.

I have spent a good many years thinking and writing about educational problems in the Third World. I have visited over thirty developing countries, often for months on end, and have lived in two. Early on I collaborated with Maureen Woodhall and Professor Richard Layard of the London School of Economics on a large-scale study of *The Causes of Graduate Unemployment in India* (1969) and this experience left me with a conviction that subsequent experience merely confirmed: the overexpansion of higher education is one of the scourges of the Third World. The first two papers in this section on developing countries will introduce the reader to the problem of educated unemployment as it manifests itself in India and the Philippines. I updated the Philippine figures when I participated in the International Labour Office's World Employment Mission to the Philippines, reaching essentially similar conclusions as in the 1972 article but on much firmer evidence.[5]

The next two articles on Thailand represent my only serious effort at calculating rates of return to education on the basis of data raised and analysed by myself.[6] They were written in the early 1970s when I was still wedded to human capital theory. My more mature thoughts on education in the Third World are summed up in the last paper of the book: 'Economics of Education in Developing Countries: Current Trends and New Priorities' (1979). The overexpansion of higher education in the Third World is associated with underinvestment in primary education and the vital importance of primary education in the development process is perhaps the principal point of agreement among virtually all economists who have ever studied the problems of education in the Third World.[7]

References

1. T.W. Schultz, 'Investment in Human Capital', *American Economic Review,* 51 (2), May 1961, reprinted in M. Blaug, ed., *Economics of Education 1. Selected Readings* (London: Penguin Books, 1968).

2. Vaizey and I spent years knocking each other in footnotes and book reviews in what was clearly a small tempest in an exceedingly small teapot. F.W. Musgrave, however, tried to make out that it was a battle of the giants: 'The Economics of Education in Britain: An Outsider's Attempt at Synthesis', *Journal of Human Resources,* Winter, 1978.

3. See S. Rosen, 'Human Capital: A Survey of Empirical Research', *Research in Labor Economics,* ed. R.G. Ehrenberg (Greenwich, Conn.: Jai Press 1977 I) for a sympathetic survey of human capital theory and see A.K. Whitehead, 'Screening and Education: A Theoretical and Empirical Survey', *British Review of Economic Issues,* Spring, 1981, and I.B. Tucker III, 'The Impact of Consumer Credentialism on Employee and Entrepreneur Returns to Higher Education', *Economics of Education Review,* 6 (1), 1987.

4. M. Blaug, 'Student Loans versus Student Grants', *Times Higher Education Supplement,* 19.12.80., p.9, and *ibid.,* 27.3.81, p. 10.

5. *Sharing in Development. A Programme of Employment, Equity and Growth for the Philippines.* Geneva: ILO, 1974, chap. 10.

6. For an updating of my calculations, see Pichai Charnsuphrindr, 'The Rate of Return to Investment in Thai Education', *Philippine Economic Journal,* 18 (3), 1979.

7. See e.g. C. Colclough, 'The Impact of Primary Schooling on Economic Development: A Review of the Evidence', *World Development,* 10 (3), 1982, and G. Psacharopoulos, 'Returns to Education: A Further International Update and Implications', *Journal of Human Resources,* 20 (4), Fall 1985.

Part I
Theory

[1]

The Rate of Return on Investment in Education in Great Britain

INTRODUCTION

A mere acquaintance with the history of economic thought is sufficient to show that the science of economics is almost as subject to fashions as the art of dressmaking. At the present time, "human capital formation," "human resource development," or, simply, "investment in human beings" is all the rage. As is so often the case with fads, the impetus has come from America. But studies of the returns from expenditures on education—to mention only the most important form of direct investment in the productivity of human beings—are not an American monopoly : the earliest work was done forty years ago in the Soviet Union and, in recent years, contributions have appeared in Mexico, Chile, Venezuela, and Israel. Rejection of this approach, however, does appear to be a national monopoly : Marshall's prescient comments notwithstanding, almost all the outspoken critics of what has come to be called the "rate of return approach" to educational investment have been British ; even the *Robbins Report*, while endorsing the investment-view of education in principle, expressed strong doubts on the side of measurement. The generally sceptical attitude in this country may account for the failure of the British Census of Population to secure the sort of information about earnings by age and education which is regularly collected by the decennial population census in the United States.

This paper is frankly intended as a defence of the investment approach to human resource development, with particular reference to formal education in a developed country like

3

Great Britain. It is not another survey of the literature.[1] Rather, it attempts to meet the many objections that have been raised against rate-of-return calculations and to demonstrate that, so far as advanced industrialised economies are concerned, none of them is really convincing.[2] In the belief that it is not enough simply to reiterate the popular dictum that "education pays," the paper includes an estimate of the private and social rates of return on educational investment in Great Britain by a staff-member of the National Economic Development Office, based, it must be admitted, on very crude data about the distribution of personal income by educational attainment that has recently become available. This article was written in the hope that we may soon have better data.[3] In its absence, there is reason to believe that policy decisions will be guided, or rather misguided, by purely notional estimates of the economic benefits of education.

I. THE RATE-OF-RETURN APPROACH

Casual impression suggests that people who remain at school beyond the statutory leaving age attain, on average, higher lifetime earnings than people of similar ability and family background who enter the labour force as soon as they

[1] For the few excellent examples of this genre, see W. G. Bowen, "Assessing the Economic Contribution of Education : An Appraisal of Alternative Approaches," *Higher Education. Report of the Committee under the Chairmanship of Lord Robbins (Robbins Report).* Cmd. 2154 (London: 1963), IV, pp. 80–94, reprinted in *Economic Aspects of Higher Education,* ed. S. E. Harris (Paris : 1964) ; A. M. Rivlin, "Research in the Economics of Higher Education : Progress and Problems," *Economics of Higher Education,* ed. S. J. Mushkin (Washington : 1962), pp. 360–73 ; F. Machlup, *The Production and Distribution of Knowledge in the United States* (Princeton : 1963), pp. 110–20 ; T. W. Schultz, *The Economic Value of Education* (New York : 1963), pp. 54–64 ; Lé Than Khôi, "Le rendement de l'éducation," *Tiers-Monde,* janvier-mars, 1964, pp. 105–39 ; and M. J. Bowman, "The New Economics of Education," *International Journal of the Educational Sciences,* I, 1, 1965, forthcoming.

[2] I am indebted to G. S. Becker, M. J. Bowman, H. L. Elvin, P. R. G. Layard, A. T. Peacock, M. Peston, T. W. Schultz, M. Steuer, J. Wiseman and M. Woodhall for suggestions and comments on an earlier version of this paper.

[3] The author is collaborating with Professor C. A. Moser, Director of the Unit for Economic and Statistical Studies on Higher Education at the London School of Economics, and Professor R. Stone of the Department of Applied Economics at the University of Cambridge in carrying out a sample survey of the adult population of Great Britain in respect of age, earnings, occupation, and education.

Rate of Return on Investment in Education in Great Britain   207

can. It is not immediately evident, however, that the extra future earnings outweigh the present costs incurred in staying at school. Therefore, the first task is to find a way of measuring the private yield of education, viewed as a type of investment by the individual in his own earning power. The standard method is to observe, for a particular year, and for different age cohorts, the net earnings differentials after tax that are associated with various amounts of education received, and then to calculate the internal rate of return which would equate the present value of these expected differentials, properly adjusted for income-determining factors other than education, to the private costs incurred in obtaining additional education. Social rates of return are derived from the private rates by allowing for the total public and private costs of education, and by adding in earnings that are taxed away. In other words, lifetime earnings are estimated from cross-section data classified by age, and we solve for the discount rate at which the present costs of extra education would yield the prospective stream of extra earnings. The argument is usually confined to different *levels* of education, but the approach is equally suitable to different *types* of secondary schools, different *channels* of higher education, and even to on-the-job training as a substitute for formal education. Similarly, separate rates of return can be calculated for arts and science graduates, males and females, whites and non-whites, and natives and immigrants. Even in America, however, lack of data has so far held back research on the effects of different kinds as distinct from the effects of more or less education.

Before turning to the policy implications of the rate-of-return approach, which is our principal concern in this paper, we must pause for a moment to consider the significance of rate-of-return calculations for private behaviour. Some American writers have postulated the existence of a rational calculus of educational and occupational choice, that is, the ability to equalise the present values of alternative lifetime income streams, differing both in amount and time-shape. The student or his parent is conceived as choosing between no less than two lifetime income profiles, one with immediate but relatively low earnings which then increase only gradually over time, the other with no earnings for several years followed by steeply rising earnings after graduation ; since future income means less than equivalent income now foregone, rational inter-temporal choice involves the comparison and equalisation, not of the *sums* of alternative lifetime income streams, but of their *present* values. As Adam Smith argued long ago, this implies relatively higher earnings in occupations that require additional schooling, or, turning it around, not obtaining additional schooling unless it leads to occupations with relatively higher earnings.[1]

Are private educational decisions economically rational in this sense ? How does one verify such an assumption ? One way is simply to ask people. But although there is a vast body of social survey data that indicates that students are principally motivated by vocational considerations in deciding to stay at school beyond the compulsory leaving age,[2] the method of testing hypotheses by inquiring directly into personal motives is inherently unsatisfactory. It is not what students or their parents think they are doing but what they actually do that concerns us. It is preferable to check assumptions about

[1]"When any expensive machine is erected, the extraordinary work to be performed by it before it is worn out, it must be expected, will replace the capital laid out upon it, with at least the ordinary profits. A man educated at the expense of much labour and time to any of those employments which require extraordinary dexterity and skill, may be compared to one of those expensive machines. The work which he learns to perform, it must be expected, over and above the usual wages of common labour, will replace to him the whole expense of his education, with at least the ordinary profits of an equally valuable capital." Adam Smith, *The Wealth of Nations*, Bk. I, Pt. I, Ch. X.

[2]E. Roper, *Factors Affecting the Admission of High School Seniors to College* (Washington, D.C. : 1949), p. XXI ; B. S. Hollinshead, *Who Should Go To College* (New York : 1952), pp. 135–85 ; C. C. Cole, Jr., *Encouraging Scientific Talent* (New Jersey : 1956), pp. 145–6, 163 ; M. Rosenberg, *Occupations and Values* (Glencoe, Ill. : 1957), pp. 11–6; Ministry of Education, 15 *to* 18. *A Report of the Central Advisory Council for Education, under the Chairmanship of G. Crowther.* (London : 1959), II, pp. 25–6 ; J. B. Lansing and C. Moriguchi, *How People Pay For College.* Survey Research Center (Ann Arbor : 1960), pp. 119–46 ; W. D. Furneaux, *The Chosen Few* (London : 1961), pp. 58–62 ; J. N. Morgan, M. H. David, W. J. Cohen, and H. F. Brazer, *Income and Welfare in the United States* (New York : 1962), pp. 356–7 ; *Robbins Report*, II(B), pp. 167–89 ; and R. Rice, "The Social and Educational Background and Anticipated Career Prospects of a Group of Students in a College of Advanced Technology," *British Journal of Educational Psychology*, November, 1964, pp. 264–5.

motives by looking at the behaviour that is predicted by these assumptions.

The private rate of return on the costs of the three years required to complete secondary school education in Great Britain in 1963, as calculated in the appendix below, is about 13 per cent.; the corresponding rate on three years of higher education is about 14 per cent. These yields are about 50 per cent. higher than those that can be earned by investing in equities and debentures. Even after allowing a considerable premium for the greater illiquidity and uncertainty of investment in human capital, it appears that private rates of return on educational investment exceed the yield of risk capital in the business sector. Now, the *Robbins Report* demonstrated the existence in this country of an excess demand for places in higher education, defined as an excess of qualified school leavers who apply for admission over the number of qualified applicants admitted.[1] This finding is consistent with the assumption that students will not voluntarily choose additional education unless the extra years of school attendance promise a rate of return significantly in excess of the yield of alternative investment opportunities ; in short, it is consistent with the hypothesis in question.[2] Unfortunately, given the artificial limitation on the

[1] For a definition of British "higher education," see *Robbins Report*, I, pp. 12–3.

[2] The reader may notice that we are switching back and forth between the language of the internal-rate-of-return or discounted-cash-flow approach (the rate which makes the algebraic sum of the discounted costs and benefits equal to zero) and that of the present-value rule (the value of the net returns when discounted to the present at a predetermined rate of interest), as if they were identical decision rules for ranking alternative investment proposals. But, in fact, the two criteria only lead to the same results if capital markets are perfectly competitive, if the contemplated proposals are completely divisible, if there is no interdependencies among the proposals, and if the benefits which are generated can be reinvested at their own internal rates of return up to the terminal date of the longer-lived alternative (for a review of the argument, see M. M. Dryden, "Capital Budgeting: Treatment of Uncertainty and Investment Criteria," *Scottish Journal of Political Economy*, March, 1963). It is obvious that the latter condition at any rate is violated with respect to earnings differentials associated with education, so that the strictly correct criterion, here as elsewhere, is the present-value rule, namely, that of accepting all income streams which have a positive present value at the market rate of interest. Nevertheless, this would give the same answers about educational choice in all the cases with which we will be concerned ; the internal-rate-of-return criterion is employed in the text simply because it is more intuitively appealing.

supply of places in higher education in Great Britain, it is hardly surprising to find evidence of excess demand : until we know what determines the position of the social supply curve of places, we cannot infer from the existence of excess demand that the private demand curve for education is a function of the "price" as defined by the yield of investment in schooling relative to the yield of all investment.[1]

Furthermore, a figure for a single year does not afford a very sensitive test of the hypothesis of a rational educational calculus. The American evidence, however, extends over two decades from 1939 to 1959 and, owing to the weight of private finance for higher education in the United States, there is virtually no rationing of places in American colleges. Looking at the private rates on return on investment in American high school and college education, as well as separate rates of return to additional years of high school and college education for white males, women, and Negroes, it is interesting to find that all of these yields are in conformity with observed changes in school attendance rates and with differential rates of entry to college on the part of different sorts of students.[2]

There are, of course, many other explanations of the phenomena under investigation. A popular alternative hypothesis accounts for the post-war "enrolment explosion" in most countries in terms of a radical shift in the taste for education, viewed as a consumer good. Unfortunately, this hypothesis will account for every observable change in the demand for education, whatever direction it takes. Another equally popular hypothesis is that a growing economy demands more skilled labour ; students are perfectly aware of this trend and realise

[1]Still, it is significant that the scarcity of university places in Great Britain first made itself felt in 1945/46 as a direct result of substantial grants for ex-service men and women under the Government's Further Education and Training Scheme (the British analogy to the American G.I. Bill). This extra demand had hardly been absorbed when the recommendations of the Minister of Education's Working Party on University Awards (1948) were put into effect, increasing the number and amounts of grants available to intending students to more than twice the pre-war levels, and thus sharply raising the private rate of return on investment in education.

[2]See G. S. Becker, *Human Capital. A Theoretical and Empirical Analysis, With Special Reference to Education.* (Princeton : 1964), pp. 91–3, 95, 101, 103.

they require additional education. But this explanation turns into the rate-of-return hypothesis, provided one grants that students also realise that extra education is not free. Still another interpretation argues that the bulge in the birthrate and the changing social composition of secondary school students are entirely responsible for all the observed facts. The data, such as it is, is not yet capable of definitely rejecting any of the contending hypothesis. What we can say at this stage is that it appears that students or their parents choose more education *as if* they were making a rational investment response to certain expected monetary and psychic returns. At any rate, no one has yet produced evidence that would falsify this assumption.[1]

The more interesting question is that of a possible conflict between the private demand for education as a function of prospective earnings and, hence, the demand from industry for educated people, and the public supply of school places as a function of the social rate of return on educational investment. The social as distinct from the private rate of return on three years of secondary schooling in this country is about 12·5 per cent. ; likewise, the social rate of return on six years of secondary and higher education is in the neighbourhood of 8 per cent. These yields are not very different from the rate of return which the State has come to expect from the nationalised industries. If the State decisions about education were rational in the same sense in which private decisions could be said to be rational, one might conclude that the recommendations of the *Robbins Report* were motivated by non-economic considerations. But that argument would beg the question : what is the maximand that determines the government's educational policy? When we calculate the social yield of education, we are not necessarily "explaining" social decisions by testing some behavioural assumption, but rather attempting to clarify the nature of these decisions and, presumably, to affect them in some way. Thus, appraisals of the private and the social rate of return on investment in education call for quite different

[1]The problem is further explored in the author's forthcoming paper : "An Economic Interpretation of the Private Demand for Extra Education," *Economica*, 1966.

criteria of judgment. Neglect of this consideration has produced considerable confusion in the literature. Associated with this confusion is the argument that the private returns do not matter because the most important benefits of education are indirect and external to the educated individual. It is not always appreciated that even if this were true, it would still leave us with the task of explaining why people choose more or less education, or one kind of education rather than another : indirect economic benefits by definition do not determine individual choice. The indirect benefits of education, however, should enter into the calculation of the social rate of return which has another *raison d'être* than that of predicting behaviour. In what follows, we will rigidly distinguish between the private and the social level of discourse.

II. An Omnibus of Objections

A review of the literature on the subject shows that the various objections that have been advanced against rate-of-return calculations fall broadly into six classes : (1) education, earnings, endowed ability, individual motivation, and social class are all intercorrelated and no one has yet succeeded in satisfactorily isolating the pure effect of education on earnings ; (2) it is assumed that people are motivated solely by consideration of the financial gains of additional school attendance, thus ignoring both the nonpecuniary attractions of certain occupations and the consumption benefits of education ; (3) the calculations depend on the projection of future trends from cross-section evidence, thus neglecting historical improvements in the quality of education as well as the effect of the secular growth of education on prospective earnings differentials ; (4) existing earnings differentials in favour of educated people reflect, not differences in their contribution to productive capacity, but rather long-established social conventions in an inherently imperfect labour market ; hence, rate-of-return studies tell us nothing about the role of education in economic growth ; (5) the direct benefits of education are quantitatively less important than the indirect spillover benefits and the latter are not adequately reflected in a social rate of return which simply relates income differentials before tax to the total

Rate of Return on Investment in Education in Great Britain 213

resource costs of education ; and (6) social rates of return have ambiguous policy implications because educational authorities have other goals than that of maximising the net national product. We will now discuss each of these objections in turn.

III. Multiple Correlations among the Income-Determining Variables

The four leading critics of the rate-of-return approach—whom we will meet again and again in the following pages—all agree in denying the possibility of attributing a definite portion of the observed differentials in earnings to education alone.[1] There is a difficulty here and it must be conceded that most of the early contributions to the literature failed to standardise in any way for various income-determining factors other than education. But as early as 1954, one American study showed that the earnings of ex-students rose with additional years of college education even after adjusting for differences in IQ scores, class rank in high school, and father's occupation.[2] Since then we have been furnished with an exhaustive analysis

[1]According to J. Vaizey, "There is a multiple correlation between parental wealth, parental income, access to educational opportunity, motivation in education, access to the best jobs and 'success' in later life. Above all, there is sheer native wit and ability which will 'out' despite all educational handicaps. It follows, then, that all the statistics may go to show is that incomes are unequal, and that education is unequally distributed ; there may be no necessary causal relationship between education and income," *The Economics of Education* (London : 1962), p. 45 ; T. Balogh and P. P. Streeten agree : "Expenditure on education is highly correlated to income and wealth of parents, to ability and motivation, to educational opportunities such as urban residence and proximity to educational centres, to access to well-paid jobs through family and other connections, any of which could either by itself or in conjunction with any of the others, account for superior earnings," "The Coefficient of Ignorance," *Bulletin of the Oxford University Institute of Economics and Statistics*, May, 1963, p. 102 ; the sole American critic carries the argument to its logical extreme: "Amount of Education is at least partly a matter of choice. As long as this is true, no matter how many factors have been considered, one can never be certain that there are not some unanalyzed variables influencing the choice which in themselves are responsible for the income differential attributed to education," H. G. Shaffer, "Investment in Human Capital : Comment," *American Economic Review*, December, 1961, p. 1030n.

[2]D. Wolfle, *America's Resources of Specialized Talent* (New York : 1954); and D. Wolfle and J. G. Smith, "The Occupational Value of Education for Superior High School Graduates," *Journal of Higher Education*, April, 1956, summarised by D. Wolfle in *Higher Education in the United States. The Economic Problem*, ed. S. E. Harris (Camb., Mass. : 1960), pp. 178–9.

of a national probability sample of heads of American households, isolating the pure effect of education on earnings with the
aid of multivariate analysis that allows separately for all the
various factors that influence the level of personal income : age,
formal   education,   on-the-job   training,   sex,   race,   native
intelligence, need-achievement drive, parents' education, family
size, father's occupation, religion, geographic region, city size,
occupational   choice,   occupational   mobility,   mortality,   unemployment,   and   hours   of   work.[1]   Multivariate   analysis
assumes that variables do not interact with one another, so
that their combined effect is simply the sum of their separate
effects.   Since the variables are themselves closely correlated,
however, there is a tendency to remove too much and therefore
to understate the pure effects of education, as the authors
themselves are the first to point out.[2]   Despite this built-in
tendency towards over-adjustment, education emerges in this
study as the single most powerful determinant of family income:
to give a concrete example, factors other than age and education
together "explain" only 40 per cent. of the gross unadjusted
earnings differentials between high school and college graduates
in the age.group 18-34, and only 12 per cent. in the age group
35-74.   As the authors conclude :   "objections to the use of
simple average earnings of different age and education groups
on   the   grounds   of   spurious   correlation   are   correct   but
quantitatively not terribly important." [3]

    In his recent book on *Human Capital*, Becker marshals all
the available American evidence on the influence of ability,
motivation, and home environment.[4]   He observes that we now

---

[1]Morgan, and others, *op. cit.*, pp. 387–427.

[2]For example, the most important factor determining the level of
    education achieved by the head of a household is not his IQ score or
    his ability measured in other ways, nor the income of his parents, but
    the educational attainment of his father (*ibid.*, pp. 359–84, 391–2,
    401–2).   In drawing conclusions about the effects of education on
    earnings, this inter-generation effect is eliminated by assuming that a
    variable like father's education influences the earnings of the head of
    the household directly without affecting his terminal education age.

[3]J. N. Morgan and M. H. David, "Education and Income," *Quarterly
    Journal of Economics*, August, 1963, pp. 436–7.   Owing to the
    tendency to over-adjust for ability and parental influences, they find
    only a modest rate of return of 4·6 per cent. on school years completed
    for a 1960 cross section of the United States.

[4]Becker, *op. cit.*, pp. 79–88.

Rate of Return on Investment in Education in Great Britain   215

have five independent studies which standardise the earnings differentials between typical high school and college graduates for various scattered measures of "ability" and "social class origins"—including a striking early study of the incomes of brothers with different amounts of education[1]—all of which suggest that college education itself is the major determinant of the extra lifetime income of college graduates. Allowing separately for IQ, high school class rank, and father's occupation, Becker concludes that the ability-cum-social-class adjustment reduces the private rate of return on college education actually received by a typical college graduate from 13 per cent. to 11·5 per cent., and the rate that may be expected by a typical high school graduate from 13 per cent. to just under 10 per cent., depending on whether we standardise the earnings of college graduates for the distribution of ability among college students or among high school students. Similarly, Denison, using much the same material, has now concluded that 66 per cent. of the gross earnings differentials between college and high school graduates is due to education alone.[2] Translating Denison's figure into rate-of-return terminology, it appears that both authors agree more or less on the magnitude of the required adjustment, leaving education substantially unaffected as a generator of higher future earnings.[3]

The British figures, given above, referred to earnings differentials *attributable* to education, that is, after multiplying the gross earnings differentials by the "Denison coefficient" alpha, varying from 0·6 for secondary school leavers to 0·66 for those with higher education, to take account of the fact that some of the observed differentials associated with extra

[1]D. E. Gorseline, *The Effect of Schooling Upon Income* (Bloomington, Ind. : 1932).

[2]E. F. Denison, "Proportion of Income Differentials Among Education Groups Due to Additional Education : The Evidence of the Wolfle-Smith Survey," *The Residual Factor and Economic Growth*, ed. J. Vaizey (Paris : 1964), p. 97.   In his book *The Sources of Economic Growth in the United States* (N.Y. : 1962), pp. 69–70, he assumed arbitrarily that the correct figure was 67·7 per cent., derived from an equally arbitrary figure of 60 per cent. of the gross income differentials between elementary school graduates and all those with additional education.

[3]See Chart III in the appendix below for a graphic method of translating from one to the other.

education are attributable to individual differences in ability and family environment. In the absence of definitive British evidence, it is not clear whether it is legitimate to apply an American alpha-coefficient to British earnings : on the one hand, the stock of education embodied in the labour force is smaller in Britain than the United States, which argues for a premium on education in this country and hence a higher value for alpha ; on the other hand, the tripartite character of British secondary education suggests that the selective effects of social class determinants operate with much greater force here than in the United States, and this argues for a lower alpha-value. On balance, it is likely that an alpha-coefficient of 0·6 for secondary school leavers is somewhat on the high side, given the finding that "early leaving" is highly correlated with social class.[1] But, in the same sense, the true alpha-coefficient for university graduates is probably much in excess of 0·66. Once students have entered advanced sixth forms, the divisive influence of social-class membership, with all that it implies in differential home background, have largely ceased to operate : the evidence shows that it has very little effect in deciding whether a student in the upper sixth applies to a university, none at all in determining whether he is accepted or not, and very little in governing his performance in university courses.[2] Social class origins is only one of the components of the alpha-coefficient ; nevertheless, it is not to be doubted that students in higher education are more homogeneous with respect to measured ability than secondary school students. In consequence, the social rate of return on investment in higher education in Great Britain, looked upon as a yield actually received rather than an anticipated yield, is nearer 9 than 6·5 per cent.[3]

Nothing we have said denies the fact that social class origins, in this country as well as in the United States, largely

[1] The evidence for Great Britain is set forth in the *Robbins Report*, I, pp. 38–84.

[2] See Furneaux, *op. cit.*, p. 71 ; *Robbins Report*, pp. 52–3 and *Robbins Report*, II(A), pp. 135–6, 155–6.

[3] The reader may check this statement for himself by reading off the rate of return corresponding to various alpha-values in Chart III.

Rate of Return on Investment in Education in Great Britain 217

determine who it is that obtains additional education ; nevertheless, they do not explain why the better educated receive higher lifetime incomes. In other words, those who stay on at school voluntarily beyond the leaving age seem to require secondary and higher education to translate favourable home background and superior measured ability into higher earnings.[1] Summing up : it is perfectly true that better educated people have better educated parents, come from smaller homes, obtain financial help more easily, live in cities, are better motivated, achieve higher scores on intelligence and aptitude tests, attain better academic grade records, gain more from self-education, and generally live longer and are healthier. But unless we adopt Shaffer's methodological position that all correlations are worthless if they are not simple correlations, we must arrive at the conclusion that the critics are simply wrong when they state that "there is no demonstrable connection between education and later earnings which is also not as close as the connection between birth and earnings."[2] Apparently it takes a university graduate to believe that endowed ability is the major cause of the higher earnings of university graduates !

We have not quite finished, however, with the problems created by multiple correlations. Apart from all their other advantages, educated people also tend to receive more on-the-job training than less educated individuals.[3] Hence, earnings differentials attributable to education include the monetary returns to associated on-the-job training. Indeed, the same is true of other forms of human capital formation : for example, the income benefits of education differ for each different level of investment in medical care. Contrary to intuitive impression,

[1] Needless to say, this is only true on average for given age cohorts. So long as abilities to learn, opportunities to learn, and quality of schools differ, some individuals with less education will earn more than their better educated contemporaries. Indeed, there is considerable variation in the rates of return within age cohorts. (See H. P. Miller, "Annual and Lifetime Income in Relation to Education," *American Economic Review*, December, 1960, p. 963 ; Becker, *op. cit.*, pp. 104–13).

[2] J. Vaizey, "The Role of Education in Economic Development," *Planning Education for Social and Economic Development*, ed. H. S. Parnes (Paris : 1963), p. 40.

[3] J. Mincer, "On-the-Job Training : Costs, Returns, and Some Implications," *Journal of Political Economy*, Supplement : October, 1962, pp. 59–60.

however, this only biases one's estimates of the rate of return on education if the yield of these other forms of investment in human beings differs systematically from the yield of education. When the yields are the same, expenditures on labour training or health simply add as much to the costs as to the returns of human capital. In the absence of any knowledge of these other rates of return, therefore, there is no reason to think that we have necessarily over or underestimated the rate of return on education.[1]

IV. THE PSYCHIC RETURNS TO EDUCATION

We will forego the pleasure of documenting the argument that rate-of-return calculations ignore the consumption-benefits of education and the nonpecuniary benefits of certain occupations that are only accessible to the highly educated : it has been mentioned not only by every critic but also by every advocate of the investment-approach to education. The standard method of dealing with the consumption aspects is either to subtract a notional consumption component from educational costs or to add some estimate of the consumption-benefits to the monetary returns.[2] In either case, of course, the effect is to increase the yield of investment in education.

However, the tacit premise that the psychic returns from consuming education are necessarily positive requires further examination. In the first place, the essential distinction that is being made is between present and future satisfactions, that is, between the enjoyment of education for its own sake and the anticipated enjoyment of a higher monetary and/or psychic income in the future. A large part of what is usually thought of as the consumption component of education is, in fact, forward-looking, involving the consumption over time of the services of a durable consumer good ; motivated as it is by utilities that accrue in the future, it is more akin to investment than to consumption. No doubt, this sort of consumption-benefit is positive and ought to be added to the rate of return on investment in education. But the same thing is not true of

[1]Becker, *op. cit.*, pp. 88–90. See also Mincer's brief discussion of the rates of return on formal education versus on-the-job training, *op. cit.*, pp. 63–6.

[2]Schultz, *op. cit.*, pp. 8, 54–6 ; Bowen, *op. cit.*, p. 89.

the current consumption of education, which, for all we know, may have negative utility for the average student.[1] And if this be granted, perhaps we ought to subtract something from the rate of return as conventionally calculated.

The more we think about it, the more we realise how arbitrary is any assertion about the consumption-benefits of education, whether they are reaped in the present or in the future. Since tastes are directly affected by schooling, we are faced with making intertemporal comparisons of utility with a yardstick that is itself constantly changing : the value for a sixth former of the future enjoyment of university education is surely different from his appraisal after university graduation ? It is true that there is an extraordinary consensus on the positive psychic benefits of education, but it is a consensus of educated people whose taste for learning has been affected by the learning process itself. It is not so much that the belief that education makes for a richer life is a value judgment but that it is *ex post facto* and, hence, of a different kind from the *ex ante* value judgment that governs the choice to acquire more education. John Stuart Mill used to say that "the uncultivated cannot be competent judges of cultivation," but he did not realise that the converse is just as true. Is it meaningful to ask someone with a Ph.D. to debate the proposition that ignorance is bliss ?[2]

It could be argued that the decision to stay at school beyond the statutory age is typically made by parents, while the choice of subjects to study is left to the student. Hence, the decision to choose more or less education is, indeed, made by someone who places an unambiguously positive value on both the present and the future consumption-benefits of education.

---

[1] The fact that the major single cause of drop-outs is poor educational performance suggests that there is enormous variation in the value that different students would assign to the present enjoyment of education.

[2] The discrepancy between expected and realised satisfactions is a familiar problem in welfare economics. It is usually slurred over by interpreting the standard assumption of constant tastes to mean perfect foresight on the part of each individual about his preferences for future as yet unexperienced satisfactions. Even if we accept this interpretation for general purposes, it seems inadmissible in treating the welfare aspects of education, for education alters rather than widens the range of choices.

In this case, the question whether we have biased the rate of return downwards by ignoring the consumption benefits turns into a question of fact : do students and parents agree about the value of remaining at school beyond the leaving age ?[1] It would seem that at this stage we simply do not know whether to add or to subtract the consumption-benefits from the investment-benefits of education. This is not to say that we can never find out. If people's choices about education were found to be inconsistent with conventionally calculated private rates of return, it might mean that they were motivated by the consumption-benefits. For the time being, however, the consumption hypothesis may be ruled out by Occam's Razor.

As soon as we tackle questions of social policy, however, the consumption-benefits come back to plague us. If the electorate is persuaded that education is a good thing in its own right, the *social* rate of return computed from earnings differentials attributable to education must be viewed as a minimum figure, to which something must be added to reflect the value of education as a consumer good. This solution will not satisfy everyone, for there are educators who appear to believe that the economist's mania for quantifying everything will lead to a perversion of the human values of education. Be that as it may, the point of calculating the social rate of return is simply that it provides a summary of the measurable economic effects of education. If it is asserted that certain immeasurable effects are more important, it does at least permit separation of the positive and normative elements in such declarations of faith.

We come now to a different kind of psychic income from education : the nonpecuniary benefits of certain occupations which require more than average education. Nonpecuniary attractions as such create no special problems for our purposes: it is true that they give rise to compensating variations in earnings but this does not matter provided the nonpecuniary

[1]Summarising all the evidence of public opinion polls taken of cross sections of the American population as far back as possible, A. J. Jaffe and W. Adams conclude : "A much smaller proportion of the children have attitudes and intentions favourable to college enrollment than do the parents" : "College Education for U.S. Youth : The Attitudes of Parents and Children," *American Journal of Economics and Sociology,* July, 1964, p. 273.

Rate of Return on Investment in Education in Great Britain   221

attraction is a feature of the job, equally attractive to all job applicants. Unfortunately, studies of the prestige-ranking of occupations suggest that more educated people attach a higher than average value to the nonpecuniary aspects of work. Thus, occupations with considerable nonpecuniary benefits are highly correlated with the distribution of education in the labour force, and to ignore this factor is to *under*state the private rate of return to education.[1]

It is not obvious that the magnitude of this bias is very large. Certainly, it is not significant enough to reverse the positive correlation between education and monetary earnings for given age groups. But once again, the problem takes on new colours when we consider the social rather than the private rate of return. From the viewpoint of social policy, non-pecuniary alternatives can be dismissed as a neutral factor. The reason for this, as Bowen explains, is that they affect only the supply and not the demand for labour, and, therefore, do not distort the relationship between earnings and a man's productive contribution to national output.[2] Employers can offer less for attractive jobs ; hence, two jobs differing in their nonpecuniary attractions, but otherwise the same, will differ in relative earnings but this difference will simply reflect the relative scarcities of labour available for the two jobs. The only exception to this is the case where nonpecuniary attractions take the form of fringe benefits that impose extra costs on the employer—for example, paid holidays, expense accounts, subsidised housing, and so forth. Since it is likely that such fringe benefits occur more frequently in education-intensive industries, an upward adjustment is required in the social rate of return to education. Thus, nonpecuniary alternatives impart a downward bias to both the private and the social rates of return, but the two biases are not uniquely related because they spring from different causes.

V. CURRENT EARNINGS AND LIFETIME EARNINGS

Rate-of-return analysis of education usually involves a time-series projection of earnings from cross-section data. But

[1]Shaffer, op. cit., pp. 1031–32.
[2]Bowen, *op. cit.*, pp. 83–4.

this is not an inherent feature of the approach. If the sixth
year of secondary schooling cost £1,000 and if the earnings
differential for the first year relative to those who left in the
fifth form is £100, the gross rate of return is 16 per cent. ; if a
5 per cent. depreciation rate is applied, the net return becomes
£50, a rate of return of 15 per cent. ; whatever happens in
subsequent years, the observed returns of that first year are
unaffected. This example treats schooling precisely as one
would an investment in a new machine. But the example is
unrealistic : the fifth former would have acquired a year of
work experience so that the earnings differential would be much
less, with the result that the net rate of return in the first year
might be negative. All this is to say that the effort to project
lifetime earnings is dictated by the extraordinary long pay-off
period from education.[1]

The diffusion of more and more education in successive age
cohorts tends, everything else being the same, to narrow
earnings differentials at any age level. There is the danger,
therefore, that future income differentials will, in fact, be
smaller than those indicated by present cross-section statistics.
This suggests that there may be an inherent upward bias in
present methods of estimating the rate of return to investment
in education, a fact which has played some role in sapping
confidence about the entire approach.

The standard answer to this objection is to point to
American evidence that the earnings differentials between high
school and college graduates have remained fairly constant
since 1939, apparently because the demand for more educated
workers has been rising at about the same rate as the supply of
college graduates. Indeed, in the last decade, the differentials
in the United States seem to have widened rather than

---

[1]This is illustrated by one of Becker's striking calculations : with a rate
of return of 13 per cent. to the 1949 cohort of male college graduates,
the rate is still negative ten years after graduation, and only about
6 per cent. after fifteen years, *op. cit.*, p. 112.

Rate of Return on Investment in Education in Great Britain 223

narrowed.[1] Thus, it seems that cross-section data do not necessarily yield irrelevant results. But this conclusion is subject to one qualification. To the extent that the quality of education is improving all the time, so that each new cohort of school leavers is better educated than the last, estimates of lifetime earnings from current earnings do *under*state the expected rate of return on education. Balogh and Streeten seem to have this in mind when they say : "Since the time-flow over a lifetime of the earnings of the educated is quite different from that of the uneducated, lifetime earnings now must be calculated as returns on education in the nineteen-twenties. To conclude from those returns anything about to-day's returns is like identifying a crystal radio set with Telstar." [2] Unfortunately, we know very little about secular changes in the quality of educational output. We cannot even agree on the meaning of "quality" in education, and so far there have been few serious efforts to measure it. Still, the best guess is that it has been improving at all levels.[3] But to compare it with improvements in the output of the radio industry over the last generation is to grossly exaggerate a well-taken point.

The possibility of error in the projection of lifetime earnings can be built directly into the calculated rates of return, in the form of an upper and lower limit for each stated error-factor. Suppose we had over or underestimated next year's earnings differentials associated with extra education by one per cent., and the following year's differentials by another one per cent., compounding the error each year by a further one per cent. ;

[1] H. P. Miller, "Income in Relation to Education," *American Economic Review*, December, 1960, pp. 967–9 ; and J. Morgan and C. Lininger, "Education and Income : Comment," *Quarterly Journal of Economics*, May, 1964, pp. 346–8. The differentials in question refer to the *absolute* income on investment in education. Since the better educated receive higher earnings, a decline in relative earnings differentials is compatible with an increase in absolute earnings differentials. Surprisingly enough, however, relative earnings differentials associated with extra education seem also to have widened in the same decade. (See Becker, *op. cit.*, pp. 52–55, 128–35, for a discussion of trends in the rates of return to education since 1900).

[2] Balogh and Streeten, *op. cit.*, p. 102.

[3] Some material indicators of the improvement are : the rise in the number of days attended per school-year ; the growth in the number of qualified teachers ; the rise in the real earnings of teachers ; the rise in current expenditures per student ; the rise in capital expenditures per student ; and so forth.

this mistake would mean that earnings differentials fifty years hence would in fact be more than 50 per cent. greater, or about 35 per cent. less, than what we had assumed. Nevertheless, as is shown in the appendix below, this would only reduce the rate of return on investment in education by about one per cent., for the simple reason that the early years get a much heavier weight. The rate of return is not sensitive to the entire age-earnings profiles of educated people ; provided we correctly project the next five or ten years' earnings, significant shifts in earning patterns in three or four decades do not substantially affect the results.

When all is said and done, cross-section data have a distinct advantage over genuine life-cycle data in that they are free from the influence of the trade cycle and implicitly provide estimates in money of constant purchasing power. Furthermore, they reflect the way in which private choices are actually made : an average person forms his expectations of the financial benefits of additional years of schooling by comparing the present earnings of different occupations requiring various amounts of education, that is, by cross-section comparisons.

Cross-section earnings data have the further advantage of providing reliable estimates of the cost of student-time as a resource input in the educational system. The appropriate measure of this input is the earnings of people of similar age, ability, and prior education who are currently in employment, and this information can be read off directly from age-education-earnings data for a given year. Students' time is, of course, only one of the inputs, the others being the time of teachers and administrators, and the use of buildings, equipment, and materials. Although the latter are measured directly by "what is put in," while the former is measured indirectly by "what is done without," the distinction is one of statistical expediency, not of theoretical principle : after all, the actual money outlays on teachers, plant, and equipment are themselves only estimates of the goods and services foregone for other purposes. Admittedly, all these estimates, including that of earnings foregone, are only reliable indicators of opportunity costs for *marginal* changes. For example, for a major shift in resource allocation, such as raising the school leaving age by a year, the use of cross-section earnings to estimate the value of students' time minimizes the consequent loss in output. Similarly, since there is evidence that the personal incidence of unemployment is correlated with the amount of education received, estimates of earnings foregone in a less than fully employed economy will tend to understate the loss in output from additional investment in education when this extra investment forms part of a general spending policy designed to secure full employment.[1]

All this may sound like a parade of well-worn truths but, alas, these truths have not won universal assent. According to Vaizey, "the inclusion of income foregone in the costs of education opens the gate to a flood of approximations which would take the concept of national income away from its origin as an estimation of the measurable flows of the economy." Furthermore, he adds, "if income foregone is added to educational costs, it must also be added to other sectors of the economy (notably housewives, mothers, unpaid sitters-in, voluntary work of all sort)"; also "it would be necessary to adjust the costs by some notional estimate of the benefits incurred while being educated, and these are usually considerable." [2] Upon close inspection, it appears that this paragraph consists of a misunderstanding of national income accounting, followed by two non sequiturs.[3] To measure the net flow of goods and services in the economy is one thing; to measure the real cost of a particular activity is another. The fallacy of identifying the two is made apparent by substituting "unemployment" for "education" in Vaizey's leading sentence. The equivalent argument then reads: it would be wrong to include incomes foregone in a calculation of the cost of unemployment because measured national income does not include the goods and services the unemployed would have produced if they had been working.

[1]For a definitive discussion of these problems, see M. J. Bowman, "The Costing of Human Resource Development," *The Economics of Education. Conference of the International Economic Association.* (London : 1965, forthcoming) ; see also B. A. Weisbrod, "Education and Investment in Human Capital," *Journal of Political Economy,* Supplement : October, 1962, pp. 122–3.

[2]Vaizey, *Economics of Education,* p. 43.

[3]See Becker, *op. cit.,* p. 74n.

These have not always been Vaizey's views.[1] In recent writings, however, he has reiterated his objections to counting earnings foregone, and his views have received some endorsement.[2] All this is very surprising from an author who, in other contexts, seems perfectly amenable to "a flood of approximations." For example, after discussing and finally rejecting the rate-of-return approach in *The Economics of Education*, Vaizey turns suddenly to cost/benefit analysis of public works, explains the methods that were used to calculate the probable costs and anticipated benefits of the London-Birmingham Motorway, and concludes "this is the most realistic procedure for calculating the returns to investment in education," without any indication of the fact that cost/benefit analysis is exactly the same thing as rate-of-return analysis![3]

We conclude that, whatever the temptation of making out the most appealing case for additional education expenditures by leaving out some of the costs, we must take account of the earnings foregone by students in calculating both the private and the social rate of return, and this, in fact, has been the standard

[1] In *The Costs of Education* (London : 1958), p. 125, he admitted that "the education accounts understate the true cost to the economy of the educational expenditure" by the amount of "the wages that people would have earned." And in an article on "Education as Investment in Comparative Perspective," *Comparative Education Review*, October, 1961, p. 99, he actually estimated the incomes foregone by students in the United Kingdom but mistakenly added to this their maintenance costs. In this article he also remarked parenthetically that "it is clearly important that investment in different levels of education should be compared with appropriate rates of return." (p. 101).

[2] See Vaizey, *Planning Education for Social and Economic Development*, p. 40 ; R. F. Lyons, "Formulating Recommendations on Educational Needs," *ibid.*, pp. 246–7 ; Balogh and Streeten, *op. cit.*, pp. 101–2 ; S. E. Harris, "General Problems of Education and Manpower," *Economic Aspects of Higher Education*, ed. S. E. Harris (Paris : 1964), pp. 13, 50–1, 56 ; J. Burkhead, *Public School Finance. Economics and Politics* (Syracuse : 1964), p. 5.

[3] *Economics of Education*, pp. 48–9.

Rate of Return on Investment in Education in Great Britain 227

practice.[1] The necessity of doing so in calculating the social yield is almost self-evident. But even with respect to the private yield, to ignore foregone earnings is to seriously misrepresent the nature of private decisions about education : it is foregone earnings that explain why so many able children from low-income families do not stay at school beyond the statutory age, despite the fact that the out-of-pocket costs of continuing school are minimal, particularly in this country. The American evidence suggests that foregone earnings constitute over half of the total resource costs of high school and college and about 75 per cent. of the private costs borne by students. In Great Britain, foregone earnings represent 34 per cent. of the total costs of higher education and nearly 100 per cent. of the private costs, given the fact that student grants now cover nearly all approved fees and maintenance costs.[2] Standard grants for maintenance even cover about 40 per cent. of earnings foregone but they still leave the average student paying indirectly for about 25 per cent. of the total costs of higher education. In consequence, even free university education would not be completely free, and the private rate of return to university education is far from being infinitely high.

VI. A Non–Competitive Labour Market ?

"The wage-system," according to Vaizey, "is, in fact a system of administered prices. Therefore, these measurements of the rate of return to education are measuring the consequences of a process of market imperfections so serious as to

[1] See Schultz, *op. cit.*, pp. 27–32. The Memorandum submitted by H. M. Treasury to the Robbins Committee allows for the fact that students would consume more if they were working by deducting from earnings foregone by students the difference between consumption as students and consumption if not students (*Robbins Report, Evidence*, I, pp. 1973–5). But this appears to be a mistake : the fact that an individual consumes less if he is a student does not reduce the loss of output involved in keeping him at school ; what it does is raise the real income of the rest of the community at the expense of the student. Unless we argue that the welfare of students counts less heavily than the welfare of the employed population, there are no grounds for treating the asceticism of students as a reduction in the resource costs of education. Even from the point of view of the private calculus, reduced consumption is one of the sacrifices of alternatives which ought to be included in our estimates of what the student foregoes to stay at school.

[2] *Robbins Report*, II(B), pp. 216–23 ; IV, pp. 148, 153.

invalidate the results."[1] Balogh and Streeten include the point
about imperfect labour markets in a more comprehensive
indictment of rate-of-return analysis : "The American data,
which are mostly used, do not provide evidence whether
expenditure on education is a *cause* or *effect* of superior incomes ;
they do not show, even if we could assume it to be a condition
of higher earnings, whether it is a *sufficient* or *necessary* condition
of growth, and they do not separate *monopolistic* and *other
forces* influencing differential earnings, which are correlated
with, but not caused by, differential education." To which they
add, a page later : "Much of the higher earnings is not a return
on education but a monopoly rent on (1) the scarcity of parents
who can afford to educate their children well and (2) the
restrictions in members permitted into a profession in which
existing members have a financial interest in maintaining
scarcity." [2]

The issue before us is, not whether there are imperfections
in the labour market, but whether these are so significant as to
invalidate rate-of-return calculations. It is not immediately
evident where to draw the line, but, presumably, what is meant
is a situation in which relative earnings do not correspond
systematically to relative marginal productivities and, hence,
do not uniquely reflect a worker's contribution to the national
product. Do the critics really mean what they say ? Vaizey, for
example, having flatly declared that wages are administered
prices, goes on to argue that a shortage of a particular skill
leads to a rise in the earnings of that skill, or to queues of firms
if market imperfections keep wages "below what they would
have been under free competition." [3] Similarly, an excess
supply leads to a decline in salaries : "teaching has become a
profession . . . whose relative salary position has deteriorated,
reflecting a growing abundance of educated talent and a decline
in the quality of teachers." [4] Thus he, at any rate, concedes
that the market mechanism governs the level of wages and

[1]Vaizey, *Economics of Education*, p. 45.

[2]Balogh and Streeten, *op. cit.*, pp. 101, 102.

[3]Vaizey, *op. cit.*, pp. 105–6.

[4]*Ibid.*, p. 110 ; also p. 112.

Rate of Return on Investment in Education in Great Britain   229

salaries, even the salaries of teachers which, after all, are administered by the State.[1] And to say that the market forces impinge upon wages and salaries is equivalent to saying that earnings are being continuously brought into line with relative productivities.

Of course, it is not enough to assert that earnings by and large reflect the push and pull of market forces. Such a defence is so vague that no observation could refute it. The major testable implications of a competitive theory of wages and salaries are (1) that positive excess demand for a skill leads to a rise in its price and (2) that the price of a skill varies directly with the cost of acquiring it. If these implications were refuted by experience, we would indeed be justified in regarding earnings as administered prices. But, as a matter of fact, there is more than enough evidence to show that earnings do rise in a seller's market and, in addition, the very data in question show that higher earnings do accrue to people who have invested in acquiring special skills. In short, the shoe is really on the other foot : if relative earnings reflect, not relative productivities, but family connections, traditional conventions, the snob-value of a university degree, nepotism, entry restrictions in trade unions and professional organisations, politically determined wage administration or any other market imperfection one might care to mention, how is it that more than 60 per cent. of gross earnings differentials are directly attributable to education alone ?

Rate-of-return analysis, despite what critics are always implying does not assume that markets are competitive. On the contrary, it affords a test of the hypothesis that labour markets are competitive. The notion that a relatively high

[1]It must be kept in mind that 45 per cent. of the 450,000 university graduates and about 60 per cent. of the 750,000 people with full-time higher education in Great Britain in 1961 were public servants, that is, worked in education, health, civil service, local government, armed forces, nationalised industries, and government research establishments, with as many as 45 per cent. of those with full-time higher education teaching in schools, colleges, and universities (see C. A. Moser, R. G. Layard, "Planning the Scale of Higher Education in Britain : Some Statistical Problems," *Journal of the Royal Statistical Society*, December, 1964, Table 6). Thus, the yield of investment in higher education is decisively influenced by salary patterns in the public sector.

rate of return to education and training in some professions is
due simply to monopolistic restrictions on entry can be verified
by a rate-of-return comparison between professions with
similar educational qualifications but different entry restrictions. In fact, a pioneering study in this field did just that
when it demonstrated that the lifetime earnings of physicians
in America exceeded that of other equally educated professionals, owing to the restrictive practices of the American
Medical Association.[1] It is ironic that the critics who attack
rate-of-return analysis because they believe labour markets are
typically non-competitive close the door to one of the models
that could test this belief.

We have been arguing as if rate-of-return analysis depended
upon the absence of significant imperfections in the labour
market. But, as a matter of fact, the only imperfections that
really matter are those that are directly related to the education
received by members of the labour force. For example, suppose
it were true that trade unions raised wages in unionised
industries relative to the unorganised sectors of the economy.
Since the majority of union members have received little extra
voluntary education, this sort of departure from a competitive
labour market would not affect the rate of return to education.
On the other hand, if business firms really do practise
"conspicuous consumption" of university graduates for reasons
of prestige, paying them more than they are really worth, as
is so often alleged, it is difficult to attach any meaning to a
calculated rate of return on investment in higher education.
But is it reasonable to believe that industry would waste £300
to £500 per annum on a quarter of a million people?

We come now to an objection which all the critics, and
particularly Balogh and Streeten, have linked with the question
of competitive labour markets : even if it is granted that more
education leads to higher earnings, rate-of-return studies do

---

[1]M. Friedman and S. Kuznets, *Incomes from Independent Professional
    Practice* (New York : 1946). For a similar treatment of scientists
    and engineers, see J. C. De Haven, *The Relation of Salary to the Supply
    of Scientists and Engineers*, The Rand Corporation P-1372-RC.
    (Santa Monica : 1958, unpublished).

Rate of Return on Investment in Education in Great Britain   231

not tell us whether education is "a sufficient or necessary condition of growth." The first point to emphasise is that rate-of-return analysis is not directly concerned with assessing the role of education in economic growth. Instead, it is addressed to the more mundane question of efficient allocation of resources among competing uses. The reason that these two questions have become hopelessly confused in the literature is, no doubt, that Denison in *The Sources of Economic Growth* used earnings differentials attributable to education as weights to construct an index of labour inputs. What he did was to ascribe a definite part of the historical improvement in the quality of labour to additional education and then to treat these and other changes in quality as equivalent to changes in the quantity of labour. Of course, the level of education of the labour force has not increased uniformly for all age cohorts and so Denison introduced three-fifths of the observed income differentials between males of similar age, classified by years of education, as weights to combine the different cohorts into a composite index.[1] Denison's book presents a model of the American economy in terms of an aggregate production function obeying the condition of constant returns to scale ; given this condition, the contribution of every input to total output or the elasticity of output with respect to that input will be identical to the input's relative share of national income. It is this corollary of a constant-returns-to-scale production function which imparts numerical precision to Denison's calculations of the various sources of economic growth, including education. It is perfectly possible to believe that earnings differentials are largely attributable to education, and even that education contributes to economic growth, without accepting the concept of an aggregate production function, much less that it is linear and homogeneous.[2] There is, indeed, no logical connection between Denison's estimate of the fraction of growth attributable to education and the finding of a

[1] For a more detailed explanation, see M. Abramovitz, "Economic Growth in the United States. A Review Article," *American Economic Review*, September, 1962, pp. 769–71.

[2] Denison later allows for increasing returns to scale as a separate source of growth but the basic model depends on the properties of a linear homogeneous production function.

particular rate of return to investment in education. It would not be necessary to say this were it not that the sins of the former are forever being visited upon the latter.

Furthermore, rate-of-return calculations as such will never establish whether education is either a necessary or a sufficient condition for growth. It can at best create a presumption that education contributes to growth, for there is always the possibility, however unlikely, that it merely redistributes an income pool, which is growing for other reasons, from the uneducated to the educated. Analogously, if the growing use of computers in industry improved the quality of the existing capital stock, a positive rate of return on investment in computers would not imply that more computers would suffice to produce growth or that the economy would not grow at all without more computers. The really disputable issue is not so much whether education is one of the sources of growth, but whether it is a more significant source than physical capital or other types of social expenditures. And in this regard, what is important is not only the rates of return on investment in human and physical capital, but also the way in which these investments are typically financed. As Denison has remarked, even if the yield of education was less than the yield of business capital, it is possible that the diversion of resources from private industry to education would raise national income and contribute to economic growth as conventionally measured if, as seems likely, private investment tends to be financed out of savings whereas additional private and public funds for education tend to be financed out of consumption expenditures.[1] Of course, the effects of an increase in taxation on saving and spending depends on the character of the extra taxes and their incidence on particular income groups. Given the British system of educational finance, it would be difficult to associate any particular tax change with a change in educational expenditures so as to distinguish the tax-elasticity of saving and of consumption. Nevertheless, the general point is that it cannot be assumed even in a fully employed economy that an extra pound sterling for education would necessarily displace an equivalent amount of investment in physical capital.

[1]Denison, *The Sources of Economic Growth*, pp. 77–8.

Rate of Return on Investment in Education in Great Britain 233

Similarly, we cannot simply multiply the cost of education by the rate of return to education to obtain a measure of education's contribution to national income. The calculated yield of investment in education depends upon the age pattern of an average differential lifetime earnings stream ; it would have to be age-specific to be the type of coefficient which can derive the contribution of an investment to national income, once the cost of the investment is known. As Mary Jean Bowman observes, in her clarification of this analytical tangle : "When the purpose is to measure education's contribution to national income growth, to discount returns is logically incorrect ; what is relevant is the sequential current inputs of Eds ("embodied education") and their contribution as these emerge in a series of undiscounted presents." [1]

Lastly, educational expenditures are counted in national income as consumption and, therefore, gross of depreciation and maintenance of the educational stock embodied in the labour force ; this ignores the fact that the existing stock is being continuously used up as time passes. In other words, we include in *net* national income the *net* additions to the stock of physical capital, as a measure of the net returns from the use of physical capital, but the *gross* additions to the stock of human capital, with the result that the contribution of education to future productive capacity, whatever it is, is always smaller than the contribution of education to national income. To reinforce the point, no allowance is made in measured national income for student-time as an investment cost of education. It follows, for all the reasons given, that we cannot jump directly from calculations of rates of return on educational investment to conclusions about economic growth.[2]

[1] M. J. Bowman, "Schultz, Denison, and the Contribution of 'Eds' to National Income Growth," *Journal of Political Economy*, October, 1964, p. 453.

[2] The converse also holds, contrary opinion notwithstanding : "I am more agnostic on the matter of the contribution of education to economic growth than a number of recent converts to the cause. I am doubtful whether, in the long run, the concept of education as 'investment' will prove much of a guide on what 'ought' to be spent on education," J. Vaizey, "Criteria for Public Expenditures on Education," *Economics of Education. Conference of the International Economic Association.* London : 1965, forthcoming.

VII. The Indirect Benefits of Education

Having rejected all existing methods of measuring the direct returns to education, Vaizey nevertheless affirms that "expenditure on education pays," by virtue of the fact that "the indirect benefits of education are so great that its direct benefits are not necessarily the most important aspect."[1] This point of view is widely shared, even by economists who, in analysing the returns to educational investment, have despaired of ever quantifying the indirect benefits of education. The critics, therefore, can hardly be blamed for seizing on this difficulty as the Achilles heel of the rate-of-return approach.

A careful specification of the variety of indirect benefits immediately reveals the cause of the despair that so many writers have voiced.[2] A less than exhaustive compilation of the indirect benefits of education that have been cited in the literature yields the following list : (1) the current spillover income gains to persons other than those that have received extra education ; (2) the spillover income gains to subsequent generations from a better educated present generation ; (3) the supply of a convenient mechanism for discovering and cultivating potential talents ; (4) the means of assuring occupational flexibility of the labour force and, thus, to furnish the skilled manpower requirements of a growing economy ; (5) the provision of an environment that stimulates research in science and technology ; (6) the tendency to encourage lawful behaviour and to promote voluntary responsibility for welfare activities, both of which reduce the demand on social services ; (7) the tendency to foster political stability by developing an informed electorate and competent political leadership ; (8) the supply of a certain measure of "social control" by the transmission of a common cultural heritage ; and (9) the enhancement of the

---

[1] Vaizey, *Economics of Education*, pp. 46, 150 ; see also Vaizey, *Planning Education for Social and Economic Development*, pp. 40, 51–2.

[2] For a similar specification to the one that follows see the suggestive paper by A. T. Peacock and J. Wiseman, "Economic Growth and the Principles of Educational Finance in Developed Countries," *Financing of Education for Economic Growth*, ed. OECD (Paris : 1965, forthcoming). See also M. J. Bowman, "The Social Returns to Education," *International Social Science Journal*, XIV, 4, 1962, pp. 647–60 ; B. A. Weisbrod, *External Benefits of Public Education : An Economic Analysis* (Princeton · 1964), pp. 28–37.

enjoyment of leisure by widening the intellectual horizons of both the educated and the uneducated. Merely to scan the list is 'to discover the difficulty : if all these are to be quantified, we are indeed defeated at the outset. But why demand more quantitative knowledge about the effects of education than economists are wont to demand from other economic phenomena ? After all, we do not give way to despair because we cannot measure the total direct and indirect benefits of industrialisation. We simply admit that economics is only "part of the story," albeit an important part, and leave it at that. Surely similar humility is in order with respect to education.

To come to grips with the problem, we must distinguish the economic from the non-economic consequences and confine ourselves to the former. A minimum demand is that we quantify the effect of better educated people on the earned income of the less educated. Ideally, we would like to quantify the economic benefits to each individual of every other individual having been educated. Unfortunately it is not immediately evident how many rounds of activity will be embraced in such an ideal calculation, with the result that interpersonal effects and intertemporal effects are straightway confused. Moreover, it is not easy to decide whether we mean that better educated people raise the total incomes of other people irrespective of their education, or the marginal incomes of other people as a function of their education. In short, even the simple concept of income spillovers is fraught with difficulties.[1]

Be that as it may, we will define the increments in the current earnings of $a, b, c, \ldots n-1$ from the additional education of n as the "first-round spillovers." It is universally believed that these are positive, though this is by no means obvious ; we have not even begun to spell out the nature of these "employment-related" external benefits, to use Weisbrod's language, but presumably they take the form of educated supervision raising the productivity of the less educated

---

[1]For example, Becker has shown that the old argument that the benefits of on-the-job training spill over to firms other than those providing it is subject to serious qualification, *op. cit.*, pp. 17–8.

members of a working team in industry.[1] If the first-round spillovers are positive, it seems to follow that we have under-estimated the *social* rate of return. But this conclusion is not justified. If the discounted value of the direct income benefits minus tax exceeds the present cost of investing in additional education, private individuals are economically justified in making the investment, even if they have to borrow the funds. Similarly, the State is economically justified in investing in education if the annual expenditure on school places can be eventually recovered by increased tax receipts following upon the increase in earning power generated by additional education. This is the argument for calculating the social rate of return from before-tax earnings differentials as a percentage yield on the total private and public costs of education. The reported earnings differentials already embody the first-round spillovers; if we could somehow remove them the absolute income differentials attributable to education would increase and, hence, the social rate of return would be higher. Therefore, we have actually *over*estimated the social yield if the social yield is narrowly interpreted as referring only to the *direct* economic benefits of education.

The use of the now well-established term "social rate of return" is somewhat unfortunate since it includes only the direct and indirect private economic benefits, and not the cultural and political benefits of education—items (7), (8) and (9) in our list. But the point is that it does include all of the private financial gains from schooling, to whomever they accrue: there are no economic benefits from education to second parties which do not raise their earnings and, thus generate increased tax receipts. Educated individuals cannot appropriate the first-round spillovers, but the State can and does *via* its taxing powers.[2] This is not to say that the distribution of tax burdens

[1]Peacock and Wiseman in *Education for Democrats* (London : 1964), pp. 19–20, are, to my knowledge, the first to question the order of magnitude usually assigned to the first-round spillovers from education.

[2]This argument ignores international and interregional spillover effects which can be very important for small countries or for federal systems of government. See Weisbrod, *External Benefits of Public Education: An Economic Analysis* which deals with the spillover of benefits among American states.

Rate of Return on Investment in Education in Great Britain 237

for the support of education is identical to the distribution of the private economic benefits of education, but simply that the incidence of the income tax broadly reflects the cash value of these benefits.

The "second-round spillovers"—that is, items (2) to (6) in the list—are not so easy to deal with. It may be doubted that more education for the present generation acts to raise the earnings of the next generation, except in so far as the children of better educated parents typically acquire more education themselves, or more education of a better quality; in either case, this tendency will be registered in time to come in the form of direct economic benefits. The intergeneration argument, if taken seriously, threatens to convert all the financial gains of education into indirect benefits.[1] Secondly, it is just as likely that certain kinds of education hinder the discovery of potential ability, impede the ability of the labour force to adjust to changing technology, foster the wrong sort of basic research, and increase the pressure on social services. Do the external diseconomies of the wrong sort of education outweigh the external economies of additional amounts of education? Surely, it would be presumptious to give a definite answer to such a question in our present state of knowledge.

The second-round spillovers have so far defied measurement but they are, in principle, measurable. In his book, Becker argues that we can get an idea of their probable magnitude without measuring them directly. He begins by deriving the social rate of return from before-tax earnings differentials as a function of the total costs of education, including foregone earnings before tax. This figure, construed as a lower limit to the true social rate of return, amounts to about 12·5 per cent. for the 1949 cohort of white male college graduates. As an upper limit, Becker takes the value of Denison's residual of "advancement in knowledge"—that part of the increase in output that is not explained either by increases in the quantity of inputs or by improvements in their quality—and attributes

[1]There are great difficulties in applying the same argument to women whose earnings differentials attributable to education exceed those for men but whose working life is typically much shorter. Much of the economic benefit of educating women is, truly, an intergeneration benefit, reflected in the greater educability of their children.

all of it to education. This gives him an upper limit of 25 per cent. The difference between 12·5 and 25 per cent., he concludes, measures our ignorance of the external effects of education.[1]

Some of the second-round spillovers clearly involve the dissemination and not the creation of knowledge—for example, items (4) or (6). Hence, these are already reflected in the lower limit of 12·5 per cent. For example, the costs of scientific research are in part included in the costs of higher education and the benefits are presumably reflected in time to come in earnings differentials. That is, Becker's procedure amounts to attributing another 12·5 per cent. to items (3) and (5). That may well be correct, but it seems difficult to believe.[2] But these are quibbles. Becker's calculation of the upper limit implies more confidence in the numerical accuracy of Denison's model of economic growth than is warranted. The upper limit of 25 per cent. may serve as a bench-mark for further argument, but it has little significance in its own right. For better or for worse, the direct economic benefits and the first-round spillovers of education remain at present the only ones capable of fairly accurate measurement ; and this is the chief, if not the only, justification for concentrating on them.

It is possible, however, to gain some impression of the effect on the rate of return of various assumptions about the magnitude of the second-round spillovers. The frequently expressed opinion that the indirect benefits of education are more important than the direct benefits is tantamount to the assertion that we should multiply earnings differentials associated with education by an alpha-value greater than 1·2, instead of 0·6 ; in other words, that the social rate of return on six years of secondary and higher education is at least 13 rather than 8 per cent.[3] But this conclusion depends on the

[1]Becker, *op. cit.*, pp. 119–21.

[2]For a vigorous statement of the belief that "the most important return from college education, viewed broadly, is additions to knowledge in contrast to transmission of existing knowledge," see H. Villard, "Underinvestment in College Education ? : A Comment," *American Economic Review*, May, 1960, pp. 376–7. The question turns on the belief that additional spending on academic research would produce a more than proportionate increase in the value of marketable scientific results.

[3]See Chart III below for C = £2,800 and $\propto > 1·2$.

Rate of Return on Investment in Education in Great Britain 239

notion that second-round spillovers do not raise everyone's incomes, including those of the more educated, by equal absolute amounts. The critics of the rate-of-return approach appear to believe that this is precisely what happens.[1] Yet it is difficult to envisage how this could come about. Take item (4) as a case in point : suppose general instead of specialised higher and further education would make it easier to retrain workers to take up new jobs ; is it likely that this would not show up in absolute earnings differentials, say, by raising all earnings equi-proportionately ? The idea that more education can raise earned income across the board without any differential impact on the more educated carries very little conviction.

For different reasons, we shall say nothing about the economic implications of literacy, political stability, and greater enjoyment of leisure—items (7), (8) and (9). It is obvious that a minimum degree of literacy is vital to the very existence of a market economy, and it is no less obvious that economic advance is impossible without a smoothly functioning political system. These are questions which can be and have been investigated by economists, and they may well be vital to the role of education in economic growth. They are not relevant, however, to allocative decisions which involve less than a total transformation of society : the rate of return to a literacy campaign of given size, yes, but not the rate of return to converting an illiterate society to a literate one. None of this denies the importance of the intangible benefits of education to the community at large. It is simply that these are not economic values at all in the ordinary sense and to assert that they are "large" or "small" is to dress up a personal value judgment. We all indulge in these judgments but it is clarifying

---

[1]This is frequently linked to an unstated objection to the use of earnings differentials, in any sense of the word, to measure the returns from education. For instance, Vaizey remarks that "if all incomes were equal it would appear to follow [from rate-of-return studies] that education as such has no direct return which is absurd ; the return would be immeasurable by this method," *Economics of Education*, p. 45. But, far from being absurd, the direct returns would indeed be zero in a society that no longer needed income differentials to encourage people with their education or to induce employers to economise on scarce educated manpower. Even in such a society, however, education might still generate indirect benefits to the community by raising all incomes together.

to keep them separate from analysis of the measurable economic gains.

Recently, however, it has been argued that the trouble with rate-of-return analysis goes deeper than that of failing to quantify the intangible benefits of education : education is a "public good" satisfying a "social want" for which conventional value and capital theory breaks down completely ; it is not simply that most production of education occurs outside the market but that, in the nature of the case, it could not be produced efficiently by a market process.[1]   The peculiar characteristic of public goods is that their benefits are indiscriminate in the double sense that no consumer can be excluded from enjoying the benefits and that consumption by one person in no ways reduces the consumption opportunities of others. Hence, public goods cannot be priced by a market mechanism because consumers have no incentive to reveal their individual preferences for these goods ; what is required is a political device like the ballot box to induce individuals to reveal their true preferences.[2]   Clearly, therefore, if education is a "public good" pure and simple, it is meaningless to calculate the rate of return, whether private or social.

The concept of a "public good," however, is far more limited than appears at first. It is not enough to have joint consumption ; the condition of equal consumption must apply to all, whether they pay or not. Furthermore, there must be no rationing problem in the supply of the good because a limitation on quantity is equivalent to a price, which creates the possibility of a solution by a price system. This leaves such things as lighthouses, national defence, noise and smoke abatement, clearance of areas that produce infectious diseases, as unambiguous examples of pure "public goods," but not internal law and order, medical care, and education.[3] Education

[1]R. S. Eckaus, "Economic Criteria for Education and Training," *Review of Economics and Statistics*, May, 1964, pp. 181–3.

[2]The argument goes back to Italian writers on public finance in the 1890's but its modern formulation is due to P. A. Samuelson, "The Pure Theory of Public Expenditures," *ibid.*, November, 1954, pp. 387–9, and R. A. Musgrave, *The Theory of Public Finance* (N.Y. : 1959), pp. 3–29.

[3]See J. Margolis, "The Pure Theory of Public Expenditures : Comment," *Review of Economics and Statistics*, November, 1955, pp. 347–8.

Rate of Return on Investment in Education in Great Britain 241

is not a pure "public good" because its economic benefits are largely personal and divisible : below the statutory leaving age, it is possible to buy more education, and above the statutory age, the number of places in higher education are rationed out in accordance with examination results. It follows that there is nothing in the nature of education as an economic service that prevents meaningful comparison of its financial costs and benefits.

It must be admitted, however, that it is not possible to confine all the benefits of education to those who have paid for it, nor is it possible to exclude the less educated from the spill-over benefits of education.[1] Education, therefore, represents what might be called a "quasi-public good" and to that extent great caution is called for in translating findings about the rate of return on educational investment into recommendations for public action. But the fact remains that education could be privately financed and even privately provided, and, in so far as the inputs and output of the educational system are bought and sold in the private market, the "prices" of teachers and students do reflect the relative scarcities of the resources involved in schooling.

We conclude that it is very unlikely that the indirect benefits of education exceed the direct benefits, at least when benefits are interpreted in a strictly economic sense. Moreover, the first-round spillovers are not ignored in rate-of-return analysis but enter into the calculation of the *social* rate of return. Lastly, knowledge of the social yield of education does not save the policy-maker the task of assessing the possible magnitude of the second-round spillovers or the duty of making value judgments about the non-economic benefits of education. Having broken the problem down into its separate components, however, the nature of the political decision will have been made explicit instead of implicit.

[1] If they could be excluded, it would be possible to charge them for the benefits, thus eliminating the spillover : see R. Turvey, "On Divergences Between Social Cost and Private Cost," *Economica*, August, 1963, pp. 309–13.

VIII. The Policy Implications of the Approach

If all the economic benefits of education accrued directly to ex-students, if there were no economies of scale in operating educational institutions, if capital markets were freely accessible to private individuals and if students were perfectly informed about job opportunities, there would be no need for public concern about the adequacy of educational expenditures. There is every reason to believe, however, that none of these conditions is fully met with. Furthermore, only part of the costs of education falls directly on students or their parents and, for this reason alone, the social rate of return on investment in education is different from the private rate. But what practical use if knowledge of the social rate of return, given the fact that it neglects the second-round spillover of education?

Since the issue is one of allocating resources among alternative uses, the first difficulty is that of finding an appropriate comparison with the rate of return on education. For private decisions, the basis of the comparison is, presumably, the yield after tax on corporate equities and debentures. For social decisions, however, the relevant alternative rate is not so obvious. What we are after is the social opportunity cost of education : the value to society of the next best alternative use of the resources invested in education, or, to put it more stringently, the present value of the consumption stream that would be created by releasing the resources now invested in education. This implies the specification of a social time preference rate, expressing the government's valuation of the relative desirability of consumption at different points of time. Some economists have proposed that the rate of interest on long-term government bonds serves that function ; others have pointed to the yield of private investment or to an average of market interest rates and business investment yields, but the issue remains unsettled.[1] The problem would be simplified if we knew the social yield of other types of government

[1]For a convenient review of the debate, see M. S. Feldstein, "Opportunity Cost Calculations in Cost-Benefit Analysis," *Public Finance*, XIX, 2, 1964, pp. 117–40, and P. D. Henderson, "Notes on Public Investment Criteria in the United Kingdom," *Bulletin of the Oxford University Institute of Economics and Statistics*, February, 1965, pp. 55–89.

Rate of Return on Investment in Education in Great Britain 243

expenditures.[1] Pending such findings, however, it seems that the best candidate for expressing social opportunity costs is some compromise between the yield of investment in physical capital and the rate at which the State can borrow.

The before-tax return on all business capital in the United States in dollars of constant purchasing power averaged about 12 per cent. for the period 1947-57, compared to an after-tax rate of 8 per cent. The *social* rate of return to white male college graduates in the same period was at least 10 and at most 13 per cent. ; the corresponding rate to all college entrants, including drop-outs, women, and Negroes, varied between 8 and 11 per cent. On the basis of these calculations, Becker concludes that the yields of investment in business capital and in education fall within the same range and, hence, that the direct benefits of education alone cannot justify an increase in public expenditures on college enrolments at the expense of investment in business capital.[2] At the same time, college education is a profitable private investment for the average American student since he earns about 10 per cent. after taxes on the private costs of four years in college. Likewise, it pays him to complete high school, which promises a rate of return of about 13 per cent. Indeed, even alternative rates as high as 10 per cent. justify the average student in completing every level of education in the United States.[3]

[1]There is a considerable body of evidence, however, on the rate of return on investment in road transport and in the nationalised industries in this country, on defence and water resource development in the United States, and on electricity generating facilities in France. For the United Kingdom, see B. R. Williams, "Economics in Unwonted Places," *Economic Journal*, March, 1965, pp. 20–30.

[2]Becker, *op. cit.*, p. 121. It must be noted, however, that the 8 per cent. return on investing in business is after corporation income taxes but not after personal income taxes paid on the earnings from business investment. In that sense, it is not quite comparable to the after-tax earnings differentials on college education.

[3]This is Lee Hansen's conclusion, after estimating the marginal and average social rates of return to education for every age from 6–21 and for every grade from elementary school to graduate school, as well as the private rates of return for every age from 14–21 and for every year of high school and college : "Total and Private Rates of Return to Investment in Schooling," *Journal of Political Economy*, April, 1963. His figures do not allow for differences in native ability and family background, and, therefore, must be reduced by 1–3 per cent. ; this does not affect his principal conclusion.

Since the social returns to education equal the sum of the gains to all individuals, it might be thought that the social yield could not possibly be less than the private yield. But, on the contrary, while income taxes substantially reduce the level of the private yield, public subsidies to schools outweigh this effect and raise the private above the social yield. American college education forms an exception to this rule owing to the considerable earnings that are foregone by 18–22 year old students. Nevertheless, even college education compares favourably with the after-tax yields of alternative investment opportunities in the United States. This implies that both high school and college enrolment would increase if better information were provided and all institutional restraints on private finance were removed. In other words, if the federal government wanted to get more resources into education for, say, non-economic reasons, it would need to do little else than to improve the flow of finance for students in the capital market. If, at the same time, it were concerned about equalising opportunities to obtain higher education, it could raise private rates of return even higher by making more generous grants to students, possibly in relation to parental income.

This argument applies doubly to the situation in Great Britain. A comprehensive analysis of all 53 British Unit Trusts or mutual funds shows that returns on equity investment in the form of dividends and capital gains have averaged 12 per cent. before tax in *real* terms for the period 1948–62, and about 8 per cent. after tax.[1] The White Paper on the *Financial and Economic Objectives of the Nationalized Industries* (1961) lays down target rates of return on total net assets for the nationalized industries, the general import of which is that new projects in the public sector should earn at least 8 per cent. We may accept the latter figure as an indicator of the social opportunity costs of education. As mentioned earlier, the social rates of return in this country in 1963 are about 12·5 per cent. to staying on at school until 18 years of age and about 8 per cent.

[1] A. J. Merrett and A. Sykes, *The Finance and Analysis of Capital Projects* (London : 1963), pp. 73–4.

Rate of Return on Investment in Education in Great Britain 245

to staying on until the age of 21 to complete higher education.[1] The implications are that the social rate of return on British university education is not strikingly higher than the yield of alternative investment opportunities, but that there is substantial under-investment of resources in secondary education and further education between the ages 15–18.[2]

As in the United States, the private rate of return to education in this country generally exceeds the social rate ; and this tendency is even greater for higher education, which is not the case in America. About 90 per cent. of the direct expenditures on teaching, research, administration, and buildings in British higher education are met from public funds; the figure is not very much lower in secondary education. For students in higher education, even indirect costs in the form of earnings foregone are largely subsidised by generous maintenance grants. The result is that British university students bear only 25 per cent. of the total cost of university education, whereas secondary school students bear about 65 per cent. of the total cost of educating them. In consequence, the private rate of return on secondary education is only a little higher than the social rate, but the private rate of return on higher education considered separately is more than twice the social rate. These private rates create a *prima facie* case for charging more of the cost of higher education to the beneficiaries, at least if the benefit principle of taxation has any validity. But even if this principle be rejected, they justify renewed consideration of the case for government-guaranteed loans to students qualified for university entrance (possibly at subsidised rates of interest with

[1]Some readers may deny that the yield of British university education can be less than that of American college education, in view of the fact that only 4–5 per cent. of the British working population are "higher-educated," as against 9 per cent. of the American working population. The explanation may lie in the much higher current cost per student in British higher education. In so far as this reflects superior quality of instruction, however, it should increase the returns no less than the costs. But much more research is needed before we can meaningfully compare rates of return to education in different countries.

[2]It is worth noting that the rate of return of 12·5 per cent. for staying on at school until the age of 18 is not just the yield of three years of extra education. Owing to the British system of selective secondary education, the 15-year-old school-leaver receives a different *kind* of education from the 18-year-old leaver. Hence, the 12·5 per cent. is a return both to a different type and to a larger amount of education.

repayment in the form of deductions through P.A.Y.E.)[1]
Since this would conflict with the goal of "equality of opportunity," loans to students in higher education ought to be
coupled with an extension of maintenance grants to secondary
school students so as to encourage more of them to reach the
levels from which university entrants are drawn.[2]

To come back to the more simple-minded implications of
the social rate of return to higher education : is it really true
that there is no case for additional public investment in higher
education ? Have we left anything out of our calculations ?
It has been suggested that we must add at each stage of the
educational ladder the cash-value of the option to obtain still
more education, suitably weighted by the probability of the
option being exercised ; in short, we must attribute to one level
of schooling the expected value of the financial rewards obtainable from the next level to the extent that these rewards exceed
the next best alternative investment opportunity.[3] In our case,
this means adding the cash-value of the option to take up postgraduate education. But what happens when the financial
rewards of the next level of education are less than the best

[1] The *Robbins Report*, pp. 211-12, dismissed the arguments for loans to
students, but see the evidence of some of the witnesses that appeared
before the committee : *Evidence*, II, pp. 136–7, 146–52. See also
W. Vickrey, "A Proposal for Student Loans" and R. Goode,
"Educational Expenditures and the Income Tax," *Economics of
Higher Education*, ed. S. J. Mushkin, pp. 268–305 ; and S. E. Harris,
Higher Education. Resources and Finance (New York : 1962),
pp. 255–63, 291–304, which discusses the replies of some 200 American
economists to a questionnaire on student loans. See also the
instructive examples of loan schemes currently in operation in The
Netherlands, Western Germany, and Sweden, *Robbins Report*, V,
pp. 97, 116, 146–7 ; and the recent American experience, Harris,
op. cit., pp. 246–83.

[2] So much for the accusation that rate-of-return studies of education
necessarily have *laissez-faire* implications : in a recent article, Balogh
inveighs against "fallacious attempts to calculate the rate of return on
capital investment in education for the individual. These have been
evolved, I suspect, for political motives, in order to substantiate a plea
for *laissez-faire* finance of education, to make it 'pay for itself,' to
abolish free education and institute a system of giving loans to
prospective students, to be paid back from the increase in their earnings
as a result of their being educated"—"The Economics of Educational
Planning : Sense and Nonesense," *Comparative Education*, October,
1964, p. 7. But as a matter of fact, the emphasis in rate-of-return
analysis on the vocational aspects of education is conducive to a
radical attitude towards educational reform.

[3] Weisbrod, *External Benefits of Public Education*, pp. 19–23, 138–43.

Rate of Return on Investment in Education in Great Britain   247

alternative investment opportunity, as appears to be the case for secondary education in Great Britain? This implies a negative option-value,[1] with the result that one might make the mistake of rejecting the second level of educational system if one could not also go on to the third. The traditional method of dealing with interdependent investment projects is to lump them together and to calculate a rate of return on the aggregate; this is what we did in calculating the yield of six years of schooling required to complete higher education. If more was known about the financial rewards of postgraduate education in Britain, the same approach could be extended to staying at school until the age of 24 or 25.

It may be convenient at this stage to recall all the other factors that we have mentioned tending to produce biased estimates of the rates of return.

	Downward Bias	Upward Bias
Private Rate of Return	1. Lower rates of return to other types of human capital formation. 2. Future consumption-benefits? 3. Nonpecuniary preferences of educated people. 4. Improved quality of education. 5. The earnings differentials necessarily include the first-round spillovers.	1. Higher rates of return to other types of human capital formation. 2. Present consumption-benefit (?)
Social Rate of Return	1. As (1) above. 2. Consumption-benefits of education. 3. Nonpecuniary alternatives taking the form of fringe-benefits. 4. As (4) above. 5. As (5) above. 6. Earnings less than marginal productivities (?) 7. Second-round spillovers?	1. As (1) above. 2. Earnings exceed marginal productivities (?) 3. No allowance for depreciation of the educational stock embodied in the labour force.

[1]The equation for the option value adds to the conventional rate of return for, say, secondary schooling, the difference between the yield of higher education and the yield of business capital, multiplied, firstly, by the proportion of secondary school-leavers who enter and complete university, and, secondly, by the ratio of the costs of the two levels of education to permit addition of the corresponding rates of return.

It is evident that the bias is mostly one way even when we ignore the broader cultural and political benefits of education. In this way a case can be made, even on narrow economic grounds, for additional public expenditures in both secondary and higher education.

If this were all we could say with the aid of rate-of-return calculations, it would hardly justify the effort. Clearly, analysis of the economic effects of various *amounts* of education must be considered a first step in a more comprehensive approach which would include the effects of various *types* of education. In the United States, there is the problem of the very uneven quality of some 2,000 Institutions of Higher Learning.[1] In this country, there is the question of the many different channels of further and higher education, not to mention the variations that must exist in the social rate of return to different subjects.[2] In addition, there is out-of-school training whose costs may well be equal to one-half of total expenditures on formal education.[3] Nothing but lack of data inhibits calculation of the rate of return to each and every type of formal and informal education. So long as the analysis is confined to amount of formal education, the approach is not given a fair chance to show its worth.

A once-and-for-all calculation of the rates of return on investment in education can only throw indirect light on the causes of early leaving : it may be due to income disabilities, or to ignorance about the returns to additional education, or to imperfections in the capital market. But as soon as steps are

[1]For the first attempt to deal with this, see S. J. Hunt, "Income Determinants for College Graduates and the Return to Educational Investment," *Yale Economic Essays*, Fall, 1963, reprinted as Center Paper No. 34, Yale University Economic Growth Center (New Haven : 1964).

[2]For example, the social costs of science students in universities is twice that of art students (*Robbins Report*, IV, p. 110) whereas their lifetime earnings differentials differ much less.

[3]This is Mincer's finding for the USA, *op. cit.*, p. 63. However, his estimates do not come directly from the accounting data of firms and do not catch the costs of training which are borne by firms rather than by workers in the form of lower wages. A much lower figure was once calculated for Great Britain by P. J. D. Wiles : "The Nation's Intellectual Investment," *Bulletin of the Oxford University Institute of Statistics*, November, 1956, p. 284.

Rate of Return on Investment in Education in Great Britain 249

taken to influence any of these causes of early leaving, rate-of-return calculations will disclose the effectiveness of the adopted policy. American studies now have the advantage of historical data for 1939, 1949, and 1959 which has, for example, made it possible to analyse the impact of the G.I. Bill for veterans.[1] Similarly, rate-of-return analysis as such cannot tell us whether education should be privately or publicly provided and financed, but it alone is capable of summarising the economic impact of changes in the mix of private and public finance. In the same way, it permits rapid calculation of the economic effect of such policy measures as raising the school-leaving age, eliminating some channel of further or higher education, altering the level of student grants, and the like. Moreover, when the same approach has been further extended to the other social services, it is bound to clarify the really important issue of the efficient allocation of resources between additions to the stock of physical capital and the stock of human capital.

Policy makers are frequently attracted to manpower forecasting as an alternative technique of educational planning, on the grounds that it avoids all the subtleties of rate-of-return analysis and, in addition, does not commit one to the assumption that earned income is an accurate measure of a worker's contribution to the net national product. But the simplicity of the manpower approach is largely a function of its narrow view of the economic ends of education. Like rate-of-return analysis, it neglects the consumption-benefits and most of the second-round spillovers of education ; in addition, it almost always ignores the costs of producing different types of educated manpower, implying that educational inputs are free goods. Of course, manpower planning is not concerned with optimising behaviour and its central objection to rate-of-return analysis is that it can at best indicate the desirable direction of change in educational policy, not its required magnitude. Unfortunately, it is precisely in spelling out the magnitude of a required change that manpower forecasting so often falls to the ground, owing largely to its failure to take account of the possibilities

[1]See H. P. Miller, "Income and Education : Does Education Pay Off ?", *Economics of Higher Education*, ed. S. J. Mushkin, pp. 129–47.

of substitution between different skills as a function of relative
wage rates. If the allocation of resources to education were
governed entirely by market forces, rate-of-return studies
would have full scope but centralised manpower planning would
have little meaning. Despite the importance of public provision
and finance of education, however, manpower forecasting is only
a useful exercise if students and their parents are in fact poor
choosers, and if elasticities of demand for particular skills, and
therefore elasticities of substitution between skills, are typically
less than unity. By its failure to pay any attention to money
costs and earnings, manpower planning stands condemned as a
brand of technological determinism.

But these are not deficiencies inherent in the manpower
approach and the fact remains that it tries to grapple with one
of the significant second-round effects of education which is
only inadequately reflected in rate-of-return calculations. The
two methods are complementary and, unless we assume that
the production of highly-qualified manpower is the only
economic purpose of an educational system, even the most
accurate manpower forecasting would not dispense with the
need for rate-of-return analysis.[1]

Is a relatively low return on teachers' training a signal to
stop educating more teachers? Is a modest social rate of return
on higher education a reason for discouraging students from
going to university? These questions have answers, but not
until they are considered in the round. As one American critic
of the rate-of-return approach put it: "it might prove
detrimental to the best interest of society (measured in terms
other than aggregate economic returns on investment) to have
government policy determined (or even substantially influenced)
by an investor's point of view."[2] It might, but we will never

[1]The strongest argument for manpower planning is simply that there is
the strong possibility, given the long gestation-period of certain
critical occupations demanding specialised education, of cob-web
cycles with periods of gluts and low salaries succeeding periods of
shortages and high salaries, and so on *ad infinitum*. If we had
historical data on the rates of return to individual fields of study, we
could test this cob-web hypothesis by checking whether the various
yields fluctuated over time.

[2]Shaffer, *op. cit.*, p. 1033.

Rate of Return on Investment in Education in Great Britain   251

know until we see what sort of policy follows from "an
investor's point of view."   Surely, it makes more sense to
advocate something on non-economic grounds after, and not
before, the implications of an economic point of view are
clearly understood ?

M. BLAUG

University of London Institute
     of Education and
London School of Economics.

[2]

Reprinted from THE ECONOMIC JOURNAL, June 1967

APPROACHES TO EDUCATIONAL PLANNING [1]

EDUCATIONAL planning is as old as state education, that is, much older than economic planning. Until comparatively recent times, however, educational planning was haphazard rather than deliberate, a matter for local rather than central government, concerned with individual educational institutions rather than entire educational systems, and no effort was ever made to state the objectives that planning was supposed to satisfy. The Second World War changed all that: the post-war explosion in the demand for education, the new interest in central economic planning, the obsession with growth rates in both developed and developing countries combined to promote a new attitude to the administration of education. Educational planning by the State with the purpose of promoting economic objectives is now as universally approved as economic planning itself. However, just as there is a world of difference between central investment planning in the Soviet Union and " indicative planning " in France and Britain, so enthusiasm about educational planning has not yet produced any consensus about the methods and techniques of planning education.

Consider the curious predicament of an educational planner who consults the fast-growing literature on the economics of education for guidance in making policy decisions. On the one hand, he is told to gear the expansion of the educational system to quantitative forecasts of the demand for highly qualified man-power. On the other hand, he is urged to project what is quaintly called " the social demand " for education, that is, the private consumers' demand, and to provide facilities accordingly. Finally, he is furnished with calculations of the rate of return on investment in education and advised to supply just enough schooling to equalise the yield of investment in human capital with the yield of investment in physical capital. Obviously, the three approaches may give different answers, and, strangely enough, the literature offers little assistance in reconciling different methods of educational planning. To add insult to injury, however, the advocates of man-power forecasting scoff at the assumptions underlying rate-of-return calculations, while the proponents of rate-of-return analysis are equally scornful of the idea that man-power requirements can be predicted accurately. In the meantime, higher education is being expanded in many countries simply to accommodate the rising numbers of academically qualified applicants, apparently on the notion that something like Say's Law operates in

[1] This is the revised text of a paper presented at last year's meeting of the Association of University Teachers of Economics in Durham (April 1966). I have benefited from the discussion at the meeting and from the comments of the staff of the Unit for Economic and Statistical Studies on Higher Education at the London School of Economics, particularly those of Mr. J. R. Crossley, Mr. H. Glennerster, Mr. R. P. G. Layard and Professor C. A. Moser.

markets for professional man-power, supply creating its own demand. All this is very confusing, and in the circumstances we can hardly blame some educational planners who are beginning to doubt the value of the contribution of economists to educational decision-making.

This paper is an attempt to resolve the issue, or at least to present it in such a way that it can be resolved. The basic thesis is that the three approaches rightly understood are complementary, not competitive. At one point the argument will involve a comparison between the United States and the United Kingdom, but this is purely illustrative and designed to clarify the problem by discussing it in a concrete setting; the thesis itself is applicable with appropriate modifications to both developed and developing countries.

I. AN OUTLINE OF THE THREE APPROACHES

The O.E.C.D. Mediterranean Regional Project provides a sophisticated example of the man-power-forecasting approach to educational planning. The method used was that of proceeding in stages from an initial projection of a desirable G.D.P. in a future year, as given by a prior economic plan, to a supply of educated man-power in some sense " required " to reach it in the target year.[1] The steps are as follows: (1) the target G.D.P. in, say, 1975 is broken down by major sectors, such as agriculture, manufacturing, transport, distribution and the like; (2) these sectoral G.D.P.s are then broken down by industries (this level of disaggregation was not attempted in the M.R.P. studies); (3) an average labour–output coefficient, the reciprocal of the familiar concept of the average productivity of labour, is applied to the sectoral or industrial G.D.P. targets, yielding a forecast of labour requirements by sector or industry; (4) the labour force is distributed among a number of mutually exclusive occupational categories; (5) the occupational structure of the labour force is converted into an educational structure by applying a standard measure of the level of formal education required to perform " adequately " in each occupation.[2] Allowances are then made for deaths, retirements and emigration, that is, for replacements as well as additions to the stock of educated man-power. The final result is a

---

[1] The M.R.P. Country Reports for Spain, Italy, Greece, Yugoslavia, Turkey and Portugal are now available from O.E.C.D. The method is explained and defended by H. S. Parnes, *Forecasting Educational Needs for Economic and Social Development* (Paris: O.E.C.D., 1962).

[2]. The method is summed up in the equation:

$$\left(G.D.P.\right)\left(\frac{G.D.P._s}{G.D.P.}\right)\left(\frac{G.D.P._i}{G.D.P._s}\right)\left(\frac{L_i}{G.D.P._i}\right)\left(\frac{L_j}{L_i}\right)\left(\frac{L_e}{L_j}\right)$$

= Workers of education e in occupation j in industry i in sector s.

where $G.D.P._s$ = G.D.P. originating in each sector;
    $G.D.P._i$ = G.D.P. originating in each industry;
    L_i = the labour force in each industry;
    L_j = the labour force in each occupation;
    L_e = the labour force with each level of education; and $L \geqslant \sum\limits^{n} L_{sije}$.

conditional forecast of the demand for educated people in 1975, conditional, that is, on the achievement of the G.D.P. target.

The difficulties in this method centre largely on steps (3) and (5), although step (4) also raises controversial questions. The standard procedure for forecasting labour–output coefficients, step (3), is to extrapolate past trends, either as a function of output or as a function of time. An alternative device is that of adopting the coefficient observed in more advanced countries, on the notion that there are definite man-power growth paths that all economies follow in the course of development; a variant is to take the labour–output coefficient ruling in the most advanced sector of the economy on the ground that the best-practice technique of that sector will eventually become the average-practice technique of all sectors. Lastly, there is the technique employed in drawing up *The National Plan* of asking employers to estimate their own future labour requirements, given a stated rate of expansion in the market for their products. We shall return to these estimating procedures later; for the moment, we simply take note that the problems involved in forecasting the productivity of labour are familiar to economists. This is not so with the difficulties encountered in step (5) of the exercise, namely, the translation of labour requirements by occupation into labour requirements by educational qualification (*The National Plan* omitted this last step, thus producing a man-power forecast without implications for educational planning). The simplest method of converting occupation into education is to apply the mean number of years of schooling currently observed in each occupation or job-cluster. Unfortunately, the concept of educational attainment is not adequately expressed by a scalar such as years of schooling. In any case, this is not what the educational planner wants to know: his decisions have to be made in terms of different types of education. The problem, therefore, is that of specifying a vector that measures the combination of varying amounts and kinds of formal education required in different occupations. So far, despite many attempts to develop such educational vectors, it cannot be said that this difficulty has been resolved satisfactorily. The difficulty is not merely technical; as we shall see, it is at the root of the inadequacy of the man-power-forecasting approach as now conceived.

We turn now to social-demand projections. Little need be said here. It is all in the Robbins Report, so to speak.[1] At this point, we need to distinguish between "forecasts" and "projections." As these terms are employed in the present paper, a "forecast" will always mean a prediction subject to the achievement of a certain economic growth target, that is, a statement of what would happen if economic growth were deliberately manipulated. In other words, man-power forecasts simply spell out the implications of an economic plan with respect to the characteristics of the labour force. "Projections," on the other hand, predict the outcome of

[1] See also O.E.C.D., *Policy Conference on Economic Growth and Investment in Education. II. Targets for Education in Europe in 1970* (Paris: O.E.C.D., 1962).

purely spontaneous forces, that is, what will happen in the normal course of events in an unplanned economy (the " normal course of events " includes the information made available by the projection). We can therefore talk about man-power projections, say, in the American economy or the British economy. Similarly, projections of the private demand for non-compulsory education, social-demand projections, attempt to predict student enrolments on the assumption that the " price " of education remains the same, whether the economy is planned or not. This " price " consists of the direct and in-direct costs of secondary and higher education, subject to the constraint of meeting entry-qualifications. Thus, social-demand projections of the Rob-bins type are contingent upon: (1) a given level of provision of secondary education, particularly of fifth and sixth forms; (2) a given standard of ad-mission into higher education; (3) a given level of the direct costs of second-ary and higher education, in particular, a given level of student grants; and (4) a given level of earnings of educated people, not only because these earnings represent an important aspect of the vocational opportunities opened up by additional education but also because they constitute the in-direct costs of staying on at school in the form of earnings forgone. Extra-polation of existing enrolment trends is the heart of the matter and, of course, the better the knowledge of the socio-economic determinants of " staying on at school," the more accurate the projection. In principle it is perfectly possible to measure the price-elasticity of the demand for education, that is, to specify the effect of changes in some of the factors that are being held equal, such as the level of student grants, but so far little effort along these lines has been attempted. All this implies that social-demand projections represent something like a minimum effort at foresight, telling the educational planner not what to do but rather what will happen if he does exactly what he has been doing in the past.

This brings us to rate-of-return analysis. Here we start with a cross-tabulation of the labour force by age, education and earnings before and after tax. From these, we construct age–earnings profiles by years of schooling, that is, we use cross-section data to project lifetime earnings associated with additional education. It is convenient to treat the costs of education as merely negative earnings, with the result that we can proceed immediately to calculate the present value of the net earnings differentials associated with extra education at different discount rates. The internal rate of return on investment in education is simply the discount rate that sums the present value of the net lifetime earnings to nought, or that equates the discounted value of the costs of a certain amount of education with the discounted value of the future earnings anticipated from it.[1] However,

---

[1] That is,

$$\sum_{t=15}^{t=65} \frac{E_t - C_t}{(1+r)^t} = 0$$

where r is the internal rate of return, E is earnings before or after tax, C is the costs of education, $t = 15$ is the legal school leaving age and $t = 65$ is the year of retirement.

266   THE ECONOMIC JOURNAL   [JUNE

an allowance must be made for the difficulty that the earnings associated with additional education cannot be entirely attributed to education alone; needless to say, individual earnings are determined partly by native ability, family background, social class origins and so forth, and to that extent take on the character of a rental payment to a non-reproducible factor of production.   On the basis of somewhat less than adequate empirical evidence, some American authorities have agreed that about two-thirds of the observable earnings differentials associated with years of schooling are statistically attributable to differences in educational attainment.   One can see why the figure of two-thirds might be an overestimate in Great Britain, given our highly selective educational system; on the other hand, higher-educated individuals are relatively scarcer here than in the United States, which argues that two-thirds is an underestimate.   Furthermore, no one has yet succeeded in giving a satisfactory quantitative expression to the considerable uncertainty and illiquidity of investment in human capital.   Nevertheless, the common-sense interpretation of the rates of return that have been calculated is that they represent something close to maximum-likelihood estimates of the average yields of additional expenditures on education.   In one sense they are merely a summary statistic expressing the prevailing relationship between the costs of more schooling and the earnings that may be more or less confidently expected to result from it.

There are many objections to this approach, some of which are worth re-emphasising in the present context.   First, it assumes that existing earnings differentials in favour of educated people reflect their superior productivity; obviously, if there is no relationship whatever between relative earnings and relative productivities rate-of-return figures are economically meaningless.   Secondly, if the demand for and supply of educated people increase at different rates in the future than in the past rates of return will differ from those that have been calculated, or, to put it into jargon, the average rate of return may not be a good guide to the marginal rate of return.   Thirdly, the approach ignores the non-monetary consumption benefits of education, and, more seriously, it ignores all the monetary benefits other than those that accrue directly to the educated individual.   This is not the place to discuss these objections,[1] although the first and second points will be taken up below.   Notice, however, that the man-power-forecasting approach is vulnerable to some of the same objections: for example, it, too, ignores the consumption as well as the spillover benefits of education.   Nevertheless, waiving all technical objections, the fact remains that the assumptions underlying rate-of-return analysis are rather different from those of man-power-forecasting and social-demand projections.   Can we some-

---

[1] For a detailed discussion of all the technical objections, see M. Blaug, " The Rate of Return on Investment in Education in Great Britain," *Manchester School*, September 1965, pp. 205–61, and Reprint Series, No. 5, Unit for Economic and Statistical Studies on Higher Education, London School of Economics.

how combine all these approaches, or must we choose one in preference to the two others?

II. A Preliminary Contrast between the Three Approaches

The first thing that strikes us about these three approaches to educational planning is that they are not on the same footing. The man-power-forecasting approach tells the educational planner how many scientists, engineers, technicians and so forth he should supply by, say, 1975 without regard either to their prospective earnings or to the relative costs of producing them. In short, it provides the planner with a forecast of one point of the 1975 demand schedule for a particular skill. If, for any reason, the supply target stipulated in the man-power forecast is not met, so that relative earnings change, the educational planner will have no way of knowing whether the error was due to an inaccurate forecast of the shift in the demand curve between 1966 and 1975 or simply to the mistaken assumption that students choose to study particular subjects with no regard for earnings prospects.[1] Similarly, a projection of the private demand for education tells the educational planner how many students with different types of professional preparation may be expected to be forthcoming by 1975. He has no way of knowing whether these students can be absorbed in the labour market without a change in the pattern of relative earnings. If relative earnings alter it is very likely that this will affect the structure of the private demand for education by fields of specialisation. At this point he may be tempted to combine the social-demand projection with a man-power forecast by providing just enough places in higher education to meet the demands of students qualified for entry, while allowing the distribution of places among faculties and subjects to be governed by a forecast of man-power requirements.

[1] Take the case of the labour market for scientists. A man-power-forecast states that the demand for scientists in 1975 will be q; as this forecast ignores the earnings of scientists, apparently the notion is that the supply of scientists is entirely a matter of the facilities made available for the study of science (hence, the supply curve is perfectly inelastic). In 1975, however, instead of q scientists at salaries s, q' scientists are forthcoming at salaries s', that is, we observe intersection B instead of C. Are we on the 1975 demand curve, the error being due to the failure to meet our educational supply target, or are we on a different demand curve?

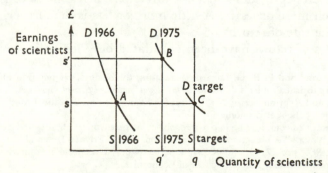

Indeed, this is more or less the approach that was adopted by the Robbins Committee.[1]   But a moment's reflection will show that this really combines the worst of both worlds: it assumes that economic growth is affected by the relative supply of skilled professionals but not by their absolute supply; it treats the fraction of the labour force that has received higher education as a consumption-decision best left in the hands of parents and students, whereas the ratio of scientists to engineers or engineers to technicians is regarded as an investment-decision that must be the responsibility of the State.   Furthermore, it is precisely in forecasting the demand for particular skills rather than in forecasting total labour requirements that man-power forecasting is weakest.   Thus, this combination of the two approaches makes poor use of the advantages of man-power forecasting, such as they are.   The outcome is a policy that is neither *laissez-faire* nor intervention, but a curious mixture of the two.   To be sure, it is not difficult to find an ideological justification for the social-demand approach in a private-enterprise economy. But consistency demands that the policy of accommodating the private demand should be applied to the choice of subject as much as to the choice of further schooling.

A logical way of combining man-power forecasting with social-demand projections would be to start with the growth of G.D.P. as a basis for the assessment of man-power requirements via estimated productivity trends, and then to reverse the procedure by forecasting the likely output of the educational system and deriving G.D.P. via labour productivity trends.   If there were a discrepancy in the two results one could then decide whether to revise the G.D.P. target or to attempt to alter the future supply of educated people; since it costs something to do either, one would probably do both in the effort to minimise the loss in resources.   As the two approaches are concerned with different sides of the labour market, however, it is difficult to see how they could be combined without some reference to relative earnings or at least hiring practices, elements conspicuously absent in the leading examples of man-power forecasting and social-demand projections.[2]   What these two approaches do have in common is that they provide the educational planner with exact magnitudes to aim at.   Rate-of-return analysis, on the other hand, merely provides a signal of direction: invest more or invest less. But how much more or less?   A little more or less is the answer, and then recalculate the rate of return.

So far, rates of return have been calculated only for entire levels of the

[1] See C. A. Moser and P. R. G. Layard, " Planning the Scale of Higher Education in Great Britain: Some Statistical Problems," *Journal of the Royal Statistical Society*, Series A, Vol. 27, Pt. 4, 1964, pp. 488–9, and Reprints Series, No. 1, Unit for Economic and Statistical Studies on Higher Education, London School of Economics.

[2] For an attempt to combine the two approaches via the earnings of educated people, see the diagram in M. Blaug, " An Economic Interpretation of the Private Demand for Education," *Economica*, May 1966, pp. 171–8, and Reprints Series No. 7, Unit for Economic and Statistical Studies on Higher Education, London School of Economics.

educational system, or, at best, for years of additional schooling. But in the United States and Canada some evidence is now beginning to emerge on rates of return to different types of professional training,[1] and for the present discussion I shall assume that such figures are available. Furthermore, present data limitations have confined rate-of-return analysis to calculations of the average rate of return on investment in education. However, with better data on the career prospects of recent graduates there is no reason why we cannot estimate marginal rates of return, which is what we really need for educational planning. At any rate, whether average or marginal yields are calculated, it is clear that rate-of-return analysis is the method of marginalism, or what Professor Popper has called " piecemeal social engineering." [2] This has long been regarded as the principal weakness of rate-of-return calculations as an instrument of planning, but in practice, it may be the source of its peculiar strength: it forces the educational planner to face the severe limitations in his capacity to foresee the consequences of present action, particularly when action involves, as it often does, the unprecedented expansion of educational facilities or changes in the entire structure of the educational system. Rate-of-return analysis as such does not forecast the demand or the supply of educated man-power. It indicates how the two are matched at present. Curiously enough, however, if man-power forecasts and social-demand projections are reliable the consequence is necessarily an implicit prediction of rates of return. Therefore, either all three methods are valid when used in conjunction with one another or there is something wrong with man-power forecasting, or social-demand projections, or both.

To argue against this conclusion, one must assert both that: (1) the costs of different types and amounts of education, and (2) the relative earnings of highly qualified man-power never vary over time. In some countries and for some periods the first assertion may be correct. The second, however, is palpably false and, indeed, can only be substantiated on theoretical grounds if: (1) Say's Law operates in all labour markets so that demand and supply shift to the right as if hooked together; or (2) relative earnings are entirely supply-determined because the supply curve of every type of scientific man-power is perfectly elastic; or (3) relative earnings are entirely demand-determined because the demand curve for every type of scientific man-power is perfectly elastic. It is easy to see that (2) and (3) are absurd assumptions. The same cannot be said of (1), which is probably the conception in the back of the minds of man-power forecasters. Unlike most

[1] See W. Lee Hansen, " The ' Shortage ' of Engineers," *Review of Economics and Statistics*, August 1961, pp. 251–6; " Professional Engineers: Salary Structure Problems," *Industrial Relations*, May 1963, pp. 33–44; " ' Shortages ' and Investment in Health Manpower," *The Economics of Health and Medical Care* (Ann Arbor, Michigan: The University of Michigan, 1965), pp. 75–92; and B. W. Wilkinson, " Present Values of Lifetime Earnings in Different Occupations," *Journal of Political Economy*, December 1966.

[2] K. R. Popper, *The Open Society and Its Enemies*, II (London: Routledge & Kegan Paul, 4th ed., 1962), p. 222.

assumptions in economics, however, this one is easy to falsify.   All we need to observe is fluctuations in the relative earnings of highly qualified man-power and Say's Law is invalidated.

Nevertheless, most educational planners react instinctively to rate-of-return analysis in the conviction that marginalism is not the appropriate technique for educational planning.   It is the length of time required to produce skilled professional people that is always cited as the rationale for long-term man-power forecasting.   Training a scientist or an engineer takes about fifteen years and the effective production-period may be even longer because the educational system is a hierarchical input–output structure: it is usually necessary first to feed back an intermediate output of teachers if we want a higher final output of scientists and engineers.[1]   In consequence, it is likely that labour markets for highly qualified man-power are subject to cob-web effects without a tendency to converge towards equilibrium.   When ex-cess demand for a specialised skill raises its relative earnings the increase in the supply of that skill, assuming students are made aware of and respond to the rise in prospective earnings, takes five or ten years to materialise.   Because of this lag in the adjustment of supply, there is every chance that market forces will overshoot the equilibrium, so that what was a shortage turns sud-denly into a glut.   As earnings fall, the reverse effect takes place.   This dynamic adjustment process may never produce market-clearance in any one period, but rather continuous fluctuations in earnings associated with successive phases of labour shortages in one field and labour surpluses in another.   Given the strong probability that there will be structural dis-equilibria in the distribution of educated man-power among occupations, and the high cost of such disequilibria when they occur, it is imperative that some central agency try to forecast the demand for scientific or technical man-power at least ten or fifteen years ahead, in the same way that the Central Electricity Board forecasts the demand for electric power before it commits itself to building a hydro-electric dam that takes almost a decade to complete.   Even if we could predict relative earnings fifteen years ahead, these would be of no help to rational investment decisions in the field of edu-cation, because these earnings simply reflect disequilibrium situations.   So runs the central argument of the proponents of man-power forecasting.[2]

   [1] For an excellent illustration of this feedback problem, see V. Stoikov, " The Allocation of Scientific Effort: Some Important Aspects," *Quarterly Journal of Economics*, May 1964, pp. 307–24.
   [2] For a powerful defence of the man-power forecasting approach along these lines, see G. Bombach, " Long-term Requirements for Qualified Manpower in Relation to Economic Growth," *Economic Aspects of Higher Education*, ed. S. E. Harris (Paris: O.E.C.D., 1964), pp. 201–23, as revised in " Manpower Forecasting and Educational Policy," *Sociology of Education*, Fall, 1965, pp. 343–74. The fact that the lead-time for the production of scientific man-power is fairly long and, hence, that markets for this type of man-power are characterised by cobweb effect does not itself prove that market forces never converge on equilibrium.   K. J. Arrow and W. M. Capron have argued that the " shortage " of engineers and scientists in the United States in recent years is gradually being eliminated by a dynamic adjustment process: " Dynamic Shortages and Price Rises: The Engineer-Scientist Case," *Quarterly Journal of Economics*, May 1959, pp. 292–309.   But Arrow and Capron

III. Two Views of the State of the World

We can now sharpen the contrast between the three approaches to educational planning by asking what the world would have to be like to make it unnecessary to forecast the demand for highly specialised man-power, despite its long production-period.   Suppose we had an educational system that did not permit students to specialise until their second or third year of higher education, that provided a perfectly general education for everyone until the ages of nineteen or twenty, that made full use of team teaching and new educational media in the interest of keeping staff/student ratios as flexible as possible and capable of ranging from $\frac{1}{10}$ to $\frac{1}{300}$.   Suppose also that vocational counselling was so efficient that students were extremely well informed of career opportunities.   Suppose further that the demand for different skills was highly elastic, that capital was an almost perfect substitute for labour and that, in addition, workers with different skill characteristics were good substitutes for one another.   In short, there were always many people who could perform a given job, and the job could almost always be displaced by a machine.   Lastly, suppose that most specialised skills were acquired on the job, not learned in schools, and that technical change demanding new and hitherto unfamiliar skills proceeded gradually without fits and starts. In these circumstances would it really matter that education is a durable asset and that the gestation-period of that asset is ten or twenty years?   To forecast man-power requirements under these conditions would be almost meaningless for the simple reason that, in this sort of world, educated man-power could never be a bottleneck to economic growth.   Projections of the private demand for education and calculations of the rate of return, however, would be perfectly meaningful in such a world, and, indeed, the only guides available to decision-making in education.

We can go to the other extreme and imagine a world created in the image of man-power forecasting: students and parents would be poorly informed of career prospects and more interested in acquiring education for consumption than for investment reasons; specialisation by subjects would start very early; student/staff ratios would be fixed and unalterable, and all school buildings and school equipment would be indivisible and highly specific in each use; the demand schedules for separate skills would be highly inelastic, and the

---

consider only lags on the demand side—such as the time it takes firms to realise that they can only obtain more qualified man-power by offering higher salaries (pp. 297–9)—and refer only briefly (p. 303) to those lags on the supply side that have been emphasised by man-power forecasters.   Even so, what is true for the United States may not apply elsewhere.   For a brilliant catalogue of all the factors that inhibit market clearance for specialised skills in both developed and underdeveloped countries—such as rigid technologies, conventions in hiring practices, ignorance of skill-substitution potentials, the high cost of spreading information both among the buyers and the sellers of skills, skill labelling by paper qualifications in response to imperfect knowledge, etc.—see H. Leibenstein, " Shortages and Surpluses in Education in Underdeveloped Countries: A Theoretical Foray," *Education and Economic Development*, eds. C. A. Anderson and M. J. Bowman (Chicago: Aldine Publishing Company, 1965), pp. 51–62.

elasticity of substitution between labour and capital, as well as the elasticity of substitution between men with different skills, would be well below unity; industry would provide virtually no training, and the pace of technical change would be so rapid that the demand curves for people with different educational backgrounds would shift through time unevenly and irregularly. Obviously, in this sort of world the private demand for education would be so unstable as to make it impossible to extrapolate existing trends, and all marginal calculations would be irrelevant. Labour–output coefficients would be technologically determined, and earnings associated with education and even the costs of supplying various skills would be ignored.

Enough has been said to suggest that the quarrel really is about the view one takes of the real world. What we have is a picture of a continuum: to the right is a neo-classical universe, characterised by substitutabilities in both the educational system and the productive system; to the left is a Leontief-type universe of fixed-input coefficients, characterised by extreme complementarities in both education and industry. Needless to say, the real world lies somewhere in between. To resolve the conflict that we are examining, we need to decide whether the world lies nearer to the right end or the left end of the continuum (right and left, of course, carry no political connotation).

IV. A Wider Conception of Educational Planning

There is much research going on both here and abroad designed to throw light on the ease of substitution among people with different educational backgrounds in particular occupational categories, on the substitutability between formal education and labour training, on hiring practices with respect to educated personnel, on the relationship between choice of technique and the skill mix of the labour force, on occupational mobility and the pattern of career opportunities and so forth.[1] In time to come these inquiries may allow us to give an unequivocal answer to the question whether the productive system is in fact characterised by variable or by fixed educational-input coefficients. But when it is realised that the answer ideally requires specification of the aggregate production function of an economy, not for output as a function of homogeneous labour and capital but as a function of labour classified by levels of education and capital classified by types of machine-operating skills, it seems obvious that educational planning will have to make do for a long time to come with very imperfect knowledge of the precise connection between education and economic growth. In these circumstances what is the planner to do? Should he act on a man-power

---

[1] The author is participating in a major study of this kind, carried out by the Unit for Economic and Statistical Studies on Higher Education of the London School of Economics, under the direction of M. Hall: for some preliminary results, see M. Blaug, M. H. Peston and A. Ziderman, *The Utilisation of Educated Manpower in Industry* (London: Oliver & Boyd, 1967).

forecast? But what if the forecast were to prompt action exactly opposite to that suggested by a projection of private demand or a calculation of the social rate of return on investment in education? We are back to the problem with which we started. Are we any nearer a resolution?

Planning has been defined as the process of preparing a set of decisions for action to be taken in the future.[1] Since it is oriented to the future, planning partakes of all the difficulties analysed in the theory of sequential decision-making under uncertainty. Educational planning is, as we have argued, particularly prone to uncertainty about the future, since even the present relationship between the supply of qualified students and the demand for educated people from industry and government is little understood. In the circumstances we are always better off if we can build into the system the kind of flexibility that allows it to adjust automatically to bottlenecks and surpluses. In short, educational planning should largely consist of action designed to move the real world closer to the right end of the continuum, characterised by a multiplicity of alternatives in producing and utilising educated man-power. For whatever is the state of the world, such action ensures a smoother adjustment of educational output to educational inputs and improves the chances of market clearance.

V. HIGHER EDUCATION IN GREAT BRITAIN AND THE UNITED STATES

To clarify the argument, let us contrast the man-power situation in Great Britain and the United States. First of all, specialisation in schools starts much earlier in Britain than in America: British students begin to concentrate on their major fields (arts or science) by the age of 15, and sometimes as early as 14; by the age of 15 or 16 the science students have largely ceased to study arts subjects, and vice versa, and by the sixth form extreme specialisation even between pure and applied science is almost universal.[2] Recently, there have been some changes in the opposite direction, but these do not affect the striking contrast between the British and American situation. Two years ago, Lord Bowden told the House of Lords: "It is almost true to say that the destiny of our universities, their whole expansion programme, and, with this, the whole destiny of this country, is at the moment in the hands of 14-year-old schoolboys,"[3] a remark which might now be amended to read " 15-year-old schoolboys." Early specialisation is said to be caused by university entrance requirements and excessive competition in sixth forms for a limited number of places in universities. But whatever the

---

[1] For an illuminating discussion of concepts of planning as applied to educational planning, see C. A. Anderson and M. J. Bowman, " Theoretical Considerations of Educational Planning," *Educational Planning*, ed. D. Adams (Syracuse, N.Y.: Syracuse University Press, 1964), pp. 4–8.

[2] The evidence is reviewed by J. A. Lauwerys, " United Kingdom," *Access to Higher Education.* II. *National Studies* (Paris: U.N.E.S.C.O., 1965), pp. 362–70.

[3] Debate on Technological Development in House of Lords, December 2, 1964: *Hansard* (House of Lords), Vol. 261, para. 1163.

reason, the undisputed fact that British students specialise at an earlier age than almost any other developed country means that the supply of, say, scientists and engineers in 1972 is already determined in Britain, whereas in the United States it will be possible to make a substantial impact on the 1972 supply by policies adopted in 1968 or 1969.   Thus, the lead-time required to produce skilled man-power in Great Britain is at least twice as long as in the United States, in consequence of which there is much stronger probability in Britain of periodic shortages and surpluses of scientists and engineers.

Added to the first consideration, and directly related to it, is the chronic excess demand for higher education in Great Britain ever since the war, defined simply as an excess of secondary school leavers qualified for entry over the number of student places available.   Higher education has been rationed in this country for twenty years, and even under the Robbins targets this situation will continue until well into the 1970s.   In the United States, on the other hand, state universities are required by law to admit all applicants with a high-school diploma, and private American universities have generally expanded facilities to keep pace with the rising number of qualified applicants.   Standards of admission vary more widely than in Great Britain and, in general, nearly all high-school graduates in America who want to go to college manage to find some institution of higher learning willing to accept them.   Paradoxically enough, British students in higher education are generously subsidised by the State, more generously than in any other developed country and certainly more generously than in the United States.   In consequence, the costs of higher education to students are much less in Britain than in the United States, and this serves further to raise the demand for places in this country.[1]

Furthermore, not only is the overall supply of places in higher education rationed in Britain but so is the allocation of places between faculties.   As we noted earlier, the policy on the balance of faculties in universities appears to have been based on the man-power forecasts of the Barlow Committee in 1946 and those of the Committee on Scientific Man-power of 1956 and 1961.[2] In consequence, there have been years when applicants for arts places have been denied entry while at the same time there were vacant places in science and technology.   Although the University Grants Committee took the view in 1958 that " student choices have shown themselves to be remarkably sensitive to prospective demand," [3] this was not allowed to affect the policy on faculty balances.   But, clearly, either students are poorly informed of

[1] Blaug, " The Rate of Return on Investment in Education in Great Britain," *op. cit.*, p. 245.

[2] Moser, Layard, *op. cit.*, pp. 510–11, and P. R. G. Layard, " Manpower Needs and the Planning of Higher Education," *Manpower Policy and Employment Trends*, eds. B. C. Roberts and J. H. Smith (London: L.S.E., 1966), pp. 86–7; see also W. G. Bowen, " University Finance in Britain and the United States: Implications of Financing Arrangements for Educational Issues," *Public Finance*, 1963, reprinted in W. G. Bowen, *Economic Aspects of Education. Three Essays* (Princeton N.J.: Princeton University Press, 1964), pp. 58–65.

[3] U.G.C., *University Development, 1952–1957* (London: H.M.S.O., 1958), p. 75.

career prospects, in which case they can be better informed, or they are well informed, in which case the argument must be that the labour market fails to produce signals of impending man-power shortages. If the latter, one would think that the State would adopt a differential student-grant policy so as to encourage students to take up those professions in which there is known to be a prospective shortage. This view implies considerable confidence in man-power forecasts; and no doubt a lack of conviction about forecasting accounts for the present inconsistent policy.

In the United States, on the other hand, students are allowed freely to choose their own subject once they have gained admission to university. They are kept informed of trends in the labour market by means of vocational counselling, and full use is made of special scholarship programmes and student loans restricted to particular subjects or fields of study that require encouragement.

It seems obvious that the supply of highly qualified man-power is more rigidly predetermined in Britain than in the United States, that students' educational choices are less firmly linked to job opportunities, and that, in general, the demands of the labour market have less influence on the structure of higher education in Britain than in the United States. If we add to this the contrast between the British tripartite secondary education, with a university stream separated from the rest by the age of 12, and the comprehensive high schools of America that allow almost 50% of the age group 16–18 to pass on to college, as well as the rigid paths of British technical education in which professional qualifications are only obtainable by passing the examination of a particular professional institution, albeit by part-time as well as full-time means, and the extraordinary variety of trade and vocational high schools, technical institutes, two-year junior colleges, four-year technical colleges and the like in the United States, we are forced to conclude that there is much less scope for short-run adjustments in the demand and supply of man-power in this country, and therefore the stronger probability of imbalances in the labour market.[1] It may be that all this is offset by differences in on-the-job training provisions in the two countries, but even here casual impression runs against Britain.[2]

---

[1] It is not easy to provide a definitive reference here because few students of comparative education have examined national systems from this point of view. For some material, however, see The Conference of Engineering Societies of Western Europe and the U.S.A. (E.U.S.E.C.), *Report on Education and Training of Professional Engineers. A Comparative Study of Engineering Education and Training in the E.U.S.E.C. and O.E.E.C. countries* (Brussels: E.U.S.E.C., 1962), I, pp. 70–6; II, pp. 11–12, 36, 39, 67–9, 79–81.

[2] To sum up our argument in terms of the ordinal continuum mentioned above:

Leontief-type universe	U.K.	U.S.A.	Neo-classical universe
‖————————————————————————‖	↑	↑	

I am, of course, ignoring all the sociological differences that underlie the two systems; I am describing, not explaining. For a suggestive sociological explanation, see R. H. Turner, " Modes of

These differences between the two educational systems go a long way to explain the American interest in rate-of-return analysis and their sceptical attitude to man-power forecasting, and exactly the reverse attitude in this country. Faced with a rigid and highly structured educational system, and aware that as much as two-thirds of university graduates and probably a similar fraction of those with G.C.E. " O " and " A " levels are employed by the public sector—the State in respect of education combining monopoly with monopsony—educational planners in Britain have seen no alternative to man-power forecasting with all its admitted shortcomings. But the price of rigidity is that errors are more disastrous. This is the great paradox of the man-power-forecasting approach : because of alleged rigidities in the educational system and imperfections in the labour market, one must forecast the demand for educated people so as to avoid structural disequilibria; but if there is indeed little synchronisation between the educational system and the labour market errors in forecasting lead to an irremediable waste of resources, not to mention the disappointment of students who cannot find employment on satisfactory terms. In short, in a Leontief-type economy there is a premium on the accuracy of forecasts, and an inaccurate forecast can aggravate instead of improve the situation. In contrast, if the economic system is sufficiently flexible to adjust to erroneous forecasts, even crude estimates of man-power requirements can serve as useful guides, but at the same time there is less reason to forecast at all, and hence the costs of making forecasts must be scrutinised more closely.

VI. Educational Reforms and an Active Man-power Policy

The way to cut through this Gordian knot is to create a safety-valve against forecasting errors by strengthening the automatic adjustment mechanism of the market-place. In the British context this means attacking the problem of early specialisation and, since this is in turn related to the keen competition for a limited number of university places, further expansion of University facilities to accommodate the unsatisfied demand. The root of the problem is the whole G.C.E. system. Although the nine G.C.E. examining boards are, strictly speaking, autonomous bodies, almost half of their members are drawn from the Universities and, hence, the remedy lies in closer co-operation between the universities and the Secondary School Examination Council. So long as places in universities are rationed, how-ever, no long-term solution is possible. Hitherto, early specialisation has been attacked on purely educational grounds. What has not always been realised is that early specialisation is also one of the major causes of man-power difficulties in Britain. Obviously, it may be expensive to redesign the educational system so as to minimise the time taken to learn professional skills, and this extra cost must enter into the decision to postpone the age of specialisation. What I contend is that the benefits of late specialisation for the elimination of man-power bottlenecks have not previously been given their proper due. Likewise, the debate on comprehensive schools, the issue of grants to secondary school students, the question of loans to students in higher education and even the Friedman–Peacock–Wiseman idea of "educational vouchers" all look somewhat different seen through man-power spectacles.

Further, every effort should be made to allow students freely to choose their faculties, concomitant with heavy investment in vocational counselling in schools. Indeed, the provision of career information both in schools and in labour exchanges ought to be a principal activity of the educational authorities. Unfortunately, in most countries this function is divided between the Ministry of Education and the Ministry of Labour, and hence there is little communication between schools and employers. For example, in Britain the Youth Employment Service is still in part under the umbrella of the Ministry of Labour, and this division of control may help to explain why facilities for vocational guidance are poorly co-ordinated and why the level of provision is well behind the United States and most other European countries.[1]

More broadly, any policy action that increases the flexibility with which resources are combined within the educational system must improve the capacity of schools to adjust to shortages and surpluses of various types of man-power. That is, any action that encourages educational innovation in school, such as constructing school buildings easily adaptable to various class sizes, training teachers to use new educational media, such as closed-circuit television and programmed instruction, must ease the man-power situation, whatever it is. Of course, the case for new educational media is not one to be decided solely or even largely on man-power grounds, but the fact remains that the more teachers are replaced by mechanical aids, the easier it is to expand enrolment or to adjust faculty balances.

Turning to the labour market, we note that shortages of particular skills, that is, the existence of unfilled vacancies at current salary levels, are overcome in the short run either by raising salaries, by lowering minimal hiring standards or by providing more on-the-job and off-the-job training. There is much less scope here for public policy than in the formal educational system. Nevertheless, in the absence of specific knowledge of the extent of a shortage, it is always possible for the State to ease the situation by altering pay scales in the public sector, by furnishing better information about the future output of the educational system to personnel officers in business enterprises in the hope of encouraging an adjustment of hiring standards and by offering

---

[1] See R. A. Lester, *Manpower Planning in a Free Society* (Princeton, N.J.: Princeton University Press, 1966), pp. 59–75, for comparative evidence.

financial incentives to industry to expand its training programmes. Recent attempts to experiment with public provision for training and retraining of adult workers, as in the Industrial Training Act in this country and the Man-power Training and Development Act in the United States, are, of course, precisely along these lines. The more we avoid placing all responsibility for man-power development on the schools alone, the less we need to pay the consequences of unemployable school leavers or economic growth held back by shortages of various skills.

What I am proposing is that educational planning should consist in part of reforms of the educational system, and, for the rest, what has been de-scribed in America as " an active man-power policy." [1] Educational planning, and particularly educational planning in developing countries, should concern itself more widely with the reciprocal impact of the educa-tional system and the labour market. It is a fallacy to think that there can be no man-power planning without man-power forecasting, and that, in the absence of forecasting, educational planning must consist of a passive atti-tude towards the economic returns from education.[2] Rather than accepting existing educational patterns and prevailing hiring policies as data in the planning process, much of the effort of educational planning should be directed at altering them so as to give full scope to the process by which industry adapts its demand to the supply of educated man-power, and the supply of students adjusts itself to the changing demands from industry.

VII. Man-power Forecasting with a Difference

None of the three conflicting approaches to educational planning has any logical priority over the others. Faced with an uncertain future, educational planning must diversify its portfolio of methods and techniques. Clearly, there are upper limits to the elasticity of substitution for certain critical skills, that is, skills involving long formal preparation and training. And no matter how late we postpone specialisation, the effective lead-time of scientific man-power is sufficiently long to create the possibility of unstable cobweb effects. It takes years to put up a complex of school buildings and, obviously, foresight is indispensable to the decision to begin building. In addition, students base their career decisions on to-day's market forces, and only a fore-cast can reveal the situation that they will confront when they eventually enter the labour market. There can be no question, therefore, about the necessity of trying to take a forward look at man-power requirements and, in

[1] See, for example, E. W. Bakke, " An Active and Positive Manpower Policy," *Active Manpower Policy. International Management Seminar. Final Report* (Paris: O.E.C.D., 1965), pp. 127–45.

[2] In a valuable new book, *Education and Social Change in Ghana* (London: Routledge & Kegan Paul, 1965), P. J. Foster shows that educational planners in Ghana have for decades insisted on providing secondary technical schools despite the fact that it proved difficult to fill all the available places and that their graduates failed to obtain employment. Students were, in practice, better informed of the poor returns from technical education than the planners themselves.

principle, one should look forward as far as possible.   However, the period over which we can usefully forecast the demand for man-power in the present state of knowledge is much more limited than is usually admitted.   All the evidence shows that we do not yet know how to forecast beyond three or four years with anything remotely resembling the 10% margins of errors that are regarded as just tolerable in general economic forecasting.   Some post-mortems on five-year and ten-year man-power forecasts in the Soviet Union, in Sweden and in Iran suggest that such forecasts invariably go wide of the mark.[1]   Unfortunately, none of these forecasts were of the type that furnished a range of estimates on various assumptions about the magnitude of the critical variables and coefficients, and single-value conditional forecasts can rarely be falsified by a simple comparison of forecast with outcome.[2]   The point is that unless the G.D.P. target itself is achieved exactly, we cannot be sure where the fault lies.   That is, there are four possibilities:

The Man-power-forecasting Hypothesis

Man-power target \ G.D.P. target	Hit	Miss
Hit	Confirmed	A bottleneck other than man-power?
Miss	Falsified	?

In the vast number of cases where single-valued man-power forecasts were made, the realised economic growth rate fell, for one reason or another,

---

[1] On the Soviet Union, N. DeWitt, *Educational and Professional Employment in the U.S.S.R.* (Washington, D.C.: National Science Foundation, 1961), and " Educational and Manpower Planning in the Soviet Union," *The World Yearbook of Education 1967. Educational Planning*, eds. G. Z. F. Bereday, M. Blaug and V. A. Lauwerys (London: Evans Bros., 1967).   On Sweden, *Educational Policy and Planning in Sweden* (Paris: O.E.C.D., mimeographed, 1964), pp. 24–5; Appendix XI, pp. 1–25.   On Iran, G. B. Baldwin, " Iran's Experience With Manpower Planning: Concept, Techniques, and Lessons," *Manpower and Education.   Country Studies in Economic Development* (New York: McGraw-Hill, 1965), pp. 140–73.   See also R. G. Hollister, *A Technical Evaluation of the First Stage of the Mediterranean Regional Project* (Paris: O.E.C.D., 1966, that demonstrates that the 1980 man-power forecasts of the M.R.P. are highly sensitive to small changes in the labour–output and in the occupation–education coefficients.   No one has yet taken a retrospective look at the many man-power forecasts that have been made in France in the last decade, but see J. Fourastié, " Employment Forecasting in France," *Employment Forecasting* (Paris: O.E.C.D., 1963), particularly pp. 71–2; and J. and A.-M. Hackett, *Economic Planning in France* (London: George Allen & Unwin, 1964), pp. 145–9, 186–8, 303–4.

[2] There are other grounds for objecting to single-value forecasts.   In the words of the *Technical Evaluation of the M.R.P.:* " educational strategy should be formulated with the uncertainties engendered by technological change clearly in mind.   In the light of such uncertainties, objectives of labour force flexibility may receive more stress in the formulation of the structure and content of education.   Manpower requirement estimates which conceal these uncertainties, by presenting single value estimates of requirements rather than ranges of alternatives, may do a great disservice to formulators of educational policy " (*op. cit.*, p. 62).

below the target growth rate, with the result that even with hindsight it proves impossible to say whether the forecast was accurate or not. Worse than this, in some instances, such as that of teacher supply, forecasts merely provided a framework for particular policy recommendations, and so were deliberately designed to be self-falsifying. Hence, repeated failures to forecast reliably in cases where G.D.P. growth targets were achieved have taught us little, and despite twenty years of experience we are not much wiser to-day about the nature of the changing demand for educated man-power. Indeed, so notorious is the unreliability of such forecasts that there is not a single country on record that has made a serious effort to implement comprehensive targets for man-power requirements.

We have spoken so far exclusively of man-power *forecasts* in the sense defined earlier. Some additional insight is gained from experience with man-power *projections* in countries such as the United Kingdom and the United States that have no commitment, or have had no commitment until recently, to a national economic plan. Suffice it to say that the British record of man-power projections is abysmal, possibly because the task was assigned to physical scientists rather than to economists.[1] The American record is more difficult to judge, as the methodology of American man-power projectors is highly eclectic,[2] and errors in prediction have been as common on the side of enrolments as on the side of employment.[3] Nevertheless, little comfort is derived from the various American efforts at predicting the demand for scientists, engineers and technicians, not to mention teachers, doctors and dentists.

The reasons for this dismal picture are several. First of all, as Kendrick has shown for the United States, the advance of both total-factor productivity and labour productivity in various sectors is quite irregular over time, and seems to exhibit no simple regular pattern that could be used by a man-power forecaster or projector.[4] Furthermore, it is doubtful, simply on theoretical grounds, whether all countries move along the same man-power growth path, that is, arrive at similar occupational distributions of the labour force for

[1] See A. T. Peacock, "Economic Growth and the Demand for Qualified Manpower," *District Bank Review*, June 1963, pp. 3–19; Moser, Layard, *op. cit.*; and the revealing evidence of Sir Solly Zuckerman to the Robbins Committee, *Higher Education. Evidence*, Pt. I, Vol. B, Cmnd. 2154–VII (London: H.M.S.O., 1963), pp. 423–52.

[2] A leading American projection simply extrapolated the ratio of employment of scientists and engineers in a given industry to total employment in that industry on the basis of evidence of a linear trend between 1954 and 1959 (*The Long-range Demand for Scientific and Engineering Personnel*. Washington, D.C.: National Science Foundation, 1961). But in two cases, the chemical industry and the electrical equipment industry, further detailed investigation threw doubt on the assumption of a stable employment fraction for scientific man-power (*ibid.*, pp. 16–17, 21–4). See also *Scientists, Engineers, and Technicians in the 1960's: Requirements and Supply* (Washington, D.C.: National Science Foundation, 1963).

[3] For a thorough review, see J. K. Folger, " Scientific Manpower Planning in the United States," *The World Yearbook of Education 1967, op. cit.*

[4] J. W. Kendrick, *Productivity Trends in the United States* (Princeton: Princeton University Press, 1961), Ch. 6, pp. 133–89.

identical levels of output per head. At any rate, there is no evidence that man-power forecasting can be based on mere imitation of a richer country.[1] Similarly, we know too little about the rate of diffusion of best-practice techniques within and between industries to make practical use of the method of " catching up " with the most advanced firm or sector of the economy. And, finally, the notion of asking business firms to forecast their labour requirements at income growth rates that they may never have experienced assumes that they can predict their market shares independently of the activities of rival firms.

Even if we could somehow predict productivity changes, we still have to cross the hurdle of occupational classifications and of converting these into educational equivalents. And here the real problem is not simply the failure to observe any unique relationship between educational background and occupational affiliation in to-day's labour force, except for those professions such as medicine and teaching where custom imposes a minimum entrance qualification,[2] but the difficulty of separating the forces of supply from the forces of demand. What we have here is the old " identification problem." After all, the schooling currently associated with each occupation is as much the outcome of the supply of educated people in the past as of the history of the demand for qualified man-power. In any economy with a high level of aggregate demand qualified man-power, however irrationally produced, will somehow be absorbed into employment: what we observe to-day may simply represent the misallocations of the past.[3] If we want to forecast the demand for educated people we cannot simply read off the existing fit of occupation and education. The task we face is to find an

[1] The case for the existence of man-power-growth paths is thoroughly canvassed with sceptical conclusions by R. G. Hollister, " The Economics of Manpower Forecasting," *International Labour Review*, 1964, reprinted in *The Economics of Manpower Planning*, ed. M. R. Sinha (Bombay: Asian Studies Press, 1965), pp. 73–103.

[2] The variance about the mean in the number of years of schooling observed in different occupations appears to be considerable: see Parnes, *op. cit.*, pp. 112–13; U.S. Bureau of the Census, *U.S. Census of Population: 1960. Subject Reports. Occupation by Earnings and Education.* Final Report PC(2)–7B (Washington, D.C.: G.P.O., 1963), pp. 244 ff; and C. A. Anderson, " Patterns and Variability in Distribution and Diffusion of Schooling," *Education and Economic Development, op. cit.,* p. 321–4.

[3] The whole point of man-power forecasting is precisely the notion that the present situation represents a malutilisation of educated people; if it does not, ordinary market forces may be trusted to give results as satisfactory in the future as in the past. By implication, man-power forecasters must assume that the market has everywhere failed to allocate man-power resources optimally. For that reason, attempts to estimate the educational structure of the labour force as a given function of national income or output per head with the aid of cross-section data for different countries falls short of solving the problem of forecasting man-power requirements (Netherlands Economic Institute, " Financial Aspects of Educational Expansion in Developing Regions," *Financing of Education for Economic Growth* (Paris: O.E.C.D., 1966); E. R. Rado and A. R. Jolly, " The Demand for Manpower: An East African Case Study," *The Journal of Development Studies*, April 1965, pp. 226–51; and P. R. G. Layard and J. C. Saigal, " Educational and Occupational Characteristics of Manpower: An International Comparison," *British Journal of Industrial Relations*, July 1966). Educational planning based on these regression equations runs the danger of reproducing the past misallocations of man-power in the more advanced countries.

independent method of estimating the optimum amount and type of education for each job-cluster. But satisfactory performance in an occupation is a complicated function of native ability, psycho-motor skills, work experience, on-the-job training and formal educational preparation, and we are far from understanding just how much the latter contributes to this mix. Furthermore, it is doubtful whether one can define the optimum education for an occupation without introducing earnings, a variable that so far has been ignored by man-power forecasters.[1]

All this has been said before, even by those who advocate long-term man-power forecasting.[2] The point is: do we brush these criticisms aside and forecast as best we can, or do we revise our basic ideas about man-power forecasting? The leading man-power forecasters insist that long-term forecasts, even of the crudest kind, distinguishing merely between occupations requiring general academic education and those requiring scientific and technical preparation, are useful in guiding the allocation of educational expenditures among levels and branches of the educational system. That would be true if one could rely on them. Unfortunately, even the forecasters themselves warn against educational expansion closely tied to

[1] There appear to be three possible relationships between education and occupation: (1) there is a minimum educational qualification for each occupation and additional qualifications have no economic value; (2) the productivity of a worker in an occupation increases with his educational qualifications, very gradually at first, then at a sharply increasing rate beyond a certain threshold level, after which it levels off again; (3) the productivity of a worker in a specific occupation increases monotonically with his educational qualifications, first at an increasing rate and then at a decreasing rate, and it never levels off. These three cases relating to a specific occupation are illustrated in the following diagram, with educational qualification measured as a scalar on the horizontal axis and productivity or performance-rating in the occupation measured on the vertical axis. The three possibilities mentioned above correspond to the three numbered curves. If the

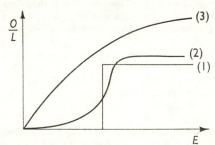

real world is correctly depicted by (1) or (2) there is no serious problem of optimisation. But if case (3) is representative of the real world the optimum amount of education is entirely a matter of the earnings associated with additional education, and cannot be defined independently of them: a man with 16 years of schooling may be twice as productive as one with 12 years, but if he costs three times as much, the optimum amount of education is nevertheless 12 years (see Blaug, Peston and Ziderman, *op. cit.*, pp. 3–4).

[2] See Parnes, *op. cit.*, pp. 19, 20, 33, 36, 38, 41, 44. But after mentioning almost every objection to long-term man-power forecasting, he nevertheless insists that the essence of his own approach is " the rather rigorous link that has been assumed between productivity levels and occupational structure on the one hand, and between occupation and educational qualification on the other " (*ibid.*, p. 51). See, in a similar vein, F. H. Harbison and C. A. Myers, *Education, Manpower, and Economic Growth* (New York: McGraw-Hill, 1965), ch. 9, pp. 189–208.

forecasts of man-power requirements.[1]   The question is not whether to forecast or not to forecast, but rather whether to forecast inaccurately as much as
ten or fifteen years ahead or to forecast three or four years ahead with a
much better chance of being accurate.   The case for long-term forecasting
is usually made on the basis of the lengthy production-period of scientific
man-power.   But, as we saw earlier, the fact that it takes fifteen years to
educate an engineer does not imply that we must predict the demand for
engineers in 1981, not unless there is one, and only one, occupation that
an engineer can fill or, at any rate, one and only one set of tasks that an engineer can perform.   We need to know much more about these questions,
but all the evidence so far suggests that there are many substitutes for professional man-power.   Human capital may take a longer time to produce
than most physical capital, but it is also less specific in use than most
machines.

The need to guide students' career choices is sometimes given as the
reason that man-power forecasts must look at least six or seven years ahead.
To be sure, students, at least British students, must think about career
opportunities six or seven years hence in choosing their major fields of study.
Suppose they were furnished with a completely accurate forecast of the
demand for a particular profession by 1972.   Would this improve their
educational choices?   Not necessarily, as they would still have to calculate
how many other students would react to the forecast in the same way.   This
is true, of course, of every student in turn.   Students are in the same position
as oligopolists who cannot decide what price to charge without knowledge
of the prices that rivals will be charging.   It is not enough, therefore, to be
told what will be the demand for engineers in 1972.   One also needs to know
the probable supply of engineering students by 1972.   Provided the student
is given the latter as well as the former, he is indeed better off: if a shortage is
forecast he need not worry much about his aptitude for engineering, as he
is likely to find employment in any case; if, on the other hand, the forecast
suggests that there will be a buyers' market he must pay stricter attention to
his own occupational aptitudes.   This argument shows that even completely
accurate medium-term man-power forecasts are not by themselves sufficient
for purposes of vocational counselling.   But, in practice, even these are

---

[1] Parnes' principal line of defence is simplicity itself: " The sceptics call attention to the large
margins of error that are likely at virtually every stage of the forecasting process: the estimate of
G.N.P. fifteen years in advance; the distribution thereof among the various sectors and branches
of the economy; the estimation of future manpower structure within each of the branches; and the
equation of occupations with required educational qualification."   But " so long as one grants that
manpower considerations are one of the elements that *ought* to influence educational decisions, then
all such decisions, if they purport to be rational, involve manpower forecast, whether or not they are
explicitly made," *Planning Education for Social and Economic Development*, ed. H. S. Parnes (Paris:
O.E.C.D., 1963), pp. 74–5.   This misses the point.   If long-term forecasts of the purely technological kind are really as subject to error as he himself admits (*op. cit.*, pp. 13, 30), it is difficult to see how
they can be justified; the fact that all educational decisions have man-power implications makes
errors more serious, not less.

284   THE ECONOMIC JOURNAL   [JUNE

rarely accurate.[1] Furthermore, they say nothing about prospective professional earnings, which is precisely what interests students.   There is a world of difference between stipulating the minimum educational requirements for realising a G.D.P. target, as in the typical man-power forecast, and predicting the employment opportunities that will most probably materialise in various fields of specialisation so as to help students to plan their careers.   The confusion between the two may perhaps account for the poor quality of vocational guidance in so many countries.

Despite everything we have said, advocates of man-power forecasting will nevertheless insist that some knowledge of the future ten or fifteen years hence, however hazy, is better than nothing.   Put like this, one can only agree. However, the implication of this view is that we ought to build the admitted haziness of long-term forecasts directly into the forecast itself.   For instance, one plausible hypothesis is that the variance around the estimated mean of the forecast increases with the square of the length of time over which we are forecasting, producing a margin of error that steadily widens as we look farther into the future.   Thus, the margin of error in predicting the demand for man-power might be $\pm 2\%$ of the 1966 figures by 1967, $\pm (0.02)^2$ of 1966 figures by 1968 and so forth, amounting to an error of $\pm 22\%$ in 10 years and $\pm 35\%$ in 15 years; the same argument, possibly with a different margin of error, applies to the supply of man-power.   The growth paths for a particular type of educated man-power might then look as follows:

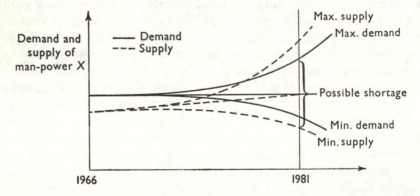

---

[1] An interesting test-case is the demand for teachers.   Here there is no problem about forecasting abour productivity, as staff/student ratios are invariably an administrative decision, nor any difficulty about specifying the minimum educational qualification for the job, as there is usually a legal minimum requirement for entry into the profession.   Nevertheless, the record of teacher forecasts is as poor as all other man-power forecasts: see W. Lee Hansen, " Human Capital Requirements for Educational Expansion: Teacher Shortages and Teacher Supply," *Education and Economic Development, op. cit.*; M. J. Bowman, " Educational Shortage and Excess," *Canadian Journal of Economics and Political Science*, November 1963, pp. 446–61; and A. M. Cartter, " A New Look at the Supply of College Teachers," *The Educational Record*, Summer 1965, pp. 267–77.   Another depressing example is the case of doctors: see W. Lee Hansen, " ' Shortages ' and Investment in Health Manpower," *op. cit.*; and J. Seale, " Medical Emigration: A Study in the Inadequacy of Official Statistics," *Lessons from Central Forecasting* (London: Institute of Economic Affairs, 1965), pp. 25–41.

In this case we would have to be satisfied by the undramatic conclusion that there will be a " shortage " of X by 1981 if we have underestimated the demand for X and overestimated its supply, and not otherwise. The diagram is, of course, purely illustrative. I do not know whether the future supply is more uncertain than the future demand or whether the errors are symmetrical around the forecast, as in the above diagram, nor whether the compounding error-term should be 1, 2 or 3%. However, until some such conception of discounting the uncertain future enters explicitly into man-power forecasting, the case for long-term man-power forecasting, particularly of the single-valued type, lacks intellectual foundation. Surely, there is some point at which the penumbra of doubt associated with a forecast becomes so large that the forecast itself misleads rather than informs?

VIII. In Conclusion

There is little point in continuing to waste resources on long-term pin-point forecasts whose results are suspect even by the forecasters themselves. These resources could be much more profitably invested in improving our knowledge of the current stock of qualified man-power and disseminating this knowledge to students and employers. It is no accident that after two decades of considerable activity in man-power forecasting only one country, namely the United States, has anything like adequate data on the distribution of the labour force by sectors, occupations, earnings and years of schooling.[1] Such data is not even expensive to collect, since it can be gathered by sample surveys. The truth is that the mystique of forecasting has discouraged investigations of the current stock of man-power on the grounds that bygones are for ever bygones.[2] But the stock of man-power is so large relative to the annual flow that most of the current stock will be with us for decades to come.

Faced with the difficulties of man-power forecasting, difficulties that seem to increase at a progressive rate the longer the time-period over which we are forecasting, the remedy is to begin modestly with short-term forecasts, extrapolated with a compounding margin of error as outlined above. As we accumulate more experience, we can begin to adjust the margin of error, gradually producing more and more reliable medium-term, and eventually long-term, forecasts. As a check on such forecasts of demand, we ought to

[1] The United States is also the only country that now has an almost complete register of professionally qualified man-power in the labour force.

[2] The almost universal neglect of earnings as a vital piece of information about trends in the use and production of man-power illustrates the effect of this mystique on data collection. For example, the *Review of the Scope and Problems of Scientific and Technological Manpower Policy*, presented last year to the British Parliament by the Committee on Man-power Resources for Science and Technology (Cmnd. 2800), listed a number of investigations now under way that are designed to supplement knowledge of the demand for and supply of scientific man-power in Great Britain, but said not a word about relative earnings. Figures on earnings by level or type of education are not collected by any official agency in Great Britain.

make continuous rolling projections of the future supply of educated people. Indeed, the forecasts of demand ought to be of the type that provides a range of alternative values for different estimates of the projected supply. If the demand for educational inputs depends in any way on its price, and this will necessarily be so if there is any substitutability between educational inputs, changes in supply are just as capable of altering that price as changes in demand, and therefore the quantity demanded of educational inputs is not independent of its supply. It follows that man-power forecasts must always be combined with social-demand projections. Similarly, social-demand projections by themselves are not a safe basis for educational planning. The tendency to upgrade skill-requirements when the labour market becomes favourable is a well-attested phenomenon.[1] It seems to have definite limits, however, as witness the incidence of " intellectual unemployment " in many countries. As we combine forecasts of demand with projections of supply, we start thinking quite naturally of earnings associated with education as indicators of impending shortages and surpluses. And since the costs of training various types of specialised man-power differ considerably, we will be led to consider variations in earnings in relation to variations in the costs of education. This is rate-of-return analysis, whether we call it that or not. By making such calculations on a year-to-year basis, we keep a continual check on labour markets for highly qualified man-power and gradually develop insights into the ways in which education interacts with economic growth.

Recent work on mathematical and computable models of the educational system may point the way to a joining of all the approaches.[2] Models of this kind are perfectly neutral instruments of planning and indispensable whatever approach is taken. They become somewhat more tendentious if specific assumptions are made about what education ought to be optimising. In a recent linear programming model of education in Northern Nigeria, for example, man-power demands were treated as exogenously determined con-

---

[1] J. K. Folger and C. B. Nam, " Trends in Education in Relation to Occupational Structure," *Sociology of Education*, Fall 1964, pp. 19–34, demonstrate a moderate but declining association between education and occupation in the United States between 1940 and 1960. Moreover, they show that most of the change that occurred in those twenty years was attributable to a rise in educational attainments within occupations, that is, to upgrading, rather than a shift from jobs requiring little to those requiring more education.

[2] The groundwork was laid by Correa, Tinbergen and Bos with a balanced-growth golden-age model, using fixed linear coefficients to relate the stock of labour with second- and third-level education to national income and the output of the third level of the educational system to the teacher requirements of the second and third level: see J. Tinbergen and H. C. Bos, " A Planning Model for the Educational Requirements of Economic Development," *Econometric Models of Education* (Paris: O.E.C.D., 1965), pp. 9–31. For a somewhat different type of model, see C. A. Moser and P. Redfern, " A Computable Model of the Educational System of England and Wales," *Proceedings of the International Statistical Institute. Bi-Annual Conference* (London: I.S.I., 1966); and P. Armytage and C. Smith, " The Development of Computable Models of the British Educational System and Their Possible Uses," *Meeting of the Ad Hoc Groups on Mathematical Models of the Educational System* (Paris: O.E.C.D., 1967).

straints and lifetime net earnings differentials associated with education as the objective function to be maximised.[1] The solutions took the form of an optimum sequence of decisions about various parts of the educational system over an eight-year time period, given different assumptions about staff/student ratios. The interesting conclusion that emerged was that the optimum pattern of resource allocation between primary, secondary and higher education was almost exactly the opposite of that advocated by previous manpower forecasts in Nigeria, not so surprising perhaps if one realises that these forecasts ignored the problem of the transition path to the target dates.[2]

We have come to the end of our story. The message has been that social-demand projections, man-power forecasting and rate-of-return analysis are reconcilable and in fact complementary techniques of educational planning, but not as these approaches are presently conceived in the literature. Above all, they must be combined with specific educational reforms and an active man-power policy designed to minimise the burden of administrative planning decisions. Economists do have a contribution to make to educational planning, but not by pressing the claims of one particular panacea, not by pretending to foresee the future accurately ten or fifteen years ahead, not by presuming to know how to promote exactly so much economic growth by just so much education. There is no reason to be apologetic about the fact that in most cases all that we can safely recommend is movement in a particular direction for a limited period of time.

M. Blaug

University of London Institute
of Education and London School
of Economics.

[1] S. S. Bowles, *The Efficient Allocation of Resources in Education: A Planning Model with Applications to Northern Nigeria* (Dissertation submitted to Harvard University, 1965).

[2] For similar evidence, see J. R. Smyth, " Rates of Return on Investment in Education: A Tool for Short Term Educational Planning, Illustrated with Ugandan Data," and E. Rado, " Manpower Planning in East Africa," both in *World Year Book of Education 1967, op. cit.*

[3]

THE CORRELATION BETWEEN EDUCATION AND EARNINGS: WHAT DOES IT SIGNIFY?

MARK BLAUG

University of London, Institute of Education
and London School of Economics, London, England

> *We seem to be ignorant in our understanding of the determinants of the derived demand for labor with different amounts of schooling.*
>
> *It is clear that, in general, employers offer higher pay to more highly educated workers, but our knowledge of what elements or ingredients of schooling make people more productive is scanty.*
>
> *Is it what they have learned in school, as measured by test scores? Or is schooling valuable for the patterns and modes of thought and behavior it develops in people? Or does schooling merely serve as a screening device that identifies the more able, highly motivated young people in our society?*

LEE HANSEN (1970)

ABSTRACT

This paper examines three alternative explanations of the basic finding that amounts of education and personal earnings are positively correlated in some 30 countries studied. Arbitrarily labelled (1) the "economic", (2) the "sociological" and (3) the "psychological" explanation, (1) argues that better-educated people earn more because education imparts vocationally useful skills that are in scarce supply; (2) propounds that they do so either because length of schooling is itself correlated with social class origins or because education disseminates definite social values which are prized by the ruling elite of a society; (3) contends that education merely selects people in accordance with their native abilities and, obviously, abler people earn more than less able ones.

The question is asked: Are these really conflicting explanations? It is concluded that a proper appreciation of the economic explanation in fact assimilates the other two. In a perfectly competitive labour market, earnings will necessarily reflect the relative scarcity of "vocationally useful skills," and the vocational skills must include the possession of values and drives appropriate to an industrial environment. In the absence of competitive pressures, however, earnings may reflect purely conventional hiring practices. In the final analysis, therefore, the question posed by the paper hinges on the strength of competitive forces in the labour markets. The question whether education contributes to economic growth turns out likewise to depend on the presence or absence of competitive labour markets.

An analysis is made of the internal logic of the three explanations. Also examined is the small quantity of direct evidence available on the link between education and the productivity of workers. An attempt is made to view familiar questions from a new angle and to relate the education-causes-growth debate to contentious issues in the field of educational planning.

Lee Hansen's words provide us with a text for this sermon.[1] We begin by noting a remarkable fact of life: between any two groups of individuals of the same age and sex, the one with more education will have higher average earnings than the one with less, even if the two groups are employed in the same occupational category in the same industry. The universality of this positive association between education and earnings is one of the most striking findings of modern social science. It is indeed one of the few safe generalisations that one can make about labour markets in all countries, whether capitalist or communist.[2] The question is: what can account for this phenomenon? It seems to me that there are basically only three explanations that merit any attention, all of which are hinted at in Lee Hansen's statement. Since it will be convenient to have labels for them, I shall arbitrarily call them the "economic explanation," the "sociological explanation" and the "psychological explanation." They correspond, roughly speaking, to three apparently conflicting propositions: (1) that education imparts vocationally useful skills that are in scarce supply; (2) that education disseminates definite social values, in effect recruiting people into the ruling elite of a society; and (3) that education merely selects people in accordance with their abilities. In so labelling these propositions, I do not mean to deny that, say, some economists believe that (2) is a better explanation of the correlation between education and earnings than (1), but simply that the three propositions seem to echo the jargon and to reflect the prevailing modes of thinking of the three respective social sciences. At any rate, nothing that follows depends in any critical way on the particular labels I have chosen.

The point of this paper is to ask: Are these really conflicting explanations, or are they all true in their own way? And if they are all true in their own way, would it make any difference if one of them were nearer the truth than the others?

1. The Economic Explanation

We may as well begin with the "economic explanation" since this is the most clearly formulated of the three views. It will be noticed that Lee Hansen complains that "our knowledge of what elements or ingredients of schooling make people more productive is scanty"; like most economists, he

---

[1] I wish to thank Richard Layard, George Psacharopoulos and Gareth Williams for helpful comments on an earlier draft of this paper.

[2] The evidence for 30 countries, 10 of which are developed countries, is briefly reviewed by Blaug (1970, pp. 23-27) and more fully documented by Psacharopoulos (1972). This sample includes no communist countries, but there are bits and pieces of evidence, particularly for the U.S.S.R., which suggest that communist countries conform to the world-wide pattern.

takes it almost for granted that schooling does raise the productivity of people, although the later reference to "a screening device" suggests that even economists have their doubts on the question.[3] Now the assertion that education renders people more productive is liable to be misunderstood. It seems to imply, first of all, that labour as a factor of production makes a definite contribution to output which can be distinguished without much difficulty from the contribution of other factors, such as management and capital equipment. But of course all factors of production participate jointly in the productive process and the separate contributions of each to final output can only be assessed at "the margin," that is, by holding constant the quantity and quality of all the other factors.

Furthermore, there are many margins: every type of machine has its own margin and, as for labour, there is a margin for each distinct attribute that enters into the hiring function of employers. A minimum list of these attributes would cover age, native ability, achievement drive, work experience, possession of specific skills, educational attainments, and on-the-job or in-plant training received. An employer cannot normally hire one of these attributes by itself, since each worker is a particular bundle of them, but he can acquire them indirectly by choosing different combinations of workers. In that sense, labour as a factor of production can be viewed as a vector of attributes, each of which has a distinct price. Thus, the proposition that "education renders people more productive" must be strictly read as "education makes the marginal worker more productive when he is furnished with the same quantity and quality of management, capital equipment and complement of all other workers as before." We can now ask if the earnings of educated labour generally exceed those of "raw labour," everything else being the same, is this evidence that the marginal product of educated labour is in fact greater that that of raw labour? Can we infer from observed earnings differentials associated with additional education that the marginal product of education is positive?

The textbook answer to this question is perfectly familiar to every student of elementary economics, and all we need to do here is to sketch its relevance to the problem at hand. It is "yes" if there is effective competition in labour markets. We must rely on competition between firms as producers for "efficient" utilisation of labour and on competition between firms as employers for "efficient" recruitment of labour. Since the demand curve for labour is simply the schedule of the (declining) marginal revenue products of labour, both of these propositions boil down to the basic rules of (1) profit

---

[3] For example, Albert Rees, in reviewing Gary Becker's *Human Capital* (Rees, 1965, pp. 958-60), mentions the possibility that the superior earnings of American college graduates are due to the prejudices of American employers rather than to the greater productivity of college-educated workers.

maximisation, (2) operating on the boundaries of the production function, and (3) hiring along *the* demand curve for a factor—these are all alternative ways of stating exactly the same thing. Similarly, we must rely on competition between workers to change jobs in the effort to maximise the "net advantages" derived from work; that is, to seek higher pecuniary returns unless they are offset by definite non-pecuniary disadvantages. Given the fulfillment of these conditions, every distinct type of labour will be paid its marginal product in equilibrium and hence we can indeed infer from the higher earnings of more educated workers that the marginal product of education is positive.

It is worth noting that this tells us little about the mechanism that produces a positive marginal product of education and, in particular, whether it is due to forces on the side of demand or on the side of supply. It is perfectly conceivable, for example, that it has nothing whatever to do with the demand for labour. Let us suppose that people with more education are always employed in "clerical" occupations, while people with less education are only employed in "manual" occupations; the marginal revenue product schedules of the two occupational categories happens to coincide, in the sense that identical increments of employment make identical contributions to output, whichever occupational class we are talking about. Nevertheless, because clerical occupations require more education and because education is costly to acquire, the relative scarcity of clerical labour will generate positive monetary returns to education (contrast W_2 and W_1 in Figure 1, ignoring D'_2 for the time being).

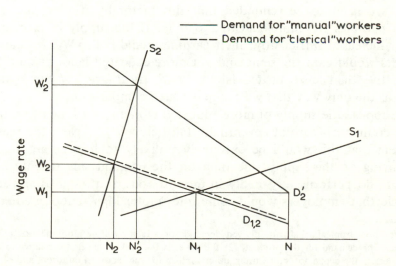

Figure 1. Demand and supply for two types of labour. Subscript 1 refers to less-educated workers; subscript 2 to more-educated workers.

The case is conceivable but it is not very likely. A glance at the Census of Population of the U.S.A. — the only country for which this kind of evidence is readily available — will show that more- and less- educated people are to be found in almost every one and two digit occupational category; occupation and education are so loosely associated that it is generally impossible to divide all occupations into two classes, confining, say, college graduates to one and elementary and high school graduates to the other.

The typical case is surely the one where both demand and supply contribute jointly to the phenomenon of higher earnings for more educated people. We can illustrate the argument by drawing the demand curve for more-educated workers, D'_2, above the demand curve for less-educated workers, D_1, in Figure 1. For the sake of simplicity, I draw straight-line demand curves, although their precise shape obviously depends on the elasticity of product demand curves and the underlying production functions of the industries that hire in this labour market. I have deliberately depicted the demand for more-educated labour as being more inelastic than the demand for less-educated labour in the effort to be realistic.[4] Likewise, the supply of more-educated labour, S_2, is depicted as being more inelastic than the supply of less-educated labour, S_1, although here both the evidence and *a priori* reasoning is more dubious than that concerning the demand for labour. The resulting relative wage rates and relative employment levels for the two types of labour are as we observe them in all labour markets of which we have knowledge, that is, $N'_2 < N_1$ and $W'_2 > W_1$.

As the diagram is drawn, more-educated labour is held to be more productive than less-educated labour at all levels of employment but, once again, we need to be reminded that this factor by itself cannot produce higher earnings for more-educated people. If the supply of more-educated labour increased sufficiently, their earnings could fall to W_1. In that case, all workers would earn the same and yet more-educated labour would be more productive than less-educated labour *at identical levels of employment*, N, which is the only way that we can make such comparisons.

Suppose the supply of more-educated workers continued to shift to the right, could their earnings eventually fall below W_1? Again, the reasons for thinking that this would be extremely unlikely to happen are much more convincing on the supply side than on the demand side. Highly educated workers do perform very badly in monotonous, routine jobs and it is conceivable that employers would sometimes prefer high school graduates even

---

[4] As we know from Marshall, the derived demand for a factor will be more inelastic (1) the more inelastic is the demand for the product, (2) the lower is the cost of the factor relative to total costs, (3) the less is the scope for substituting other factors for the factor in question, and (4) the more inelastic are the supply curves of substitute factors. One would defend the proposition in the text in terms of the special relevance of conditions (2), (3) and (4) to educated labour.

if they could get college graduates for less. At the moment, such cases are probably exceptional, occuring only in certain occupations and industries; their effects wash out when we aggregate the demand curves of industries into market demand curves, such as those of Figure 1. In general, it is probably true to say that more-educated workers are good technical substitutes for less-educated workers, but not *vice versa*, and this suffices to prevent W_2 from falling below W_1. But whatever we think of this argument, it is actually the restricted supply of educated people that keeps their earnings above those of "raw labour."

As every economist knows, to call one factor more productive than another is merely a different way of saying that it is relatively scarcer: There must be something that keeps the supply of educated labour low in relation to the demand for it, whatever it is, in contrast to the plentiful supply of "raw labour" in relation to the separate demand for it. This "something" is simply the costs of formal education to the individual in the form of fees (if any) and earnings foregone while studying. If people only demand education for consumption motives, the fact that it is costly will alone keep the demand within limits and will result in fewer people having, say, 15 years rather than 10 years of education. If the extra years of schooling then render people more productive, or at least if it opens up job opportunities hitherto closed to them, those with more education will find themselves earning more than those with less. This creates an investment motive in acquiring education, at least for some, and in consequence we get an additional demand for education. Nevertheless, it is a striking fact that the absolute supply of more-educated people is in all countries smaller than the absolute supply of less-educated people—even in the U.S.A. which practises a virtual open-door policy in secondary and higher education—clearly revealing the inhibitory effect of the private costs of education.[5]

If employers took no account of educational qualifications in hiring labour, the fact that the acquisition of education is costly would not of course suffice to generate a monetary return to additional years of schooling. Even a positive marginal product of education as such is only a necessary but not a sufficient condition. We have to add the existence of profit-maximising employers to get both necessary and sufficient conditions for the positive correlation between earnings and education. In short, the higher earnings of

---

[5] There is an additional supply consideration that may help to account for the higher earnings of more-educated workers. It is true that mean earnings generally increase with years of education but so does the variance of earnings: Some college graduates do earn less than high school graduates, even if we include the monetary value of fringe benefits in earnings. Educated people are more efficient at job searching, and since wage dispersion for identical occupations is a normal feature of labour markets, more-educated people are more likely to find a higher wage offer than less-educated people (Stigler, 1962).

more-educated people is proof of their superior productivity if and only if labour markets are competitive.

This is really all there is to the "economic explanation." The economist does not have to address himself directly to productivity as a variable intervening between education and earnings. Provided labour markets function competitively, earnings are a satisfactory measure of productivity and indeed in the limiting case of perfect competition, they are an exact measure. But this is precisely the point at which the misgivings begin. It is said that firms do not really strive to maximise profits: They maximise sales, or their market share, or they simply "satisfice," all of which may well leave them operating inside their production-possibility frontier.[6] Even if it is conceded that, whatever their motives, a Darwinian struggle to survive leads firms "best fitted" to survive to be profit maximisers, it is argued that labour markets among all markets are peculiarly prone to imperfections of all sorts.

The imperfections of the labour market with which we are concerned for present purposes are not those that usually crop up in textbook discussions of skilled and unskilled labour, such as the influence of collective bargaining on wage determination or the notorious disinclination of workers to explore job opportunities outside their own geographical area. It is rather those imperfections that seem particularly to characterise professional labour markets. In general, when a certain type of labour is in short supply, the employer must decide whether to offer the going wage while relaxing his hiring standards, or whether to maintain his hiring standards and to offer higher rates of pay. Alternatively, he can do neither and instead attempt to make the job appear more attractive by promising to provide in-plant training. All three methods of attracting labour are costly and the marginal re-

---

[6] There is the further contention associated with some Cambridge economists (Cambridge, England, not Cambridge, Massachusetts) that the concept of a production function is untenable, either because technical change is typically "embodied" in capital accumulation, so that the function shifts as we move along it (Kaldor, 1961, pp. 204–207), or because the stock of capital cannot be defined independently of the rate of interest or profit (Robinson, 1953); hence, all talk of marginal productivity must be ruled out as meaningless. These criticisms have been advanced in the context of aggregate growth theory and it is not entirely clear whether they are also meant to apply at the microeconomic level; indeed, the refusal to discuss the microeconomic foundations of macroeconomic proportions has become the hallmark of Cambridge economics.

Suffice it to say that even if all capital investment involved technical change, which is doubtful, we might still wish to retain the concept of a production function in the theory of the firm as a useful taxonomic device in analysing the various elements of a production decision. Furthermore, a production function should logically define all inputs in terms of flows, not stocks (Georgescu-Roegen, 1967, pp. 45–56); the decision to measure the stock of capital rather than the flow of machine-hours is merely an empirical compromise. The rate of interest or profit is strictly speaking irrelevant to the notion of a production function; it is only needed when we want to talk about the prices of machines, in which case we have to bring in the forces of thrift in addition to productivity considerations. All this is not to say that production function measurement is easy, or even that the idea of aggregate production functions is as meaningful as the concept of microeconomic production functions, but merely that the question we are posing cannot be ruled out as irrelevant on Kaldor-Robinson grounds.

cruitment costs are likely to be greater, the less specific the skill that is being hired. In the circumstances, employers tend to "hoard" their professional workers, that is, to treat their salaries as overhead costs and to resort to conventional rules-of-thumb in hiring them that have proved to be effective discriminants in the past. One plausible rule-of-thumb is to hire more-educated workers for complex jobs that involve initiative and drive, and less-educated workers for everything else; in short, to lean heavily on educational qualifications as an index of certain personal characteristics.

This brings us squarely to one of the principal economic functions of educational systems, namely, to certify the competence of students, if only competence to pass examinations. "Skill labelling" by paper qualifications, as Harvey Leibenstein (1965; 1969) calls it, is a useful social invention because it reduces hiring costs in labour markets by eliminating the need to test the type and degree of skill on every occasion the skill is bought. But there is obviously a great deal of history and tradition in skill labelling which is only remotely connected to current demands in the labour market. It is hard to believe, for example, that the length of courses, which in most cases has remained the same for generations, is now optimal for the particular skills that are labelled. It is also obvious that the "professionalisation" of certain occupations, like medecine, dentistry, teaching, law and accountancy invariably leads to longer courses and more technical syllabuses, thus effectively limiting entry to the profession by raising the minimum requirements for qualification. This acts to reduce the number of skills that are being labelled and thus narrows the range of potential substitution possibilities between different skills, all of which is to say that skill labelling in the real world is far from optimal; what started out as an effective device for reducing the costs of obtaining information ends up all too frequently as a potent source of the malutilisation of labour.

On the supply side, there are all the inherent difficulties of rapidly diffusing information about alternative job offers throughout labour markets, as well as the patent inadequacy of vocational counselling in schools and the weight of non-vocational factors in choosing careers. Besides, educational cycles are long, and in many countries it is difficult to change courses or fields of study half-way through the cycle. The longer we think about such elements in the situation, the less we are willing to believe in the free play of competitive forces that supposed to bring labour markets automatically into equilibrium.[7]

---

[7] Shortages (excess demand for labour) mean that people are paid less than their marginal products, and surpluses (excess supply of labour) mean that they are paid more. This follows from the fact that the feasible wage-employment region in a Marshallian diagram of the labour market is bounded by the demand curve at wage rates above the equilibrium rate and by the supply curve at wage rates below the equilibrium rate.

There is the further difficulty that in most countries anything from one-thirds to two-thirds of all highly qualified manpower is employed in the public sector at administered pay scales, which gear earnings directly to paper qualifications without any effort to check whether more education means better job performance.[8] If the private sector sets the rate of pay for the public sector, the fact that the marginal product of labour is difficult to define in the public sector raises no special problems: Earnings in the public sector will reflect the marginal revenue product of labour in the economy. But the public sector may decide to pay more than the marginal revenue product of labour to ease its recruitment problems—as appears to be the case in Britain (Scitovsky, 1966, Table 9)—or to pay less to create employment opportunities—as in many underdeveloped countries. Our only test of "more" or "less" is the marginal product of labour in the private sector. The concept of the marginal productivity has no meaning in the public sector, not so much because the government does not sell its output, so that an increment of output cannot be valued in monetary terms—we could get round that by using some weighted bundle of physical indicators—but because governments are not profit-maximisers and hence can produce any output of public services that Parliament approves. Governments may or may not utilise labour efficiently within a given budget, but the size of the budget itself lacks any economic rationale. Thus, to talk about the marginal productivity of the civil service is to abuse technical language. It follows that the larger the proportion of educated people employed in the civil service or the armed forces of an economy, the less likely it is that government salaries will be passively adapted to salaries in private industry. Once they are set free from the constraint of having to compete for labour with the private sector, the shoe is on the other foot. The tendency to force artificially high pay scales on private industry is checked in the long run by the decline of private investment and the disappearance of tax revenues; and the tendency to pay below the private sector ultimately defeats itself in a drain of labour out of the public into the private sector. However, these tendencies may take decades to work themselves out and in the meanwhile, the higher earnings of better-educated people may bear little relationship to the marginal product of education, whatever it is. Fortunately, the private sector in most countries does pay highly qualified manpower above the pay scales prevailing in the

---

[8] It is not possible to give precise figures for Britain. To the best of our knowledge – the most recent evidence dates from the Robbins Report in 1963 and even that is not available in the form required to answer the question – about 35 per cent of all those with higher education in the labour force are teachers and another 10 per cent are employed in the civil service, the nationalised industries and government research stations. U.G.C. figures on the *First Employment of University Graduates* in recent years show that 40-45 per cent of *new* graduates take up employment in the public sector.

public sector[9] and, in that sense, the marginal product of labour in private industry remains a key element in determining the actual structure of salaries in the economy. Nevertheless, the high proportion of qualified people employed by governments around the world must sap our confidence in the competitive model of professional labour markets.

All this is purely speculative. Is there no empirical evidence that we can bring to bear on the question? What in fact are the results predicted by a competitive model of labour markets? In one sense, the model is not very powerful: it predicts that excess demand will raise and excess supply will lower relative earnings either per job or per man; it predicts that labour of the same type will fetch the same price in any local labour market but not if that labour is employed in different occupations and under different working conditions, a qualification that is frequently overlooked; it also predicts that skills which are costly to acquire will tend to command higher earnings. The simple textbook theory of competitive labour markets is silent, however, about the length of time it takes to produce a response in situations of disequilibrium and it is even silent about the exact nature of this response. [10] This is precisely why the theory is difficult to test and why the evidence to date fails to convince sceptics.

Arrow and Capron (1959; see also Folk, 1970; Richardson, 1969) have demonstrated that persistent excess demand for American engineers and scientists over a decade or so has raised their relative salaries, and others (Blaug, Layard and Woodhall, 1969) have shown that chronic excess supply of graduates in a country like India has steadily eroded the real earnings differentials associated with higher education. Moreover, if the word "skill" is used in its broadest sense to refer to acquired abilities of any kind, the fact that more-educated people earn more the world over is itself evidence in favour of the competitive model. But other interpretations of these findings are possible. At any rate, the notion that market forces broadly govern the determination of wages and salaries, and that therefore competitive pressures do make themselves felt in labour markets, has been categorically dismissed time and again, particularly by British writers.[11] One commentator has gone

---

[9] This is true even in Tropical Africa and South-East Asia, although the contrary is often asserted. Some African governments in the 1950's did pay graduates more than they could earn in the private sector, but the stickiness of public sector pay scales and the growth of private industry has by now reversed these differentials to conform to the general pattern around the world.

[10] But a recent collection of essays (Phelps, 1970) has at long last broken the ice in developing a dynamic theory of labour market adjustments.

[11] Perhaps the most famous dismissal is Wootton's (1954). A recent example is Routh (1965, pp. 144–47) who rejects "the theory of demand and supply" on the basis of wath is, at best, thin evidence of rigidities in the British occupational pay structure since 1900; no reference is made in the book to the existence of a well-behaved Phillips curve in the inter-war period, and the concept of occupations on which the argument is based, namely, the Registrar General's five social classes, is so broad as to be almost useless for testing any theory about the structure of pay.

so far as to note that "it is, indeed, bad form, even to use the word 'market' in association with labour, among British manpower administrators and legislators" (Crossley, 1970, p. 127). Recent discussions of a voluntary or statutory incomes policy has further encouraged the man-in-the-street view that we can make wages and salaries just about anything we want them to be.[12]

This is not one of those questions that can be settled with a yes/no answer. There seems to be some consensus among labour economists that competitive wage theory is successful in predicting long-run changes in occupational wage differentials but, on the other hand, it has a poor record in predicting short-run changes in interindustry wage differentials.[13] Be that as it may, we may sum up by underlining the fact that the "economic explanation" of the correlation between education and earnings ultimately depends on a broad, empirical judgement in favour of the competitive hypothesis. It must, in the nature of the case, be a complex judgement because we are dealing with a whole series of labour markets, and statements that we can make about some do not necessarily apply to others. There is clearly a world of difference between the labour market for secondary school leavers and that for graduates, to give only one example, and I myself am tempted by the idea that the relatively high cost of graduates to employers and the relatively high mobility of graduates make graduate labour markets more subject to competitive pressures than markets for unskilled labour. But this is an idea that yet remains to be clearly demonstrated.

---

[12] A beautiful illustration of this tendency is a recent outburst by Peter Hall, an eminent geographer: "We shall have to ask why I, a university professor, am paid five times as much as a dustman (and have just been given a 10 per cent increase, representing a sum which, given to the dustman, would keep him in comfort for years). We shall need to ask also why X, a company director, is paid five times as much as I am. It will be no good, is no good now, trying to answer this question in economic terms. I don't earn more than the dustman by reason of the resources put into my education (that hoary old myth of the educational economists, which is purely question begging). Nor do I earn more by reason of the demand for my services, which in the last resort is far less than that for dustmen. (Finally, I need the dustman, while, save in a strictly metaphysical sense, he doesn't need me.) No: the reason I get more is that somewhere society has formed a half-developed notion on this subject, and has then cemented it by social and political pressures. We shall need to find a way of breaking these lazy notions of consensus, and starting the whole argument from the beginning" (Hall, 1970). I count three major and two minor fallacies in this passage, which is not of course to say that the present differential between the earnings of university professors and dustmen is due to competition, pure and simple. Economic theory has almost nothing to say about the precise magnitude of earnings differentials, but it does predict a positive differential between university professors and dustmen, even when both (as in this case) are employed in the public sector and paid on pre-determined scales.

[13] See Pierson (1957); Ross (1957); Perlman (1969, chs. 4 and 5) and, as the best single source, the papers in Burton *et al.* (1971).

2. Direct evidence

Since it is so difficult to test the proposition that labour markets are subject to competition, perhaps we should look for direct evidence of the "economic explanation." The well-known finding that the same job category as invariably filled by people with a wide range of educational qualifications suggests immediately that we cannot expect to discover a simple link between schooling and the contribution of an individual to final output. There is also the difficulty, that we spoke of earlier, of isolating the specific contribution of a worker, not to mention the contribution of education as distinct from other attributes of labour. Undaunted by these difficulties, however, a recent study by Ivar Berg (1970), revealingly entitled *Education and Jobs: The Great Training Robbery,* collects all the available evidence for the United States on the link between education and productivity, concluding that education generally does *not* raise the productivity of workers.

Berg started out by interviewing employers and found that they typically justify their emphasis on educational qualifications by claiming that years of schooling are good evidence of the ability to get along with others—the "sociological explanation"—but they also made frequent reference to the notion that more-educated workers have a greater potential to be promoted to more responsible jobs (Berg, 1970, pp. 72–80)—the "economic explanation." Somewhat more conclusive, however, is his finding that employers in such diverse industries as steel, rubber, textiles and packaging rarely analyse their own hiring practices and indeed do not even record the educational qualifications of all workers on their personnel record cards (Berg, 1970, pp. 78–79, 92–94, 117).[14] The absence of some sort of manpower planning at the factory level is indeed strongly suggestive of purely conventional hiring practices.

Next, Berg examined evidence from "job analysis," that is, the attempt to delineate and quantify the skill content of jobs and to relate these to minimum educational requirements for effective performance in jobs. He made liberal use of a carefully designed study of "worker trait requirements" by the United States Employment Service. It examined the minimum requirements of a job in terms of what was called "general educational development" (GED) and "specific vocational preparation" (SVP) categories, covering a wide sample of about 4,000 jobs listed in the American *Dictionary of Occupational Titles* in both 1956 and 1966. A brief word of explanation of the method is required to grasp the use that Berg made of the data: The GED scale covers reasoning ability, mathematical skills and language

---

[14] A similar finding is reported for some British electrical engineering firms (Blaug, Peston and Ziderman, 1967, p. 27).

competence; each of these is measured separately on an ordinal scale in seven steps, and the final estimate of the requirements of a job is simply the highest rating the job receives on each of the three scales. Because of variations in the quality of schooling throughout the 50 States of the Union and because of the possibility that work experience can make up for any lack of GED, the Employment Service disavowed any attempt to translate GED into years of schooling, although SVP was in fact expressed in terms of training weeks. Some years ago, Richard Eckaus (1964) translated the GED categories in the first of the two surveys into what he believed to be equivalent years of schooling and combined these with the length of time specified for the SVP categories; applying these estimates to the American occupational census of 1940 and 1950, he classified the entire labour force in each major sector of the economy by its "education and training requirements" in the two census years and arrived at the dramatic finding that there was a "surplus" of high school graduates in 1950 but a "shortage" of college graduates.

Berg extends Eckaus' method to the 1966 version of the worker traits requirements study, but he goes well beyond Eckaus in presenting multi-valued rather than single-valued conversions. He admits candidly that the results depend entirely on how "requirements" are matched with "achievements," that is, on the actual relationship of GED and years of schooling, which is of course precisely what we want to know. To surmount this difficulty he uses a range of plausible equivalences and comes to the conclusion that "whether there is a shortage or an 'excess' of college graduates [in 1966] depends on whether jobs requiring a GED of 5 are regarded as jobs for college graduates or as jobs that can be performed adequately by persons who have graduated from high school and have undergone some college training" (Berg, 1970, p. 51). In plain language, you can make the answer come out any way you want to! In extending Eckaus' methods, Berg has in fact undermined this approach to measuring the educational requirements of jobs.[15]

The rest of Berg's evidence is even less persuasive of his basic thesis: it shows that more-educated workers have higher turnover rates and that their use therefore imposes unsuspected costs on employers; unfortunately, this seems to prove, not that educated labour is no more productive than "raw labour," but that they must be much more productive if employers go on hiring them. The upshot of Berg's book is to cast doubt, not so much on the "economic explanation" of the correlation between earnings and education,

---

[15] As he puts it diplomatically: "The problem in estimating the nature of the utilization of educated manpower in the United States by the 'direct approach' are, at the very least, a good deal more complex than might be supposed from a reading of the earlier and groundbreaking studies, even after allowing for their cautious stipulations concerning the adequacy of the data" (Berg, 1970, pp. 58–59).

as on the effort to measure the productivity of individual workers in purely physical terms.

We turn now to a completely different way of tackling the problem, namely, by interfirm, interindustry and international comparisons. A recent cross-section study by Richard Layard and others (1971) compares the educational structure of a random sample of 68 plants employing 26,000 non-manual workers in the British electrical engineering industry with various indicators of the economic performance of establishments. The industrial census divided the electrical engineering industry into six minimum list headings by type of product produced, such as electronic equipment, heavy electrical goods, wires and cables, etcetera. Within these headings, plants are producing more or less the same product, which ought to mean that at any point in time, they operate with the same capital–labour ratio and with the same combinations of different types of labour. But of course the plants are not all of the same age or size and therefore we might expect some to use more up-to-date equipment than others, which would lead to differences in the occupational and educational composition of their work force. And indeed there are wide disparities in the proportions of people with different educational qualifications employed by different factories making the same products. Now if education does raise the productivity of people, we might expect that education-intensive plants would enjoy either higher profit rates, or larger sales per unit of capital, or faster rates of growth of sales, or higher outputs per unit of labour, or lower unit costs. But none of these expectations is borne out by the evidence. Differences in the educational and occupational structure of the labour force of plants within sub-categories of the electrical engineering industry in Britain are not statistically related to any of the factors mentioned above, nor even to capital–labour ratios, or the type of productive process employed, or the size and country of origin of the parent firm.

Likewise, efforts to estimate either Cobb-Douglas or CES production functions for each of the six minimum list headings, where the labour force is broken down into four types of labour depending on its level of education (namely, graduates, professionally trained people, H.N.C.'s and O.N.C.'s), yielded statistically insignificant coefficients for educated labour; to put it more precisely, the estimates could not reject the hypothesis that all the labour inputs are perfect substitutes.[16] What is even more surprising is the

---

[16] These estimates by Denis Sargan are the first to introduce education into cross-section measurements of production functions by disaggregating labour in terms of educational attainments. Previous efforts to do so for time-series data are difficult to interpret for our purposes because they have almost always introduced education as a pure labour-augmenting index, the weights of which are the very earnings differentials by levels of education that we want to explain. The literature in this area is too vast to survey adequately in a footnote: For some references, see Griliches (1970).

fact that the estimates only improved slightly when labour was divided into only two types, namely, "H.N.C. and above" and "less than H.N.C."

The almost wholly negative results of the Layard study can be interpreted in at least five different ways. Firstly, we can deny that output is really homogeneous in the electrical engineering industry even within minimum list headings; in other words, the plants in question were not on the same production function. This explanation receives some support from the fact that the only statistically significant regressions in the entire study are those in which the proportions of educated labour in plants are regressed on four dummy variables that reflect the product mix of plants. Secondly, we can deny the implicit assumption of the study that all plants at the same point in time are optimally adjusted to given factor and product prices: If it takes time to adjust to changes in product and factor markets, some plants might adjust more quickly than others and this would explain why we do not discover any systematic relationships between economic variables across plants. Thirdly, we can assert that certain things which are in fact important to the economic performance of factories, such as the character of their management, or their pricing policy, or their research-orientation, are not included in the regressions and this is why no definite relationships emerge. Fourthly, we can argue, somewhat speciously, that the results show that more-educated workers are indeed perfect substitutes for less-educated workers; although educated workers make a disproportionate contribution to output, this contribution is exactly offset by their higher earnings.[17] Lastly, we can give up the fight and admit that the Layard results are evidence against the notion that firms are efficient in utilising labour: if labour is hired haphazardly, or if hiring is governed by rules-of-thumb which vary from firm to firm, or if there is "conspicuous consumption" of educated workers because employers derive utility from working with highly educated employees, we would get precisely the results produced by the Layard study. In short, we must conclude that our confidence in the "economic explanation" is now somewhat shaken.

Consider finally an OECD study (1970) which compares entire sectors of an economy across 52 countries. Here the regression results are not quite so dramatic. Nevertheless, no definite and unambiguous relationships emerge between the proportions of labour with different years of schooling and output per head, capital per worker, energy consumption per worker and even composite social indicators of living standards. I find it difficult to interpret these findings because they do not correspond to any recognisable theory of the relationship between economic variables: Economic theory does *not* lead one to expect that there is any unique relationship between the educational

---

[17] For a formal analysis of this case, see Johnson (1970).

density of an entire sector of an economy and output per worker or capital per worker in the sector (see my comments set out at greater length in OECD, 1970, pp. 283–286). The only way to make sense of the OECD regression is to assume that different countries are on the same sectoral production functions, although at different points on these production functions. Although this is a standard assumption of modern international trade theory, at least for the traded goods of identical industries if not for identical sectors of different countries, the mind boggles at the factors that are typically excluded in production-function measurements which are surely not invariant between countries, such as natural resource endowments, the quality of management and the work habit of the labour force. At any rate, those who are still naive enough to believe that education is *the* key to economic growth will find sufficient grounds in the OECD study to think again.

3. What Difference Does It Make?

We turn to the explanation of sociologists and psychologists. We have to invent the "sociological explanation" of the correlation between education and earnings because sociologists have not in fact addressed themselves directly to the problem. Reading between the lines, however, the argument seems to fall into two parts, the first of which simply dismisses the correlation as spurious.

It asserts that the correlation between native ability and earnings, or between acquired ability and earnings—the formulation depends on the view taken of the nature versus nurture debate—is at least as high as between education and earnings. To put it very bluntly, clever and/or middle class children get more schooling than stupid and/or working class children, and later they earn more simply because they have had all the advantages in life, of which more education is only one and not even the most important one. Now it is clear that what we have here is a straightforward empirical question which calls for multiple regression analysis of the determinants of personal earnings. A great deal of work of this kind has in fact been carried out in the United States, as well as in Sweden, Mexico and Kenya (for a review, see Blaug, 1970, pp. 32–54). The broad implication of these studies is to show that education does raise earnings, even if we hold constant father's occupation, father's and mother's education, IQ of the individual taken at an early age and school examination scores. A fair summary of the evidence to-date is to say that Denison was not far wrong in *The Sources of Economic Growth* (1962, pp. 69–70) when he attributed three-fifths of the earnings differentials between elementary and high school graduates and between college and high school graduates in the United States to the pure effect of extra years of schooling; this American finding seems to stand up fairly well even in other countries.[18] It would be naive to assert that the question is now settled and that all must agree that the correlation between education and earnings cannot be explained away in terms of social class origins. However, for present purposes it is interesting to note that even if everyone accepted the Denison finding, there is still scope for a "sociological explanation" of the earnings differentials that are attributable to education.

The argument rests on the fact that all organisations are hierarchically managed so that as we descend from the apex, the number of superiors and the extent of accountability to those higher up in the chain of command continually increases, while the number of underlings and the degree of independence from the supervision of others continually decreases.[19] Those who stand at the top of each layer, and particularly those who occupy positions in the upper layers, must have the personal confidence to command others and must share a common loyalty to the organisation if the organisation is to survive at all. It is no accident that the members of what Galbraith calls "the technostructure" are usually highly educated people because anyone who has crossed the successive hurdles of secondary and higher education is likely to have acquired the appropriate personality traits of independence and self-reliance; they have become accustomed, as it were, to thinking of themselves as members of an intellectual elite, and they are not likely to quibble at joining an elite within an organisation.

This argument looks very plausible if we confine our attention to business executives, government officials and administrators of all kinds, but at this level it is difficult to distinguish it from "the economic explanation." Economists would say that these people earn more because they are more productive: They continually have to assess new information and to take non-routine decisions, and it is precisely their education that has equipped them for these tasks. The difficulty is that of applying the "sociological explanation" across-the-board. What we must explain is not just why univer-

---

[18] It may be worth scotching a frequent misunderstanding of Denison's "three-fifths assumption," or what I prefer to call "the alpha-coefficient": It refers to a proportion of the difference between two earnings streams, not to a proportion of absolute earnings. Thus, the common finding that schooling as such contributes little to educational performance in standardised tests—e.g. the Plowden evidence that only 26 per cent of the "explained" variance in children's performance on a reading comprehension test in British primary schools is due to differences in the quality of schools (Plowden, 1967, p. 33)—is perfectly compatible with a large alpha-coefficient. Suppose that the Plowden result also held in both lower and upper secondary schools but that performance nevertheless improves as children go from Fourth Forms to Sixth Forms. In that case, if sixth form leavers earn more than fourth form leavers—which they do—most of this *difference* may be due to additional schooling.

[19] The crucial concept is what Elliott Jacques (1956) calls the "time span of discretion," namely, the length of time for which workers are exempt from supervisory review, which he argues ought to be made the basis of the pay structure of a company. The "sociological explanation" says in effect that the "time span of discretion" is already the basis of the pay structure of most organisations.

sity graduates earn more than secondary school leavers, but why secondary school leavers earn more than those who leave at 15. More generally, in underdeveloped countries where some children do not attend school at all, and others start working at the age of 10, 12, 14, and so on, we have to explain why positive earnings differentials emerge even for an additional sixth, seventh and eighth year of education.[20] If graduates earn more because they are "leaders of men," are we expected to believe that this also applies to high school graduates and even to primary school leavers?

These difficulties do not exist for the "psychological explanation," which is indeed perfectly general. Assume once again that organisations are hierarchically arranged,[21] not only because of the nature of decision-making but also because of the technical characteristics of the production process. The structure of occupations and the corresponding structure of rewards in industry takes on the shape of a pyramid; the further up the pyramid we go, the greater is the degree of responsibility imposed on job incumbents, and the greater is the degree of initiative required from them. Employers are not sure that they can measure the particular bundle of attributes required to rise up the pyramid, but they have found from past experience that there is a general concordance between such abilities and educational attainments. In that sense, educational credentials act as surrogates for qualities which the employer regards as important: They predict a higher level of performance without necessarily making any direct contribution to it. From the point of view of students, on the other hand, this characteristic of educational credentials provides an urge to obtain more education as the only way of securing a competitive advantage in the labour market: An additional paper qualification acts in effect as a "union card" for entry into the apex of the occupational pyramid.[22] This explanation neatly accounts for the fact that

---

[20] It is noteworthy that there is African and Asian evidence that significant earnings differentials only occur once a worker has acquired 4-5 years of schooling; having only a few years of primary education seems to make little difference to earnings prospects.

[21] The argument that follows is a generalisation of the work of Simon and Lydall (1968, pp. 125–133), which invokes the hierarchic hypothesis to show that the distribution of salaries in an organisation will follow the Pareto Law.

[22] For a succinct statement of "the psychologist's explanation" we have to go to the writings of an economist: "To be sure, economic growth is *associated with* higher education, but which is cause and *which* effect? Who is to say that Enoch Powell is wrong?—higher education might be simply a consumption good for which rich communities develop a taste as much as rich individuals like foreign travel. The so-called economic yield on higher education might be due to little more than this: Clever people usually get more money than stupid people, but they will also compete for degrees and pre-empt university places once a prejudice in favour of degrees has been established. And such a prejudice might be initially due to nothing more than the convenience to employers of a free external testing system: The universities, already existing in adequate numbers, happen to be able to certify, at an absurdly great cost, which *are* the clever ones. So employers demand degrees, and from there on the whole expansion might be a vicious circle" (Wiles, 1969, p. 195; see also Nelson, 1967).

education and earnings are positively correlated; it even explains why so many educational qualifications appear to be unrelated to the type of work that individuals take up and why the returns to the terminal year of a cycle of education are frequently disproportionately larger than the returns to earlier years, the so-called "sheepskin effect."

The general implications of the "psychological explanation" are devastating. Since the economic returns to society on this argument are merely those of providing a screening device for employers, and since the provision of education everywhere entails considerable subsidies to students, the net contribution of education to national output must be negative. Education is not a form of investment in economic growth and to provide more education simply increases the scramble for top jobs without adding anything to productive capacity; in short, education is a service, the supply of which automatically creates its own demand by virtue of the flexibility of hiring standards for jobs. To put it slightly differently, the fact that more-educated people earn more simply means that they "exploit" the less-educated: Since educated labour is paid more than its marginal product, "raw labour" must be paid less.[23]

These conclusions are subject to some possible qualifications. Firstly, education may generate production-externalities such that more education for some, while in no way adding to their own marginal product, nevertheless, raises the productivity of others who have not enjoyed additional education. Although we know very little about the external effects of education (Blaug, 1970, pp. 105–114), the case in question is utterly implausible because it is impossible for an employer to select one set of abilities on the basis of paper qualifications without excluding another set; it is hardly likely, therefore, that less-educated people would somehow benefit from the presence of more-educated people. Secondly, there is some suggestive evidence that highly educated workers in the U.S. economy actually receive more on-the-job and in-plant training than less-educated workers (Mincer, 1962, pp. 59–61). If this were found to be true elsewhere, it would allow us in some sense to combine the "economic" and the "psychological explanation": Educated labour is more productive but only because education increases the likelihood that a worker will benefit from job-related instruction; employers quite rationally treat educational credentials as an index of trainability, although formal education as such has no significance from the point

---

[23] It is conceivable of course that educated labour "exploits" capital rather than raw labour. Lester Thurow (1969, pp. 163–168) produces evidence, based on a time series estimate of the aggregate production function for the American economy, that the earnings of the average American worker are less than the marginal product of labour; in other words, it is capital that has been "exploiting" labour. But these estimates throw no light on the gap between the earnings and marginal products of labour by levels of education.

of view of output. Thirdly, it is conceivable that the main economic importance of schooling is not its direct contribution to the marginal product of labour but rather its indirect effect on the marginal product of physical capital, or better still, on the quality of all inputs in the productive process. For example, Welch (1970) has shown that much of the impact of added schooling in U.S. agriculture, at least with respect to college, although not with respect to high school education, derives from the dynamic character of changing technology, that is, from the tendency of better-educated farmers to adopt innovations more readily. Nevertheless, despite evidence of overall slack in certain industries and even in entire sectors of modern economics (Leibenstein, 1966; Mack, 1968, pp. 47–54), which emphasizes the importance of managerial inputs, it is questionable that this argument is sufficiently general for the purposes at hand: once again, it must be emphasised that the positive correlation between education and earnings is not confined only to those in executive or managerial positions.

We may conclude, therefore, that the "psychological explanation" is in fact destructive of the investment view of education: The educational system is merely an extremely expensive selection mechanism which forces people through finer and finer sieves without adding anything to them along the way. No doubt, employers need some device for discovering skills and abilities, and no doubt it is economical to certify skills once and for all so as to avoid repeated testing every time a worker changes jobs. But surely it ought to be possible to do the job more cheaply by completely divorcing the certification of skills from formal schooling? Why not certify skills once-for-all by means of nationally administered tests at the point of first employment, regardless of how the skill was obtained?

To pose the question is to see the difficulties. First of all, it would shift the cost of certification from general tax funds to employers themselves and employers would of course resist such a change. But waiving that point, what evidence do we have that there exists any set of psychological tests that could certify skills and abilities as effectively per unit of costs as an educational qualification? It is precisely the length of a typical educational cycle leading up to a final credential that is one of its strengths: Students are examined not once but repeatedly by a large number of people in the performance of a diverse set of tasks. For all its shortcomings, a degree or diploma may in fact provide a more sensitive test of a person's general abilities than any number of psychological aptitude and intelligence tests.

The "psychological explanation" goes too far: It virtually implies that ability and drive are innate capacities that require no development, only discovery. It ignores the whole area of professional and vocational education which does impart specific skills that cannot be acquired except by formal preparation. More to the point, it simply ignores the fact that firms often promote from within and only hire new workers at the bottom of their pay scales, partly to maintain morale and partly because much better information is available on their own employees than on new recruits to the firm. Although very little reliable information is available on this point, it appears that educated people change jobs five or six times over a lifetime in contrast to some thirty or forty occasions on which they receive a salary increment from the firm in which they are currently employed. When a worker is internally promoted, there is no reason whatever to rely heavily on educational credentials as an indicator of his skills, abilities and values, and this may well explain why Berg and others have found that many employers do not even bother permanently to record a worker's educational attainments.[24] In short, the "psychological explanation" is at best only part of the story.

4. Conclusion

It is time to draw the threads together. As we suspected all along, there is a sense in which all three explanations hold simultaneously. Employers pay educated people more, even when their education has taught them no specific skill, because they are more achievement-motivated, more self-reliant, act with greater initiative in problem-solving situations, adapt themselves more easily to changing circumstances, assume supervisory responsibilities more quickly, and benefit more from work experience and on-the-job training. They pay them more not only when they hire them but they go on paying them more throughout their working life. In short, they expect them to be more productive than less-educated people and the expectation is borne out. The weakness of the "sociological" and "psychological explanation" is precisely that the advantages of more-educated people show up at every age throughout working life. Now we cannot have it both ways: Either the educational system is a superb discriminant of the sort of abilities industry demands, in which case we must conclude that this is the economic role of education until such a time that a better screening device is invented,

---

[24] In a remarkable book that came my way after this paper was completed, Doeringer and Piore (1971) distinguish between the "internal labour market" of an enterprise, within which the pricing and allocation of labour is governed by administrative procedures, and the external labour market of conventional economics. The two are connected by certain job categories which mark entry and exit points to and from the internal system; the remainder of jobs within the internal labour market are filled by the promotion or transfer of workers who have already gained entry. This is precisely the point of the remarks in the text above. Although their book deals largely with blue-collar workers in manufacturing, their analysis is extremely suggestive for the question of earnings differentials among white-collar workers. See, in particular, Doeringer and Piore (1971, pp. 3, 47, 76–7, 103–7, 194).

or it is only a crude way of selecting people that misinforms as frequently as it informs, in which case it is not clear why employers do not correct their initial hiring mistakes. But of course that assumes that employers are continually tightening up the allocation of labour, which they would only do if they were subject to competitive pressures. We come back full circle, therefore, to the question of competition in labour markets. It is the action of competition in a labour market that allows all three explanations to hold simultaneously. Contrariwise, the less are the pressures to compete, the weaker is the "economic explanation" and the stronger are those of the sociologist and psychologist. Thus, the much-publicised idea that education contributes directly to economic growth by the formation of "human capital," rather than indirectly by changing basic values and attitudes, rests ultimately on the belief that competition is at work in labour markets; without that, there is only presumption, not proof.[25]

LA SIGNIFICATION DE LA CORRELATION ENTRE L'EDUCATION ET LE REVENU

Résumé

Cette étude examine trois explications possibles d'un fait fondamental: dans la trentaine de pays sur lesquels a porté l'investigation, le niveau d'éducation est en relation étroite avec le salaire des individus. (1) L'explication "économique" revient à dire que les individus à fort niveau d'instruction gagnent davantage parce que l'éducation procure les compétences techniques qui sont aujourd'hui les plus rares. (2) L'explication "sociologique" explique le même phénomène par le fait que la longueur de la scolarité est elle-même fonction de l'origine de classe, ou par le fait que l'éducation diffuse les valeurs sociales les plus valorisées par l'élite dirigeante de la société. (3) L'explication "psychologique" affirme que l'éducation ne fait que sélectionner les individus selon leurs aptitudes innées, en sorte que les plus capables gagnent plus que ceux qui le sont moins.

On se demande si ces explications sont vraiment contradictoires. On montre qu'une appréciation adéquate de l'explication économique implique les deux autres. Sur un marché de travail, où jouerait une concurrence pure,

---

[25] It is ironic that Enoch Powell, who elsewhere displays great faith in the efficacy of the market mechanism, denies that higher education contributes to growth: "the growth theory of education is bunkum . . . economic growth is no more caused by the increase of education than by the prevalence of leisure or of motor cars" (Powell, 1968). This denial, we now see, amounts to the repudiation of the model of perfect competition applied to labour markets. But in that case, what becomes of the faith in free markets?

les salaires indiqueraient nécessairement la rareté relative des "compétences techniques qui sont professionnellement utiles"; d'autre part la compétence professionelle devrait comprendre la possession des valeurs et des motivations qui conviennent au milieu industriel. Mais, en l'absence d'une concurrence pressante, il peut se faire que les salaires se fondent sur des estimations purement conventionnelles. En définitive, la force de la concurrence sur le marché du travail est le pivot de la question. La question de savoir si l'éducation contribue à l'expansion économique renvoie-t-elle aussi à la présence ou à l'absence de rivalité sur les marchés du travail.

On procède à une analyse de la logique interne des trois explications. On examine aussi les quelques données disponibles qui pourraient prouver la liaison entre l'éducation et la productivité des ouvriers. On essaie de renouveler ces questions en mettant en rapports le débat de l'éducation et de la croissance avec les questions débattues dans le domaine de la planification de l'enseignement.

References

Arrow, K. J. and Capron, W. M. (1959). "Dynamic Shortages and Price Rises: The Engineer-Scientist Case," *Q. J. Econ.* (May).

Berg, I. (1970). *Education and Jobs: The Great Training Robbery.* New York: Praeger.

Blaug, M. (1970). *An Introduction to the Economics of Education.* London: Allen Lane the Penguin Press.

Blaug, M., Layard, R. and Woodhall, M. (1969). *Causes of Graduate Unemployment in India.* London: Allen Lane the Penguin Press.

Blaug, M., Peston, M. and Ziderman, A. (1967). *The Utilization of Educated Manpower in Industry.* London: Oliver & Boyd.

Burton, J. F. Jr., *et al.* (1971). *Readings in Labor Market Analysis.* New York: Holt, Rinehart and Winston.

Crossley, J. R. (1970). "Theory and Methods of National Manpower Policy," *Scott. J. Polit. Econ.* (June).

Denison, E. F. (1962). *The Sources of Economic Growth in the U.S. and the Alternatives Before Us.* Committee for Economic Development.

Doeringer, P. B. and Piore, M. J. (1971). *Internal Labor Markets and Manpower Analysis.* Boston: D. C. Heath.

Eckaus, R. S. (1964). "Economic Criteria for Education and Training," *Rev. Econ. and Statist.* (May).

Folk, H. (1970). *The Shortage of Scientists and Engineers.* Heath Lexington Books.

Georgescu-Roegen, N. (1967). "Chamberlin's New Economics and the Unit of Production," in Kuenue, R. E., ed., *Monopolistic Competition Theory: Studies in Impact.* New York: Wiley.

Griliches, Z. (1970). "Notes on the Role of Education in Production Functions and Growth Accounting," in Hansen, W. L., ed., *Education, Income and Human Capital.* New York: Columbia University Press.

Hall, P. (1970). "It is a Moral Issue," *New Society* (December 17).

Hansen, W. L. (1970). "Introduction," in Hansen, W. L., ed., *Education, Income and Human Capital.* New York: Columbia University Press.

Jacques, E. (1956). *Measurement of Responsibility.* London: Tavistock Publications.

Johnson, G. E. (1970). "The Demand for Labor by Educational Category," *South. Econ. J.* (October).

Kaldor, N. (1961). "Capital Accumulation and Economic Growth," in Lutz, F. A., *The Theory of Capital.* New York: Macmillan.

Layard, P. R. G., Sargan, J. D., Ager, M. E. and Jones, D. J. (1971). *Qualified Manpower and Economic Performance.* London: Allen Lane the Penquin Press.

Leibenstein, H. (1965). "Shortages and Surpluses in Education in Underdeveloped Countries," in Anderson, C. A. and Bowman, M. J., eds., *Education and Economic Development.* Chicago: Aldine Press.

Leibenstein, H. (1969). "Economics of Skill Labelling," in Lauwerys, J. A. and Scanlon, D. G., eds., *World Year Book of Education 1969. Examinations.* London: Evans Brothers.

Leibenstein, H. (1966). "Allocative Efficiency vs. '*X-Efficiency*'," *Am. Econ. Rev.* (June).

Lydall, H. (1968). *The Structure of Earnings.* London: Oxford University Press.

Mack, R. P. (1968). "Ecological Processes in Economic Change: Models, Measurement and Meaning," *Am. Econ. Rev.* (May).

Mincer, J. (1962). "On-the-Job Training: Cost, Returns, and Some Implications," *J. Polit. Econ., Supplement* (October).

Nelson, R. R. (1967). "Aggregate Production Functions and Economic Growth Policy," in Brown, M., ed., *The Theory and Empirical Analysis of Production.* New York: Columbia University Press.

OECD (1970). *Occupational and Educational Structures of the Labour Force and Levels of Economic Development.* Paris: OECD.

Perlman, R. (1969). *Labor Theory.* New York: Wiley.

Phelps, E. S. *et al.* (1970). *Microeconomic Foundations of Employment and Inflation Theory.* New York: W. W. Norton & Co.

Pierson, F. C. (1957). "An Evaluation of Wage Theory," in Taylor, C. W. and Pierson, F. C., eds., *New Concepts of Wage Determination.* New York: McGraw-Hill.

Plowden (1967). *Children and Their Primary Schools.* Vol. 1: Report, H. M. S. O. Central Advisory Council for Education (England).

Powell, E. (1968). "Speech at the Annual Conference of the Conservative National Advisory Committee on Education," June.

Psacharopoulos G. (1972). "Rates of Return Around the World," *Comp. Educ. Rev.* (February).

Rees, A. (1965). "Review of Becker, *Human Capital,*" *Am. Econ. Rev.* (September).

Richardson, V. A. (1969). "A Measurement of Demand for Professional Engeneers," *Brit. J. Ind. Relat.* (March).

Robinson, J. (1953). "The Production Function and the Theory of Capital," *Rev. of Econ. Stud.* XXI (2): No. 55.

Ross, A. M. (1957). "The External Wage Structure," in Taylor, G. W. and Pierson, F. C., eds., *New Concepts of Wage Determination.* New York: McGraw-Hill.

Routh, G. (1965). *Occupation and Pay in Great Britain.* London: Cambridge University Press.

Scitovsky, T. (1966). "An International Comparison of the Trend of Professional Earnings," *Am. Econ. Rev.* (March).

Stigler, G. J. (1962) "Information in the Labor Market," *J. Polit. Econ., Supplement* (October).

Thurow, L. C. (1969). *Poverty and Discrimination.* Washington: Brookings Institution.

Welch, F. (1970). "Education in Production," *J. Polit. Econ.* (January/February).

Wiles, P. (1969). "Die Bauchschmerzen eines Fachidioten," *Anarchy and Culture.* London: Routledge & Kegan Paul.

Wootton, B. (1954). *The Social Foundations of Wage Policy.* London: Allen and Unwin.

[4]

The Empirical Status of Human Capital Theory:
A Slightly Jaundiced Survey

By MARK BLAUG

*University of London Institute of Education
and London School of Economics*

*I owe thanks to F. Bosch-Font, M. J. Bowman, R. Layard, G. Psach-
aropoulos, the participants of the 1975 Conference of the International Institute of Public Finance, and several anonymous referees
of this journal for helpful comments on an earlier version of this
paper. However, being obdurate by nature, I have not taken account
of all their comments. They are therefore in no way responsible for
what follows.*

THE BIRTH OF human-capital theory was announced in 1960 by Theodore Schultz. The birth itself may be said to have taken place two years later when the *Journal of Political Economy* published its October 1962 supplement volume on "Investment in Human Beings." This volume included, among several other path-breaking papers, the preliminary chapters of Gary Becker's 1964 monograph *Human Capital,* which has ever since served as the *locus classicus* of the subject.[1] Thus, the theory of human capital has been with us for more than a decade, during which time the flood of literature in the field has never abated and seems, if anything, to be increasing lately at an increasing rate.[2] The first textbook exclusively devoted to the subject appeared in 1963 [87, Schultz, 1963].[3] After a lull in the mid-sixties, the textbook industry started in earnest: between 1970 and 1973 as many as eight authors tried their hand at the task, not to

[1] Earlier papers by John R. Walsh [98, 1935] and Jacob Mincer [64, 1958], and particularly the Milton Friedman–Simon Kuznets book on *Income from Independent Professional Practice* [37, 1945], provided some of the key elements of the new theory. Hints and suggestions of the theme of human-capital formation occur all through the eighteenth and nineteenth centuries but these *obiter dicta* were never tied together before Schultz and Becker; a reading of Bernard F. Kiker [52, 1968], the standard history of human-capital doctrines since Petty, leaves no doubt on that score; see also Blaug [10, 1976].

[2] A fairly comprehensive annotated bibliography by Blaug [11, 1976], published in 1966, contained 800 items; the second edition of this bibliography, published in 1970, contained 1,350 items, and the third 1976 edition contains almost 2,000 items. In an analysis of all articles in 114 major economic journals, published between 1970 and 1974, Naomi W. Perlman and Mark Perlman [73, 1976] show that articles on "human capital" rose from 1.34 to 1.75 percent of all classified articles, which they characterize as an extremely rapid rate of growth. During the same period, articles in the "economics of education (consumption side)" rose from 1.31 to 1.69 percent, an almost identical level and rate of growth to health economics. To put these figures into perspective, compare the corresponding figures for urban economics, 3.26 to 2.73, regional economics, 3.80 to 4.15, and trade unions, 2.54 to 3.73.

[3] Earlier textbooks on the economics of education by Charles S. Benson [6, 1961] and John E. Vaizey [97, 1962] paint a wider canvass and deal only parenthetically with human-capital theory.

mention the appearance of seven anthologies of classic articles on human-capital-and-all-that.[4] It may be time therefore to ask what all this adds up to. Has the theory lived up to the high expectations of its founders? Has it progressed, in the sense of grappling ever more deeply and profoundly with the problems to which it was addressed, or are there signs of stagnation and malaise?

I adopt the Popperian methodological position that all theories must be judged ultimately in terms of their falsifiable predictions, a position to which almost all modern economists subscribe—and which some even take seriously. What I hope to do in this paper is to assess what Sir Karl Popper calls the "degree of corroboration" of human-capital theory. "By the degree of corroboration of a theory," Popper explains, "I mean a concise report evaluating the state (at a certain time t) of the critical discussion of a theory, with respect to the way it solves its problems; its degree of testability; the severity of the tests it has undergone; and the way it has stood up to these tests. Corroboration (or degree of corroboration) is thus an evaluating report of past performance" [76, Popper, 1972, p. 18].

Such an "evaluating report of past performance" can never be absolute: a theory can only be judged in relation to its rivals, purporting to explain a similar range of phenomena. Even such a relative comparison is never final because we cannot accurately predict the future evolution of a theory. Moreover, it is inappropriate to appraise individual theories in isolation of the general framework in which such theories are typically embedded. What ought to be appraised are clusters of interconnected theories, or what Imre Lakatos has called "scientific research programs." In the process of testing the predictions of a particular research program, some fal-

sifications are invariably encountered, and all scientific research programs tend to be continuously reformulated to avoid refutation. Borrowing from the post-Popperian methodological writings of Lakatos, we may distinguish between the "hard core" and "the protective belt" of a scientific research program: the "hard core" consists of the set of purely metaphysical beliefs that inspire and define the research strategy of the program; it is in "the protective belt," however, that this "hard core" is combined with auxiliary assumptions to form the specific testable theories with which the research program earns its scientific reputation.[5] We may further distinguish "progressive" and "degenerating" research programs: the former consists of programs whose successive reformulations contain "excess empirical content" in the sense of predicting novel, hitherto unexpected facts; the latter, on the other hand, accommodate whatever new facts become available by endless additions of *ad hoc* "epicycles."

Armed with these methodological distinctions, we may now reformulate the aims of the paper. What is the "hard core" of a human-capital research program, whose abandonment is tantamount to abandoning the program itself? What refutations have been encountered in the "protective belt" of the program, and how have the advocates of the program responded to these refutations? Lastly, is the human-capital research program a "progressive" or a "degenerating" research program, which is virtually like asking, has the empirical content of the program increased or decreased over time?

I. *Hard Core Versus Protective Belt*

The so-called "theory" of human capital is of course a perfect example of a research program: it cannot be reduced to one, sin-

---

[4] For a complete list, see Blaug [11, 1976].

[5] For references and further discussion of Lakatos' philosophy of science in relation to economics, see Blaug [12, 1976].

gle theory, being in fact an application of standard capital theory to certain economic phenomena. The concept of human capital, or "hard core" of the human-capital research program, is the idea that people spend on themselves in diverse ways, not for the sake of present enjoyments, but for the sake of future pecuniary and nonpecuniary returns. They may purchase health care; they may voluntarily acquire additional education; they may spend time searching for a job with the highest possible rate of pay, instead of accepting the first offer that comes along; they may purchase information about job opportunities; they may migrate to take advantage of better employment opportunities; and they may choose jobs with low pay but high learning potential in preference to dead-end jobs with high pay. All these phenomena—health, education, job search, information retrieval, migration, and in-service training—may be viewed as investment rather than consumption, whether undertaken by individuals on their own behalf or undertaken by society on behalf of its members. What knits these phenomena together is not the question of who undertakes what, but rather the fact that the decision-maker, whoever he is, looks forward to the future for the justification of his present actions.

Having said this much, it takes only an additional assumption, namely, that the decision-maker is a household rather than an individual, to extend the analogy to family planning and even to the decision to marry.[6] We are not surprised to see life-cycle considerations applied to the theory of saving, but prior to what Mary Jean Bowman has aptly called "the human

[6] We will omit discussion in this paper of the recent extension of the human-capital research program by Becker and others to the "economics of the family." For a highly critical review of the population aspects of this extension, see Harvey Leibenstein [57, 1974] and the instructive reply by Michael C. Keely [51, 1975].

investment revolution in economic thought," it was not common to treat expenditures on such social services as health and education as analogous to investment in physical capital, and certainly no one dreamed in those days of finding common analytical grounds between labor economics and the economics of the social services.

There is hardly any doubt therefore of the genuine novelty of the "hard core" of the human-capital research program. Nor is there any doubt of the rich research possibilities created by a commitment to this "hard core." The "protective belt" of the human-capital research program is replete with human-capital "theories," properly so labeled, and indeed the list is so large that we can hardly hope to give an exhaustive account of them. But few human-capital theorists would, I think, quarrel with those we have selected for emphasis.

In the field of education, the principal theoretical implication of the human-capital research program is that the demand for upper secondary and higher education is responsive both to variations in the direct and indirect private costs of schooling and to variations in the earnings differentials associated with additional years of schooling. The traditional pre-1960 view among economists was that the demand for post-compulsory education was a demand for a consumption good, and as such depended on given "tastes," family incomes, and the "price" of schooling in the form of tuition costs. There was the complication that this consumption demand also involved an "ability" to consume the good in question, but most economists were satisfied to leave it to sociologists and social psychologists to show that both "tastes" and "abilities" depended in turn on the social class background of students, and particularly on the levels of education achieved by their parents. Since this pre-1960 theory of the consumption demand for education was never used to explain real-world attendance rates in high schools and colleges, it makes little difference what particular formulation of it we adopt. The point is that the notion that earnings forgone constitute an important element in the private costs of schooling and that students take a systematic, forward-looking view of earnings prospects in the labor market would have been dismissed in the pre-1960 days as implausible, on the grounds that students lack the necessary information and that the available information is known to be unreliable. The human-capital research program, on the other hand, while also taking "tastes" and "abilities" as given, emphasizes the role of present and future earnings, arguing in addition that these are much more likely to exhibit variations in the short term than the distribution of family background characteristics between successive cohorts of students.

The difference between the old and the new view is therefore fundamental and the auxiliary assumptions that convert the "hard core" of the human-capital research program into a testable theory of the demand for upper secondary and higher education are almost too obvious to require elaboration: students cannot easily finance the present costs of additional schooling out of future earnings; they are aware of the earnings they forgo while studying and hence demand more schooling when there is a rise in youth unemployment rates; current salary differentials by years of schooling provide them with fairly accurate estimates of the salary differentials that will prevail when they enter the labor market several years later; *et cetera, et cetera.* Furthermore, the theory comes in two versions: it claims modestly to predict total enrollments in post-compulsory schooling, and, more ambitiously, to predict enrollments in specific fields of study in higher education, and even enrollments in different types of institutions at the tertiary level.

As originally formulated by Schultz, Becker, and Mincer, the human-capital research program was characterized by "methodological individualism," that is, the view that all social phenomena should be traced back to their foundation in individual behavior. For Schultz, Becker, and Mincer, human-capital formation is typically conceived as being carried out by individuals acting in their own interests. This is the natural view to take in respect of job search and migration, but health care, education, information retrieval, and labor training are either wholly or in part carried out by governments in many countries. However, familiarity with private medicine and private education, and the almost total absence of government-sponsored training schemes in the American context (at least before 1968), gave support to an emphasis on the private calculus. But when health and education are largely in the public sector, as is the case in most of Europe and in most of the Third World, it is tempting to ask the question of whether the human-capital research program is also capable of providing new normative criteria for public action. In education at any rate, the human-capital research program did indeed furnish a new social investment criterion: resources are to be allocated to levels of education and to years of schooling so as to equalize the marginal, "social" rate of return on educational investment, and, going one step further, this equalized yield on educational investment should not fall below the yield on alternative private investments. However, this normative criterion was not advocated with the same degree of conviction by all adherents of the human-capital research program. Furthermore, the so-called "social" rate of return on educational investment is necessarily calculated exclusively on the basis of observable pecuniary values; the nonpecuniary returns to education, as well as the externalities associated with schooling, are invariably accommodated by qualitative

Blaug: A View on Human Capital Theory   831

judgments, and these differ from author to author [8, Blaug, 1972, pp. 202–05]. Thus, the same observed "social" rates of return to investment in education frequently produced quite different conclusions about the optimal educational strategy.

Being normative, the cry to equalize the "social" rate of return to education raises no questions of empirical testing. In the mood of positive economics, it may be interesting to ask whether governments do indeed allocate resources to the educational system so as to equalize the social yield to all levels and types of education, but few human-capital theorists would commit themselves to a definite prediction about the outcome of such a calculation.[7] In the absence of any generally accepted theory of government behavior, the advocates of the human-capital research program may be forgiven for slighting the normative implications of their doctrines.[8] Unfortunately, it seems difficult to test any positive prediction about the demand for post-compulsory schooling without taking a view of the norms that underlie government action in the field of education. The world provides few examples of countries in which the

demand for post-compulsory education is not constrained by the supply of places that governments decide to make available. In testing predictions about private demand, we therefore end up testing predictions about the supply function as well as the demand function. To give the human-capital research program a run for its money, therefore, we must go to such open-door systems of higher education as exist only in the United States, Japan, India, and the Philippines.

These comments no doubt help to explain why almost all empirical work about the demand for education has been confined to the United States. But even with respect to the United States, it is surprising how little attention has actually been devoted to an explanation of the private demand for schooling. As we shall see, almost nothing with any cutting edge was accomplished before 1970 or thereabouts, and even now the demand for education remains a curiously neglected subject in the vast empirical literature exemplifying the human-capital approach.

We turn now from formal schooling to labor training. Almost from the outset, the human-capital research program was as much preoccupied with the phenomenon of training as with that of education. Becker's fundamental distinction between "general" and "specific" training produced the startling prediction that workers themselves pay for "general" training via reduced earnings during the training period, thus contradicting the older Marshallian view that a competitive market mechanism fails to provide employers with adequate incentives to offer optimum levels of in-service training. Predictions about the demand for training fitted neatly with predictions about the demand for education because formal schooling is an almost perfect example of "general" training; indeed, Becker's model has the virtue of correctly predicting that employers will rarely pay directly for the schooling acquired by their em-

[7] Similarly, it is interesting to ask what impact education has on economic growth, irrespective of the motives that lie behind the provision of formal schooling. The attempt to answer this question was at the center of the burgeoning literature on growth accounting in the early 1960's, but recent doubts about the concept of aggregate production functions have virtually dried up all further interest in the question: e.g., see Richard R. Nelson [69, 1973] but also Edward F. Denison [26, 1974]. In retrospect, it seems doubtful in any case whether growth accounting of the Denison-type has much to do with the crucial issues in human-capital theory [8, Blaug, 1972, pp. 99–100].

[8] Besides, what needs to be explained about formal schooling is not so much why governments subsidize it as they do, but why they insist on owning so much of it in every country around the world. On this crucial question we get no help, and cannot expect to get help, from the human-capital research program, even when it is supplemented by the theory of externalities and public goods of modern welfare economics. The answer, surely, lies elsewhere, perhaps in voting behavior and the internal logic of public bureaucracies?

ployees, a generally observed real-world phenomenon unexplained by any alternative research program (except perhaps that of Marx).

The distinction between two kinds of post-school learning soon led to fruitful discussion about the extent to which training is or is not fully vested in individual workers, but it largely failed to inspire new empirical work on labor training in industry [7, Blaug, 1972, pp. 191–99]. In part, this was due to the inherent difficulty of distinguishing costless on-the-job learning from both informal on-the-job and formal off-the-job-but-in-plant training. (I say nothing about formal off-the-job-out-of-plant training, the so-called manpower retraining programs, whose evaluation raises different problems not especially related to Becker's distinction). For the rest, Becker's emphasis on training as the outcome of an occupational choice by workers seemed to ignore complex questions about the supply of training by firms with well-developed "internal labor markets." All in all, it can hardly be said that the human-capital approach to labor training has yet been put to a decisive empirical test (on which more anon).

The subject of migration gives rise to similar difficulties in assessing degrees of success or failure. There is a rich economic and sociological literature on geographical migration going back to the nineteenth and even eighteenth century, to which the human-capital approach adds little except a pronounced emphasis on the role of geographical disparities in real incomes. There is little doubt that recent empirical work on migration has been deeply influenced by human-capital considerations, but an appraisal of the empirical status of the human-capital research program in the field of migration is by no means straightforward. We shall simply ignore this area because it has been surveyed again and again by others: e.g., see Michael Greenwood [39, 1975].

This leaves us with health, job search, and labor market information networks. We shall say little about the human-capital approach to health because the virtual explosion of health economics in recent years would require a paper by itself to do justice to the theme: but, e.g., see Herbert E. Klarman [53, 1965] and Michael H. Cooper and Anthony Culyer [25, 1973]. Likewise, George J. Stigler's pioneering article on "Information in the Labor Market" in the 1962 supplement volume of the Journal of Political Economy [93, 1962], in conjunction with work on the Phillips curve, sparked off a long line of papers on what has come to be known as the "new theory of voluntary unemployment," or the "microeconomic foundations of employment theory." To survey this area would take us far afield—but, e.g., see Edmund Phelps et al. [75, 1970] and David Whipple [102, 1973]—and the precise relationship between these developments in labor economics and the human-capital research program is in any case somewhat tenuous.

Taking all these together, the program adds up to an almost total explanation of the determinants of earnings from employment, predicting declining investments in human-capital formation with increasing age, and hence lifetime earnings profiles that are concave from below. No wonder the bulk of empirical work inspired by the human-capital framework has taken the form of regressing the earnings of individuals on such variables as native ability, family background, place of residence, years of schooling, years of work experience, occupational status, and the like—the so-called "earnings function." It is sometimes difficult in all this research to see precisely what hypothesis is being tested, other than that schooling and work experience are important and that native ability and family background are not. Apart from earnings functions, some effort has also been devoted to explaining the size distribution of personal earnings, culminating in the somewhat surprising conclusion that the joint effect of years of schooling and years of work experience alone accounts for as much as half of the observed variance in the distribution of earnings. If true, this is perhaps the most powerful test of the human-capital research program that it would be possible to find. There is reason to believe, however, that this result depends on the assumption that labor markets are sufficiently competitive to equalize the private yields on all types of education and training. Alas, the empirical evidence leaves little doubt that these yields are not in fact equalized at the margin.

In summary, it may be said that the human-capital research program has displayed a simply amazing fecundity, spawning new research projects in almost every branch of economics. Nevertheless, we hope to show in the pages that follow that the program is actually not very well corroborated. That is of course no reason for abandoning the human-capital research program. To believe that scientific research programs are given up the moment a refutation is encountered is to fall victim to "naive falsificationism." What is required to eliminate a scientific research program is, first of all, repeated refutations, secondly, an embarrassing proliferation of *ad hoc* adjustments designed to avoid these refutations, and thirdly, and most importantly, a rival program that purports to account for the same evidence by a different but equally powerful theoretical framework. Such a rival to the human-capital research program may now have made its appearance: it travels under the name of the "screening hypothesis" or "credentialism," and it is linked up in some of its versions to the new theory of "dual labor markets," or labor market "segmentation." Its origins lie in the theory of decision-making under uncertainty and its impact derives from the discovery

that the process of hiring workers is merely a species of a larger genus, namely, the problem of selecting buyers or sellers in the presence of inadequate information about their characteristics. The issue, however, is whether this "screening hypothesis" is truly a rival framework, or instead a complement to the human-capital research program, which may in the end subsume rather than displace it. At any rate, the appearance of the screening hypothesis has at long last presented the human-capital research program with a challenge on its own grounds, making it necessary to ask: what precisely is the empirical status of human-capital theory?

II. *Demand for Schooling*

We begin our review of the evidence by considering the demand function for formal schooling. Becker's *Human Capital* noted that observed changes in American school and college attendance rates over the last thirty years can be satisfactorily explained by the persistently high yield of educational investment to individuals [3, Becker, 1975, pp. 169–73, 179–81]. No doubt, if his calculations had yielded negative or absurdly low private rates of return, the human-capital research program would have died there and then. On the other hand, it can hardly be said that his test was a severe one: an almost infinite number of alternative theories can easily account for the enrollment changes in question.

Robert Campbell and Barry N. Siegel [18, 1967] were the first to attempt to estimate the demand function for higher education in the United States: they regressed the fraction of the age group enrolled in institutions of higher education over the period 1919 to 1964 on time-series data of real tuition costs and real disposable incomes per household. Apart from their rather unconvincing attempt to "identify" a demand rather than a supply function, they failed to include either forgone earnings or any measure of expected future earnings as independent variables in their regression, and hence ended up testing, not the human-capital explanation of the demand for higher education, but rather the standard consumption explanation. The fact that they obtained a good fit with an $R^2 = 0.93$ suggests immediately that the concept of "education as investment" may be less promising than was imagined at first.

Two years later, Harvey Galper and Robert M. Dunn [38, 1969] improved this estimate by introducing distributed lags in their regressions. Their only independent variables were high school enrollments, household incomes, and the size of the armed forces. Even without tuition costs, they obtained an excellent fit on 1929–65 data. Once again, therefore, their results refute the human-capital model, at least by implication.[9] Oddly enough, when enrollment data are taken state by state on a cross-section basis, good results are obtained using such independent variables as parental education, test scores, tuition fees, and current earnings by levels of education [32, Feldman and Hoenack, 1969], thus confirming a weak version of the human-capital explanation of the demand for higher education.[10] On the other hand, Leonard S. Miller [63, 1971], using a similar approach, found significant differences between low and high achievers, with high achievers displaying few of the cost-conscious characteristics of students in the human-capital image of the world;

in other words, the human-capital research program may be said to apply to the lower half of the American ability range.

With Freeman [34, 1971] attention shifted away from the explanation of the total demand for higher education to the demand for specialized fields of study and, in particular, to the career choices of engineers and scientists. Freeman introduced five new elements into the analysis: firstly, he allowed for the fact that earnings today can only influence the supply of graduates four years later; secondly, he intended to discount expected lifetime incomes, thus treating the present value of earnings as the relevant explanatory variable; thirdly, he found empirical counterparts for certain nonpecuniary factors affecting occupational choice; fourthly, he took account of expected lifetime incomes in alternative occupations; and fifthly, he allowed for the effects of employers' demand in the labor market by including the output of industries hiring scientists and engineers. His entire model formed a recursive structure that first explained the number of first-year enrollments in, say, B.Sc. engineering courses, then the number of engineers graduating with a B.Sc. degree four years later, and, finally, the starting salaries of graduate engineers.[11] Furthermore, the distributed lag structure of his equations made it possible to estimate the speed at which the model attained an equilibrium solution.

Freeman's results for engineers, accountants, chemists, and mathematicians constitute a striking confirmation of human-capital theory: all the coefficients have the expected signs and the wage elas-

[9] See, likewise, the latest attempt in this area by Sandra Christensen, John Melder, and Burton A. Weisbrod [23, 1975]; see also Michael L. Handa and Michael L. Skolnik [42, 1972] for a review of similar Canadian studies, and George Psacharopoulos [77, 1973] for a study of Hawaii.

[10] For stronger evidence, see Handa and Skolnik [43, 1975] for Canada and Richard B. Freeman [35, 1975] on the recent downturn in American college enrollment rates. But Handa and Skolnik's results are marred by poor earnings data and Freeman concedes that recent changes in the draft law may be responsible for some of his findings.

[11] This summary of his procedure is too terse. Actually, he estimated three models: a recursive cobweb model; a recursive but "incomplete adjustment model"; and a simultaneous equation model. The manner in which he moves back and forth between these models, substituting estimated variables from one model into the equations of another model, create difficulties in interpreting his results.

ticity is well above unity; the entire model is stable and yields a rapid adjustment to equilibrium. Furthermore, he produced additional findings from a survey of students in the Boston area to show that the typical student is indeed attentive and responsive to variations in occupational earnings. Nevertheless, the usual gap between the hypothesis to be tested and the variables employed in empirical estimation do raise doubts about his findings. In the absence of lifetime earnings profiles for all his professional categories, Freeman treated starting salaries as a proxy for lifetime earnings and thus failed in fact to test the hypothesis that students take a lifecycle view of career opportunities. Even the dynamic structure of his model is purely mechanical, reflecting the four-year production period of engineers, and not the tendency of students and employers to form a particular set of adaptive expectations about the future course of prices and quantities. To be sure, the use of arbitrarily distributed lags in the estimation of economic relationships is well established in the econometric literature. But the absence of a truly dynamic theory of the formation of expectations is particularly damaging here: what is at issue in the theory of human capital is precisely whether students take *any* forward view of economic variables. As a matter of fact, Alan N. Freiden and Robert J. Staaf [36, 1973] manage to successfully predict the pattern of subject changes by students in a particular American college, not by invoking the theory of human capital, but by applying the standard theory of consumer behavior.[12]

Let us pause for a moment to note that there is a world of difference, at least for the United States, between an explanation of the entry demand for a specialized field of study and an explanation of the num-

bers actually graduating in that field of study. About 40 percent of freshman students in American colleges switch their major subjects somewhere between the freshman and the senior year: over the four-year period, such subjects as engineering and natural science are net losers, while education and social science subjects are net gainers, which is to say that the net flow is from subjects with higher to subjects with lower income expectations. The explanation for this phenomenon has clearly much to do with the lower probability of surviving a course in engineering and natural science, owing to the fact that these subjects have higher grading norms than education and social science. In so far as Freeman explains such switches of majors by relative wages and salaries, he must be assuming that relative nonpecuniary benefits (including the chances of surviving a course) do not change across majors over the period of observation. But Freiden and Staaf [36, 1973], followed at book-length by McKenzie and Staaf [62, 1974], argue that the distribution of grades across majors changes much more frequently than do relative salaries, and they therefore explain the switches between majors by the economic logic of consumer behavior theory applied to the student's choice between university subjects. This line of argument may not refute the human-capital explanation of the supply of professional manpower but it certainly complicates it.

Indeed, when John F. O'Connell [70, 1972] carried Freeman's analysis one stage further, many of Freeman's sharp results evaporated. O'Connell concentrated attention on the supply of graduate engineers, irrespective of the point at which students have decided to study engineering; he also provided something like a fully specified demand function for engineers; and he estimated a simultaneous equation model rather than a recursive model. He found that the supply of engi-

[12] See also the damaging evidence of low elasticities in reference to costs and earnings in Walter Fogel and Daniel J. B. Mitchell [33, 1974].

neers was indeed responsive to absolute although not to relative earnings differences, duplicating one of Freeman's results, but also that the demand for engineers was fairly insensitive to relative wage differences. However, his results are extremely unstable: the signs and the magnitudes of the coefficients, as well as the levels of statistical significance, change from one specification of his model to the next and, in particular, from one engineering field to another. All this is to say that despite Freeman's impressive early results, the problem of developing a satisfactory model of the American labor market for engineers, not to mention the demand for engineering as a field of study, remains unresolved.

In European countries, the effective rationing of higher education by the State makes it virtually impossible to test the hypothesis that subject choice in higher education is sensitive to earnings.[13] Worse than that, there is actually no convincing data outside the United States to show that students are informed of the pattern of earnings in the labor market, much less that they take them into account in reaching educational decisions, even when the earnings in question are currently forgone rather than expected in the future. There are of course innumerable European surveys to indicate that students and parents are principally motivated by "vocational factors" or "financial considerations" [8, Blaug, 1972, pp. 181, 187–88], but such vague replies to questionnaires should provide little comfort to human-capital theorists. After all, sociologists do not deny that people are generally aware of the fact that additional education opens the door to high-paying occupations; it is

simply that they consider this to be a minor factor in the demand for post-compulsory schooling.[14] Even in the United States, this type of direct survey evidence leaves much to be desired.

As for actual behavior apart from knowledge and information, we have seen that the empirical evidence for the human-capital explanation of the demand for schooling is far from unambiguous: it is true that it has never been decisively refuted on its own grounds, but on the other hand it has only been corroborated in its weaker versions. Moreover, alternative economic models have yielded equally good and even better results. When we consider that the private demand for formal schooling is, as it were, at the center of the human-capital research program, the results to date begin to raise doubts as to whether the program is indeed "progressing."

III. *Labor Training*

From the earliest formulations of the human-capital model by Schultz, Becker, and Mincer, it was on-the-job training and not formal schooling that was taken to be the paradigm case of self-investment. In the absence of post-school investment, lifecycle earnings profiles were assumed to show neither appreciation as a result of learning-by-doing, nor depreciation as a result of biological aging and obsolescence of knowledge; in graphical terms, the picture was that of a series of perfectly horizontal profiles, each higher profile being associated with an additional year of schooling. It was argued, however, that individuals tend to invest in themselves after completing schooling by choosing occupations that promise "general training"; in so doing, they lower their starting salaries below alternative opportunities in

---

[13] See Ruth Klinov-Malul's [54, 1971] totally negative results for Britain and Frank A. Sloan's [89, 1971] finding that applications to American medical schools are positively related to the supply of places, medical education being the one clear case where the supply of American higher education is rationed in terms of quantity rather than quality.

[14] The major factor, much neglected by human-capital theorists, may well be demographic forces: *e.g.*, see Douglas L. Adkins [1, 1974] and Stephen P. Dresch [27, 1975].

exchange for higher future salaries as the training begins to pay off. Provided a sufficient number of workers with a given level of education behave in this fashion, the model predicts that the age-earnings profiles of different educational cohorts that we actually observe will be concave from below, a prediction that was immediately confirmed by American census evidence and that has since been confirmed again and again by evidence for some forty countries around the world.

Unfortunately, any psychological theory of "learning curves," in which appreciation over time is partly but only partly offset by depreciation and obsolescence, will likewise account for concave age-earnings profiles. Furthermore, it is not easy even in principle to separate off-the-job-in-plant "general" and "specific" training, which clearly implies a direct cost that must be borne by either workers or employers, from either on-the-job-learning-by-doing or on-the-job-doing-under-supervision. Both learning-by-doing and doing-under-supervision are costly in terms of output forgone, but the former is unavoidable and hence is not subject to individual choice. In short, it is difficult to see how individuals can choose more or less learning-by-doing, although no doubt business firms will want to minimize the number of inexperienced workers, everything else being the same. Of course, entry into certain professions, such as medicine, law, and accountancy, do entail long periods of learning-by-doing at low rates of pay. But this kind of post-school investment is artificial, in the sense of being the result of the restrictive practices of professional associations. The difficulty is that of believing that occupational choice is generally characterized under competitive conditions by the choice of low-paying occupations whose learning potential (apart from formal training) will subsequently raise earnings to more than justify the period of low pay. On this absolutely fun-

damental question, Mincer's new book, *Schooling, Experience and Earnings,* has little to add to Becker's earlier arguments in *Human Capital:* "The assumption of costless opportunities for augmenting productivity, which is sometimes implied in the notion of 'learning by doing,' cannot be descriptive of labor markets where labor mobility is the norm rather than the exception" [67, Mincer, 1974, p. 65; also p. 132]. Granting the point about labor mobility as the norm rather than the exception, it is nevertheless doubtful that all interoccupational, and even more intraoccupational, movements of labor can be reduced to the action of sowing and reaping the advantages of labor training, widely defined so as to include not just formal in-plant training and learning under supervision, but also learning by experience.[15] The use of such portmanteau terms as "on-the-job-training" or "work experience" to cover what is in fact a number of quite distinct phenomena merely adds to our doubts.

The question is further complicated by the introduction of Mincer's new concept of "overtaking." According to human-capital theory, all individuals with a given level of schooling choose occupations, so

---

[15] If alternative techniques for producing a given product involve more or less learning-by-doing, and if firms can predict these learning characteristics of alternative techniques (a big if), learning-by-doing would indeed become a decision variable for firms. Workers, on the other hand, would have to be able to predict the learning characteristics of different techniques ruling in different industries, so as to make it possible by choice of employment to invest in more or less learning-by-doing. I know of no evidence to suggest that this is a realistic picture of the elements that enter into occupational choice. As George Psacharopoulos and Richard Layard [81, 1976] put it: "Is costless learning impossible? For this to be the case there must always exist a job at which no learning occurs and at which we could currently produce more (net) than in any job where we can learn anything. There need not actually be anybody doing this job, though in a perfect market it would be surprising if someone were not doing it . . . We have spent some years trying to think what this job is . . . But we have found it impossible to think of any such job."

as to equalize the present value of lifetime earnings (this conveniently ignores the nonpecuniary attractions of different occupations); since individuals have different time preferences, the effect of these post-school investment decisions is to produce an initial dispersion of earnings by levels of education. It follows from the logic of the equalization of present values that the dispersion must decline subsequently, only to increase again in the later stages of working life; in other words, the different profiles must cross each other at some point. The time at which the dispersion of earnings is minimized is called the point of "overtaking" and Mincer shows that, in the United States at any rate, the cross-over years are bunched together at about 7–9 years after entry into the labor force, that is, at ages 23 to 33, depending on what level of education we are talking about. The point of "overtaking," by the way, is also the point at which the effects of formal schooling on earnings are maximized: at this point the returns on post-school investments just about equal their current costs to individuals in terms of earnings forgone. In other words, if we concentrate attention on a cohort of men with 7–9 years of work experience, Mincer argues, we can in fact explain about one-third of the inequality in earnings solely by differences in formal schooling [67, Mincer, 1974, pp. 133–34].

The problem with the concept of "overtaking" is similar to that of distinguishing costly on-the-job training from costless learning-by-doing, namely, the failure to observe the lifetime earnings profiles of individuals who have neither invested in nor received any post-school training. Mincer assumes that these base-line earnings profiles would remain perfectly horizontal throughout working life, but no such profiles have ever been observed for any category of individuals. He further assumes that rates of return to investment in formal schooling are identical to rates

of return to post-school investment, and it is particularly the latter assumption that allows him to separate the costs from the returns to post-school investment [8, Blaug, 1972, pp. 197–98]. The finding that the "overtaking point" occurs about 7–9 years after completion of schooling is therefore dependent both on the assumption of a once-and-for-all effect of schooling on earnings (no net appreciation of human capital from costless work experience) and on the assumption that general equilibrium is actually attained in human-capital markets. Alas, there is simply overwhelming evidence, both for the United States and for other countries, that private rates of return to successive years of formal schooling are not equalized at the margin; indeed, they decline with successively higher levels of schooling [80, Psacharopoulos and Hinchliffe, 1973]. Mincer's attempt to reinterpret this evidence is not entirely convincing[16] and without the assumption of equality in all private rates of return to formal schooling, there would seem to be no way of disentangling the effects of investment in schooling from the effects of post-school

---

[16] He argues that differences in the amount of time worked per year account for almost all of the observed differences in rates of return to levels of schooling: rates of return calculated from hourly or weekly rather than annual earnings do not differ significantly by levels of schooling [67, Mincer, 1974, pp. 54–55]. This result is actually rather paradoxical. It is a fact that average weeks worked per year increase with levels of schooling [67, 1974, p. 121]. Hence, if we standardize for the numbers of weeks worked per year by calculating rates of return to schooling from weekly rather than annual earnings, the decline in rates of return to successively higher levels of schooling should increase, not decrease, the more so as there is some evidence that weekly earnings tend to be positively correlated with weeks worked per year [67, 1974, p. 94]. Mincer's own conclusion seems to be based on what happens to the negative squared coefficient of schooling in his earnings function when he adds in the effect of weeks worked [67, 1974, pp. 54, 93]. For the reasons given above, however, I am inclined to argue that this result is due to a misspecification of the model. On the general question of standardizing rates of return for time worked per year, see also Richard S. Eckaus [29, 1973] and Cotton M. Lindsay [58, 1973].

investment. Furthermore, his earlier attempt to compare estimates of the returns
to formal schooling with some independent estimates of the returns to training, so
as to show that they are indeed roughly
equalized [65, Mincer, 1962, pp. 63–66],
is vitiated by the fact that the training
studies in question refer to apprenticeship
programs, an amalgam of learning-by-
doing and doing-under-supervision, sometimes but not always involving off-the-job-
in-plant courses.

Enough has now been said to suggest
that the human-capital explanation of labor training founders on the failure to provide a testable theory of occupational
choice. Nothing is said about the nonpecuniary attractions of alternative occupations, the costs of gaining adequate
information, and the imperfections of
the capital markets, which inhibit some
individuals from financing their desirable occupational choices. Moreover, the
model concentrates all its attention on the
supply of human capital, while virtually
ignoring the nature of demand in labor
markets. But the earnings function, from
which all the basic results are derived, is
itself a "reduced-form" equation, the outcome, that is, of an interaction of the
forces of demand and supply.

In distinguishing between "general"
and "specific" training, Becker conceded
that employers can vary the turnover of
labor in a plant by a variety of devices: the
lower the turnover, the greater the willingness of firms to pay for training and,
hence, the more "specific" the training,
whatever its content.[17] Thus, the nearer
we approach the monopsony model of
firm behavior, the less likely the relevance
of a worker self-investment approach to
the question of labor training. Sherwin
Rosen [84, 1972; 85, 1972] has indeed generalized the Becker-Mincer approach by

recasting the problem in terms of an implicit market for learning opportunities,
overlapping the explicit market for jobs:
in effect, employers attempt to sell training services as a way of inducing people
to work for them and, of course, the price
of such services is a lower wage than workers could have obtained in alternative employments. Given the market price for
learning on-the-job, however, employers
can frequently redesign jobs so as to maximize the net returns from a given work
force.[18] What emerges from this extension
of the Becker-Mincer thesis is a more general conception of the training process,
giving due scope both to the recruitment
and hiring practices of firms and to the
sequential job choices of workers over
their working lives, a process in which the
trade-off between learning and earning is
gradually altered in favor of the latter.

We are left, therefore, with two un-
solved riddles. The first is how to separate
appreciation of human capital over time
due to costless learning-by-doing from appreciation due to costly self-investment by
workers, both of which tend to be offset
as time passes by the natural deterioration
or obsolescence of human capital. The second is how to square the picture of workers choosing between jobs with different
earning-learning ratios with the notion of
firms jointly producing goods and services
for their customers and learning opportunities for their employees. These un-
solved riddles have so far spoiled all efforts
to solve the problem of human-capital formation at a still higher level of abstraction
than that adopted by Becker and Mincer.
The process of investment in schooling followed by investment in job search and
post-school training is in effect a sequential process of individual decisions, subject
at each stage to the constraints of past
decisions and the stock of human capital

---

[17] Donald O. Parsons [72, 1972] and Masatoshi
Kuratani [55, 1973] have attempted to develop these
ideas into a testable theory of quit and lay-off rates.

[18] The work of James Scoville [88, 1972] has laid
particular emphasis on the much-neglected variable
of job design.

accumulated to date. Expressed in this way, the natural technique to apply to the problem is optimal control theory. In Yoram Ben-Porath's [4, 1967] pioneering application of optimal control theory to human-capital formation, every individual begins with an initial endowment of human capital, capable of generating earnings at a declining rate through time, subject to an exogenously determined rate of deterioration; this endowment can be invested throughout the lifecycle either in learning or in earning but, unfortunately, not in both. The empirical implications of this model are not very rich. It predicts the typical concave shape of age-earnings profiles, and it implies that investment in learning will be concentrated in the early years of the lifecycle. Subsequent attempts by Ben-Porath [5, 1970] to test the model on earnings data proved to be unsuccessful: apart from the failure to isolate the depreciation-obsolescence parameter, he found it impossible to allow for the possible jointness of earning and learning in the post-school investment process.[19]

All in all, the question of labor training continues to haunt the human-capital research program. It is ironic to realize that the program was first developed in its most general form with reference to training, of which formal schooling is only a special case. Nevertheless, the bulk of the work in the human-capital research program has been devoted to investment in education; to this day we have had to make do with rates of return to educational investment that are actually averages of rates of return to schooling and rates of return to training, in the fond belief that the yields on all types of human-capital formation are more or less equalized in the labor market. As we have seen, there is little empirical evidence to support this belief, and there is a great deal of evidence that flatly contradicts it.

IV. *Private and Social Rates of Return*

Calculations of the rates of return to investment in formal schooling have proved to be the bread-and-butter of the human-capital research program: literally hundreds of such studies have now been carried out around the world in both developed and developing countries and even the recent comprehensive survey by George Psacharopoulos and Keith Hinchliffe [80, 1973] is already badly out of date: *e.g.*, see Richard S. Eckaus, Ahmad El Safty, and Victor D. Norman [30, 1974] and Carnegie Commission [19, 1974]. Nevertheless, despite considerable refinements in recent calculations, certain anomalies in the reported rates have largely escaped notice.

The vast majority of calculated rates have fallen within the range of 5–15 percent, although private rates as high as 80 percent for primary education in certain developing countries and as low as minus 2–3 percent for certain types of graduate education in the United States have been reported: *e.g.*, see Psacharopoulos and Hinchliffe [80, 1973] and John M. Campbell and Thomas D. Curtis [17, 1975]. The modal figure of 5–15 percent has been generally interpreted as reflecting a certain underlying rationality in both private and public decisions about schooling. This picture of social harmony is somewhat marred by the persistent observation of unequal private rates of return to successive years of schooling and, in particular, by the "sheepskin" effect of higher rates of return to the last years of schooling in a given educational cycle compared to the earlier years.[20] In general, private rates of return tend to decline monotonically with additional years of schooling, thus implying a chronic tendency on the part of individuals to over-invest in their education as a function of the acquisition of previous schooling. There are, of course, no dearth

---

[19] For a more detailed discussion of this and other optimal control models, see Bowman [16, 1974, pp. 214–19, 225–29].

[20] For new American evidence, see Richard Raymond and Michael Sesnowitz [83, 1975].

of *ad hoc* explanations of this phenomenon, most of which involve imperfections in the human-capital market, that is, the absence of banking institutions that will furnish students with unlimited funds to finance their education at a constant rate of interest. But there is no general theory which can predict how self-financed students will behave in the face of a given pattern of the private returns to schooling. Moreover, there is the suspicion that family finance is highly intercorrelated with academic ability and achievement drive, thus opening the door to another rich source of *ad hocery*, easily derivable from the voluminous writings of sociologists of education.

Furthermore, the variance of rates of return by years of schooling between individuals is more significant for the private calculus than the average rates for educational cohorts highlighted in rates-of-return studies. The fact that rates of return by levels of education display considerable variance has, of course, been known ever since Becker drew attention to it [3, 1975, pp. 181–90]. But the problems this creates for interpreting private rates of return have been generally ignored. The rates that motivate students are expected rates of return, and there is no reason to think that risk aversion is uniformly distributed among the members of a particular educational cohort. Thus, even when we know both the mean and variance of *ex post* returns and, in addition, assume that students will treat these *ex post* returns as best estimates of *ex ante* returns, we still cannot predict how they will behave in choosing schooling without taking a view of their attitudes toward risk. Recent attempts to show that risk differentials among individuals in respect to educational and occupational choices are not very important [100, Weiss, 1972], have begged as many questions as they have answered [45, Hause, 1974] and, on balance, it must be concluded that the human-capital research program has so far

evaded the problem of portfolio selection in human-capital formation.

If all this were not enough, there is evidence that the relative constancy of private rates of return in the United States between 1939 and 1971 was associated with significant shifts in age-earnings profiles by levels of education in certain years during that 30-year period [49, Johnson and Hebein, 1974; 20, Carnoy and Marenbach, 1975]. If there were perfect capital markets for educational loans, this would make little difference to our interpretations of the private calculus. In the absence of perfect capital markets, however, we cannot treat direct costs and forgone earnings on the same footing as expected earnings. In abandoning this principle, however, we virtually abandon the human-capital interpretation of private rate-of-return calculations.

Lastly, there is the unresolved problem that students choose, not just schooling, but schooling of a certain type and quality, and few rate-of-return calculations have succeeded in successfully standardizing the calculated yields for quality of educational institution. Most of the American work in this area has been confined to interstate differences in the quality of elementary and secondary education, quality being measured by average per pupil state expenditures on education, with only an occasional glance in higher education at two-year junior colleges and particular graduate programs, employing measures of quality that are frequently indistinguishable from measures of the average ability of the relevant student body.[21] So far, very little has been done to calculate private rates of return for particular colleges or groups of colleges in a contiguous area. A recent calculation for the Philippines, however, estimated the private rate of return to college education, not only by field of study but even by individual insti-

[21] For a useful survey of these findings, see Psacharopoulos [79, 1975, ch. 4] and Paul Wachtel [99, 1975].

tution attended [47, International Labor Office, 1974, pp. 317–18, 632–44]. Although the estimates are crude, being based only on the first 4–6 years of employment suitably projected over the lifecycle, they reveal that an over-all, average private rate of return of 9 percent to university education is perfectly compatible with negative rates of return to certain fields of study at certain low-quality institutions. If it is going to be argued that students are quite rational to demand college education because the private rate of return is 9 percent as against an interest rate of 8–10 percent in the organized money market, it will have to be conceded that some students are quite irrational in demanding a college education whose yield is negative, unless, of course, they are poorly informed, or risk lovers, or well endowed with family finance, or. . . .

The hallmark of a "degenerating" research program is the capacity to account for all the facts, whatever they are. The endless rate-of-return calculations of human-capital theorists have turned up plenty of anomalous facts crying out for explanation, such as the low or even negative private rates of return to graduate education in the United States. The steadfast refusal to exploit these anomalies in a further burst of fruitful theorizing is perhaps the best indication we have that the human-capital research program may indeed have started to "degenerate."

V. *The Earnings Function*

This brings us quite naturally to a famous question so far neglected, namely, the influence of native ability and family background on earnings. It is sometimes argued [40, Griliches, 1970, pp. 100–3] that we can safely ignore these factors in calculating social rates of return to educational investment, at least if our motive in making such calculations is to induce marginal policy changes in the allocation of resources between different educational

sectors. Even if that argument is accepted, it is perfectly clear that we cannot ignore all of nature and so much of nurture for other purposes, in particular for the measurement of the contribution of schooling to earnings differentials. Only a few years ago, most investigators were content to follow Edward F. Denison by making the so-called "two-thirds assumption," that is, to attribute two-thirds of the earnings differentials associated with different amounts of education to the pure effect of schooling, ascribing the rest to some amalgam of genetic endowment and social origins: *e.g.,* see Blaug [8, 1972, pp. 51–52]. But the present view is either that Denison underestimated the pure effect of education, as Zvi Griliches has argued, or that the interaction effect between native ability and family background on the one hand, and schooling on the other, exceeds the separate effect of each.

The bewildering flood of literature in recent years on earnings functions defies anything less than a book-length summary.[22] Our aim here, however, is merely to suggest that the battle lines are now clearly drawn, and to venture the prediction that the eventual outcome of this ongoing debate may be as surprising to advocates of the human-capital research program as to most of its critics.

The classic stance of the human-capital research program is to play down the influence of preschool factors on lifetime earnings, be it native ability or preschool investment of family time, or at any rate to claim that the combined effect of preschool factors and the subsequent influence of these on academic achievement is greatly exceeded by the separate effect of sheer duration of formal schooling and training. Needless to say, the human-capi-

[22] For literature surveys and commentaries largely confined to the United States and a few European countries, see Lewis C. Solmon [90, 1973], F. Thomas Juster [50, 1975], and Psacharopoulos [79, 1975]. There are, in addition, some half-dozen studies of earnings functions in less developed countries.

Blaug: A View on Human Capital Theory   843

tal model in no way denies the interaction of all of these factors, but it does claim that whatever interaction there is still leaves considerable room for the purely additive effects of the various explanatory variables. This classic position continues to be upheld by many—*e.g.*, see John Conlisk [24, 1971] and Zvi Griliches and William M. Mason [41, 1972]—and it is more or less endorsed by the authoritative work of Peter M. Blau and Otis D. Duncan [7, 1967] on occupational mobility in the United States (see sequel by O. D. Duncan, D. L. Featherman and B. Duncan [28, 1972]). However, most empirical work in this area lacks measures of native ability at an early age, much less measures taken in the preschool years, and the measures of family background that are invoked rarely go beyond father's occupation, father's or mother's education, and place of residence; what is conspicuously lacking are reliable measures of family income and wealth. It is difficult, therefore, to be entirely confident about the many findings that confirm the classic position.

Within the ranks of the human-capital research program, however, there are some who continue to emphasize the quantitative importance of the interaction between inborn ability and schooling [44, Hause, 1972; 46, Hause, 1975; 95, Taubman and Wales, 1974] and outside these ranks, there are others equally insistent that genetic endowment as measured by I.Q.'s counts for little because family background counts for so much [13, Bowles, 1972; 14, Bowles, 1973]. That says nothing about Christopher Jencks [48, 1972] who purports to demonstrate that nothing counts except luck, a finding that is almost entirely due to the fact that he explains, not the distribution of age-specific earnings from employment, but rather the distribution of total income averaged over people in four ten-year age groups, switching on unspecified occasions to all people aged 25 to 65.

The major shortcomings of all these investigations may perhaps be summarized under three headings: the identification problem; the problem of proxy-variables; and the problem of data sources. Take first the identification problem, of which we have already had occasion to speak. An earnings function is a reduced-form equation and in the absence of estimated structural parameters of the underlying simultaneous-equation model, we have every reason to suspect that the coefficients of the single equation are biased. This suspicion is borne out by Robert D. Morgenstern [68, 1973], who estimates both a nonrecursive, single-equation earnings function for the United States and a recursive model to explain the distribution of years of schooling in the labor force, as well as the distribution of earnings from employment. He shows that schooling certainly exerts a strong independent influence on earnings but, on the other hand, home background exerts weak direct as well as strong indirect effects on earnings, and this produces a bias in the schooling coefficient of single-equation earnings function.

The next heading is the problem of proxy-variables. First, there are the difficulties already referred to of measuring family background as an index of the environment in which children are brought up. Whether measured in terms of income, occupation, or education, we can never be sure whether the reported measures of family background refer to preschool investment, to later investments complementary with schooling, to postschool influences, or simply to certain attitudinal changes that provide children in certain homes with a set of self-fulfilling aspirations. Native ability is an even better example of a variable we cannot measure satisfactorily because there is simply no agreement about what we are supposed to be measuring. Is I.Q. really relevant, or instead should we be measuring "achievement motivation"? [61, McClelland, 1961]. To date, most of the work on earnings functions has been satisfied with measuring variables one way and one way only, as if any proxy will do. If we hope to make any progress in this area, the time has surely come to fit earnings functions with alternative proxies of the crucial variables.

The last heading is that of data sources. Virtually all fitted earnings functions have made use of either cross-section or time-series data, aggregated over cohorts. Only two or three studies have employed longitudinal or genuinely individualized data, although the temporal order of such variables as native ability, family background, formal schooling, occupational status, and personal earnings points to longitudinal data as the natural empirical framework for the analysis. The latest example of a longitudinal study of the economic benefits of education amply conveys the power of this type of data [31, Fägerlind, 1975]. Fifteen thousand individuals from Malmö, Sweden, were followed up from the age of 10 in 1938 to the age of 43 in 1971; I.Q. was measured at ages 10 and 20, and information on scholastic achievements was obtained throughout their period of schooling; occupational careers were monitored year by year, and information about earnings before tax were gathered from the tax records. The data were analyzed by means of path analysis, which is basically linear regression with standardized variables, but interaction terms were added in an effort to go some way towards a multiplicative model. The basic findings of the study directly contradict the conclusion of Jencks that "neither family background, cognitive skill, educational attainment, nor occupational status explains much of the variance in men's incomes" [48, 1972, p. 226]. Jencks explained only 22 percent of the variance in income among males

aged 25 to 65.[23] The Fägerlind study, using almost the same explanatory variables as Jencks, explains only 2 percent of the variance in earnings of males aged 25; there is a steep rise in variance explained, however, after the age of 30, reaching 30 percent at age 35, and more than 50 percent at age 43, thus confirming Mincer's view that the correlation between schooling and earnings is maximized at the "overtaking point."[24]

The direct effect of years of schooling on earnings is insignificant, except for earnings at age 43 when the effect is nevertheless very weak. But type of schooling does exert a strong and increasing effect on earnings, both directly and indirectly as a mediator of family background and early cognitive ability. Family background, on the other hand, exerts only a minor influence on earnings independently of education, and the same thing is true of early cognitive ability, which seems to interact with type rather than quantity of schooling. Fägerlind's summary of his results is nothing but judicious [31, 1975, p. 78]:

It is not possible to endorse conclusions that formal education is nearly insignificant in determining adult success in occupational status and earnings. On the other hand, the view advanced that amount of formal education is the main explanatory factor in status attainment and earnings cannot find full support from this investigation either, since other factors such as family background and cognitive ability play important indirect roles. The overall conception of the relationship between earnings and the various predictors included here is the following: The resources the individual has access to in early childhood, mainly family resources and personality assets, are converted into "marketable assets" mainly through the formal educational system. The present study reveals that although the direct effects of early cognitive

[23] As calculated from Jencks [48, 1972, Fig. B-7, p. 346].

[24] Fägerlind's overtaking point, however, occurs almost 10 years after Mincer's. A longer overtaking point than 7–9 years also emerges in the British data [81, Psacharopoulos and Layard, 1976].

ability on earnings are either small or insignificant, their indirect effects are relatively strong. Later assets, such as the quality of education, have both strong direct and indirect effects on earnings. . . . The school system alone is [therefore] not an adequate instrument for equalizing opportunities. This is because educational benefits are best used by those who come from advantaged backgrounds. Without some kind of equalization of home and child-care resources the educational system will function as a stratifier, wherein successful performances in one socializing setting are used to justify different and more advantageous treatments in the next.

The picture that emerges from studies such as these does not marry well with the so-called "schooling model" explanation of income distribution in the writings of Becker, Mincer, and Chiswick, which, it must be emphasized, is one and only one human-capital interpretation of the income distribution problem: *e.g.*, see Mincer [66, 1970] and Chiswick [22, 1974, ch. 3]. The schooling model necessarily implies the paradoxical conclusion that an increase in the average level of schooling of the population, given a constant distribution of schooling and a constant private rate of return to investment in education, causes the distribution of income to become more unequal. This conclusion depends critically, however, on the assumption of an equal rate of return to all types of human investment, an assumption which, as we have seen, is denied by the evidence [59, Marin and Psacharopoulos, 1976].[25]

[25] It is ironic to observe that a recent Marxist critique of human-capital theory, after berating the human-capital research program for its superficial approach to labor market phenomena, commits itself to two and only two predictions: "there is no reason at all to expect equality in rates of return, either among different types of schooling or between schooling and other forms of investment"; and "reduction in inequalities in the distribution of schooling might lead to changes in income inequality in any particular direction" [15, Bowles and Gintis, 1975, pp. 80, 81]. It is, however, difficult to find any connection between these predictions and the Marxist research program adopted by the authors.

Moreover, the schooling model explains the distribution of earnings by the distribution of accumulated human capital, and it explains the latter in turn by the exogenously determined distribution of "abilities" and "opportunities." But the "distribution of abilities and opportunities" is merely shorthand for the effects of early cognitive ability and parental background on the demand for formal schooling, both of which are endogenously determined variables in any intergenerational view of the process of human-capital formation [71, Oulton, 1974]. Thus, at best, the schooling model is incomplete and, at worst, it is misleading.

After ten years of work on earnings functions, all we have is a dim light at the end of a tunnel: everyone has been wrong and everyone has been right because the problem has proved to be more complicated than was originally imagined. This has proved to be a "progressive" research program in the sense that the basic model has come to be better specified, the variables better measured, and the range of statistical techniques gradually widened beyond classical least squares regression of a single equation. Nevertheless, the fact remains that no one has so far succeeded in specifying and testing the simultaneous demand and supply equations that generate the earnings function, without which empirical work on earnings function amounts to little more than trying to walk on one leg.

VI. *The Screening Hypothesis*

We come, at long last, to the screening hypothesis as a possible substitute or complement to the human-capital research program. According to human-capital theory, the labor market is capable of continually absorbing workers with ever higher levels of education, provided that education-specific earnings are flexible downwards. Since the educational hiring standards for an occupation is itself a decision variable, it matters little whether better educated workers are absorbed into lower-paying occupations, while holding average earnings per occupation constant, or into the same occupations as before, while reducing earnings by occupation. In any case, there is sufficient variance of earnings within 2-digit and even 3-digit occupations [60, Mayhew, 1971] to suggest that both of these effects occur simultaneously; in addition, occupations can be redesigned so as to destroy any basis of comparison between old and new occupations. In short, nothing is more alien to the human-capital research program than the manpower forecaster's notion of technically-determined educational requirements for jobs.

These self-regulating labor markets may or may not work smoothly, in the sense of keeping the demand for educated manpower continuously in line with its supply, but they will not work at all unless employers prefer more to less educated workers, everything else being the same. The human-capital research program is silent on why there should be such a persistent bias in the preferences of employers: it may be because educated workers possess scarce cognitive skills, it may be because they possess desirable personality traits, such as self-reliance and achievement-drive, and it may be because they display compliance with organizational rules. But whatever the reason for the preference, the fact remains that all of these desirable attributes cannot be known with certainty at the time of hiring. The employer is therefore faced with a selection problem: given the difficulties of accurately predicting the future performance of job applicants, he is tempted to treat educational qualifications as a screening device to distinguish new workers in terms of ability, achievement motivation, and possibly family origins, that is, in terms of personality traits rather than

cognitive skills; cognitive skills are largely acquired by on-the-job training, and employers are therefore fundamentally concerned with selecting job applicants in terms of their trainability. This may not be the whole story but it is, surely, a good deal of the story. If so, the observed correlation between earnings and length of schooling, which figures so prominently in the writings of human-capital theorists, disguises a more fundamental correlation between schooling and the attributes that characterize trainability. The contribution of education to economic growth, therefore, is simply that of providing a selection device for employers, and the way is now open to consider the question of whether formal schooling is indeed the most efficient selection mechanism that we could design for the purpose. This is the so-called "screening hypothesis" or "theory of credentialism," which, in one form or another, has now been expounded by a large number of writers [74, Phelps, 1972; 2, Arrow, 1973; 86, Rothschild, 1973; 95, Taubman and Wales, 1974; 96, Thurow, 1974; 91, Spence, 1973; 92, Spence, 1974; 103, Wiles, 1974; 94, Stiglitz, 1975].

This thesis runs into the serious objection that it accounts at best for starting salaries and not for the earnings of long-time employees in different firms. Earnings are not only highly correlated with length of schooling but also with years of work experience. An employer has ample opportunity with long-time employees to acquire independent evidence of job performance without continuing to rely on educational qualifications. Besides, the evidence suggests that the correlation between earnings and length of schooling actually increases in the first 10–15 years of work experience, a fact difficult to explain by this weak version of the screening hypothesis [9, Blaug, 1972, pp. 73–75; 21, Chiswick, 1973; 56, Layard and Psacharopoulos, 1974; 78, Psacharopoulos, 1974].

A stronger version of credentialism,

however, surmounts these difficulties by adding the consideration that job performance is typically judged within firms on a departmental basis [82, Rawlins and Ulman, 1974]. Each hierarchically-organized department operates its own Doeringer-Piore "internal labor market," whose principal function is to maintain output in the face of unpredictable variations in demand, while minimizing the costs of labor turnover to the firm as a whole. In consequence, departments operate with enough manpower slack to ensure every new recruit a well-defined sequence of promotions throughout his working life. In this way, the kind of statistical discrimination based on paper qualifications that operates to determine starting salaries in the weak version of credentialism is hereby extended to lifetime earnings. The argument is strengthened by the introduction of various "institutional" factors such as (1) the tendency of monopsonistic employers to share the costs of specific training with workers, (2) the lagged response of firms to cyclical contractions, (3) the effects of collective bargaining in promoting substitution of more for less educated workers, and (4) the phenomenon of "seller's credentialism," whereby professional associations press for increased educational requirements under state licensing laws [82, Rawlins and Ulman, 1974, pp. 224–32].

The theory of credentialism, especially in its stronger version, appears to have radical implications for educational policy. It suggests, for example, that educational expansion is unlikely to have much impact on earnings differentials because an increased flow of college graduates will simply promote upgrading of hiring standards: college graduates will be worse off in absolute terms but so will high school graduates, and hence earnings differentials by education will remain more or less the same. However, there is nothing about this argument that is incompatible with

human-capital theory. The question at issue is whether upgrading can be carried on indefinitely, implying that college graduates are perfect substitutes for high school graduates, and high school graduates for elementary school leavers, and therefore that the educational system is merely an arbitrary sorting mechanism. Even in this extreme version of credentialism, we are still left with an explanation of the demand for schooling that is the same as that of human-capital theory: screening by employers in terms of educational credentials creates an incentive on the part of employees to produce the "signal" that maximizes the probability of being selected, namely, the possession of an educational qualification, and this signaling incentive is in fact conveyed by the private rate of return to educational investment.

If college graduates are not perfect substitutes for high school graduates, and so on down the line, it may well be that the true "social" rate of return to educational investment is positive. In that case, what the theory of credentialism amounts to is the charge that human-capital theorists have been measuring the wrong thing: the social rate of return to educational investment is a rate of return to a particular occupational selection mechanism, and not the yield on resources invested in improving the quality of the labor force. However, no advocate of credentialism has so far succeeded in quantifying the social rate of return understood in this sense.

The screening hypothesis is clearly much less ambitious than the human-capital research program: it is silent on questions of health care and geographical migration. It is also obvious that the screening hypothesis concentrates its fire on the demand side in the labor market, whereas the human-capital research program is strong, where it is strong, on the supply side. Thus, it may well be true that the two research programs are complements, not substitutes. Indeed, Finis Welch has observed: "the fundamental notion of human capital, of foregoing current income for the prospect of increased future earnings, assumes only that the schooling-income association is not spurious. As such, it is fully consistent with the screening view that schools primarily identify pre-existent skills and with the view that market skills are produced in school" [101, 1975, p. 65]. If the difference between the two explanations is indeed that of discovering whether schools produce or merely identify those attributes that employers value, the empirical evidence that would be capable of distinguishing between them is presumably evidence about what actually happens in classrooms. However, both sides have instead looked to labor market data with which to assail their opponents. For example, Paul J. Taubman and Terence Wales attempt to vindicate the screening hypothesis by comparing the distribution of education within occupations with what the distribution would have been if employers had selected workers solely on the basis of measures of general ability (such as I.Q. scores and scores on tests of mathematical competence) [95, 1974]. But what if employers actually select workers on the basis of occupation-specific abilities? Why assume that employers screen all workers for the same attributes? If individuals have different comparative advantages in carrying out different tasks involved in different occupations, and if education is an efficient sorter of these comparative advantages, screening by educational qualifications may in fact be highly productive. Indeed, so far not a single convincing piece of evidence has been produced to show that the educational system is not an efficient sorter of students according to their manifest aptitudes and abilities.

Mincer on the other hand, throws cold water on credentialism by citing American survey data that show that seniority is a relatively minor factor in the promotion of white-collar workers and that educational qualifications are rarely mentioned as a factor in promotion in most major collective bargaining agreements [67, 1974, pp. 80–82]. But if credentialism creates self-fulfilling expectations in both employers and employees, evidence relating to seniority provisions in employment practices may prove little one way or the other. As Layard and Psacharopoulos point out, no simple market test is likely to discriminate between human capital and screening explanations because the question is not whether schooling explains earnings, but rather why it does [56, 1974].

One is left with the uneasy feeling that the advocates of credentialism are largely content to verify their theory by pointing to "educational inflation" without committing themselves to a decisive prediction that might falsify it. The point of a testable theory is to define states of the world that cannot occur if the theory is true. It is sometimes difficult to see what states of the world are excluded by credentialism, particularly as credentialists have so far studiously avoided any investigation of "educational production functions." But this is not to say that the debate is merely a tempest-in-a-teapot. What is at issue is whether the labor market generates private signals to individuals that are totally at variance with social signals. The debate is about the meaning of the social rather than the private rate of return on investment in human capital. In this sense, the argument is about normative values: do we want to select individuals for the world of work by means of educational credentials because, surely, it is not beyond the wit of men to concoct other devices for sorting workers for purposes of assigning them to particular occupations?

But as is so often the case with normative problems, there is an underlying positive issue to be settled first: how efficient *is* the educational system in assigning people to jobs? Before joining Illitch in "deschooling society," we ought to try to answer that question.

VII. *Conclusion*

We began by asking: is the human-capital research program "progressing" or "degenerating"? Having reviewed the development of the program over the last decade, are we any nearer to an answer?

A research program, as we said, can only be adequately appraised in relation to its rivals of roughly equal scope. The human-capital research program, however, has no genuine rival of equal breadth and rigor. The standard, timeless theories of the behavior of consumers and firms provide some explanation of such phenomena as school enrollments and on-the-job training, but they are powerless to account for the sharing of training costs between employers and workers. Classic sociology certainly furnishes alternative explanations of the correlation between education and earnings, and quasi-sociological theories of dual or segmented labor markets undoubtedly poach in the territory staked out by human-capital theorists. The difficulty here is one of lack of precision in formulating hypotheses and, in particular, of commitment to new, falsifiable hypotheses outside the range of the human-capital research program. The screening hypothesis presents similar difficulties because its advocates seem largely satisfied with providing different causal explanations for facts discovered by the human-capital research program. The Marxist research program, on the other hand, has hardly begun to attack the question of earnings differentials and thus in effect fails to compete in the same terrain with human-capital theory.

We are thus condemned to judge the human-capital research program largely in its own terms, which is strictly speaking impossible—even the flat-earth research program, judged in its own terms, is not faring too badly! There are certainly grounds for thinking that the human-capital research program is now in something of a "crisis": its explanation of the private demand for education seems increasingly unconvincing; it offers advice on the supply of education, but it does not begin to explain either the patterns of educational finance or the public ownership of schools and colleges that we actually observe; its account of post-school training continues to underemphasize the role of costless learning-by-doing as a simple function of time, not to mention the organizational imperatives of "internal labor markets"; its rate-of-return calculations repeatedly turn up significant, unexplained differences in the yields of investment in different types of human capital, but its schooling-model explanation of the distribution of earnings nevertheless goes on blithely assuming that all rates of return to human-capital formation are equalized at the margin. Worse still, is the persistent resort to *ad hoc* auxiliary assumptions to account for every perverse result, culminating in a certain tendency to mindlessly grind out the same calculation with a new set of data, which are typical signs of degeneration in a scientific research program.

At the same time, we must give credit where credit is due. The human-capital research program has moved steadily away from some of its early naive formulations, and it has boldly attacked certain traditionally neglected topics in economics, such as the distribution of personal income. Moreover, it has never entirely lost sight of its original goal of demonstrating that a wide range of apparently disconnected phenomena in the world are the outcome of a definite pattern of individual decisions, having in common the features of forgoing present gains for the prospect of future ones.[26] In so doing, it discovered novel facts, such as the correlation between education and age-specific earnings, which have opened up entirely new areas of research in economics. Whether this momentum can be maintained in the future is, of course, anybody's guess, but it is noteworthy that the screening hypothesis first emerged in the writings of adherents to the human-capital research program, and to this day the most fruitful empirical work in the testing of credentialist hypotheses continues to emerge from the friends rather than the enemies of human-capital theory.

Nothing is easier than predicting the future course of scientific development —and nothing is more likely to be wrong. Nevertheless, let me rush in where angels fear to tread. In all likelihood, the human-capital research program will never die, but it will gradually fade away to be swallowed up by the new theory of signaling, the theory of how teachers and students, employers and employees, and indeed all buyers and sellers select each other when their attributes matter but when information about these attributes is subject to uncertainty. In time, the screening hypothesis will be seen to have marked a turning point in the "human investment revolution in economic thought," a turning point to a richer, still more comprehensive view of the sequential lifecycle choices of individuals.

---

[26] The emphasis on individual choice is the *differentia specifica* of the human-capital research program. It has been argued that education improves allocative efficiency in production and in consumption; it accelerates technical progress; it raises the saving rate; it reduces the birth rate; and it affects the level as well as the nature of crime: *e.g.*, see Juster [50, 1975, chs. 9–14]. But unless these effects motivate individuals to demand education, they have nothing whatever to do with the human-capital research program.

REFERENCES

1. ADKINS, DOUGLAS L. "The American Educated Labor Force: An Empirical Look at Theories of its Formation and Composition," in *Higher education in the labor market.* Edited by MARGARET S. GORDON. New York: McGraw-Hill, 1974, pp. 111–46.
2. ARROW, KENNETH J. "Higher Education as a Filter," *J. Publ. Econ.,* July 1973, *2*(3), pp. 193–216.
3. BECKER, GARY S. *Human capital.* Second edition. New York: Columbia University Press, [1964] 1975.
4. BEN-PORATH, YORAM. "The Production of Human Capital and the Life Cycle of Earnings," *J. Polit. Econ.,* Part I, August 1967, *75*(4), pp. 352–65.
5. _____. "The Production of Human Capital Over Time," in *Education, income, and human capital.* Edited by W. LEE HANSEN. New York: National Bureau of Economic Research; distributed by Columbia University Press, 1970, pp. 129–47.
6. BENSON, CHARLES S. *The economics of public education.* Boston: Houghton Mifflin, 1961.
7. BLAU, PETER M. AND DUNCAN, OTIS DUDLEY, *The American occupational structure.* New York and London: Wiley, 1967.
8. BLAUG, MARK. *An introduction to the economics of education.* Baltimore and Middlesex, England: Penguin Books, 1972.
9. _____. "The Correlation Between Education and Earnings: What Does it Signify?" *Higher Education,* Feb. 1972, *1*(1), pp. 53–76.
10. _____. "The Economics of Education in English Classical Political Economy: A Re-Examination," in *Essays on Adam Smith.* Edited by ANDREW S. SKINNER AND THOMAS WIL-

Blaug: A View on Human Capital Theory   851

SON. London: Oxford University Press, 1976.

11. _____. *The economics of education: An annotated bibliography*. Third edition. Oxford: Pergamon Press, 1976.

12. _____. "Kuhn versus Lakatos, or Paradigms versus Research Programmes in the History of Economics," *Hist. Polit. Econ.*, Jan. 1976, *8*(1), pp. 399–433.

13. BOWLES, SAMUEL. "Schooling and Inequality From Generation to Generation," in *Investment in education: The equity-efficiency quandary*. Edited by THEODORE W. SCHULTZ. Chicago: Chicago University Press, 1972.

14. _____. "Understanding Unequal Economic Opportunity," *Amer. Econ. Rev.*, May 1973, *63*(2), pp. 346–56.

15. _____ AND GINTIS, HERBERT. "The Problem with Human Capital Theory—A Marxian Critique," *Amer. Econ. Rev.*, May 1975, *65*(2), pp. 74–82.

16. BOWMAN, MARY JEAN. "Learning and Earning in the Postschool Years," in *Review of research in education*. Edited by FRANK N. KERLINGER, JOHN B. CARROLL. Itasca, Illinois: Peacock, 1974, pp. 202–44.

17. CAMPBELL, JOHN M., JR. AND CURTIS, THOMAS D. "Graduate Education and Private Rates of Return: A Review of Theory and Empiricism," *Econ. Inquiry*, March 1975, *13*(1), pp. 99–118.

18. CAMPBELL, ROBERT AND SIEGEL, BARRY N. "The Demand for Higher Education in the United States, 1919–1964," *Amer. Econ. Rev.*, June 1967, *57*(3), pp. 482–94.

19. CARNEGIE COMMISSION ON HIGHER EDUCATION. *Higher education: Who pays? Who benefits? Who should pay? A report and recommendations.* New York: McGraw-Hill, 1973.

20. CARNOY, MARTIN AND MARENBACH, DIETER. "The Return to Schooling in the United States, 1939–69," *J. Human Res.*, Summer 1975, *10*(3), pp. 312–31.

21. CHISWICK, BARRY R. "Schooling, Screening, and Income," in *Does college matter?* Edited by LEWIS C. SOLMON AND PAUL J. TAUBMAN. New York: Academic Press, 1973, pp. 151–58.

22. _____. *Income inequality: Regional analysis within a human capital framework*. New York: National Bureau of Economic Research; distributed by Columbia University Press, 1974.

23. CHRISTENSEN, SANDRA; MELDER, JOHN AND WEISBROD, BURTON A. "Factors Affecting College Attendance," *J. Human Res.*, Spring 1975, *10*(2), pp. 174–88.

24. CONLISK, JOHN. "A Bit of Evidence on the Income-Education-Ability Interrelation," *J. Human Res.*, Summer 1971, *6*(3), pp. 358–62.

25. COOPER, MICHAEL H. AND CULYER, ANTHONY H. *Health economics.* Penguin Modern Economics Readings. London: Penguin Books, 1973.

26. DENISON, EDWARD F. *Accounting for U.S. growth, 1929–1969.* Washington: The Brookings Institution, 1974.

27. DRESCH, STEPHEN P. "Demography, Technology, and Higher Education: Toward a Formal Model of Educational Adaptation," *J. Polit. Econ.*, June 1975, *83*(3), pp. 535–69.

28. DUNCAN, OTIS DUDLEY; FEATHERMAN, DAVID L. AND DUNCAN, BEVERLY. *Socioeconomic background and achievement.* New York: Seminar Press, 1972.

29. ECKAUS, RICHARD S. "Estimation of

the Returns to Education with Hourly Standardized Incomes," *Quart. J. Econ.*, Feb. 1973, *87*(1), pp. 121–31.

30. _____; SAFTY, AHMAD EL AND NORMAN, VICTOR D. "An Appraisal of the Calculations of Rates of Return to Higher Education," in *Higher education and the labor market.* Edited by M. S. GORDON. New York: McGraw-Hill, 1974, pp. 333–72.

31. FÄGERLIND, INGMAR. *Formal education and adult earnings.* Stockholm: Almqvist & Wicksell International, 1975.

32. FELDMAN, PAUL AND HOENACK, STEPHEN A. "Private Demand for Higher Education in the United States," in *The economics and financing of higher education in the United States.* U.S. Joint Economic Committee, 91st Congress, 1st session. Washington: U.S.G.P.O., 1969, pp. 375–95.

33. FOGEL, WALTER AND MITCHELL, DANIEL J. B. "Higher Education Decision Making and the Labor Market," in *Higher education and the labor market.* Edited by M. S. GORDON. New York: McGraw-Hill, 1974, pp. 453–502.

34. FREEMAN, RICHARD B. *The market for college-trained manpower.* Cambridge: Harvard University Press, 1971.

35. _____. "Overinvestment in College Training," *J. Human Res.*, Summer 1975, *10*(3), pp. 287–311.

36. FREIDEN, ALAN N. AND STAAF, ROBERT J. "Scholastic Choice: An Economic Model of Student Behavior," *J. Human Res.*, Summer 1973, *8*(3), pp. 396–404.

37. FRIEDMAN, MILTON AND KUZNETS, SIMON. *Income from independent professional practice.* New York: National Bureau of Economic Research, 1945.

38. GALPER, HARVEY AND DUNN, ROBERT M., JR. "A Short-Run Demand Function for Higher Education in the United States," *J. Polit. Econ.*, Sept./Oct. 1969, *77*(5), pp. 765–77.

39. GREENWOOD, MICHAEL J. "Research on Internal Migration in the United States: A Survey," *J. Econ. Lit.*, June 1975, *13*(2), pp. 397–433.

40. GRILICHES, ZVI. "Notes on the Role of Education in Production Functions and Growth Accounting," in *Education, income, and human capital.* Edited by W. LEE HANSEN. New York: National Bureau of Economic Research; distributed by Columbia University Press, 1970, pp. 71–115.

41. _____ AND MASON, WILLIAM M. "Education, Income and Ability," in *Investment in education: The equity-efficiency quandary.* Edited by T. W. SCHULTZ. Chicago: Chicago University Press, 1972, pp. 74–103.

42. HANDA, MICHAEL L. AND SKOLNIK, MICHAEL L. "Empirical Analysis of the Demand for Education in Canada," in *Canadian higher education in the seventies.* Edited by SYLVIA OSTREY. Ottawa: Economic Council of Canada, 1972, pp. 5–44.

43. _____ AND SKOLNIK, MICHAEL L. "Unemployment, Expected Returns, and the Demand for University Education in Ontario: Some Empirical Results," *Higher Education,* Feb. 1975, *4*(1), pp. 27–44.

44. HAUSE, JOHN C. "Earnings Profile: Ability and Schooling," in *Investment in education: The equity-efficiency quandary.* Edited by T. W. SCHULTZ. Chicago: Chicago University Press, 1972, pp. 108–38.

45. _____. "The Risk Element in Occupational and Educational Choices: Comment," *J. Polit. Econ.*, July/August 1974, *82*(4), pp. 803–08.

46. _____. "Ability and Schooling as Determinants of Lifetime Earnings,

or If You're So Smart, Why Aren't You Rich?" in *Education, income and human behavior.* Edited by F. THOMAS JUSTER. New York: McGraw-Hill, 1975, pp. 123–49.

47. INTERNATIONAL LABOUR OFFICE. *Sharing in development: A programme of employment, equity, and growth for the Philippines.* Geneva: ILO, 1974.

48. JENCKS, CHRISTOPHER, ET AL. *Inequality: A reassessment of the effect of family and schooling in America.* New York: Basic Books, 1972.

49. JOHNSON, THOMAS AND HEBEIN, FREDERICK J. "Investments in Human Capital and Growth in Personal Income 1956–1966," *Amer. Econ. Rev.,* Sept. 1974, *64*(4), pp. 604–15.

50. JUSTER, F. THOMAS. "Introduction and Summary," in *Education, income and human behavior.* Edited by F. T. JUSTER. New York: McGraw-Hill, 1975, pp. 1–43.

51. KEELY, MICHAEL C. "A Comment on Leibenstein's 'An Interpretation of the Economic Theory of Fertility'," *J. Econ. Lit.,* June 1975, *13*(2), 461–68.

52. KIKER, BERNARD F. *Human capital: In retrospect.* Columbia: University of South Carolina, Bureau of Business and Economic Research, 1968.

53. KLARMAN, HERBERT E. *The economics of health.* New York: Columbia University Press, 1965.

54. KLINOV-MALUL, RUTH. "Enrolments in Higher Education as Related to Earnings," *Brit. J. Ind. Relat.,* March 1971, *9*(1), pp. 82–91.

55. KURATANI, MASATOSHI. "A Theory of Training, Earnings, and Employment: An Application to Japan," unpublished Ph.D. thesis, Columbia University, 1973.

56. LAYARD, RICHARD AND PSACHAROPOULOS, GEORGE. "The Screening Hypothesis and the Returns to Education," *J. Polit. Econ.,* Sept./Oct. 1974, *82*(5), pp. 985–98.

57. LEIBENSTEIN, HARVEY. "An Interpretation of the Economic Theory of Fertility: Promising Path or Blind Alley?" *J. Econ. Lit.,* June 1974, *12*(2), pp. 457–79.

58. LINDSAY, COTTON M. "Real Returns to Medical Education," *J. Human Res.,* Summer 1973, *8*(3), pp. 331–48.

59. MARIN, ALAN AND PSACHAROPOULOS, GEORGE. "Schooling and Income Distribution," *Rev. Econ. Statist.,* forthcoming 1976.

60. MAYHEW, ANNE. "Education, Occupation and Earnings," *Ind. Lab. Relat. Rev.,* Jan. 1971, *24*(2), pp. 216–25.

61. MCCLELLAND, DAVID C. *The achieving society.* Princeton, N. J.: Van Nostrand, 1961.

62. MCKENZIE, RICHARD B. AND STAAF, ROBERT J. *An economic theory of learning.* Blacksburg, Virginia: University Publications, 1974.

63. MILLER, LEONARD S. *Demand for higher education in the United States.* Stony Brook, New York: Economic Research Bureau, State University of New York, 1971.

64. MINCER, JACOB. "Investment in Human Capital and Personal Income Distribution," *J. Polit. Econ.,* August 1958, *66*, pp. 281–302.

65. ———. "On-the-Job Training: Costs, Returns, and Some Implications," *J. Polit. Econ.,* Supplement, Part 2, Oct. 1962, *70*(5), pp. 50–79.

66. ———. "The Distribution of Labor Incomes: A Survey with Special Reference to the Human Capital Approach," *J. Econ. Lit.,* March 1970, *8*(1), pp. 1–26.

67. ———. *Schooling, experience and earnings.* New York: National Bureau of Economic Research; distributed by Columbia University Press, 1974.

854 *Journal of Economic Literature*

68. MORGENSTERN, ROBERT D. "Direct and Indirect Effects on Earnings of Schooling and Socio-Economic Background," *Rev. Econ. Statist.*, May 1973, *55*(2), pp. 225–33.

69. NELSON, RICHARD R. "Recent Exercises in Growth Accounting: New Understanding or Dead End?" *Amer. Econ. Rev.*, June 1973, *63*(3), pp. 462–68.

70. O'CONNELL, JOHN F. "The Labor Market for Engineers: An Alternative Methodology," *J. Human Res.*, Winter 1972, *7*(1), pp. 71–86.

71. OULTON, NICHOLAS. "The Distribution of Education and the Distribution of Income," *Economica*, Nov. 1974, *41*(164), pp. 387–402.

72. PARSONS, DONALD O. "Specific Human Capital: An Application to Quit Rates and Layoff Rates," *J. Polit. Econ.*, Nov./Dec. 1972, *80*(6), pp. 1120–43.

73. PERLMAN, NAOMI W. AND PERLMAN, MARK. "The Changing Modes of Data in Recent Research," in *The organization and retrieval of economic information*. International Economics Association Symposium. Edited by MARK PERLMAN. New York: Macmillan, 1976.

74. PHELPS, EDMUND S. "The Statistical Theory of Racism and Sexism," *Amer. Econ. Rev.*, Sept. 1972, *62*(4), pp. 659–61.

75. _____, ET AL. *Microeconomic foundations of employment and inflation theory*. New York: Norton; London: Macmillan, 1970.

76. POPPER, [SIR] KARL. *Objective knowledge: An evolutionary approach*. Oxford: Clarendon Press, 1972.

77. PSACHAROPOULOS, GEORGE. "A Note on the Demand for Enrollment in Higher Education," *De Economist*, 1973, *121*(5), pp. 521–25.

78. _____. "College Quality as a Screening Device?" *J. Human Res.*, Fall 1974, *9*(4), pp. 556–58.

79. _____. *Earnings and education in OECD countries*. Paris: OECD, 1975.

80. _____ AND HINCHLIFFE, KEITH. *Returns to education: An international comparison*. Amsterdam: Elsevier Scientific; San Francisco: Jossey-Bass, 1973.

81. _____ AND LAYARD, RICHARD. "Human Capital and Earnings: British Evidence and a Critique," London School of Economics, Department of Economics, mimeo., 1976.

82. RAWLINS, V. LANE AND ULMAN, LLOYD. "The Utilization of College-Trained Manpower in the United States," in *Higher education and the labor market*. Edited by M. S. Gordon. New York: McGraw-Hill, 1974, pp. 195–236.

83. RAYMOND, RICHARD and SESNOWITZ, MICHAEL. "The Returns to Investments in Higher Education: Some New Evidence," *J. Human Res.*, Spring 1975, *10*(2), pp. 139–54.

84. ROSEN, SHERWIN. "Learning and Experience in the Labor Market," *J. Human Res.*, Summer 1972, *7*(3), pp. 326–42.

85. _____. "Learning by Experience as Joint Production," *Quart. J. Econ.*, August 1972, *86*(3), pp. 366–82.

86. ROTHSCHILD, MICHAEL. "Models of Market Organization With Imperfect Information: A Survey," *J. Polit. Econ.*, Nov./Dec. 1973, *81*(6), pp. 1283–1308.

87. SCHULTZ, THEODORE W. *The economic value of education*. New York: Columbia University Press, 1963.

88. SCOVILLE, JAMES. *Manpower and occupational analysis: Concepts and measurements*. Lexington, Mass.: Heath, Lexington Books, 1972.

89. SLOAN, FRANK A. "The Demand for Higher Education: The Case of Medical School Applicants," *J. Hu-*

man Res., Fall 1971, *6*(4), pp. 466–89.

90. SOLOMON, LEWIS C. "Schooling and Subsequent Success," in *Does college matter?* Edited by LEWIS C. SOLMON AND PAUL J. TAUBMAN. New York: Academic Press, 1973, pp. 13–34.

91. SPENCE, MICHAEL. "Job Market Signaling," *Quart. J. Econ.,* August 1973, *87*(3), pp. 355–74.

92. ———. *Market signaling.* Cambridge: Harvard University Press, 1974.

93. STIGLER, GEORGE J. "Information in the Labor Market," *J. Polit. Econ.,* Part 2, Oct. 1962, *70*(5), pp. 94–105.

94. STIGLITZ, JOSEPH E. "The Theory of 'Screening', Education and the Distribution of Income," *Amer. Econ. Rev.,* June 1975, *65*(3), pp. 283–300.

95. TAUBMAN, PAUL J. AND WALES, TERENCE. *Higher education and earnings: College as an investment and a screening device.* New York: McGraw-Hill, 1974.

96. THUROW, LESTER C. "Measuring the Economic Benefits of Education," in *Higher education and the labor market.* Edited by M. S. GORDON. New York: McGraw-Hill, 1974, pp. 373–418.

97. VAIZEY, JOHN E. *The economics of education.* New York: Free Press of Glencoe; London: Faber & Faber, 1962.

98. WALSH, JOHN RAYMOND. "Capital Concept Applied to Man," *Quart. J. Econ.,* Feb. 1935, *49*, pp. 255–85.

99. WACHTEL, PAUL. "The Returns to Investment in Higher Education: Another View," in *Education, income and human behavior.* Edited by F. THOMAS JUSTER. New York: McGraw-Hill, 1975, pp. 151–70.

100. WEISS, YORAM. "The Risk Element in Occupational and Educational Choices," *J. Polit. Econ.,* Nov./Dec. 1972, *80*(6), pp. 1203–13.

101. WELCH, FINIS. "Human Capital Theory: Education, Discrimination, and Life Cycles," *Amer. Econ. Rev.,* May 1975, *75*(2), pp. 63–73.

102. WHIPPLE, DAVID. "A Generalized Theory of Job Search," *J. Polit. Econ.,* Sept./Oct. 1973, *81*(5), pp. 1170–88.

103. WILES, PETER. "The Correlation Between Education and Earnings: The External-Test-Not-Content-Hypothesis (ETNC)," *Higher Education,* Feb. 1974, *3*(1), pp. 43–58.

[5]

Where Are We Now in the Economics of Education?

MARK BLAUG

Netherlands Institute for Advanced Study and University of London Institute of Education,
56 Gordon Square, London WC1H 0NT, U.K.

Abstract — This essay offers a bird's eye view of new directions in the economics of education. An increasing awareness of the socialization function of education, of the screening hypothesis, of the 'incomplete' employment contract and of labour market segmentation is leading, it is argued, to a picture of the economic value of schooling which is simply miles removed from the old-fashioned belief that education enhances cognitive knowledge and that employers pay educated people more because they know more. The new way of looking at the economic value of schooling is illustrated by the example of youth training and work experience programmes.

INTRODUCTION

THE ECONOMICS of education, conceived either as a specialized branch of economics or as a separate area of educational studies, was born somewhere around 1960. Its heyday was the decade of the 1960s, reaching a peak at, say, 1970 or thereabouts: those were the days when Denison's sources-of-growth accounting was generally believed to have demonstrated the precise quantitative contribution of education to economic growth, when Becker's *Human Capital* (1964) was widely acclaimed as opening up new vistas in labour economics, when every discussion of educational planning revolved around the respective merits of the 'social-demand approach', the 'manpower-requirements approach' and 'rate-of-return analysis'.[1] Those were, in short, the 'golden years' of the economics of education when no self-respecting Minister of Education would have dreamed of making educational decisions without an economist sitting at his right hand.

The early 1970s witnessed a profound change in the dominant role of economists in educational policy making. The enrolment explosion that had marked the history of educational systems all over the world since 1945 began to slow down. The earlier optimism that the expansion of education would effectively equalize life chances in industrialized societies gave way to a new pessimism about the possibilities of altering the distribution of incomes by educational means. Best-sellers like Jencks *et al.*'s *Inequality* (1972) were harbingers of the new scepticism about education that now swept through the First and Third Worlds. Influential studies like the Fauré Report, *Learning to Be* (Fauré *et al.* 1972), assumed without question that the prevailing system of education was largely dysfunctional and then went on to pin their faith on new educational structures which would alternate schooling and work throughout the lifetime of individuals. But the movement towards what has come to be called 'recurrent education' failed to catch on. Worried about inflation, youth unemployment and the actual or impending glut of highly educated people, most governments in the 1970s cut back on educational expenditure and hence were reluctant to venture forth to any significant extent into the unchartered territory of recurrent education (Blaug and Mace, 1977). What enthusiasm survived for educational reform now came to be increasingly devoted to qualitative reform rather than quantitative expansion. In promoting qualitative improvements in education, however, economists were found to be

Editor's note: This is the second paper in our series of invited papers. [Manuscript received and accepted 19 July 1984.]

17

18   *Economics of Education Review*

less useful than psychologists and psychometricians. No wonder then that economists were less prominent on the educational scene in the 1970s than in previous years.

Nevertheless, the economics of education did not die out in the 1970s as a field of academic study. On the contrary, the decade saw a vigorous development of the subject into new directions, such that we can now distinguish a well-defined second, as contrasted with a first, generation of economists of education.[2] The second generation no longer believes that the projection of private demand — the so-called 'social demand approach' — provides a sufficient basis for quantitative educational planning. Such projections almost always take for granted the existing patterns of finance for education and the second generation is keen to re-examine the prevailing patterns of educational finance. The second generation has likewise abandoned manpower forecasting as a planning tool if only because it begs too many questions about the relationship between the structure of occupations in an economy and the educational requirements for jobs, not to mention the notorious inaccuracy of such forecasts for any period in the future that is longer than 1 or 2 years. As for rate-of-return analysis, even first-generation economists of education were reluctant to employ it wholeheartedly for purposes of public policy making, a reluctance which is now enforced by the general endorsement of some version of the 'screening hypothesis' among second-generation economists of education. Gone, too, is the facile notion of the earlier generation that more education would steadily erode the income advantages of the highly educated, so that educational expansion would inevitably entail greater equality. The effect of education on income distribution is now understood to rest as much on the distribution as on the level of schooling in the population and, depending on how education is financed, it is now appreciated that more schooling can actually increase observed inequalities in income.

But perhaps the most far-reaching changes in the economics of education have come from the work of institutional and radical economists in the United States, emphasizing the 'socialization' function of schooling in contrast to its vocational function in teaching cognitive skills, the 'segmentation' of labour markets which generates different economic values of schooling to identical individuals and,

more generally, the 'invisible handshake' between employers and workers, which governs the personal rewards of education and training. Adding all these elements together, the 'new' economics of education is hardly recognizable as the same subject which ruled the roost in the 1960s. Of course, elements of the 'old' economics of education survive and even the recent pages of this journal can be employed to demonstrate that human capital theory and earnings regressions still serve many as suitable paradigms for studying the economic effects of education. Nevertheless, I claim that the vital parts of the subject lie elsewhere, linking up with similar developments in labour economics.

What follows, therefore, is not a review of the state of the arts in the economics of education but a deliberately provocative bird's-eye view of new directions in thinking among economists concerned with educational issues.

THE SOCIALIZATION FUNCTION OF SCHOOLING

The year 1976 saw the publication of a book by Samuel Bowles and Herbert Gintis entitled *Schooling in Capitalist America* (1976), which immediately became something of a minor educational classic among radical economists and sociologists. The centrepiece of the Bowles–Gintis book is the argument that the economic value of education in a capitalist economy has been grossly misunderstood by orthodox economists of education. The widely observed association between personal earnings and schooling is usually attributed to the influence of education on the levels of cognitive knowledge in the working population. But effective performance in most jobs, argue Bowles and Gintis, depends very little on directly usable cognitive skills and much more on certain non-cognitive personality traits. Moreover, these personality traits are also rewarded in the classroom and hence are systematically encouraged by the educational system.

What are these non-cognitive, affective outcomes of schools? At the risk of oversimplification, we can divide them into two broad categories. In the wide spectrum of lower level occupations to which unqualified school leavers are largely condemned they are the behavioural traits of punctuality, persistence, concentration, docility, compliance and the ability to work with others. However, the top of the occupational pyramid, accessible largely to university graduates, calls for a different set of personality traits, namely, self-esteem, self-reliance, versatility and the capacity to assume leadership roles. In a nutshell, we may say that elementary and secondary education breed the foot-soldiers, while higher education trains the lieutenants and captains of the economy.

Indeed, schools under capitalism are mini-factories and promote the same values which are prized in the labour market. Capitalist factories are hierarchically organized, and so are capitalist schools; capitalist factories require obedience and subservience to a central authority, and so do capitalist schools; capitalist factories 'alienate' workers from the products of their labour, and capitalist schools 'alienate' students from the products of their learning; workers are motivated, not by the intrinsic value of work, but by the promise of pay, and students are likewise motivated by the extrinsic reward of examination grades; and competition rather than co-operation, self-interest rather than comradeliness, governs the relations among workers as it governs the relations among students. In short, according to this view there is a nearly perfect correspondence between the educational system and the capitalist economic system: the educational system lacks any administrative and intellectual autonomy of its own, shining as it were only by reflected light emanating from the labour market. As Bowles and Gintis express it in their favourite Althusserian jargon: "the social relations of schools reproduce the social division of labour under capitalism".

Unfortunately, this entire line of argument, even if it were valid as it stands, is not very original. Ever since Emile Durkheim, mainstream sociologists have underlined the fact that 'socialization', that is, the inculcation of definite values and attitudes in children, is one of the principal functions of the educational system in any society. Bowles and Gintis complain that the school system has played an important role in preserving the capitalist order, but surely this is an obvious and even trivial proposition? Does the school system in a socialist society not play a similar role in preserving the socialist order? The viability of any economic system depends on citizens respecting 'the rules of the game', whatever they are, and clearly schools play a major part in legitimizing these rules.

Nevertheless, Bowles and Gintis are perfectly correct to reject cognitive development and, in-cidentally, the development of psychomotor skills as the central economic function of schools. The notion that most jobs in a modern economy require high levels of literacy and numeracy, and increasingly so as industry becomes more sophisticated, has been productive of a whole series of misdirected educational reforms. It lies behind the frequent tendency to 'vocationalize' secondary education in the fond belief that this will increase the employability of school leavers. The familiar finding of the low economic returns to vocational schooling, vocational school graduates being frequently less employable than academic school graduates (Psacharopoulos, 1980), is easily explained when it is remembered that most employers, whether public or private, care less about what potential workers know than about how they will behave. The very distinction between 'academic' and 'vocational' education, in which only the latter is supposed to be geared to the needs of the labour market, falsely suggests that much, if not most, education is economically irrelevant. But the 'hidden curriculum' of teacher–pupil relations in academic-style education has as much to do with the world of work as the explicit curriculum of mental and manipulative skills in vocational education. The frequently repeated research finding that few workers ever make specific use of the cognitive knowledge acquired in schools (Gintis, 1971) thus indicates, not some sort of monstrous mismatch between education and work, but the pivotal role of affective behavioural traits in job performance. The truth of the matter is that most jobs in a modern economy require about as much cognitive knowledge and psychomotor skills as are used to drive an automobile!

I am, of course, exaggerating. It is not to be denied that many professional qualifications do involve an indispensable element of cognitive knowledge and that, say, an oil company employing a chemist is looking for a minimum level of competence in the science of chemistry. But even at the level of professional studies, the cognitive knowledge which is said to be indispensable frequently consists of perfectly general communication skills and problem-solving abilities rather than occupation-specific competences; and to that extent implies a combination of particular personality traits and certain cognitive achievements. If this were not so, it would be difficult to explain the widespread employment of sociology and history graduates in public and private sector jobs. There are occupations, like that of the aeroplane pilot or the brain surgeon, where, indeed, nothing matters except cognitive judgement and psychomotor skills. Additional examples where cognitive knowledge looms large are accountants, lawyers, computer scientists — and perhaps even university teachers. Even here, however, success has frequently more to do with achievement-motivation — the motivation to excel in whatever one does for its own sake — than with factual or conceptual knowledge; and, surely, achievement-motivation is a personality trait? At any rate, all that we are claiming in endorsing Bowles and Gintis is that none of the occupations just mentioned are typical modes of employment in a modern economy. The vast bulk of jobs in an industrial economy involve competences that are acquired on the job in a few weeks and require, not a given stock of knowledge of facts and concepts, but the capacity to learn by doing.

Bowles and Gintis are also correct in asserting that first-generation economists of education, and particularly those advocating the theory of human capital, frequently implied in so many words that the economic value of education is due entirely to the effects of cognitive learning in schools. That is not to say, however, that mainstream economists of education committed themselves explicitly to this view. To a surprising extent they viewed schooling as a 'black box': without pretending or even caring to know what went on in classrooms, they simply insisted that passing through schools increased the earning power of people independently of differences in both family origins and inborn or acquired mental abilities (see Blaug, 1976, pp. 847–848). Nevertheless, their writings lent themselves naturally to the cognitive-knowledge interpretation. Furthermore, human capital theory with its rates of return to educational investment flourished alongside an extensive body of research on 'educational production functions', all or almost all of which related the inputs into schools to an 'output' consisting solely of scores of students on tests of cognitive achievement.[3] At the same time, another line of work attempted to forecast the educational requirements of particular patterns of economic growth. While these forecasts rarely asked the question of the sense in which the growth of certain jobs depended rigidly on the growth of educational qualifications, the implicit notion was always that each job entailed a definite complement of cognitive skills which could only be acquired via formal schooling. The moment we argue that the chief contribution of education to economic growth is to complement the socialization function of families in instilling values and attitudes requisite to adequate job functioning in an industrial society, we necessarily jettison the concepts of any precise quantitative relationship between the growth of the economy and the growth of the educational system. The question is no longer whether manpower forecasts are accurate or not, which is typically how the issue was posed in the 1960s, but whether the entire exercise is not perhaps misconceived in its very foundations.

No doubt there remains the problem of assessing the future supply of accountants, lawyers, doctors, computer scientists, etc., that is, professions which necessarily involve training in specific cognitive skills. This type of training typically requires long-cycle education, lasting 5–7 years. But manpower forecasts over periods of such length are hopelessly inaccurate and little better than guesswork (see Ahamad and Blaug, 1973). In the circumstances, what scope is there for educational planning? One general answer to the inherent imperfection of manpower forecasting is to shorten educational cycles so as to make it unnecessary to forecast 5 or 7 years into the future. But the professions in question are dominated by professional associations who have steadily lengthened the training period required to reach entry standards and who see any move to lower the training period as a threat to their monopoly power. That leaves us with the possibility of using the short-term signals of labour markets — unemployment rates, vacancy rates, wages rates, etc. — to register trends in the pattern of employment. This is not an entirely satisfactory solution to the problem of educated manpower but it is the best available. Fortunately, private demand for professional qualifications is sensitive to short-term indicators of labour market prospects and, indeed, has proved better at forecasting future trends than most public authorities. The best guide to policy in this case would actually seem to be *laissez-faire, laissez-passer*, and certainly doing nothing is preferable to engaging in meaningless forecasts of the demands for educated manpower 5–10 years hence.

THE SCREENING HYPOTHESIS

To return to Bowles and Gintis: the emphasis in our schools on affective behaviour rather than mental attainments is not, they argue, the unintended consequence of schooling carried out for other purposes. So long as production is hierarchically organized along capitalist lines, what is required at the bottom of the job pyramid is the ability to take orders, while at the top of the pyramid what is required is the ability to give orders. Teachers are perfectly aware of this spectrum of vocational demands and hence reward students in classrooms accordingly. Employers, on the other hand, have learned from past experience that there is a general concordance between the attributes required at various levels of the educational pyramid and educational attainments. In that sense, educational credentials act as surrogates for qualities which employers regard as important, predicting a certain level of job performance without, however, making any direct contribution to it. This 'screening hypothesis' neatly accounts for the fact that earnings rise with additional education; it even explains why so many educational qualifications appear to be unrelated to the type of work that students eventually take up; and it certainly helps to explain why the educational explosion of the last 35 years has had so little effect on equalizing the distribution of income.

If education acts merely as a filter to separate the chaff from the wheat, the steady expansion of higher education dilutes the significance of a degree and induces employers to upgrade the hiring standards of jobs previously filled by university and college graduates; graduates will then be worse off in absolute terms. But if secondary schooling is expanding at the same time, so that high school leavers are likewise being squeezed into lower-level jobs, earnings differentials between the two cohorts may nevertheless remain more or less the same. What is true of these two categories of labour is true of every category — the expansion of post-compulsory education is simply passed down the line and ends up in a chronic core of unemployed school leavers without, however, much visible effect on the distribution of earned income from employment.

The 'screening hypothesis' clearly has dramatic implications for educational policy. The difficulty with the hypothesis is that it comes in two versions, a strong version and a weak one. In its strong version it is virtually untenable, whereas in its weak version it is difficult to pin down with any precision. The strong version of the screening hypothesis asserts that education merely identifies students with particular attributes, acquired either at birth or by virtue of family background, but does not itself produce or in any way improve those attributes. It is difficult to conceive how this strong version of the hypothesis could be true. After all, schools screen twice, once when they select students for admission and a second time when they pass or fail students at the end of an educational cycle. If there is screening in the strong sense, only the first screen serves any useful economic function, the second being a piece of window-dressing designed purely to create employment for teachers. But as every teacher knows, the correlation for any individual student between predicted and actual education success is by no means perfect: selection for admission to courses is wrong almost as often as it is right. In other words, 'good' students have to be discovered and it takes a protracted sequence of hurdles, such as any educational cycle provides, to identify the traits and attributes that lead to success. The notion that they are present, only waiting to be sifted out by some ingenious filter, and that any filter will do, schooling being simply one, is a naïve psychological fallacy.

Moreover, the strong version of the screening hypothesis implies that there is little reward to an incompleted degree or certificate, or at any rate that the extra rewards of, say, 2 years of university education are much less than two-thirds of the rewards of a university degree completed in 3 years. In other words, educational credentials act like a 'sheepskin' that disguises the true difference between dropouts and graduates. Similarly, strong screening implies that, whatever differences in starting salaries between university graduates and secondary school leavers, the gap in the two salary streams gradually disappears with additional years of work experience: employers may use educational qualifications as a screen at the time of hiring when they are ignorant of the true abilities of potential workers, but as time passes they can actually observe their job performance and reward them in accordance with their true personal abilities. Finally, strong screening makes it difficult to understand why employers have not sought to replace the educational system by a cheaper screening mechanism. Surely, it is cheaper to incur the personal costs of independently testing the abilities of individual workers, say, by a battery of psychological aptitude tests, than to pay all university graduates more simply because they are university graduates.

Thus the strong version of the screening hypothesis carried with it at least three definite empirical implications. All of these three implications, however, are firmly refuted by the evidence (Layard and Psacharopoulos, 1974). Firstly, the private rate of return to education for university dropouts sometimes actually exceeds the yield of a completed university degree. Secondly, the effect of years of education on personal earnings generally rises rather than falls with additional years of work experience. Thirdly, business firms and government departments do sometimes test individual workers at the point of recruitment; nevertheless, in no country in the world have such independent testing services effectively replaced the role of educational credentials in screening out job applicants. Furthermore, strong screening additionally implies that education has no effect on personal earnings when it comes to the self-employed since there is little point in self-screening. However, the impact of years of education on earnings is as great for self-employed accountants, doctors and lawyers as it is for wage and salary earners. Of course, that may be due to screening by the customers of self-employed professionals, which in turn leads professional associations of accountants, doctors and lawyers to press for increased educational qualifications under state occupational licensing laws. Nevertheless, the evidence on the association between education and earnings for the self-employed does cast some doubt on screening in its stronger versions (see Lazear, 1977; Whitehead, 1981).

All these refutations, however, fall to the ground if we give the screening hypothesis a weaker interpretation. After all, employers face considerable information costs in recruiting suitable workers and assigning them appropriately to different tasks. Every new worker takes days or weeks to reach an adequate level of performance and thus mistakes in hiring are costly in terms of output forgone, not to mention the administrative costs of posting vacancies, sorting applicants and inducting successful recruits. No wonder, then, that employers resort to stereotypes like sex, colour, ethnic background, educational credentials, marital status, age and previous work experience, indicators which experience has shown to be good predictors of job performance, at least on average. Obviously, for crucial jobs like those of supervisors, junior managers and executives, it may pay to engage in expensive search procedures, including the use of aptitude tests, to select a particular candidate from among a group of job applicants with similar characteristics. But for most jobs it is cheaper to rely

on group characteristics and to run the risk of occasional errors. Thus 'educational credentialism' or the use of educational qualifications as a hiring screen is a species of a larger genus of 'statistical discrimination' in the hiring of labour: the costs of truly identifying the talents of potential workers forces employers to discriminate against atypical members of social groups. The fact that educational qualifications stand out among all the other stereotypes as being legally permitted and generally approved — most people nowadays regard educational meritocracy as being perfectly fair and legitimate — only encourages screening by education on the part of the employers.

So interpreted, the 'screening hypothesis' is a label for a classic information problem in a labour market. So far, however, we have only dealt with hiring at the point of recruitment and we have said nothing to explain the association between education and earnings right through the entire working life of individuals. Granted that employers will pay more to better educated workers when they know nothing about their individual aptitudes, why should they almost invariably continue to do so when they have had ample opportunity to monitor their performance over long periods of time?

One explanation may be the existence of what is called 'internal labour markets' in many business firms and government departments. It does not pay any large organization with a complex occupational structure to recruit every vacancy from an external labour market. Instead, most vacancies are filled by internal promotion and external recruitment is confined to a few 'ports of entry' at the bottom and the top of the occupational pyramid (Doeringer and Piore, 1971). This confers a double advantage: it promotes the morale of the workforce by providing a number of lifetime careers within the organization and it enhances the efficiency of recruitment because hiring is always confined to the same categories of jobs. However, once such an 'internal labour market' takes a firm foothold in an enterprise, it creates claims to eventual promotion among all workers in the firm at the time of hiring. In short, workers tend to be recruited in such enterprises not to a job but to a career path, and this means that any advantages at the point of recruitment tend to be converted into persistent advantages throughout a working life with the company. In this way the use of educational qualifications as a screen at the point of hiring becomes an effective screen throughout the period of association with a particular enterprise. Even if he or she leaves the company to work elsewhere, the next employer is likely to give credit both for previous experience and for previous earnings, which perpetuates the earlier link between schooling and earnings. To sum up: the notion of 'statistical discrimination' in hiring and the presence of 'internal labour markets' taken together are perfectly capable of explaining why highly educated people *on average* earn more than less educated people even though they may not be inherently more productive.

I say 'on average' advisedly. Clearly, employers do make mistakes in hiring and do discover in due course that, say, some university graduates are worse than others; these they will not promote or will only promote more slowly; alternatively, they may rotate them to a different job from the one for which they were recruited; contrariwise, the jobs of 'high flyers' may be enriched as time passes or combined with other jobs into a new job title. Therefore, when we study the structure of personal earnings by education and occupation in any modern economy, we observe: (i) a strong positive association between earnings and education when expressed in terms of averages; (ii) considerable variance in the association between education and earnings, such that the worst paid university graduates actually earn less than the best paid secondary school leavers, and so on for all other educational cohorts; and (iii) a considerable variance for every occupational category, however finely defined, in the years of schooling of incumbents of that occupation — such evidence is accountable by an element of 'statistical discrimination' at the hiring stage and the presence of 'internal labour markets' of various degrees of strength in many private companies and government departments.

THE INCOMPLETE EMPLOYMENT CONTRACT

We now take the argument a step further. Just as educators have always objected to the phrase 'human capital' to describe personal investment in education because it appears to demean education, so trade union leaders have long objected to the economist's habit of writing about labour problems as if labour was a commodity like any other to be bought and sold in the market place. But labour under capitalism is not in fact a commodity like any

other because its hiring contract is typically 'incomplete'. A contract of employment typically specifies the duration of work and the rate of pay for that work in terms of hours per day and days per week. What is most important in the hiring decision, however, is not written into the contract, namely, the intensity and quality of the effort to be expended, if only because there appears to be no dimension in which to express this effort. Obviously, if it is possible to isolate what each worker produces, workers are paid by the piece and the employment contract is complete. But in most production processes it is impossible to attribute every portion of final output to the contribution of some individual worker; production is carried out jointly by teams of workers, in which case the rate of pay must be expressed in terms of time. The famous slogan 'a fair day's pay for a fair day's work' highlights this double dimension of the employment contract of production systems in which output cannot be unambiguously traced to individual workers.

Thus for the bulk of manufacturing and service industries, not to mention the civil service and local government, the hire of labour implies the conscious willingness to work at a minimum level of intensity which simply cannot be fully spelled out in a contractual agreement. To secure the co-operation of workers in the production process, employers must prevent shirking by constant monitoring and policing, backed up by the promise of promotion and the threat of summary dismissal. Nevertheless, in the final analysis employers are forced to rely on what has been aptly named 'the invisible handshake' of trust and loyalty to replace 'the invisible hand' of competition that secures the effective provision of most other goods and services.

Experts in industrial relations will hardly be surprised by this concept of the incomplete employment contract. Economists, however, have, so to speak, forgotten it, or perhaps have never learned it until recently. Economists have, of course, long recognized that the business firm as a whole is a particular non-market institution in which authoritarian allocation replaces allocation by the price system, but they have neglected to analyse the principles which govern this internal allocation system (see Williamson, 1975). Thus, when certain labour economists developed the concept of 'internal labour markets' in the early 1970s, the very term 'internal labour *markets*' was misleading in suggesting a market mechanism rather than an administrative and organizational procedure for minimizing the potential sources of conflict in the employment relation. Similarly, economists have largely tended to treat trade unions as extra-economic forces having no reason for being in a competitive economy. But the incomplete labour contract makes it all too easy to account for the rise of trade unions as an attempt on the part of workers to choose collective rather than individual labour contracts in order to countervail the employer's control over the production process.

It is obvious that employers are at a disadvantage in completing the labour contract if workers act in concert. It will be to the interest of employers, therefore, to 'divide and rule'. One way of doing so is to buy individual loyalty by the promise of eventual promotion and treat all promotions as a race between a number of competitors. Another is to capitalize on the socially legitimate or illegitimate indicators that are employed in the hiring process and to assign men and women, married men and single men, whites and blacks, youths and adults, school leavers and university graduates, etc. to different lifetime career paths in the enterprise. This brings us squarely to the last element in our story, the concept of 'labour market segmentation'.

LABOUR MARKET SEGMENTATION

The theory of segmented labour markets (SLM) started out as a contrast between two *sectors* of the modern economy, the so-called 'primary' labour markets of large corporations, trade unions, job security and steady career prospects, and the 'secondary' labour markets of small businesses, no unions and dead-end jobs. It was designed to explain the fact of significant earnings differences between males and females and between whites and blacks even when age, schooling and years of work experience are held constant, and the persistent failure of education and training programmes specifically directed at low-paid workers to erode these differences. However, theories of SLM have since been radicalized and in such books as the *Contested Terrain* (1979) by Richard Edwards, segmentation of labour is not so much a matter of two or three contrasting *sectors* of economic activity as of many contrasting *categories* of workers within each and every capitalist enterprise in every sector of the economy.

As with the screening hypothesis, theories of SLM

seem to imply certain definite predictions. Firstly, they imply that if we select some index of the quality of jobs, made up, for example, of starting wages, turnover rates, bouts of unemployment, increments of pay with the same employers and so forth, it will prove to be bimodally or multimodally distributed across different but well-defined categories of workers; in other words, 'good' jobs are not randomly assigned to workers whatever their personal characteristics. Secondly, and more importantly, SLM theories imply that there will be very little mobility over time between these well-defined job clusters. The last of these two implications has been pretty well refuted, at least for the American economy. The first implication, however, has been generally corroborated, although the dust has by no means settled in this controversial area.[4]

Internal labour markets and segmentation of labour markets destroy much of the elegant simplicity of Becker's famous distinction between 'general training' and 'specific training'. *General* training was said to raise the trainee's productivity, not just in the firm providing the training but in any firm whatsoever; private firms have no incentive to pay the costs of such training because they cannot guarantee that they will be able to retain workers who have received such training; in consequence, general training will only be provided if trainees pay for it themselves in the form of reduced earnings during the training period. The classic example of such general training is, of course, apprenticeship training, not just in industry but also in the professions. *Specific* training, on the other hand, raises the productivity of trainees only in the firm providing the training, so that firms do have an incentive to finance such training. Leading examples of this universal class of training are induction programmes for newly hired workers coupled with probationary periods of supervision. The question now is: is training, whether on or off the job, largely general rather than specific? This is like asking: who actually pays for most training, firms or workers? The difficulty with the question is that business firms may well pay for some portion of general training if they can thereby retain labour and reduce turnover costs. Once a firm is committed to sharing even general training costs with its workers, labour training may become a fringe benefit in an 'internal labour market', another method of bidding away labour from rivals. We are left at the end of the story with no general guidance on the financing of training, whether general or specific: in some firms it is paid for by the company and in others it is paid for by workers; it all depends on the strength of internal labour markets in certain lines of economic activity and on the degree to which the work force in an enterprise is segmented or not.

SOME IMPLICATIONS

If we now add together the vital 'socialization' function of schools, the 'screening hypothesis' in the sense of statistical discrimination, the concept of the 'incomplete' employment contract, the phenomenon of 'internal labour markets' and the notion of labour market 'segmentation', we arrive at a picture of the economic value of schooling that is simply miles removed from the old-fashioned belief that education makes workers more productive and that employers pay them more because they are more productive. The basic problem in hiring workers is to induce them to co-operate in carrying out the tasks to which the enterprise is committed. At the same time, there is the information problem of discovering the potential aptitudes of individual workers so as to combine them together into a loyal team. The need for artificial filters or screens arises not just because genuine hiring search procedures are costly but also because they are socially divisive. The beauty of such filters as age, sex, race, marital status, years of work experience and, above all, educational qualifications is that at least some of them are generally regarded as socially legitimate, 'just', 'fair' and so on. Educational credentials, in particular, are widely held to be the product of individual effort and to that extent their use in recruitment and promotion meets with the approval of workers, employers and customers alike — a perfect social consensus!

It may be that schooling increases the productivity of individuals by making them more effective members of a production team or better able to handle machines and materials, but it would matter little if it were not so provided everyone thought it was so — which, of course, they do. What is important is that every worker accepts the principles on which some are paid more and some are paid less. Even if these payments are in reverse order of the true spot marginal products of individual workers, assuming that the marginal product of an individual worker can even be identified, the maximization of the output and minimization of the

costs of the firm depend critically, not on the scale of individual rewards, but on the mutual co-operation of all workers in the enterprise. In short, screening by educational qualifications is economically efficient not because 'good' students are always 'good' workers but because educational credentialism avoids the inherent conflict of interests between workers and employers.

What follows from all this for educational policy? Firstly, we have said enough to show why labour markets tend to react to changes in effective demand by adjusting quantities rather than prices, numbers employed rather than wages: layoffs in a lump threaten the morale of the workforce less than an across-the-board cut in wages, particularly if the layoffs are concentrated among certain 'inferior' groups, like youngsters, women, blacks, etc.; likewise, fresh hiring in a boom generates the expectation of promotion among older workers, which is even more effective in raising morale than an actual promotion. Thus labour markets are inherently capable of continually absorbing workers with ever higher levels of education simply by adjusting the customary educational hiring standards for jobs. However, such adjustments, precisely because they must win, and must be seen to win, general approval, take time. A rapid flooding of a labour market with, say, university graduates may well produce graduate unemployment, whereas the same numbers could have been absorbed if they had been forthcoming at a slower rate. Similarly, a sudden glut of university graduates produces graduate unemployment because employers have misgivings about hiring overqualified applicants who tend to feel underutilized, making them ineffective workers. But declining job opportunities for university graduates forces degree holders to adjust their job aspirations downwards. In time, therefore, BAs will cease to feel themselves to be overqualified for, say, a secretarial post and in that sense the original objection to hiring them for such jobs will lose its force. Once again, it is not an absolute oversupply of university graduates but a rapid increase in that supply that causes graduate unemployment.

Contrariwise, there is no real sense in which a given level of education in the economically active population of a country can be said to be technically 'required' to permit the achieved level of economic growth of that country. That sort of argument grossly exaggerates the contribution of manipulative and cognitive skills in the performance of economic functions, ignores the fact that such skills are largely acquired by on-the-job training, and utterly neglects the vital role of suitable personality traits in securing the 'invisible handshake' on which production critically depends. In short, educational policies may be fitted to literally any level or rate of economic growth and cannot be justified in terms of those patterns of growth. Education does make a contribution to economic growth, not as an indispensable input into the growth process, as first-generation economists of education used to argue, but simply as a framework which willy-nilly accommodates the growth process.

One is tempted at this point to provide numerous illustrations of the powerful policy implications of this new way of looking at the economic value of schooling. A single but telling example, however, must suffice for present purposes. One of the outstanding social problems of recent years has been the rising incidence of youth unemployment which has everywhere accompanied the appearance of slumpflation since the early 1970s. Most governments in industrialized countries have reacted to this problem by expanding training and work-experience programmes for out-of-school youngsters aged 16–19 years (Magnussen, 1977). Indeed, if we add all public expenditure on such schemes to those that directly subsidize the employment of young people, we reach figures for government expenditure on the employment and training of 16- to 19-year-olds that in some European countries equal the levels of expenditure on college and university education.

The motive for these programmes is sometimes taken to be simply that of removing as many people as possible from the unemployment rolls so as to put the best face on deflationary policies. But that is perhaps an unduly cynical interpretation. Governments themselves defend training and work-experience programmes for youngsters as repairing the deficiencies of formal schooling. In other words, their theory of why there is now so much youth unemployment is that secondary schools have failed to inculcate the requisite skills and positive attitudes that render a school leaver employable. From our standpoint, it is highly significant that many youth training programmes include training, not just in the three Rs and in low-level manipulative skills, but also in techniques of interviewing and presentation of biographical information, thus recognizing that employability depends as much on personality traits as on physical competence and cognitive knowledge.

However, the difficulty with this quasi-official theory of youth unemployment is that it fails utterly to account for the emergence of heavy youth unemployment all over the industrialized world in the last half of the 1970s except by the implausible assumption that the quality of secondary education suddenly deteriorated badly in 1973 or thereabouts.

There is nothing new about the fact that in a recession the rates of joblessness for young people exceed those for adults. What is new about youth unemployment in recent years is that the gap which always opens up between the two unemployment rates in a recession has never been as large as it is today in most countries, and this despite a steady upward trend in the proportion of young people staying on in schools beyond the compulsory leaving age. Even when we standardize the figures for demographic changes and for changes in labour force activity rates, the size of the gap seems to be without historical precedent: in almost all capitalist countries unemployment for people under the age of 21 constitutes 40 and sometimes 50% of total unemployment (see Sorentino, 1981). The true causes of this problem still remain somewhat mysterious: it is as if employers all over the industrialized world became strangely reluctant after about 1973 or 1974 to hire young people for regular, full-time jobs; moreover, in some countries, like France, Germany, Sweden, Italy, and the U.K., this reluctance actually manifested itself as early as the late 1960s (Sorentino, 1981).

One can go some way towards explaining this phenomenon by taking account of the world-wide shift in the pattern of demand from the industrial sector to the service industries but this phenomenon still leaves unexplained a considerable proportion of youth unemployment. A more significant factor may be the gradual strengthening of job security provisions for adult workers in most industrialized countries. Traditional management prerogatives in dismissing labour have been substantially curtailed everywhere, and increasingly so in the 1970s — consider, for example, the successive impact in Britain of the Redundancy Payments Act of 1965, the Industrial Relations Act of 1972 and the Employment Protection Act of 1975 — and this has encouraged the substitution of older, experienced workers for younger, inexperienced workers in order to minimize rates of labour turnover. At the same time, a general narrowing of wage differentials between youth and adult workers, frequently as a result of minimum wage legislation and union pressure, has tended to price youngsters out of the labour market. But a final element in the explanation of rising youth unemployment must be the phenomenon referred to earlier, namely, that of educational inflation in which the educational hiring standards of jobs are continually raised to absorb the ever-growing number of educated entrants into the labour force, a process which has no natural halting place other than the legal school leaving age. In other words, the problem of youth unemployment is to a considerable extent the product of the post-war explosion in post-compulsory education.

Be that as it may, current training, work-experience, job-creation and job-subsidization programmes for the age group 16–19 years continue to expand in most countries under the impetus of untested if not implausible hypotheses about the collapse of formal schooling coupled with half-baked ideas about the long-term training requirements of growing economies which private industry is somehow incapable of providing. There is, surely, a world of difference between creating jobs for which labour can be trained when it is recruited (with appropriate assistance from a relevant government department) and training people via special programmes for jobs which do not exist and may never exist. This elementary distinction is almost totally neglected in the recent world-wide upsurge of out-of-school programmes for youngsters aged 16–19 years.

If this much is accepted, we have illustrated a more general thesis, namely, that effective educational planning must be based on a realistic assessment of the operations of labour markets. Such markets are in a continuous state of flux, particu-larly in terms of employment patterns rather than relative wage differentials, and with the best will in the world it is difficult to avoid a situation in which every educational reform is addressed to curing yesterday's rather than today's ills. Economic growth and technical progress are just as capable of de-skilling existing jobs as of generating new jobs and new skills: consider, for example, the way in which the development of hand-held calculators and word processors has reduced the importance of functional numeracy and literacy in the work force and increased the importance of favourable affective attitudes to computer aids. The expansion of new industries and the contraction of old ones, changes in employment legislation, changes in trade union regulations, etc. are capable of rapidly altering existing patterns of recruitment. No method of educational planning can keep pace with this kaleidoscope and in this sense there is a real economic merit in general, academic education as a hedge against technical dynamism. The old battle cry for vocational job-specific education, which at first glance might seem to be the rallying grounds of economists, is actually the very opposite of what is implied by the 'new' economics of education. Here, as in so many other educational debates, the enemy is a Neanderthal economics of education concocted of a vulgar version of first-generation economics of education and old-fashioned shibboleths about the alleged economic value of schooling.

Acknowledgements — This paper was originally commissioned by the Organization for Economic Co-operation and Development (OECD) Directorate for Social Affairs, Manpower and Education (SME/ET/82.29) and was subsequently published (in a slightly different version) in a series of special public lectures by the University of London Institute of Education (1983).

NOTES

1. My own textbook (Blaug, 1972) reflects those concerns almost perfectly.
2. See Carnoy (1977), the first to suggest that the 1970s saw some sort of watershed in the subject.
3. For some attempt to include non-cognitive outcomes see Bridge *et al.* (1979, pp. 59–67, 205–212) and Cohn (1975). On the general distinction between cognitive and non-cognitive outcomes of schooling, see Bloom *et al.* (1956).
4. See Cain (1976), Carnoy (1980), Gordon *et al.* (1982) and Blaug (1983, pp. 225–227).

REFERENCES

AHAMAD, B. and BLAUG, M. (1973) *The Practice of Manpower Forecasting: a Collection of Case Studies.* Amsterdam: Elsevier.
BECKER, G. S. (1964) *Human Capital.* Princeton, NJ: Princeton University Press.

28   *Economics of Education Review*

BLAUG, M. (1972) *Introduction to the Economics of Education*. London: Penguin Books.
BLAUG, M. (1976) The empirical status of human capital theory: a slightly jaundiced survey. *J. econ. Lit.* **14**, 827–855.
BLAUG, M. (1983) A methodological appraisal of radical economics. *Methodological Controversy in Economics. A Historical Perspective* (Edited by COATS, A.W.). Greenwich, CT: JAI Press.
BLAUG, M. and MACE, J. (1977) Recurrent education — the new Jerusalem. *Higher Educ.* **6**, 277–300.
BLOOM, B. S. *et al.* (1956) *Taxonomy of Educational Objectives*. New York: David McKay (2 vols).
BOWLES, S. and GINTIS, H. (1976) *Schooling in Capitalist America*. New York: Basic Books.
BRIDGE, R. G., JUDD, C. M. and MOOCK, P. R. (1979) *The Determinants of Educational Outcomes*. Cambridge, MA: Ballinger.
CAIN, G. C. (1976) The challenge of segmented labor market theories to orthodox theory: a survey. *J. econ. Lit.* **14**, 1215–1257.
CARNOY, M. (1977) Education and economic development: the first generation. *Econ. Dev. cult. Change* **25** (Suppl.), 448–488.
CARNOY, M. (1980) *Education, Work and Employment, II. Segmented Labour Markets*. Paris: UNESCO — International Institute of Educational Planning.
COHN, E. (1975) *Input–Output Analysis in Public Education*. Cambridge, MA: Ballinger.
DOERINGER, P. B. and PIORE, M. J. (1971) *Internal Labor Markets and Manpower Analysis*. Lexington, MA: D.C. Heath.
EDWARDS, R. C. (1979) *Contested Terrain: The Transformation of the Working Place in the Twentieth Century*. New York: Basic Books.
FAURÉ, E. *et al.* (1972) *Learning to Be*. Paris: UNESCO.
GINTIS, H. (1971) Education, technology and the characteristics of worker productivity. *Am. econ. Rev.* **61**, 266–279.
GORDON, D. M., EDWARDS, R. C. and REICH, M. (1982) *Segmented Work, Divided Workers: The Historical Transformation of Labor in the United States*. London: Cambridge University Press.
JENCKS, C. *et al.* (1972) *Inequality*. New York: Basic Books.
LAYARD, R. and PSACHAROPOULOS, G. (1974) The screening hypothesis and the returns to education. *J. polit. Econ.* **82**, 985–998.
LAZEAR, E. (1977) Academic achievement and job performance. *Am. econ. Rev.* **67**, 252–254.
MAGNUSSEN, O. (1977) *Education and Employment: the Problem of Early School-leavers*. Paris: Institute of Education of European Cultural Foundation.
PSACHAROPOULOS, G. (1980) *Higher Education in Developing Countries: a Cost–Benefit Analysis*. Washington, DC: World Bank.
SORENTINO, C. (1981) Youth unemployment: an international perspective. *Monthly Labor Rev.* **38** (July), 73–98.
WHITEHEAD, A. K. (1981) Screening and education: a theoretical and empirical survey. *Br. Rev. econ. Issues* **2** (8), 44–62.
WILLIAMSON, O. E. (1975) *Market and Hierarchies: Analysis and Antitrust Implications. A Study in the Economics of Internal Organization*. New York: The Free Press.

Part II
The First World

[6]

RECURRENT EDUCATION – THE NEW JERUSALEM*

MARK BLAUG and JOHN MACE

*University of London Institute of Education,
Research Unit in the Economics of Education,
London WC1H ONT.*

ABSTRACT

The origins of the concept of recurrent education and the claims presently made for it are analyzed. The recurrent education policies presently pursued in six OECD countries are described. The theory of recurrent education and relevant empirical data are reviewed. The authors conclude that the concept of recurrent education requires clarification and that the costing of proposals for recurrent education should be undertaken.

Introduction

Educators the world over seem to climb on new bandwagons every five years or so: in the early 1960s, manpower forecasting and vocational education were in fashion; in the late 1960s, programmed learning and comprehensive secondary education; in the early 1970s, functional literacy and nonformal education in developing countries; and in the late 1970s, it is clearly recurrent education. All these bandwagons have one thing in common: they cannot be implemented without increasing educational expenditure. This much is certainly true of the latest mania — recurrent education. Indeed, if the recurrent education movement were to succeed, it would prove to be the most expansionary educational proposal that the world has ever seen. Fortunately, there is very little danger that it will succeed. Its potential is strictly limited and at best it will complement rather than replace the present system of education.

The basic theme of the recurrent education movement is that full-time schooling, which hitherto has been experienced by most individuals as one

---

* The research for this paper was sponsored by the United States Education Policy Research Center for Higher Education and Society under HEW Contract No. 300–76–0026. The views expressed in it are not necessarily those of the Center. Our thanks are due to J. Froomkin for valuable comments on an earlier draft.

278

uninterrupted sequence, will henceforth recur again and again throughout an individual's working life. This notion of life-long, permanent, recurring education (RE) is defended on grounds of equity, efficiency, and human rights — and usually on all three. We hope to show that none of these grounds offers any secure basis for advocating a system in which everyone will continually alternate work and study after completing an initial period of compulsory schooling. The objection may be raised that this is only one extreme version of the concept of RE. Another version, that of second-chance education for adults who left school at the statutory leaving age, and this may be both equitable and efficient, not to mention the fulfilment of a legitimate "human right"? The objection neatly illustrates the difficulties of analyzing so elastic a concept as RE and emphasizes the need for some terminological clarification.

We will begin, therefore, with a sorting out of both the concept itself and the claims that are made for it. This is followed by a description of RE policies presently pursued in six OECD countries, which will hopefully help to nail down what we are discussing. At this point we are ready to consider the "theory" of RE, followed by a discussion of what little empirical evidence is presently available to elucidate the probable effects of RE. Our analysis of the theory as well as the review of the evidence demonstrates that RE is nothing but a gigantic political balloon, which collapses as soon as it is pricked. There are of course aspects or versions of RE which it is easy to support — for example subsidized part-time adult education, or subsidized government retraining schemes, or even paid educational leave for workers financed by payroll taxes — but nothing is gained by bundling these together under the portmanteau label of "recurrent education", thus creating the impression that there is a single Master Plan which will cure all the ills of the present educational system. RE is not only a misleading label, it is a dangerous one because it inhibits clear thinking about specific educational proposals.

Historical Background

The idea of RE was literally invented by the Swedish U68 Educational Commission Reports of 1969 and 1970. The commission was charged with the responsibility for developing an overall plan for post-secondary education in Sweden. Consequently it advanced the notion that this stage of education should be postponed to a later age and acquired in a modular form during interrupted periods of full-time employment. In this way, post-secondary education would also become accessible to adults who had earlier rejected it (U68, 1973). Here, at the outset, we have the double-pronged idea that has ever since characterized the RE movement: postponement of

279

post-compulsory schooling, in effect educating older rather than younger individuals; and second-chance education for an adult clientele, in effect educating older individuals who have never been educated at all under present arrangements.

The commission recognized that they were proposing a far-reaching global reform which would require changes in the structure of both secondary and higher education. Their aim was to satisfy certain objectives, such as reducing the inequality in educational attainments among the generations, strengthening the sense of a common set of values in the community, improving the motivation of students, and linking the educational system more closely to the world of work (Bengtsson, 1972, pp. 10–17). These objectives between them span the grounds of equity and efficiency but go beyond them to include the objective of promoting social cohesion via the schooling process; almost all subsequent writings on RE have claimed as much or more.

The commission made certain definite proposals to encourage the adoption of a system of RE: secondary schools would introduce vocational subjects in their curriculum; admission criteria to higher education would be altered to allow credit to be given for work experience; educational facilities would be more widely dispersed in what the Swedes call "out-reach" centers, so as to give a wider range of adults ready access to schooling; teaching was to be offered on a part-time basis in both secondary schools and universities; and workers were to be allowed to absent themselves from work without loss of earnings or pension rights. The costs of these changes were not calculated and, as we shall see, only some of these changes have actually been adopted in Sweden. Nevertheless, these proposals and the issues raised by them have remained the basis of all subsequent thinking on RE throughout Europe and the United States.

Despite the undoubted influence of the U68 Commission Reports, the first sign that RE was more than a "Swedish fad" was the wholesale adoption of the concept of RE in the so-called Faure Report of 1972 (*Learning To Be*, 1972). The report condemned the present system of education as being dysfunctional and urged its replacement by a new structure in which schooling is interspersed with work throughout the lifetime of an individual. The new structure was said to require radical changes in both curricula and institutions but the report failed to explain how these educational reforms were to be realized. Indeed, the report was as weak in its diagnosis as it was lame in its prescriptions (Simmons, 1973). Nevertheless, the Faure Report was widely read and we may date the launching of RE into the center of the educational stage from the publication of the report in 1972.

A year later, the principle of educational leave from work with pay, not only for vocational training and trade union instruction, but also for

280

purposes of acquiring general education, was promoted at the 49th Session of the International Labour Conference as a new labor right. The conference adopted a resolution which advocated,

> the access of workers to various types of *paid* [our italics] educational leave, as distinct from holidays with pay for recreational purposes, in order to give them the opportunity and incentive to acquire the further education and training which they need to carry out their duties at the workplace and assume their responsibilities as members of the community (CERI, 1976, p. 17.)

The demand for RE in this form has since been repeated by other international organizations, such as OECD and the Council of Europe. Evidently, within only four years the ideas of the U68 Commission have been converted into a world-wide drive to reallocate drastically the current resources used for educational purposes.

The Definition of RE

The concept of RE is like a chameleon, its appearance changing with every observer. According to OECD, "recurrent education is *formal,* and *preferably full-time,* education for adults who want to resume their education, interrupted earlier for a variety of reasons" (CERI, 1971). But UNESCO (1971) takes a wider view:

> The term "lifelong education" covers a very wide field. In some cases it is applied to strictly vocational education . . . It may also cover much the same ground as adult education .... . But more and more frequently it is being applied to new activities and fields of research which . . . express a desire for evolving a new style of education.

Further definitions may be found in Stoikov (1975, p. 2). At bottom, all definitions involve the idea of postponing post-compulsory formal education to a later stage of life, but it is not always clear whether the postponement is to be made once and for all, or whether schooling should be spread in many small dosages over a person's entire lifetime, either on a full-time or on a part-time basis; whether it is higher education that is to be postponed, or whether the same considerations apply to post-compulsory secondary education; whether postponement is to be made mandatory, or whether it is to be left entirely to the voluntary decisions of individuals; whether we are postponing a decision that would have been made earlier or whether we are encouraging a second chance in later life for people who would never have made the decision earlier; and particularly whether it is to be financed privately or publicly, and if the latter, whether both direct costs and indirect costs in the form of earnings forgone are to be reimbursed by the state. Even the simple idea of post-compulsory education which is

281

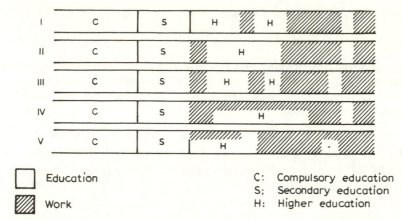

Fig. 1. Some possible alternatives for recurrent education in Sweden.

basically recurrent and not sequential is subject to a variety of interpretations, as is made clear by Figure 1 which depicts a diagram of alternative models for recurrent higher education which are now under consideration in Sweden (Bengtsson, 1972, p. 8).

Model I is reminiscent of the British "sandwich course" in interposing
work between the second and the final years of higher education; it goes
further, however, by providing a refresher course in later life. Model II
interposes a gap between secondary and higher education, but higher education is nevertheless completed in one sequence; again there is a refresher
course later in life. Model III is recurrent all the way through, but periods of
education are still periods of full-time education. Models IV and V make
higher education part-time and concurrent with employment, differing
mainly in that Model IV includes a full-time refresher course, while Model V
allows for a final year of full-time higher education, topped by a part-time
refresher course at a later stage. In essence there appear to be two notions of
RE here. The first is where individuals alternate between work and education, e.g. Models I-III. The second is where education and work are somehow
integrated, e.g. Models IV-V.

The extraordinary flexibility of the concept of RE (certainly these five
models do not exhaust all the possibilities) makes analysis virtually impossible, and perhaps this is the reason that so much of the literature about RE
is, at best, inspirational and, at worst, vague. Nevertheless, for purposes of
this paper we adopt Stoikov's (1975, pp. 5–6) definition of RE as

> a global system containing a variety of programmes which distribute
> education and training of different levels (primary, secondary and tertiary),
> by formal and nonformal means, over the life-span of the individual in a
> recurring way, that is, alternated with work or other activities.

282

As Stoikov remarks, this is the widest possible definition of RE because it includes

> any education and training effort which sets in after an initial education followed by a period of employment or other occupation. So adult education at various levels and retraining, for instance, are regarded . . . as an integral part of any recurrent education system.

At present no such global system exists anywhere but elements of it do exist in a number of countries. We turn now to a brief description of these elements of RE in Sweden, Germany, France, Yugoslavia, the United Kingdom, and the United States.

Elements of RE in Six Countries

Sweden: Sweden has in recent years taken two important steps toward realizing the proposals of the U68 Commission Reports. The first concerns the development of "out-reach" centers and the second the provision of educational leave from work. The number of out-reach study centers has risen from 47,333 in 1970 to 79,779 in 1973 and the number of students in these centers has risen from 445,799 to 716,225 over the same period (CERI, 1976, p. 195). Provision for evening classes at municipal high schools has been extended to half of all municipalities in Sweden. There are two national schools for adults which now follow the nation-wide curriculum for grades 7–9 of the compulsory school; they also offer subjects taught in the secondary schools. Correspondence courses are available at both of these national schools. In addition, there exist people's high schools where the courses are broadly comparable to the last three grades of compulsory school, complementing the courses available at study centers.

A law on study leave came into effect in 1975, securing the principle of the right of all public and private employees to leave for educational purposes during working hours, provided he or she has been employed for at least 12 months during the last two years, and guaranteeing the right to return to the same job as before after completion of the course (the employer has the right to postpone leave for up to 6 months but thereafter the local trade union must approve any postponement). However, the law fails to guarantee paid educational leave because it includes no provision for financing a leave of absence. Although limited assistance to leavers is available in the form of study grants from the central government, these are much less than the average wage rate for unskilled workers in Sweden. It is doubtful, therefore, that many workers will take up the option of a study leave that involves a considerable loss of income. Thus, Sweden may be said now to have legislated some of the letter but little of the true spirit of RE.

283

Germany: The situation in Germany is complicated by a division of functions between the *Länder* and the *Bund,* or the state governments and the central government, but a number of existing provisions at both levels of governments are consistent with our definition of RE. First, there is the *Bildungsweg* (adult evening institutes), which provides a standard curriculum leading to a high school diploma. The *Berufsaufbauschule* (vocational evening institutes) provides evening courses part-time for two years, full-time for the third. From these, students can proceed on a full-time basis to the *Fachschule*(technical high schools). More relevant to the concept of RE are the *Telekolleg* courses developed in certain *Länder*. These follow the secondary school curriculum but use carefully written material for self-study. They offer monthly tutorial meetings and make use of television. There are also many private institutions, which tend to cater to either vocational or general education at the secondary level, typically involving full-time study for students of all ages. The *Volkshochschulen* (people's high schools), which are found throughout Germany, have recently adopted the policy of counting work experience as a possible entry qualification in addition to certain minimum educational qualifications, and practically all of them are now prepared to certify units of uncompleted courses, allowing the student to alternate periods of study with periods of work. This is nothing less than the American college credit system applied to high school education but it marks a considerable innovation in German education in the spirit of RE.

However, these developments in the formal educational system are not matched by recent legislative efforts in Germany to promote educational leave from work. As one OECD report on Germany puts it: "the idea of lifelong learning that underlies the concept (of RE) is inadequately met in any of the existing forms of education leave" (Rudolph et al., 1972, p. 11). The year 1969 saw the passage in Germany of the Vocational Training Act, the Labor Market Promotion Act, and the Industrial Education Assistance Act. The Vocational Training Act gave recognition to the public responsibility for vocational training. However, it focused its attention on initial vocational training and made no provisions for funding these activities. The Labor Market Promotion Act does provide aid for individuals undertaking full-time vocational training at the rate of 1.25 to 1.72 Dm per hour, provided the training is truly vocational and does not exceed 10 days per year. Lastly, the Industrial Education Assistance Act gives workers the legal right to financial assistance, subject to qualifications and need, to attend courses in general education at the secondary level. A later act, the Federal Educational Assistance Act of 1971, established that such assistance should be inversely related to the level of family income.

As a result of these four acts, an agreement about study leave from work for 2.2 million German workers had been reached by 1973, but only a fraction of these workers are to receive paid leave (CERI, 1976, p. 157). The

284

financial arrangements differ between the four acts, but the Labor Promotion Act obliges both employers and employees to contribute together 2 percent of fixed monthly earnings. Since the amount paid is a function of income earned, this provision militates against low-paid workers. Moreover, given the fees that are charged by most secondary educational institutions in Germany, a 4 percent monthly payroll contribution, even when accumulated over 5–10 years, is not adequate to pay for more than a few months of full-time study. As in the case of Sweden, we see that it is not difficult to legislate educational study leave for workers but it is very difficult to finance such leaves without imposing most of the costs on the workers themselves.

France: More than in any other country, the concept of RE has made deep inroads in recent years in France. The Orientation Law of 1968 enjoined universities to actively promote the education of adults and it authorized the admission of non-baccalaureats if there was evidence of work experience. In 1970, the universities, in conjunction with industrialists and trade unionists, proposed that adults should be able to enter university, classes should be composed of people of all ages, a modular credit system should be introduced, and experiments should be conducted with different types of course, as for example summer courses to accommodate part-time students.

In 1971 new laws were passed that recognized technical certificates coupled with work experience as a qualification for entry to higher education. In addition, it ratified an agreement already reached between employers and trade unions concerning educational leave. This was followed in 1973 by a law to regulate correspondence courses. The same law established a government agency which was to stimulate and encourage any and all programs that alternate work and study.

Individual training of workers is supported by three laws passed in 1966, 1968 and 1969. The first law taxed employers at the rate of 0.4 to 0.6 percent of their total salary bill, the proceeds of which are to be paid into a Fund for Vocational Training and Social Mobility. The second law established the right of workers to take unpaid leave up to a period of one year. And the third law established the circumstances under which state aid to workers taking leaves might be forthcoming, as for example, retraining after loss of employment, vocational promotion, and updating of obsolescent knowledge. As a direct result of these three laws, the number of workers taking leave from work for either full-time or part-time study rose from 190,000 in 1969 to 620,000 in 1973, and outlays of the Fund for Vocational Training and Social Mobility for the remuneration of trainees rose from 402 million francs in 1971 to 1000 million francs in 1975 (CERI, 1976, pp. 127–8).

These developments were given a new push with the law of 1971,

285

whose grandiose title, "The Organization of Continuing Vocational. Education Within the Framework of Permanent Education," leaves no doubt of the source of its inspiration. This law guaranteed the right of employees to one year's full-time or 1200 hours part-time paid study leave (subject to certain conditions) and it provided various encouragements to employers to develop leave programs. However, state aid to workers on leave was only to be given if it prevented unemployment, if it entailed vocational upgrading, or if it constituted pre-training for first-job seekers between the ages of 16 and 18. Furthermore, the number of workers taking educational leave in any one year in an enterprise was limited to 2 percent of the total work force. The state agreed to provide the training facilities but firms for their part have to donate 2 percent of their wage bill to cover the costs of providing training.

In 1974 the state spent 2,323 million francs under the provisions of the law of 1971, and private firms spent almost four million francs more. In consequence, worker participation in state-run courses is estimated to have risen from 283,000 in 1971 to 421,000 in 1974 (CERI, 1976, p. 133 and p. 135). But a survey of these schemes showed that there was a much higher rate of participation among workers for large firms than from small ones; there was also a markedly lower participation rate among unskilled than among skilled workers, and among female than among male workers (CERI, 1976, pp. 135–7). Since one objective of RE is to equalize education and training opportunities between different social groups, this particular objective does not seem to have been successfully achieved in France.

Furthermore, virtually the whole of the expansion of paid study leaves in France in recent years has been concentrated in the field of vocational training. There are very few general education courses available to adult workers and under the law of 1971 only staff personnel are entitled to be paid to participate in such courses, on the grounds that academic education is in fact vocational training for the professions. Despite the impressive achievements of their legislation, therefore, the French are still a longer way from realizing the original aim of the RE reformer: to postpone post-compulsory formal education to the later years of a working life and to provide general education for adults who for one reason or another had missed the chance to study earlier on.

Oddly enough Sweden seems to have achieved one strand of RE — the idea of open-ended, formal education accessible to adults — but only by reneging on the concept of educational leave with pay, while France has more or less achieved the other strand of RE — the ideal of paid study leave — but only by renouncing the principle of making formal, academic education available to all regardless of age. But perhaps this is not at all puzzling. To secure both strands is to guarantee a run-away inflation of educational expenditure.

286

Yugoslavia: If Western educators have made extravagant claims for RE, these claims are as nothing compared to what the Yugoslavs hope to achieve by RE. The objectives of RE in Yugoslavia are stated to be that it

> (1) offers equal educational opportunity to people of different ages;
> (2) prolongs the individual's active career and increases his labour output;
> (3) guarantees the adaptability of education to the social needs of highly qualified manpower; [and] (4) gives better opportunities for integration of education in the self-management system (CERI, 1972, pp. 21—25).

In the light of these objectives, the present system of education in Yugoslavia is being thoroughly overhauled so as virtually to abolish the concept of sequential, uninterrupted schooling for all stages of education beyond the primary one.

Study leave from work in Yugoslavia is presently encouraged by the legal right to attend courses during working hours with entitlement to full pay during such study periods. Nevertheless, of the 4.3 million workers in the state-owned sector, only about 530,000, or 12 percent, enrol annually for various forms of education and training, and of these, the bulk of enrolments are for purposes of vocational and professional preparation (CERI, 1976, pp. 218—9). No doubt, these modest results are derived from the fact that the right to leave of absence is administered in practice by the worker-management committees of individual enterprises and these are more likely to give a sympathetic hearing to vocational rather than self-enrichment arguments. In any case, given the strong official support for RE in Yugoslavia, the Yugoslavian evidence begins to sow seeds of doubt about the magnitude of the potential demand for formal study among adults, even when it costs them virtually nothing but leisure time forgone.

United Kingdom: Little is said about RE in British educational debates, though Houghton and others (1974 and 1976) have contributed to the discussion. Some would say that this is because so many of the elements of RE already exist in the U.K. Consider, for example, the so-called "further education colleges". Courses at these colleges are full-time or part-time, evening or day-time, vocationally or academically oriented, and they are available to anyone over the compulsory school leaving age of 16; furthermore, they vary from recreational, non-examinable courses to accredited degree courses at polytechnics, fully equivalent to degree courses at universities.

In 1973 there were approximately 3,700,000 students attending further education colleges in the United Kingdom. Of these only 8 percent were attending full-time. The remaining 92 percent were divided between evening and day classes in the proportion of 3:1 (D.E.S., 1975, p. 21), which is to say that 2,572,000 or 70 percent of all FE students were not alternating study and work but were in fact studying and working concurrently. Similarly 17 percent of all students in FE Colleges in 1973 were released by their employers for interrupted periods of study and three-quarters of these were 21 years of age or less (D.E.S., 1975, pp. 32–3). That is, only 4 percent of all "day-release" and "sandwich" students attending FE institutions are over 21. Thus, if RE is a system of study leave from work on a continual basis throughout the working lives of adults, Britain has the form but none of the substance of RE.

Non-examinable adult education of the liberal arts variety is provided by the Worker Educational Services and by extra-mural departments in universities. A recent influential report on adult education, the so-called Russell Report (1973), made only a passing reference to the concept of RE. It did give pride of place in the system of adult education to second-chance examinable courses for adults, but it did not raise the issue of adult education as an alternative to increased provision of higher education along traditional lines which is the essence of the concept of RE.

The Open University is the best known and perhaps the most important British innovation along RE lines. OU courses are mainly provided through correspondence texts, coupled with radio and television programs. They are expressly designed for adults and although the content is more or less identical to what is found in the undergraduate degree programs of traditional universities, the curriculum design and methods of teaching have strong elements of RE; in addition, some nondegree, "post-experience" courses were launched in 1972. The Open University has now over 70,000 students, the great majority being between the ages of 25 and 45, and as many as 25,000 of them lack the minimum qualifications for entry into higher education in Britain. In addition to the Open University, private correspondence courses in the United Kingdom are said to cater to some 500,000 adults, of whom 75,000 are studying for some professional qualification (Glatter and Wedell, 1971). In the words of one observer:

> Clearly, the adult education sector (in the United Kingdom) cannot be said to be organised on a recurrent basis. Nonetheless, equally clearly it includes a number of developments . . . which incorporate many of the features of recurrent education. To that extent, if it were decided to establish systematic provision of education on a recurrent basis, the elements of such a system already exist within adult education in the United Kingdom (Cantor, 1974, pp. 22–3).

In the area of paid educational leave, Britain has neither the form nor the content of RE. There is nothing in the statute books in Britain that gives workers a legal right to study leave, whether paid or unpaid. A precedent was set in 1975 with the passing of the Employment Protection Act, giving trade union officials the legal right to paid leave for training in industrial relations, but this act has not yet passed into law. In addition the Industrial Training

288

Act of 1964 designated Industrial Training Boards in several industries to monitor and design formal, in-plant training courses, paid for by the firms themselves through a levy scheme. Similarly, the Manpower Services Commission operates a Training Opportunities Scheme, which is intended to cater to 60–70,000 young people over the age of 19. But these and some other programs are clearly designed to provide adequate on-the-job training, and not leave from work to take up either vocational or non-vocational courses in formal education institutions. In short, Britain lags far behind other European countries in implementing the recommendations of the International Labour Conference on paid educational leave.

United States: The Carnegie Commission Report, *Toward a Learning Society: Alternative Channels to Life and Work* (1973) demonstrated that the total educational effort after high school in America is divided almost equally between full-time degree work in colleges and universities, on the one hand, and part-time, nondegree work in colleges, business firms, the armed forces, and various privately owned "proprietary" schools, on the other. Furthermore, they predicted that the latter half would grow more rapidly in future years than the former half, a development which they applauded. Thus, in the words of one commentary on the Carnegie Commission Reports, "the conversion of the Carnegie Commission to the doctrine of recurrent education seems to be complete" (Embling, 1974, p. 216). Ever since, the idea that RE might provide an alternative to the present structure of formal education has been gaining ground in the United States. The American educational scene, however, is complicated because it varies from state to state. We will therefore cite some recent developments in the State of New York as an illustration of a trend that is also at work in other states (Regan, 1972).

Many of the evening courses offered to adults at universities in the State of New York, such as the Brooklyn College of General Studies and Syracuse University, are identical in content and teaching methods to daytime courses offered to youngsters in the college-going age group. But elsewhere in the State some of the Community Colleges and Technical Institutes have modified the curriculum to suit people of different ages and backgrounds; entry can take place at any time; work experience counts; and the courses are offered at a variety of geographical centers. Likewise, degrees can now be obtained by correspondence at the University of the Air and at so-called Learning Centers which are found all over the State.

Leave of absence to acquire education is not regulated in the U.S.A. as it is in Western Europe by legislation, with the singular exception of employees in the public sector. For that reason, no comprehensive information is available concerning the numbers of workers taking leave, the length of leaves, and the extent to which leaves are paid for by firms. Nevertheless, it

289

is possible to infer from some available evidence that paid educational leave of the type that alternates work and study is relatively rare; that large firms employing 500 or more workers authorize leave more frequently than small firms, and that leave is typically granted for strictly vocational reasons (Nollen, 1976). A number of agreements between unions and firms specifically include the right to paid educational leave, a leading example being the 1970 agreement between the Kaiser Foundation Hospital and the Hospital and Institutional Workers Union Local 250, AFL–CIO. The latter provides for paid educational leave of one week for every year of work after the second year. Once again, little is known about participation rates in these schemes but hearsay has it that they are low and that courses are taken up entirely for purposes of vocational updating (CERI, 1976, pp. 72–5 and Levine, 1975).

Theory of RE

We learn several things from this bird's-eye view of RE developments in six countries. Firstly, there is a steady tendency everywhere to create new opportunities for adults to acquire education but no country has yet succeeded in effectively postponing either secondary or higher education to a later stage in life. Secondly, the legal right of workers to obtain study leave has now been secured in most of Western Europe and seems likely to spread around the world in the next decade or so, but the concept of paid study leave is meeting with considerable resistance. Even countries that have adopted it are making sure that it will not amount to more than a few months in the entire working life of an individual. Thirdly, no progress whatever has been achieved in securing the principle of paid study leave for purely personal reasons, such as self-renewal or cultural enrichment: country after country has confined study leave to vocational updating and/or retraining. In this sense, the RE movement has so far failed to achieve some of its main objectives.

In the light of these comments, we turn now to the theoretical arguments for and against RE. In most discussions about RE its potential for reducing inequality between the generations, between the sexes, and between social classes is emphasized (See CERI, 1975; Emmerij, 1974 especially ch xii; Kallen, 1973). The present school system is said to perpetuate these inequalities and to be incapable of appropriate reform. Although one can easily show that the formal educational system does indeed have a poor record of equalizing the educational chances of individuals, one may question whether RE is going to be any more successful in this respect. If we are talking about unequal educational chances between the generations, it would appear that there is simply no other remedy except

290

RE. But recall our earlier definition of RE as "a global system" for distributing education over the lifespan of individuals in a recurring way. That we simply have to overturn the whole of the existing educational system in order to provide adults with the opportunity of catching up on young people is far from obvious. What would be wrong with gradually expanding adult education, possibly going so far as to bribe adults to attend evening classes by a time-equivalent reduction in the work week? Coupling this with the introduction of daytime courses in adult education centers to take advantage of the current expansion of paid study leave in industry might eventually induce some youngsters to postpone their formal education until they are older. In this way we will approach RE by evolution rather than revolution.

The point is that to induce adult men and women from underprivileged homes to take up RE is not going to be any easier than it is to induce girls and boys from working-class homes to stay on in the formal educational system. The experience with adult education in all countries is that most students are middle-class professionals. This is hardly surprising. If the courses are given in the evenings, it takes a great deal of motivation to attend classes after work. If instead the courses are available on a daytime basis, only high-earning professionals can afford to sacrifice their earnings while attending an adult education center. All this is no argument against attempting to induce adults to take up formal education on a recurrent basis. It is simply a warning against expecting miracles in this area. And we certainly do not need to abolish sequential formal schooling merely to boost adult education.

Similarly, it is doubtful whether the existing educational inequalities between the sexes and between social classes cannot be dealt with more directly by positive discrimination at the stage of post-compulsory schooling, say, by differential grants and loans to girls as well as to all students from poorer homes (Billings, 1975). The notion that is current in the RE literature — provide the facilities for alternating study and work and leave questions of finance till a later date — is almost certain to reproduce the inequalities generted by the existing educational system. Furthermore, the evidence shows that employers tend to regard better-educated workers as more trainable and hence provide them with the bulk of on-the-job training made available (Nollen, 1976). In other words, training is viewed as complementary to formal education, which means consequently that even the wholesale adoption of RE would still tend to favor those who had acquired their stock of general knowledge at an earlier age. Therefore if we are concerned with equalizing the distribution of income by means of equalizing the opportunities to acquire education and training, there may be no substitute for doing so before entry into the labor market.

The second major argument for RE is concerned with the relationship between the educational system and the world of work. All the advocates of

291

RE argue that it will lead to a more effective relationship between schooling and the labor market: students with work experience will be better motivated and will make better educational choices; new skills can be learned when the present ones become obsolete; any mismatch between educational qualifications and occupational requirements can be rapidly remedied; etc.

To do justice to this line of "efficiency" arguments we must carefully distinguish between the question of "postponement of education" and the question of "investing in older individuals" (Stoikov, 1975, p. 11). Consider, first of all, the question of postponement. What can we say about it in general terms?

To postpone the cost of schooling, everything else being the same, releases resources in the present which will be less valuable in the future; the net effect is to save resources. They will be less valuable in the future because, in a growing economy, resources are always less scarce tomorrow than they are today. In short, on efficiency grounds, we are always better off if we can postpone a cost.

On the other hand, to postpone the benefit of schooling, everything else being the same, results in a net loss of resources and precisely for the same reason: future benefits in a growing economy are always worth less than present benefits. Moreover, the fact that the length of one's working life is limited reduces the benefits of education incurred in late life compared to those of education taken at an earlier age simply because it reduces the number of years over which the benefits can be collected. In other words, that education and training are typically acquired early in life is no accident. To sum up, the cost argument runs in favor of postponing education but the benefit argument runs against it.

Unfortunately, the favorable cost argument is less favorable the moment we consider the difficulty of satisfying the condition of "everything-else-being-the-same". The major cost of education, both to the individual and to society, is earnings or output forgone. Obviously, older men or women earn more and can produce more than inexperienced youngsters; thus, society loses more from a year of study when the student is 40 years old than when he is 20. Therefore, the prima facie case against RE as postponement rests as much on considerations of costs as on considerations of benefits.

Nevertheless, the knot in the case of postponement derives from the difficulty of believing that the benefits of education, whatever they are, would be absolutely the same at whatever age schooling was acquired. Cognitive knowledge rapidly depreciates with age, and if the economic value of education resides in what educated people know (which we doubt) there is a clear case for postponing some education until a later age, or at least there is a case for topping-up forgotten knowledge at a later age. Besides, the

292

uncertainty of the future and particularly the uncertainty of the technological future, which is often invoked to justify late rather than early
specialization in sequential formal education, is just as capable of justi-
fying the deferment of formal education as a whole. It is true that there are
certain skills, such as those of mathematicians and musicians, which do seem
to require early development and uninterrupted study for their full fruition.
But these are special cases and most professional people would probably
benefit from some discontinuities in their formal preparation. Thus, the
advocates of RE have a real case to make on the benefit side, which perhaps
more than outweighs prima facie arguments against postponement. And that
is as far as perfectly general theoretical arguments will take us.

None of this has anything to do with the question of "investing in older
individuals". Perhaps the benefit-cost ratio for postponing higher education
for 10 years is too low to justify the action, but that is a completely
different question from providing higher education for 28-year-olds. Just
because the first benefit-cost ratio is low, there is no reason to think
that therefore the second benefit-cost ratio will also be low. Furthermore,
we can invest in older individuals by part-time, on-the-job training schemes,
by full-time, off-the-job retraining programs, or by full-time leave of absence
from work for purposes of formal instruction. So long as we confine ourselves to "efficiency" arguments, there is nothing very interesting to be said
in general, although, as we shall see, there is some relevant evidence to consider. However, training and retraining programs have a long history and we
hardly need the concept of RE to justify them. It is rather the latter concept of study leave which belongs properly to RE.

Since no costs are being postponed when we decide now to invest in
older rather than younger people by granting study leave, the cost argument
is neither here nor there, although how the costs are shared between
employers, employees and taxpayers does make a difference. On the benefit
side, the arguments previously considered respecting the depreciation and
obsolescence of knowledge apply just as much to "investing in older individuals" as to "postponement of education". These are issues of empirical
evidence and we will resist the temptation to speculate.

That brings us to arguments about RE grounded either on the concept
of human rights or on the concept of social cohesion. To base the case
for RE on the question of a human right to lifelong education is to close a
debate, not to open it. We cannot prove anyone wrong who appeals to RE as
a human right but we may pose some awkward questions. Human right at
the expense of the general taxpayer, or human right at one's own expense? A
human right financed out of general taxes which only some people exploit —
and we know who these people will be — is hardly a way to redress
inequalities. And a human right that is paid for out of one's own pocket is
simply market-provided RE, in which case one is entitled to ask why the

market has not spontaneously provided for RE. Besides, the right to paid study leave is typically coupled with the right to return to one's old job after completion of the course of study. But presumably the motive to take up study leave is often dissatisfaction with one's present job. Are we really prepared to subsidize workers to upgrade their qualifications, and then, after possibly failing to get a better job, to lay claim to their old position which originally drove them to acquire more education? Such issues have simply never been squarely faced in the RE literature.

As for social cohesion, all the great sociologists of the nineteenth century used to argue that it was best secured by providing formal schooling for all children. In fact, this argument lay behind the movement to make primary and eventually lower secondary education compulsory and it continues to buttress the present drive towards comprehensivization of secondary education in Western Europe. Now we are told that the argument is invalid for 16 to 22-year-olds but that, nevertheless, it becomes valid once again for older people. Why working at a mature age is divisive, while studying at a mature age is cohesive, is not made clear. But since the social cohesion argument for RE crops up only occasionally, we may perhaps pass it by without further comment.

Empirical Evidence

No country has yet adopted RE as a full-fledged system. As we saw earlier, however, bits and pieces of RE do exist in several countries. Even these bits and pieces, however, have never been adequately evaluated. What evidence there is refers largely to increased provision, increased expenditure, and participation rates in various schemes. As Stoikov (1975, p. 30), the only economist to have attempted a comprehensive assessment of RE, observes; "apart from a study of village-level workers in India, there is almost no empirical information on the direct effects of recurrent education and training ... A great deal is claimed for recurrent education, but serious empirical research has been scarce." Nevertheless, let us see what the evidence tells us.

Take first the question of equity. We have seen that the Swedish and German legislation on educational leave from work make inadequate provision for reimbursing workers for the earnings they forego. In these countries, therefore, little can be expected by way of equalizing the disparity in educational attainments between the generations. In France and Yugoslavia, on the other hand, workers are fully compensated for study leave. Nevertheless, men in France have been quicker to take advantage of these opportunities than women and, likewise, salaried employees have responded more readily than wage earners. Furthermore, in France as in Yugoslavia,

294

study leave has been largely devoted to formal vocational training and hence has failed to bridge the gap in general education level among various age groups.

Elsewhere too, recent years have seen a considerable expansion of manpower training schemes under government auspices, which has generally been given a clean bill of health by economists on "efficiency" grounds (Goldstein, 1972; Ziderman, 1969). However, it is rarely argued that such training programs, given their costs, can do much to close the enormous gap in the formal educational qualifications of young people and adults. The idea of study leave from work is precisely that it would close that gap, although in practice it seems invariably to turn into vocational training and retraining pure and simple. There is certainly a case to be made for manpower training programs financed by government but to suggest that this is RE is to play hard and fast with language. The equity argument for RE. conceived as the provision of opportunities for adults to take leave from work in order to engage in full-time study, is hardly to be taken seriously. Even Stoikov (1975; p. 32 and c.f. p. 48) has to concede that those demanding and obtaining RE are those who have had much previous schooling.

For further evidence of the difficulties of reducing the educational inequalities between generations by the mere provision of second-chance opportunities, we have the experience of the Open University in Britain. An analysis of the educational background of registered students in the Open University shows that two-thirds of them enter the Open University with qualifications that would have entitled them in any case to admission to university in Britain (McIntosh and Morrison, 1974). In short, the OU is only a second-chance university for the remaining one-third. Of the 65.5 percent who in 1974 were qualified for admission to a university, roughly a quarter were qualified teachers whose salaries as teachers will rise automatically after receipt of a university degree. That leaves 37.8 percent of qualified, registered students who are grasping the opportunity to study part-time by correspondence, radio and television, an opportunity which would not be available but for the existence of the Open University. This is no mean achievement, to be sure, but it is nevertheless limited.

Further analysis of the sex and class composition of Open University students shows that the Open University does attract a larger proportion of women (42.5%) than do conventional universities (34%) (McIntosh, 1975; McIntosh and Woodley, 1974). It is also claimed that the percentage of students with fathers from manual occupations is much higher at the Open University than at either conventional universities or polytechnics (McIntosh, 1975; McIntosh and Woodley, 1974). Considering that the average age of an Open University student is about 35, one would think that the more relevant statistic is the occupation of the student himself. When the comparison is drawn in terms of this statistic (McIntosh and Woodley, 1974,

p. 9, Table 5), it appears that the Open University is only slightly more open than the conventional university: the Open University clearly attracts some students who have moved from a working-class home to a middle-class occupation, which is quite a different result from the one that was claimed earlier. Furthermore evidence shows that the more qualified students have a greater chance of obtaining a credit (McIntosh and Woodley, 1974), which is hardly surprising when we realize that the curriculum of the Open University is very similar to that of traditional higher education in Britain. All of this adds up to a dubious conclusion when considering the Open University merely as an equalizing device between social classes.

We turn now to the question of postponement versus investment in older individuals, considered strictly on efficiency grounds. Taking data about the costs of college education in the United States, and assuming that the benefits of higher education are fully reflected in age-specific, pre-tax earnings, Stoikov has calculated the net present value of postponing college education for 18-year-olds by 5, 10 and 20 years, in contrast to providing college education to individuals now aged 23, 28, and 38, at various discount rates ranging from 0 to 8 percent, and at various growth rates for age-specific earnings ranging from 0 to 3 percent. On the basis of these calculations, he concludes that there is a clear case for "investing in older people" but, on the other hand, "there appear to be no valid reasons for considering a recurrent education system which includes an option of postponement for a substantial number of years, where substantial means anything over five years" (Stoikov, 1975, p. 16).

This conclusion may be regarded as too severe in view of the fact that postponement might lead to better educational and occupational choices. On the other hand, there is the counter-argument that postponement for as much as five years breaks the study-habit which makes formal learning so easy for young people and so difficult for older people. On balance, therefore, the Stoikov conclusion carries conviction: higher education might be more efficiently provided if there were a 2 to 3 year break between secondary and higher education and, similarly, higher education on a full-time or part-time basis for individuals who are now in their late 20s or 30s might well be a profitable social investment. This conclusion is based on the present curriculum and on present teaching methods, geared as they are to the 18–22 year age group. If higher education could be cheaply transformed to meet the rather different learning styles of older people, we get an even stronger efficiency argument in favor of "investing in older people".

We now complicate the argument by considering the problem of deterioration and obsolescence of knowledge, requiring maintenance investment of the RE type. Stoikov provides an able survey of the evidence on deterioration of sensory, psychomotor and cognitive functions as a result of ageing, concluding that there is little evidence of deterioration until the sixth

296

decade of life (Stoikov, 1975, pp. 37—43).

He turns next to obsolescence, where he argues that formal course work is successful for those recently educated but almost useless for those who lack a recent academic background:

> The richer the educational background (in terms of quantity and quality) the smaller is the risk of obsolescence. In general, technical and specific education and training are more subject to obsolescence than general education and knowledge. Consequently, priority clients for recurrent education would be those with a relatively small educational background in technical trades and occupations rather than those with a large educational background in the professions (Stoikov, 1975, p. 49).

Notice that this is both an argument for not postponing general education, and at the same time for repairing the educational deficiencies of older people who left school early. Even so, the positive argument for older people is at best one for short, in-service training courses rather than long leaves of absence from work to acquire formal education, as Stoikov readily concedes (1975, pp. 49—50).

> The optimal role of recurrent education as an antidote for human capital obsolescence seems to be preventive rather than curative. Efficient programmes which would maximise the possibility of the non-obsolete (or not-yet obsolete) individuals to keep abreast of current technology (optimally through a series of many sessions) are more attractive than attempts to isolate obsolete individuals and to enroll them in formal course work.

To sum up, in older people, an investment may be profitable, everything else being the same. On the other hand deterioration and obsolescence of skills and knowledge as a result of ageing does not strengthen the argument for study leave from work, at least if the leave is long enough to complete a cycle of higher education. It merely strengthens the standard claims for in-service training. Did we not know that before the RE revolution?

Conclusion

Stoikov (1975, p. 112) in his largely sympathetic study of RE reaches the following cautious conclusions:

> (1) Formal general education, including higher education for both men and women, should not be postponed for more than two to three years. Systems involving a longer postponement become very inefficient and therefore costly, and furthermore cannot be justified on grounds of equity. In the case of the "hard" sciences and mathematics even a postponement of two to three years becomes difficult to justify . . ..

297

(2) Formal general education, including higher education, could be provided to older persons, both men and women, who have not had the opportunity to receive such education earlier. Such programmes are not too inefficient and can be justified on grounds of equity.
(3) Programmes of intermittent education and work at the higher education level appear quite sensible except in the "hard" sciences.
(4) Programmes of recurrent training for workers of almost any age appear efficient in general, particularly under employment systems which reward seniority. . . .
(5) No serious argument has been found against recurrent training programmes for workers threatened by obsolescence. The training cost can usually be amortised over the lifetime of the value of the training.

If this package of five points is indeed what is meant by RE, we can hardly quarrel with his conclusions. But notice that points 4 and 5 concern the training and retraining of workers either on-the-job or off-the-job and we are not aware that it requires a radical change in our thinking to accept that such programs may frequently but not invariably prove to be a profitable investment for employers, employees, and society. What is new is point 1, the postponement of higher education by "two to three years". Likewise, point 2 about the provision of formal education to older individuals is new but to argue its desirability is quite different from predicting its success in overcoming educational inequalities by age. Again, Stoikov gives qualified support to "intermittent education and work at the higher education level" (point 3), although here too one may doubt whether the idea will be adopted in large numbers once the opportunity is created.

Points 1–3 are all that is left of the grandiose claims made on behalf of "a global system containing a variety of programmes which distribute education and training. . . . by formal and non-formal means, over the lifespan of an individual in a recurring way" — to quote Stoikov's definition of RE once again. By all means let us encourage universities to give priority in admission to individuals who have worked two or three years in the labor market. Let us also export the American credit system to Europe so that European students, like American students, can acquire their higher education at intervals interrupted by periods of work. Similarly, let us expand adult education to supplement evening by daytime courses, including such adult extension centers as the Open University, employing the facilities of radio and television, and taxing employers to pay workers to take advantage of these new opportunities. But let us not call that RE. To do so is to plant the suggestion that the present educational system should be abandoned in favor of an entirely new structure, which will miraculously equalize the educational participation rates of all, gear the educational system directly to the changing requirements of the labor market, and bind the body politic together in the self-enriching experience of formal learning continued throughout working life. To call it RE is to invite the emotive arguments

298

that we have been handed in recent years by one international organization after another.

Most governments these days are worried about an impending glut of too highly educated individuals. To solve the problem by restricting higher education would seem to be politically unacceptable. In that context, RE may be understood as a movement which seeks to regulate the expansion of higher education by directing attention to yet another underprivileged group in modern society whose educational claims have even greater priority. Unfortunately there is absolutely no evidence of any burning demand on the part of that group for formal education. Nothing is more dangerous to rational educational planning than recipes for improvement which have not been fully thought out: the RE recipe is certainly guilty on that score.

The time has come to ask the education lobby to put its cards on the table. If they want RE, let them tell us what kind of RE, when, and paid for by whom. On the other hand, if they have some concrete proposal to make about the education of older people, let them make it without the glow of RE language.

References

Bengtsson, J. (1972). *The Swedish View of Recurrent Education.* Paris: OECD/CERI (Center for Educational Research and Innovation).

Billings, B. B. (1975). "Income contingent loans for recurrent education," *Recurrent Education,* S. J. Mushkin (ed.) Washington: National Institute for Adult Education, U.S. Department of Health, Education and Welfare.

Cantor, L. M. (1974). *Recurrent Education. Policy and Development in OECD Member Countries. United Kingdom.* Paris: OECD/CERI.

CERI (1971). *Equal Educational Opportunity 1.* Paris: OECD/CERI.

CERI (1972). *Recurrent Education in Yugoslavia.* Paris: OECD/CERI.

CERI (1975). *Recurrent Education: Trends and Issues.* Paris: OECD/CERI.

CERI (1976). *Developments in Educational Leave of Absence.* Paris: OECD/CERI.

D.E.S. (1975). *Educational Statistics for the United Kingdom 1973.* London: H.M.S.O.

Embling, J. (1974). *A Fresh Look at Higher Education. European Implications of the Carnegie Commission Reports.* Amsterdam: Elsevier Publishing Co.

Emmerij, L. (1974). *Can the School Build a New Social Order?* Amsterdam: Elsevier Publishing Co.

Glatter, R. and Wedell, G. (1971). *Study by Correspondence.* London: Longmans.

Goldstein, J. (1972). *The Effectiveness of Manpower Training Programs: A Review of Research on the Impact on the Poor.* Washington: Government Printing Office.

Hamermesh, D. S. (1971). *Economic Aspects of Manpower Training Programs.* Lexington, Mass.: D.C. Heath & Co.

Hardin, E. and Borus, M. E. (1971). *The Economic Benefit and Costs of Retraining.* Lexington, Mass.: D.C. Heath & Co.

Houghton, V. and Richardson, K. (Eds.) (1974). *Recurrent Education.* London: Ward Lock Educational.

299

Houghton, V. (1976). "Recurrent Education – the Immediate Future," *Teaching at a Distance* No. 6.

Kallen, D. (1973). *Recurrent Education: A Strategy for Lifelong Learning.* Paris: OECD/ CERI.

Learning To Be: The World of Education Today and Tomorrow, (1972). Paris: UNESCO. (It is known as the Faure Report because it contains the findings of the International Commission on the Development of Education established by UNESCO under the chairmanship of Edgar Faure, former Prime Minister and Minister of Education of France.)

Levine, H. A. (1975). "Labor-Management Policies on Educational Opportunity," *Recurrent Education*, S. J. Mushkin (ed.) Washington: National Institute of Adult Education, U.S. Department of Health, Education and Welfare.

McIntosh, N. E. (1975). "Open Admission – An Open Door or a Revolving Door," *Universities Quarterly* March.

McIntosh, N. E. and Morrison, V. (1974). "Student Demand, Progress and Withdrawal: Open University's First Four Years," *Higher Education Review* Autumn.

McIntosh, N. E. and Woodley, A. (1974). "The Open University and Second Chance Education – An Analysis of the Sexual and Educational Background of Open University Students," *Paedagogica Europaea* IX.

Nollen, S. D. (1976). "Paid Educational Leave: U.S. Pilot Study." Paris: OECD/CERI, unpublished.

Regan, P. F. et al. (1972). *Recurrent Education in the State of New York,* Paris: OECD/CERI.

Rudolph, H. et al. (1972). *Recurrent Education in the Federal Republic of Germany.* Paris: OECD/CERI.

Russell Report (1973). *Adult Education. A Plan for Development.* London: H.M.S.O.

Simmons, J. (1973). "The Report of the Faure Commission: One Step Forward and Two Steps Back," *Higher Education* II: 4.

Stoikov, V. (1975). *The Economics of Recurrent Education and Training.* Geneva: ILO.

U68. (1973). *Higher Education: Proposals by the Swedish 1968 Educational Commission* (summary in English). Stockholm: Allmänna Förlarget.

UNESCO. (1971). "Lifelong Education in a Changing World." In *Investment in Human Resources and Manpower Planning.* New York: United Nations, p. 75.

Ziderman, A. (1969). "Costs and Benefits of Adult Retraining in the United Kingdom," *Economica* November.

[7]

PATTERNS OF SUBSIDIES TO HIGHER EDUCATION IN EUROPE*

MARK BLAUG

University of London Institute of Education

MAUREEN WOODHALL

Institute for Research and Development in Post Compulsory Education, University of Lancaster

ABSTRACT

The patterns of government subsidies to higher education in France, Germany, Netherlands, Sweden, and the United Kingdom (UK) are compared and contrasted. The subsidies are subsequently evaluated in the light of stated policy objectives, with particular attention to the objectives of efficiency and equity. Two extreme models of financing are considered; one in which public subsidy covers 100 per cent of the private costs of higher education, including income forgone by students, the other in which public subsidy to students is kept at a minimum. The study concludes that the ideal package from the standpoint of efficiency and equity is (1) a grants system in the last few years of secondary education; (2) a system of fees equal to about 30—50 per cent of institutional incomes and (3) an income contingent loan scheme (or graduate tax) for both undergraduate and postgraduate students.

Higher education throughout Europe is heavily subsidised by the state: the direct costs of tuition are subsidised by grants to colleges and universities so as to allow fees to be reduced to minimal levels, and the indirect costs of tuition (in the sense of earnings forgone) are subsidised by grants or loans to students. While the general pattern of subsidies to higher education is the same throughout Europe, there are significant differences between countries. In some countries, all colleges and universities are administered as well as financed by government; in others, there are private as well as public institutions. Most European countries provide aid to students by means of a mixture of grants and loans but the mix varies considerably from country to country: at one extreme is the UK where students receive grants but no loans, and at the other is Sweden where the bulk of student aid takes the

* The research for this paper was sponsored by the United States Education Policy Research Center for Higher Education and Society under HEW Contract No. 300-76-0026. The views expressed are not necessarily those of the Center. Our thanks are due to J. Froomkin for valuable comments on an earlier draft.

166

332

form of loans. A rather different pattern of aid is found in France, where the provision of subsidised meals and subsidised accommodation, as well as tax relief and allowances paid to students' families, represent a far greater proportion of total student aid than either grants or loans.

The purpose of this paper is, first of all, to compare and contrast patterns of government subsidies to higher education in five European countries: France, Germany, the Netherlands, Sweden and the UK, distinguishing between aid to institutions and aid to students. Our second purpose is to assess these subsidies in the light of the stated objectives of governments, having particular reference to the objectives of efficiency and equity. For that reason we pay special attention to recent changes in the pattern of subsidies to higher education in the five countries under examination.

I. The Existing Pattern of Subsidies

Although there are certain differences between countries in policies regarding tuition fees, it is true to say that fees generally play an insignificant part in the finance of European higher education. This is just as true in countries where there are private institutions as in those where virtually all universities or colleges are owned and administered by the state. In France and Germany, for example, only 4 per cent of students enrolled in higher education in 1970 were in private institutions, whereas in the Netherlands the proportion was as high as 47 per cent (National Center for Education Statistics, 1976, p. 264). However, government subsidies to educational institutions were and are as significant in the Netherlands as in France and Germany. Thus, the distinction between public and private universities in Europe does not have the same meaning as in the USA, where sources of finance for institutions depend critically on whether they are publicly or privately owned.

Most European countries have a long tradition of free education and, indeed, the promise of free education at all levels, including higher education, is an integral feature of the national constitution of several European nations. Even when fees are charged, as they are in a few cases, they are almost always nominal. There are no fees for any form of higher education in Germany and Sweden. In France students do pay minimal registration fees but in the Netherlands, where public and private universities and colleges have always charged a low fee, there is the intention of abolishing fees altogether in the near future.

The one exception to the general European trend to abolish tuition fees is the UK where fees have recently been sharply increased, accompanied by the introduction of higher fees for postgraduates than for undergraduates. Nevertheless, the large majority of British students have their fees paid in full by Local Education Authorities (who are reimbursed in turn by central government), so that the recent increase in fees affects only a minority of students who are for one reason or another not eligible for student grants (mainly overseas students and some postgraduates with poor first degrees).

The overwhelming pattern in Europe, therefore, is to meet the direct costs of higher education either wholly or in large part by means of institutional grants from public funds. In addition, European governments also subsidise the indirect costs of education by means of aid provided to students. However, there are numerous differences between countries in the magnitude of these kinds of subsidies to students and also in the type of student aid provided [1]. France, Germany, Sweden and the Netherlands all make some use of student loans but only in combination with grants and scholarships. The UK is unusual in providing only grants and successive British governments have opposed the very idea of student loans. Most countries apply some form of "means test", so that the amount of financial aid awarded to a student depends upon the level of his parents' income. The assumption is that parents should contribute towards their children's living expenses if they can afford to do so. In return, parents are eligible for tax relief, and in some cases to family allowances, while their children are in full-time education. The one exception to this pattern is Sweden, where students are entitled to study assistance regardless of the income of their parents or the income of their spouse; Swedish parents of students in higher education are not eligible for tax relief and the only means test which is applied relates to the student's own income. The Swedish system is based on the legal premise that young people are financially independent from the age of 19, whereas in other European countries the age of financial independence that is legally recognised is 25 or even 27.

Apart from grants or loans to students, and income tax relief for the parents of students, most governments provide additional subsidies for students in the form of low-cost accommodation, travel facilities, free medical care or health insurance, and in some cases subsidised food and books. Such indirect subsidies typically amount to about 10–20 per cent of direct student aid in the form of grants and loans, except in France where they actually exceed the sums provided directly to students.

Most of the countries have recently introduced, or are planning to introduce, fairly radical changes in their system of student aid. For instance, Germany has recently re-introduced student loans after experimenting for some years with a system based entirely on grants, and Sweden has abolished the means test which used to be applied to the income of a student's spouse, and has also introduced interest charges for student loans in place of the former system under which graduates repaid their loans at zero interest in

334

terms of constant purchasing power (which amounts to an interest charge equal to the rate of price change). Similarly, the Dutch government plans shortly to co-ordinate all forms of student aid into a single system of grants and loans, which will be available to all students in post-secondary education. Clearly, the pattern of subsidies for students in Europe is changing and it is noteworthy that European governments appear more ready to introduce changes in student aid schemes than to alter the system of financing institutions. The general picture seems to be one of flexibility in aiding students combined with inflexibility in aiding institutions, an issue to which we will return below.

After this general sketch of the pattern of subsidies to higher education throughout Europe, we turn now to a more detailed account of the methods of aiding both institutions and students in each of the five countries. (Table VII provides an oversimplified summary of the main features of student aid in the five countries under examination).

1. FRANCE

Despite the existence of certain private institutions of higher education in France, such as the Catholic University, some of the *grandes écoles* and a few private technical colleges, the bulk of all expenditure on French higher education is financed by central government (see Table I).

Each year a certain sum is allotted in the government budget for higher education, and the Secretariat of State for Universities (a government department with full Ministerial power), in association with certain other bodies, then allocates a sum to each university. Thereafter, it is left to each university council to draw up a detailed budget for the coming year. These

TABLE I

Sources of Finance for Current and Capital Expenditure on Higher Education, France, 1975

	Million francs	%
State subsidies	4,977	96.2
Local authorities	147	2.8
Students' fees	50	1.0
Total	5,174	100.0

Source: Orivel (1977).
Note: the figures exclude private contributions, which are believed to be small.

university councils typically consist of elected representatives of the teaching and administrative staff as well as the students of the university. The university budget is then submitted to the Secretariat and, once it has been approved, no expenditure is permitted which falls outside the budget. Thus, university expenditure in France is subject to more detailed central control than is the case in other countries in Europe.

The French university budget covers all current expenditure except teachers' salaries, which are paid directly by central government; all capital expenditure in higher education is also paid directly by central government. Private institutions of higher education in France also receive grants through the Secretariat and, in addition, certain other Ministries provide subsidies of their own; some of the *grandes écoles* also receive financial support from Chambers of Commerce, religious organisations and business firms but very little information is available on these private sources of finance.

As we have already noted, France is unusual among European countries in providing a high proportion of subsidies in the form of low-cost housing and meals for students, as well as family allowances and tax relief for their parents. The amount made available directly to students as scholarships, grants and loans is very limited and only about 15 per cent of students benefit from such schemes. Another unusual feature of the French system is the payment of salaries for "pre-employment contracts" to certain students who intend to become teachers or public servants. This form of aid is highly selective: it is offered as a reward for ability and as an inducement to the most able students to enter particular occupations. In other words, the objective of the scheme is to recruit manpower which is thought to be in scarce supply rather than to assist low-income students. Those who receive such payments undertake to work in the public sector for a certain period; if they later break this undertaking, the money must be repaid. Pre-employment contracts are declining in importance: in 1960 they accounted for 20 per cent of all government aid to students but in 1974 the proportion had declined to 12 per cent (Orivel, 1975).

Table II shows that scholarships and grants accounted for less than half of the total aid to French students. A small number of short-term loans are also available at 5 per cent interest. But these direct forms of aid amount to very little more than the government's expenditure on subsidised housing, subsidised catering, and free medical facilities for students under the social security system. Even more important are the various types of aid to students' families. When these are added to the aid provided to students given in Table II they are seen to exceed the financial assistance given directly to students (see Table III).

Since such a high proportion of aid goes in the form of tax relief to students' parents, it would appear that the pattern of aid to students in France is biased in favour of high income families. Although scholarships

336

TABLE II

Distribution of Aid to Students, France,
1974 (percentages)

Scholarships, loans and grants	46
Pre-employment contracts	12
Food and housing subsidies	35
Medical subsidies	7
Total	100

Source: Orivel (1975)

TABLE III

Distribution of Total Student Aid, France,
1974 (percentages)

Scholarships, loans and grants	23
Other subsidies to students	27
Tax relief for students' parents	32
Family allowances for children in full-time education	18
Total	100

Source: Orivel (1975)

are means-tested and are awarded only to students from low income families, pre-employment contracts are awarded on the basis of academic merit rather than financial need, and subsidised housing and food benefits only those students who choose to live in the *cités üniversitaires* rather than at home. Tax relief, on the other hand, is available to all but its value necessarily increases as parental income increases. The result of this mixture of selective and universal subsidies makes it difficult to convincingly demonstrate the true incidence of the benefits from student aid in France, but on balance it must surely be the richer rather than the poorer students who benefit most. At any rate, one study of the equity implications of French educational expenditure concludes that student aid has had little tendency to equalize access to higher education (Levy-Garboua, 1975; see also Eicher and Mingat, "Education et égalité," in OECD, 1975; and Mingat, 1977, chapter 3).

In the past few years, the amount of aid in the form of scholarships and loans has not kept pace either with rising student numbers or with rising prices. The result is that state aid per student has been declining in real terms. Orivel (1975) estimates that it fell from Frs. 2,019 in 1965 to Frs. 1,309 in 1975. This implies that the private costs of higher education in France have been rising. In 1975, total state aid for students in higher education amounted to about Frs. 2,500 million, and it was estimated that student expenditure was about Frs. 10,000 million, so that state subsidies covered only a quarter of students' actual money outlays. In addition, one estimate for 1970 suggested that earnings forgone represent 70 per cent of the total resources cost of higher education in France and that direct subsidies to French students covered only 12 per cent of these earnings forgone; in short, if earnings forgone are taken into account, students and their families contribute about half the total resource costs of higher education in France (Orivel, 1975; Levy-Garboua, 1977).

2. GERMANY

The German constitution originally placed all responsibility for financing and administering higher education in the hands of the eleven states, or *Länder,* that together form the Federal Republic. In 1969, however, the constitution was amended to make the financing of university buildings a joint task of the Federal government and the *Länder,* and in 1970 this amendment was extended to include all tertiary education institutions (see OECD, 1972). The past few years in Germany have, therefore, seen a radical extension of central government involvement in higher education. Nevertheless, the bulk of all expenditure on German higher education still derives from the *Länder* rather than the central government. In 1975, for example, the *Länder* contributed 90 per cent of all expenditure on higher education (including student aid) with the Federal government contributing only 10 per cent. Municipal governments, which provide a large share of the public funds for compulsory schooling, do not contribute to the finance of higher education in Germany. Nor do students make any direct financial contribution since all tuition fees have now been abolished.

All higher education in Germany is provided in state institutions and traditionally students did pay low fees which went to supplement the salary of the professor in charge of their teaching. This system was abolished during the 1960's and professorial salaries were increased concomitantly to compensate professors for their loss of income. In 1970, examination fees, which were the last remaining fees charged in German higher education, were also abolished. There have been some suggestions in Germany that fees should be reintroduced to supplement teachers' salaries (Roeloffs, 1976), but there are no indications that any of the *Länder* are willing to reconsider their policy of providing free tuition at all levels of education, including higher education.

Financial aid to students in Germany, like financial aid for university building, was designated in 1969 as the joint task of both the Federal and state governments. The Federal government passed a new Educational Support Bill (*BAfög*) in 1971, which set up a new system of grants for students in higher education to replace the old system of loans (Roeloffs, 1976). For the first few years of its operation, the *BAfög* scheme relied solely on grants but in 1974 a loan element was introduced. A student who is entitled to the maximum support now receives about 20 per cent of aid in the form of a long term interest-free loan, with the remainder of aid being given in the form of a grant. All student aid is means-tested, however, and if a student receives less than the maximum award, the loan may account for more than 20 per cent of his total aid (all students repay the same amount, being about DM 80 a month). This scheme is administered by the *Länder* but it is financed jointly by the Federal government and the *Länder,*

338

with 65 per cent of the expenditure coming from the center and the rest from state governments.

To repeat: all German student aid is awarded on the basis of family income and 45 per cent of all students in higher education in 1974–75 received awards. A student is not regarded as financially independent in Germany until the age of 27 but when the scheme was first introduced, students were permitted to take out low-interest loans if their parents refused to give them financial support. However, this option was eliminated in 1976 and parents can now be taken to court if they refuse to support their children when the authorities judge that they can afford to do so. In order to simplify the job of calculating a student's entitlement to a grant or loan, the amount of support due to a student is calculated on the basis of his parents' income two years earlier; as a result, income tax assessments can be used as a basis for the calculation. In exceptional cases, a student's entitlement may be assessed on the basis of his parents' current income and the past few years have seen a considerable increase in the number of such applications.

After graduation, the student begins to repay his loan at the rate of DM 80 a month, but those with low incomes may pay less and those who are unemployed, voluntarily or involuntarily, are excused repayment. Thus, there is no negative-dowry problem for married women who do not work. Some graduates repay their interest-free loans in about five years but those with low incomes, or those who received all their support in the form of a loan (because they changed courses or took a second qualification) may take up to 20 years to complete their payment.

When the loan element was introduced into the system in 1974, the bitter pill was sweetened by an increase in the level of support available. The original *BAfög* Bill of 1971 stipulated that levels of support would be adjusted every two years, so that another increase was due in 1976. However, this increase has been postponed as part of the Federal government's measures to reduce public expenditure.

3. NETHERLANDS

All public and private universities in Holland are governed by the University Education Act of 1961 and the University Administration Reform Act of 1970. Both these Acts declare that public and private universities should be financed in the same way. At present, all universities are fully financed by the Dutch government, although students pay a small tuition fee of Fl. 600 (about $80) a year. Higher vocational schools are financed in the same way, the only difference being that fees in these schools are related to parental income up to a maximum of Fl. 600 a year (the level of university fees), but they are administered in ways that are quite different from those of universities.

· However, the Dutch government has announced its intention of abolishing the division that now exists between universities and other institutions of higher education, so as ultimately to create a unified system of higher education. A recent government memorandum on the *Contours of a Future Education System in the Netherlands* called for a halt to university expansion and a reduction in university costs, principally by means of the introduction of shorter university courses (Government of the Netherlands, 1976). At present, Dutch university courses last between six to nine years, in part because of the tradition of working while studying part-time, compared with three to four years at higher vocational schools. Universities have been asked to submit proposals for new four-year degree courses, or five-year courses in exceptional circumstances, but this proposal has led to bitter opposition (Council of Europe, 1977). Attempts to reform higher education in the Netherlands are, therefore, running into considerable difficulties but neither the reforms nor the resistance to it is significantly connected with the way institutions are financed. The only change in financing procedures proposed by the government is a change in the student aid system, accompanied by the abolition of tuition fees.

The existing system of student aid in Holland includes grants, low interest loans, subsidised housing and meals, and fax relief and family allowances for students' parents (see Table IV). Students from low-income families receive aid in the form of grants and interest-free loans in the proportions 3:2. All aid is means-tested and students with higher family incomes receive no aid at all except for tax relief and family allowances given to their parents. This system has been criticised as inequitable because tax relief is worth more to families with higher incomes, while students from low-income families are driven to incur debts. The Dutch government has therefore proposed a new system of student aid, which will abolish tax relief and family allowances, instead providing all students with a basic

TABLE IV

Distribution of Total Student Aid, the
Netherlands, 1974–75 (percentages)

Grants to students	27
Interest subsidy for student loans	12
Tax relief for students' parents	8
Family allowances for children in full-time education	53
Total	100

Source: Council of Europe (1976)

340

grant towards living expenses. There will also be means-tested, supplementary grants for students from low-income families and, in addition, any student may choose to take a government-guaranteed loan from a commercial bank at subsidised interest rates (in 1976 the rate of interest on student loans backed by a government guarantee was 8.75 per cent).

The Dutch government's proposal for a new system of student aid is not expected to involve any extra expenditure. In 1974—75, revenue from fees amounted to less than 5 per cent of total expenditure on student aid. Under the new system, all tuition fees will be abolished but the lost revenue will be deducted from the total student aid budget, so that, in the words of a Ministry of Education information sheet, "a collective tuition fee will be charged" (Council of Europe, 1976). Most of the amount allocated for student support will now be given in the form of grants but a smaller proportion than before will be given as interest subsidies for voluntary loans from commercial banks.

It is interesting that the Dutch government actively considered introducing a graduate tax to replace tuition fees on the grounds that this would be more equitable than the present system of state subsidies. This proposal had to be dropped for "practical reasons" but a report submitted by the Dutch Ministry of Education to the Council of Europe states:

> The Netherlands Government regrets that it has not proved possible to recover through taxation a substantial amount of the cost of their education from graduates, more especially as the government considers that in any case it is desirable to do something about the privileged position of higher education students by some such means. The government's intention of abandoning the above method is based purely on practical considerations. Government policy in this respect will be pursued by some other means (Council of Europe, 1976).

4. SWEDEN

All higher education in Sweden is financed by the state and since the 1950s all institutions of higher education have been owned and administered by the state. Recent educational reforms, designed to unify all forms of post-secondary education in Sweden along the lines of the recommendations of the U68 Commission, will affect the way institutions are administered but will not radically change their methods of finance. Institutions will continue to receive all their income from government grants but there will be changes in the way in which these funds are allocated. One of the objectives of the reforms is to decentralise decision-making. A new National Board of Universities and Colleges was created in 1976 to take charge of general planning and co-ordination of all branches of post-secondary education, including the submission of budget proposals for higher education (National Board of Universities and Colleges, 1976).

341

The budget for 1977–78, for example, distinguishes between allocations for (1) research, (2) basic general courses of higher education, and (3) local and special courses of education and training. Funds for research will be allocated on the basis of faculties and subject areas, corresponding to traditional academic disciplines, but they will no longer be given exclusively to universities – all institutions of higher education are expected to engage in research. Similarly, funds for basic general courses will no longer be allocated in terms of university faculties or subject areas but in terms of five vocational areas. Finally, funds for local and special courses will be distributed between six regional boards, reflecting the recent division of Sweden into six higher education regions. Membership of the regional boards includes representatives of teachers, students, and the "public interest", including local businesses, trade unions, and political parties (Duckenfield, 1977). It is too early to say how this new form of organisation will affect the distribution of funds in practice. What seems clear is that the autonomy of university departments or faculties in Sweden will be lessened, with funds being distributed on the basis of vocational criteria and local labour market conditions rather than individual student demand for traditional academic disciplines.

The question of how much student demand should be allowed to influence planning decisions has caused bitter controversy in Sweden. The old system of higher education in Sweden included "closed" faculties where the number of students admitted each year was strictly limited, such as medicine and engineering, and "open" faculties where there were no restrictions on the number of students admitted. The original Parliamentary proposals, endorsing the recommendations of the U68 Commission, would have extended the policy of restricted admissions to all areas of higher education, so as to impose admission ceilings on such "open faculties" as humanities, social sciences and theology. After an acrid debate, a compromise was reached under which the old distinction between "closed" and "open" courses is maintained. However, institutional revenue will no longer be automatically linked with student numbers as it was in the past. Whether this will mean that admissions to higher education will in fact be restricted in the future depends on whether total funds will be allowed to grow and on how these total funds will be allocated by the National Board and regional boards. The new organisational structure of higher education may make it easier for the Swedish government to impose numerical ceilings by means of financial controls rather than by decree creating more "closed" faculties.

The Swedish government provides three forms of financial support for students: (1) upper secondary school pupils receive *studiehjälp* (study aid); (2) students in higher education receive *studiemedel* (study means); and (3) adults who take leave from work to take part in full or part-time education or training receive *studiepenning* (study benefit). Apart from the fact that part-time students in Sweden are entitled to financial assistance, two

342

other features distinguish the Swedish system of aid for students from the other countries we have described; loans are not a supplement to grants but in fact constitute the bulk of aid provided and, furthermore, financial assistance is given to all students regardless of parental means. Swedish students are assumed to be financially independent at 19 and as of 1976 even a husband's or wife's income is disregarded when assessing a student's eligibility for aid. In 1974—75, the proportion of students who received state aid was 70 per cent and this proportion is likely to be even higher in 1977—78 as more married students are now eligible. All students receive a basic grant to which a long-term loan is added. When the present scheme was first introduced in 1964, the grant amounted to a quarter of aid per student and the remaining 75 per cent took the form of loans. Since 1964, the total amount of aid has risen each year in line with the cost-of-living index but the level of the grant has remained fixed. This means that the loan element has increased; in 1968 it accounted for 78 per cent of aid per student, and in 1975 for as much as 85 per cent of the total.

When the loan system was first established, all graduates repaid their loans in terms of constant purchasing power. This was done by expressing their debt in terms of the "base amount" of the social security system. All social security payments, including pensions, unemployment benefit, and student aid itself are expressed in terms of this base amount, which is linked automatically to the cost-of-living index. Thus, if prices rise, students receive more but at the same time the debt of graduates is also increased. Because this method of repayment takes account of inflation, no interest was charged for the loan. This system worked well during the 1960s when inflation rates were modest, but in recent years, when the cost-of-living has risen sharply, students have become reluctant to undertake the open-ended commitment which such a scheme implies. In consequence, the system was changed to a conventional loans scheme charging interest at 3.2 per cent a year. Thus, while 85 per cent of student aid is given in the form of a loan, there is still a considerable element of subsidy because of the low interest charge.

The loans are also very long term: graduates must repay the debt by the time they reach 50, which means that in practice most graduates have up to 25 years in which to repay. There is an important "insurance" element built into the system. Graduates who have low incomes, or who are ill or unemployed, are automatically excused repayment if their income falls below a minimum level; in 1974, about 13 per cent of all graduates postponed repayment for such reasons.

The level of student aid is high in Sweden compared with most other countries, at least when expressed as a proportion of per capita incomes in Sweden (see Table VII). A Swedish survey of student income and expenditure (Swärd, et al., 1968) showed that more than 60 per cent of the average student income in 1968 was derived from government aid and the proportion is probably higher today. Critics of loans schemes in other countries claim that loans will deter both working-class and female students from entering higher education. This does not appear to have happened in Sweden where the social class composition of students in higher education compares very favourably with other advanced countries in the world and where female labour force participation rates are relatively high (Woodhall, 1970).

5. UNITED KINGDOM

The finance of higher education in the UK differs from the pattern in other European countries in two important respects: (1) the division of expenditure between central and local government; and (2) the contribution of fees to total university income. Whereas state subsidies are provided almost wholly by the central government in France, and predominantly by the *Länder* in Germany, the burden of financing higher education in the UK is shared between central and local government. At the same time, fees account for a larger share of university income than in any of the countries we have so far considered.

There are two sectors of higher education in the UK, as there are in several other countries, but the two sectors are financed quite differently. British universities are financed from central government revenue through the University Grants Committee (UGC). The UGC is often described as a "buffer" between the central government and the universities; it is responsible in the first instance to the Department of Education and Science, and its function is to advise the Department on university matters and to distribute to universities the current and capital grants allocated by governments. In the past, the grants for current expenditure were announced five years ahead but this system of quinquennial grants has been temporarily suspended due to recent public expenditure cuts. At present, British universities receive annual allocations for both current and capital expenditure on the basis of their submissions to the UGC. Once the current grant is awarded, universities are free to allocate it between departments or faculties as they like; however, they are expected to take account of the "Memorandum of Guidance" issued by the UGC, which consists largely of targets for student numbers and, in particular, the balance of numbers between "arts" and "science" students.

British universities are possessive of their independence and proud of their freedom to allocate funds without direct government interference. There is much disagreement, however, about the extent of the freedom in practice. Some critics argue that the UGC now acts like a traditional department of government rather than a buffer (Pratt, 1975; Crowther-Hunt, 1976), and others contend that the present method of channelling government sub-

344

sidies through the UGC leads to inefficiency, with each university trying to maximise its grant rather than to minimise costs and to maximise student output (Prest, 1966; Verry, 1977a). The question of how far British universities are really free from government control has been brought sharply to the fore by the government's recent decision to increase student fees. In 1973–74, fee income amounted to only 4 per cent of all British university income (see Table V), having fallen from over 30 per cent in 1939 to 15 per cent in 1951. However, a new structure of fees was introduced in 1977 which increased fees for British undergraduates from £182 to £500 a year, and for British postgraduates from £182 to £750 a year; overseas students pay higher fees: £650 for undergraduates and £850 for postgraduate courses. British universities were generally opposed to such large fee increases but since most home students have their fees paid in full by Local Authorities, the students themselves accepted the new fees while protesting at the unfair treatment of foreign students. Under the new arrangements, fee income will account for about 20 per cent of all university income

TABLE V

Sources of University Income, UK, 1973–74

University Grants Committee	£'000	%
Non-recurrent grant for building	51,536	8.7
Furniture and equipment grants	38,926	6.6
Recurrent grant	349,734	58.5
Rates grant	13,094	2.2
Other income mainly from public sources		
Research grants (from research councils but also private foundations, etc.)	52,626	8.8
Fee income (mainly paid by LEAs or research councils)	23,437	3.9
Other Income		
Payments for services rendered	13,532	2.2
Receipts from catering and residential services	39,807	6.5
Other general income (including trust funds)	15,914	2.6
Total	598,606	100.0

Source: Department of Education and Science (1976a)

but most of this will come from public funds rather than from students or their parents.

Other public "maintained" institutions of higher education in the UK, such as polytechnics and colleges of higher education, are administered by Local Education Authorities and receive grants directly from them. But a large proportion of the funds of this "maintained" sector comes indirectly from central government through the so-called "rate support grant", even though the institutions in question are owned and administered by local authorities. It is impossible to say exactly how large the proportion is since the rate support grant is a general grant, covering all items of local authority expenditure, and the allocation of resources between different services varies between authorities. Moreover, since higher education is assumed to be a service which brings national rather than local benefits, polytechnics and colleges of education are at present financed by means of a common fund, known as the "pool", to which all local authorities contribute. However, a recent official committee (the Oakes Committee) has recommended modifications to the present arrangements for pooling expenditure, and has proposed that a new national body should be set up to manage colleges and polytechnics: the bulk of finance would be channelled through that body on analogy to the UGC in respect of universities.

When all these complications of British local government finance are taken into account, it appears that well over half of all expenditure on higher education comes from central government revenue, either directly or indirectly. However, the fact that different types of institutions receive government grants from different sources means that they are subject to different types of financial control. Local authority institutions must satisfy more detailed regulations than universities. This has led to suggestions that the scope of the UGC should be extended, so that it covers all forms of higher education, but this raises complex questions about whether different methods of finance necessarily lead to differences in the degree of government control.

Britain is alone in Europe in providing all student awards in the form of grants rather than loans; the proportion of students receiving grants (90—92 per cent of full-time students) is also much higher than in most other countries. All British undergraduates who qualify for a mandatory award receive a basic grant of £50 but any additional award is dependent on parental income. In 1972—73, about 8 per cent of all student award holders received the minimum grant because their parents' net income was relatively high, and 21 per cent received the maximum grant because their parents' income was relatively low; the remaining 71 per cent received amounts varying according to the parental means test. In addition to these mandatory awards, there are certain other discretionary grants awarded by local authorities, typically for lower-level courses. All students' grants are administered by Local Education

346

Authorities but a very high proportion of the finance comes ultimately from central government through grants to the local authorities.

In recent years, the means test has been much criticised in Britain on the grounds that many parents cannot afford to pay the "assessed contribution" which is assumed for purposes of calculating the level of a student's grant. The National Union of Students (NUS) in Britain argues that it is quite unreasonable to expect parents to contribute towards students' living expenses until they reach the age of 25 when young people in fact reach their legal majority in Britain at the age of 18. A number of surveys of students' income have shown that many British parents in fact contribute less than their "assessed contribution" (Department of Education and Science, 1976b; Rudd, 1975; and Rudd, 1977) and the abolition of the means test now has a very high priority on the list of NUS demands. However, it was estimated in 1973 that it would cost about £40 million to abolish the means test, representing about 27 per cent of government expenditure on student grants. Parents do receive income tax relief, which is assumed to compensate them for contributing towards students' living expenses; in fact, the total cost to public funds of this type of tax relief is considerably smaller than the total "parental contribution" assumed in student grant calculations.

Since it is clear that some students do suffer because their parents are unable or unwilling to contribute sufficiently to their living expenses, some British writers have suggested that loans should be made available to supplement grants. Many others have advocated more widespread use of loans but there are as many opponents as advocates of student loans in Britain (see Woodhall, 1970; Maynard, 1975). On the whole, the British debate about loans is characterised by heat rather than light. Assertions and counter-assertions are presented without much evidence. In particular, the experience of other European countries with loans is steadfastly ignored in British discussions. Indeed, the fact that loans are common throughout continental Europe is not generally appreciated in the UK. In 1973, the Expenditure Committee of the House of Commons recommended that loans should be introduced for postgraduate students, coupled with free tuition and a basic maintenance grant exempt from any means test. In other words, what was recommended was very close to the Swedish model. Without explaining any of the details of the foreign experience with loans schemes, the Expenditure Committee concluded: "We are satisfied that such loans schemes are practicable, that they help to contain public expenditure and that they could contribute to a reordering of priorities in education expenditure to promote equality of opportunity" (Expenditure Committee, 1973). However, in 1976 the British government announced that "it had no present intention of introducing a loans scheme in partial or complete substitution for grants," and it denied that the saving involved in a loans scheme for postgraduates would be large enough to outweigh its "unpredictable effects" and "potentially dangerous consequences in terms of social equity" (Department of Education and Science, 1976c, pp. 7–8).

The fact that all British student aid is in the form of grants and tax relief for students' parents, together with the fact that British student grants cover a higher proportion of earnings forgone than in most other countries, implies that British students enjoy greater subsidies than in most other European countries. Some calculations in 1969 suggested that state subsidies, that is, the maintenance award plus tax relief for parents, compensate undergraduates for over half of net earnings forgone, compared to only 22 per cent for a secondary school pupil staying on for a year after the minimum school-leaving age (see Table VI). These calculations are by now somewhat out of date because the real value of student grants has significantly declined since 1969 (Williams, 1974). Nevertheless, it is still true

TABLE VI

Estimates of Earnings Forgone and Public Sector Contribution to Students and their Families UK, 1969

	For a 15-year old	For an under-graduate
Earnings forgone		
Gross pay	315	815
Less vacation and teaching earnings	–	60
Less national insurance and income tax payable	280	585
Public subsidies		
(a) Tax relief to parent	60	70
(b) Maintenance award, less element for books and parental contribution	–	265
Total	60	335
Balance carried by individual or his family	220	250
As a % of net earnings forgone	78	43
State subsidies as % of net earnings forgone	22	57

Source: Calculated from Department of Education and Science (1970, p. 28).

348

TABLE VII

Summary of Student Aid Schemes in the Five Countries, 1974–75

	France	Germany	Netherlands	Sweden	U.K.
Type of direct financial aid to students	Grants, Loans, and Pre-employment Contracts	20% Fixed Loan + 80% Supplementary Grant	60% Basic Grant + 40% Loan	15% Fixed Grant + 85% Supplementary Loan	All Grants
Percentage of students receiving direct state aid	15	45	38 (universities), 50 higher vocational)	70	92
Maximum award per student (at exchange rates in December, 1974)	$2,099	$2,489	$2,988	$3,086	$1,500
Are awards related to parental income?	Yes	Yes	Yes	No	Yes
Do students' parents receive tax relief or family allowances?	Yes	Yes	Yes (to be abolished)	No	Yes
Tax relief as % of direct aid to students	180	X	16	–	25
Indirect aid (housing, food subsidies, health, etc.) as % of direct aid to students	100 (of expenditure on grants)	20	X	12	18

Are fees charged?	Yes but low	No	Yes but low (to be abolished)	No	Yes but covered by grants
Interest Rate on Loans (%)	5	None	None, pro-posed 8.75	3.2	—
Maximum period of re-payment of loans	Variable	Variable up to 20 years	10 years	Variable up to age 50	—
Does repayment of loans vary with student's future income?	No	Yes for low and zero incomes	No	Yes and re-payment post-ponable if income low	—
Percentage of average student income derived from state aid	25 (inclu-ding indirect subsidies)	40	65	over 60	54 (70 during term time)
Average award per student as percentage of per capita GDP (1975)	23	X	15	43	36
% of age group entering university-type higher education (1970)	15.0	10.4	8.3	23.5	10.6

Source: Woodhall (1978)
Notes: — = not applicable; X = not available

350

to say that state subsidies to students represent a greater proportion of earnings forgone in the UK than in, say, France. In terms of per capita incomes, the level of average award per student in Britain is only some-what less than it is in Sweden and it is far greater than it is in France and the Netherlands (see Table VII).

All this implies that the financial barriers to more schooling in Britain are concentrated at the point of finishing secondary education rather than at the point of entry to higher education [2]. This helps to explain why the proportion of working class pupils that drop out of the educational system is not very different in Britain from elsewhere in the world [3]. Since unemployed school leavers in Britain are now eligible for allowances under the new Youth Opportunities Programme, there is growing support in the UK for a policy of increasing maintenance allowances for 16—19 year olds in full-time education, so as to provide adequate financial incentives to students to stay on at school beyond the legal leaving age of 16. The government has announced its approval of such a policy in principle but there are no immediate plans to put it into effect in view of the estimated cost of between £500 to £1,000 million.

II. Implications of Alternative Patterns of Subsidy

So much for the description of facts. We move now to the analysis of issues. We have seen that the predominant method of subsidising higher education in Europe is by means of grants to universities and colleges to cover virtually all tuition costs combined with grants and loans to students to help them to finance from a quarter to as much as two-thirds of their living costs (see Table VII). This pattern of subsidies has been criticised on three grounds: (1) higher education institutions are liable to government control, whatever the ideology of state action in a country, if all or most of their income derives from government; (2) it is inefficient to give subsidies mainly in the form of grants to institutions since this provides them with no incentives to allocate their resources efficiently; and (3) it is inequitable to force taxpayers to finance the bulk of higher education costs because the average taxpayer has a lower income than the average graduate of tertiary education [4]. These criticisms raise two quite different questions. Firstly, what should be the optimum level of subsidy for higher education and, secondly, what is the best method of providing that subsidy?

Why should governments subsidise higher education at all? The economic case for subsidising higher education is typically posed in terms of a comparison between the social rate of return and the private rate of return to higher education. The invariable tendency of the former to fall below the latter is taken to be a sign that subsidies are excessive unless offset by (1) positive marginal externalities; (2) positive non-pecuniary benefits that exceed the psychic disutility of studying; and (3) capital-market imperfections that inhibit potential graduates from borrowing against the future returns of higher education. Unfortunately, little progress has been made in quantifying (1) and (2) and the force of (3) is dissipated wherever there is some system of student loans in a country. Hence, every economist is likely to reach a different judgement about the optimum level of subsidy of higher education in the light of his casual assessment of the magnitudes of (1) and (2) [5]. In short, economic analysis at best affords a presumption on grounds of efficiency that the level of subsidy to higher education is almost everywhere too high but it cannot convincingly demonstrate its claim against all possible objections.

Moreover, governments subsidise higher education, not just for efficiency reasons but also for reasons of equity, not to mention various other social and political objectives, and the order of priority among these multiple objectives is subject to constant change. The point is well expressed in the Dutch government memorandum on the *Contours of a Future Education System in the Netherlands,* emphasising the shifts that have taken place in the aims of educational legislation in the Netherlands since the end of World War II: "At first the over-riding consideration was the protection of the most defenceless members of society against exploitation; later the emphasis fell on the need for skilled and professional manpower, while in the last years especially, the right of the individual to develop his full potential and the need to prepare him for a place in society in the broadest sense have gained the upper hand" (Government of the Netherlands, 1976). It is vain to pretend, therefore, that we can appeal to any general principles that would specify an optimum level of subsidy to higher education, much less to general principles that would prove that the present level of subsidy in Europe is somehow excessive.

But suppose it were agreed that the optimum level of subsidy to higher education is some positive number, one might still ask whether the existing subsidies to higher education are excessive in the light of alternative optimum subsidies to health, housing, public transport, etc. In short, let us compare the social rate of return to higher education with the social rate of return to health care, to municipal housing, to highway construction, and so forth, because investment in higher education must ultimately compete for public funds with every other type of investment.

Of course, this route to an answer along these lines is beset by even more difficulties than those that confront the quantification of the externalities and net psychic benefits of higher education. Nevertheless, there is no doubt that recent fears of rising public expenditure in the face of inflationary pressures have caused opinion in some countries to swing against the further expansion of higher education almost as if a crude comparison

352

of alternative rates of return to various components of public expenditure had revealed the fact of overinvestment in higher education. In Germany, Sweden, and the Netherlands, as we have seen, there have been moves in recent years to seek ways to restrict admissions to higher education (see Gordon, 1976). Curiously enough, such moves are rarely accompanied by reductions in the level of subsidy that might discourage demand for higher education. To the extent that subsidies have been reduced, they have been reduced by stealth: student grants have not kept pace with inflation in either Britain, France, or Germany. But no European government has advocated a fall in the real value of student aid as a matter of policy. Governments appear to be unalterably committed to maintaining the present level of subsidy to students despite the fact that it could probably be lowered almost everywhere without significantly diminishing private incentives to acquire higher education. It is clear that governments prefer to control the size of tertiary education by administrative fiat rather than by the private purse.

The obvious explanation of this phenomenon is that equity considerations have usually taken precedence over efficiency considerations in determining the appropriate level of subsidy to higher education. Most European governments argue that it is necessary to provide free education at all levels and also to subsidise students' living expenses in post-secondary schooling so as to guarantee "equality of educational opportunity". But there is ample evidence that the provision of free tuition, combined with grants and low-interest loans for tertiary students, has not in fact achieved greater equality, at least as measured by trends in the social class composition of students in higher education throughout Europe (see OECD, 1975). Besides, since those that bear the costs of the subsidies are not identical with those that enjoy their benefits, there is always the question of whether the existing pattern of subsidies to higher education actually contributes towards the equalisation of incomes.

All of which is to say that the debate about the equity of alternative methods of financing higher education has confused two quite separate questions: (1) how can we equalise opportunities for students from high and low income families?; and (2) how should the costs of education be shared between high and low income taxpayers? For example, the case for aiding students by means of grants rather than loans is based on the notion that poorer students are discouraged by a loans scheme from undertaking higher education, being risk averters who lack confidence that higher education will indeed result in higher incomes. But if repayment of loans is made income-contingent, or if instead the loan is financed by a graduate tax, it is not at all obvious that loans would in fact discourage students from low income families. Income-contingent loans are, after all, a form of insurance against the risk of low income and it is precisely low income families who are likely to be affected by those capital-market imperfections for which a government loans scheme provides a remedy. Thus, it is at least plausible to argue on a priori grounds that a greater reliance on loans rather than grants would actually improve the social class composition of students in colleges and universities (Verry, 1977b, pp. 84–5).

Be that as it may, if the objective of the subsidy system is to create "equality of educational opportunity", its success ought to be judged solely in terms of the social class composition of students independently of the taxes paid to finance the subsidies. If, on the other hand, the objective is the more ambitious one of equalising the distribution of personal income, then of course both the incidence of benefits received and the incidence of taxes paid must be included in a total assessment of subsidies. And in that case what is relevant is, not just the current distribution of beneficiaries and taxpayers, but the distribution of lifetime incomes of both beneficiaries and taxpayers. The oft-encountered proposition that subsidies to higher education must operate to make the distribution of income more unequal because the average taxpayer is poorer than the average beneficiary of the subsidies is simply wrong: it ignores the fact that some of the poor taxpayers of today may become the rich taxpayers of tomorrow precisely because of the benefits of higher education. If the subsidy system constitutes an inter-generational transfer of income, as it surely does, the argument must take account of lifetime tax and lifetime income streams [6].

Nevertheless, it is important to ask what could be inferred from annual data on taxes and subsidies because we are never likely to be furnished with appropriate longitudinal data. Let us, therefore, divide the problem into two parts: (1) what would be the distributional effects of subsidies to higher education if the present size distribution of family incomes remained invariant over time; and (2) what are its actual effects, taking account of intergenerational movements in the distribution of family incomes?

There is a prior question, however, that must be disposed of. In the first instance, the subsidy system represents a transfer of income from single people and childless couples to families with children of school-going ages. If family size varied monotonically with family income, we could derive a clear-cut conclusion about the distributional effects of the subsidy system. However, an examination of the demographic evidence belies any simple relationship between family size and family income (e.g. Miller, 1966, p. 34). We are justified, therefore, in assuming that family size, or more precisely the number of children in a family aged 18–22, is randomly associated with levels of family income. This leaves us with the problem of distinguishing between all taxpayers, on the one hand, and those taxpayers who derive positive benefits from subsidies to higher education, on the other.

Let us now rank all families that pay taxes by their annual incomes and then let us rank the same families again by the higher education subsidies

354

they now receive (many of the entries in this ranking will of course be zero) [7]. We can then express the degree of "progression" in these two distributions by the average propensity to pay tax (the tax-income ratio) in the first ranking and the average propensity to receive higher education subsidies (the subsidy-income ratio) in the second ranking. If the slope of the subsidy-income ratio exceeds the slope of the tax-income ratio (see Fig.1), we have the necessary but not sufficient conditions for the subsidy system to worsen the distribution of family income.

The sufficient conditions for greater inequality in the distribution of family income involve the net movement of taxpayers from low to high income families in the course of a lifetime, possibly but not necessarily because of the tendency of higher education to raise the lifetime income of graduates above those of their parents. To sum up: subsidies to higher education will redistribute income towards greater inequality if (1) the degree of "progression" of subsidies is greater than that of all taxes taken together (see Fig.1); and (2) the number of "poor" taxpayers in the present generation that rise to become "rich" taxpayers in the next generation exceeds the obverse tendency of some taxpayers to fall in the income hierarchy as time passes.

There is longitudinal evidence for the USA and for some European countries that condition (2) generally obtains: the net movement over time is upwards (see Duncan, et al., 1972). But there is no comprehensive data for any country that would allow us to say that Fig.1 correctly depicts the typical situation around the world in respect of condition (1). There is, however, a good deal of evidence for the USA and some countries in Europe that suggests that tax systems are only "progressive" in the upper tail of the income distribution, being roughly proportional to income throughout the entire range of incomes from the second to the ninth decile of the income distribution (see OECD, 1975, I, pp. 27–8, II, pp. 200–1) [8].

Since the subsidy-income ratio almost certainly rises with levels of

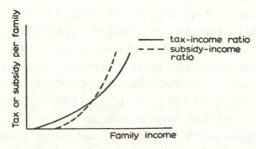

Fig. 1. An illustration. Note: Because of indirect taxes, we may assume that all families pay some tax. If the tax system is "progressive", the tax-income ratio will rise with family incomes, as shown above; the subsidy-income curve may be similarly interpreted.

family income [9], there is the strong presumption that both of our conditions for an adverse distributional effect of the subsidy system are met in most of the countries with which we are concerned. It follows that the burden of proof in the equity argument for grants as against loans rests on those who would defend grants as equalising incomes.

Apart from the question of aiding students by grants rather than loans, there is also the question of how to provide the aid that is regularly furnished to institutions. There are those who argue that it would be efficient to give a much greater share of the total subsidy to students rather than to institutions, so as to force institutions to compete with each other for students and therefore for funds (see Crew and Young, 1977). But it is not obvious that such a change taken by itself would produce that effect. For example, British universities have recently increased the level of fees but the majority of British students have their fees paid in full from public funds, which means that the government will still be the principal source of university income. Thus, the policy of paying grants to students to cover fees will work in the same way in Britain as a policy of making grants to institutions based on student numbers. The main effect of the change will be to make the size of the subsidy more obvious and this, of course, is no small difference: open rather than hidden subsidies promote the accountability of institutions. Nevertheless, to give bite to the policy of aiding students rather than institutions, fees would have to be related to the widely varying costs of tuition in different subjects, and this is an idea that apparently strikes most European Ministries of Education as too radical to be entertained.

Conclusion

In drawing conclusions about the current pattern of subsidies to higher education in Europe, it is convenient to set out two extreme models, one in which the level of subsidy is maximised to cover 100 per cent of the private costs of higher education both direct and indirect, and another in which the level is minimised but not necessarily set equal to zero (because, say, the externalities of higher education are thought to be positive, or because some subsidy is regarded as necessary to provide equality of access). The first model might be represented as a more extreme example of the British case in that the majority of UK higher education students are subsidised for the whole of their fees and up to half of their gross earnings forgone. The second model cannot be represented, even in exaggerated terms, by any individual country. It is a model in which all higher education institutions would charge fees that covered the total cost of educating a student in a particular subject and in which students would be provided with publicly guaranteed loans at commercial rates of interest. No student and no institution of higher educa-

356

tion would be subsidised directly and all subsidies to higher education would therefore disappear except insofar as defaults on loans would have to be financed.

In between these two extreme models, we have a hierarchy of levels and types of subsidies ranging from the maximum to the minimum of the continuum. As we have seen, the tendency throughout Europe is to abolish tuition fees and this immediately implies a definite level of subsidy, depending on the costs of tuition in different countries and the distribution of students between high-cost science subjects and low-cost liberal arts subjects. But given this definite level of subsidy to institutions, the level of student aid that is added on top of this may approach either end of the continuum. Student aid may consist solely of grants that in effect constitute a living wage and students' parents may be provided with generous tax relief, thus maximising subsidies to students. Alternatively, the system of student aid may consist entirely of loans, as is the case in Japan, thus minimising subsidies to students.

It is evident that most countries on the continent of Europe fall somewhere in between the two extremes on the issue of student aid. There is a general tendency to lean more heavily on loans and there is also a universal tendency to subsidise loans by charging interest rates below commercial levels. But there is no consistent pattern in the fraction of students aided directly by grants or loans and indirectly by food and housing subsidies; there is also no consistent pattern in the level of tax relief afforded to students' families (see Table VII). What appears to be missing in all the recent changes that are taking place in student aid schemes throughout Europe is some set of general principles that could distinguish between more and less desirable changes.

We bring our argument to a close by setting out one such set of principles. We argue, first, that all higher education institutions should charge tuition fees that represent a significant proportion of the total costs of education — the argument here is one of institutional autonomy and internal efficiency. Next, we argue that the ideal type of student aid involves a mixture of grants and loans — the argument here is one of efficiency in studying, equity in treatment, and practical politics. Lastly, we argue that both fees, the size of grants and loans, and the repayment of loans should be related to income: to present parental income in the case of fees, grants and loans, and to future graduate income when it comes to the repayment of loans. Several countries have established elements of this general policy of means-tested, income-related student aid schemes (see Table VII) but none have adopted it wholeheartedly.

But if all higher education institutions in Europe charged some tuition fees and then related these fees to the family income of students, and if at the same time, governments supplemented means-tested basic grants by income-contingent loans, or better still loans financed by a graduate tax, both subsidies and the burden of financing them would be shared more equitably than at present. Another virtue of such a comprehensive income-geared policy is that it could be made far more flexible than the present system of subsidies. The details of the policy could be adapted to achieve different objectives of social policy. If governments wished to encourage particular courses of study for manpower reasons, a differential level of fees could provide suitable incentives. Similarly, if the aim was to reduce the length of study in particular areas, then fees could increase steeply after, say, three or four years. If it was felt that certain groups might be discouraged from accepting loans, for instance women, then the repayment terms might be varied for them.

Such a scheme would not solve problems overnight. It is easy to claim too much for a new method of financing. It would certainly pose new administrative problems and it appears to conflict with the general tendency in industrialised countries of lowering the voting age. Indeed, we have now reached the paradoxical position in Europe of giving the vote to 18 or 19 year olds, and recognising their age of majority for purposes of entering into legal contracts, while continuing to regard them as children dependent on parental support for purposes of providing financial aids to schooling. When we consider how frequently university students earn while studying, particularly on the continent of Europe, and how frequently parents refuse to support them once they are in receipt of a study grant, the conviction grows that it is high time that student aid schemes are brought into line with electoral practice. But if all countries were to follow the Swedish example of totally disregarding parental income when subsidising either students or institutions, the attractive notion of gearing both fees and grants to parental incomes would have to go by the board, and the entire weight of the equity argument would have to fall on income-contingent loans.

There is an escape from this dilemma, however. Social inequalities of access to higher education have their roots in pre-school family background factors, which are then exacerbated by implicit and explicit achievement testing throughout primary and secondary education. Since all European countries compel school attendance until the age of 16, direct aid to students, or even indirect student aid in the form of remission of fees or tax relief cannot affect enrolments until the stage of upper secondary education is reached. Thus, there is a strong case for grants to equalise access to higher education, not after admission to higher education, but at the ages 16–18 or 17–19, the stage at which the dropouts from the school system are concentrated. And yet, in all European countries except France, grants for secondary school pupils are less generous than subsidies for tertiary education [10]. If loans in higher education were coupled with grants in

358

upper secondary education, the last remaining argument against loans schemes would fall to the ground.

The ideal package, therefore, from the standpoint of both efficiency and equity is (1) a grants system in the last few years of secondary education; (2) a system of fees in higher education equal to, say, 30 to 50 per cent of institutional incomes; and (3) an income-contingent loans scheme or graduate tax for undergraduates and postgraduates coupled with a minimum basic grant. We would argue that this package has overwhelming economic, social and educational merits. It might also be popular with the electorate of Europe if adequate preparations were made for its introduction. The first task would be a publicity campaign to inform the electorate of the family origins of the beneficiaries of existing subsidies to higher education. The next task would be to mobilise opinion in favour of an increase in the system of grants to secondary school pupils. Because of pressures on public expenditure, such an expansion of the grants system at the lower end of the schooling distribution might imply a curtailment of grants at the upper end. However, as grants in higher education are cut back, existing loans schemes may be expanded, and student opposition could be neutralised by an agreement to freeze grants at their current money value, while allowing loans to expand to preserve the real value of maintenance in the face of inflation. Alternatively, grants and loans in higher education might be preserved at existing levels with the extra funds for grants to secondary school pupils being generated by the introduction of a graduate tax, supplementing the standard income tax. A graduate tax differs from a loans scheme in that participation in the system is compulsory; hence, a graduate tax raises more revenue, everything else being the same, than a loans scheme. A graduate tax might be difficult to introduce in a federated country like Germany or the USA but, even in such countries, there is scope for a graduate tax on the local level.

We venture to predict that, as higher education in Europe continues to expand in the 1980s, the tendency to move in the general direction that we have outlined will come increasingly to dominate debates on educational finance.

Notes

1 For a more detailed examination of student aid policies in Europe, as well as in Australia, Canada, Japan and the USA, see Woodhall (1978).
2 This point is further developed by Paichaud (1975).
3 For some recent comparative data, see Verry (1977b, pp. 67–71).
4 See Verry (1977b, p. 56) for references to the European literature on the grants-loans debate.

5 The recent popularity of the "screening hypothesis" has complicated that assessment: if firms screen potential employees in terms of educational credentials, each individual is motivated to obtain additional education to provide a "signal" of his superior qualities; as more and more individuals of a given ability attain a certain level of education, those with superior abilities are induced to attain still higher levels of education; the inevitable result of screening, therefore, is overinvestment in education and its remedy is a reduction in subsidies to higher education. The validity of the screening hypothesis, however, remains controversial.

6 See Miklius (1975), summing up the inconclusive American debate on the distributional effects of public higher education; see also Conlisk (1977).

7 Families also receive many other kinds of subsidies and transfers, which we may properly ignore when assessing the specific effects of higher education subsidies.

8 In short, the tax-income ratio in Fig.1 is a straight line throughout most of its range. It is true, of course, that the entire tax-transfer expenditure system is slightly progressive in most countries (OECD, 1975, I, pp. 143–7, II, pp. 201–4, 330–32) but that is irrelevant for our purposes.

9 There is a recent Dutch study for 1975, confirming American findings along similar lines: Ritzen, et al., 1977, pp. 82, 85, 100–1.

10 In Germany, financial aid for upper secondary school pupils amounts to less than a third of government expenditure on student aid; in the Netherlands, the proportion is 18 per cent; and in Britain, it is only 5 per cent. France is unique in Europe in providing more financial aid for secondary school pupils than for students in higher education.

References

Conlisk, J. (1977). "A Further Look at the Hansen-Weisbrod-Pechman Debate", *Journal of Human Resources* (Spring).

Council of Europe, Committee for Higher Education and Research (1976). *Financial Aid to Students: Netherlands.* Strasbourg: Council of Europe, mimeographed. (Report submitted by the Netherlands Ministry for Education and Science to 33rd Meeting, 12–14 May).

Council of Europe. (1977). *News Letter.* Strasbourg: Documentation Centre for Education in Europe, No. 2.

Crew, M., Young, A. (1977). *Paying By Degrees.* London: Institute of Economic Affairs.

Crowther-Hunt, Lord (1976). *Times Higher Education Supplement* (May 28).

Department of Education and Science (1970). *Output Budgeting for the Department of Education and Science.* Education Planning Paper No. 1. London: HMSO.

Department of Education and Science (1976a). *University Grants Committee Annual Survey, Academic Year 1974–75.* London: HMSO.

Department of Education and Science (1976b). *Undergraduate Income and Spending.* London: HMSO.

Department of Education and Science (1976c). *Expenditure Committee: Government Observations on Third Report 1973–74.* London: HMSO.

Duckenfield, M. (1977). "U68: Decentralised Decisions and an End to the Binary System," *Times Higher Education Supplement* (May 13).

360

Duncan, O. D., Featherman, D. L. and Duncan, B. (1972). *Socioeconomic Background and Achievement.* New York: Seminar Press.

Expenditure Committee of the House of Commons, Session 1973–4 (1973). *Postgraduate Education.* London: HMSO.

Gordon, A. (1976). "Trends in European Higher Education," *Higher Education Bulletin* (Winter).

Government of the Netherlands (1976). *Contours of a Future Education System in the Netherlands.* The Hague: Government of the Netherlands.

Levy-Garboua, L. (1975). "La justice distributive de l'école," *Consommation: Annales du CREDOC* (Centre de Recherche pour l'Etude et l'Observation des Conditions de Vie), No. 2.

Levy-Garboua, L. (1977). "Les dépenses d'enseignement en France," *Educational Expenditure in France, Japan and the U.K.* Paris: OECD.

Maynard, A. (1975). *Experiment with Choice in Education.* London: Institute of Economic Affairs.

Miklius, W. (1975). "The Distributional Effects of Public Higher Education: A Comment," *Higher Education,* 4: 351–355.

Miller, H. P. (1966). *Income Distribution in the United States. A 1960 Census Monograph.* Washington, D. C.: US Government Printing Office.

Mingat, A. (1977). *Essai sur la demande de l'éducation.* Thèse présentée le 12 novembre, 1977, à l'Université de Dijon. Dijon: Université de Dijon, Faculté de science économique et de gestion, mimeographed.

National Board of Universities and Colleges (1976). *The National Swedish Board of Universities and Colleges: A New Government Agency.* Stockholm: U.H.A. (Universitets – och Högskoleämberet).

National Center for Education Statistics (1976). *The Condition of Education 1976 edition.* Washington: U.S. Government Printing Office for the National Center for Education Statistics.

OECD (1972). *Educational Policy and Planning: Germany.* Paris: OECD.

OECD (1975). *Education, Inequality and Life Chances.* Paris: OECD.

Orivel, F. (1975). "Origines et objectifs du système Francais d'aide aux étudiants," *L'aide aux étudiants en France: faits et critique.* Dijon: Institut de recherche sur l'économie de l'éducation (IREDU), Université de Dijon, mimeographed.

Orivel, F. (1977). *Côut et financement de l'enseignement supérieur.* (A summary of part of a doctoral thesis presented in 1975 to the University of Dijon by B. Millot and F. Orivel, *L'Allocation des ressources dans l'enseignement supérieur Francais: evaluation et rationalité*). Dijon: IREDU, mimeographed.

Paichaud, D. (1975). "The Economics of Educational Opportunity," *Higher Education,* 4: 201–212.

Pratt, J. (1975). "The UGC Department," *Higher Education Review* (Spring).

Prest, A. R. (1966). *Financing University Education.* London: Institute of Economic Affairs.

Ritzen, J. M. M., Pommer, E. J., Roelse, W. and Ruitenberg, L. W. (1977). *Profijt van de Overheid* (Benefits from Government). The Hague: Sociaal en Cultureel Planbureau.

Roeloffs, K. (1976). *Financial Aid to Students in Germany.* Paris: OECD, mimeographed.

361

Rudd, E. (1975). "Parents Should Not be Forced to Pay," *Times Higher Education Supplement* (October 24).

Rudd, E. (1977). "Student Grants: No Worse, But Little Better," *Times Higher Education Supplement,* (June 10).

Swärd, G., Larsson, J., Persson, R. and Gesser, B. (1968). *Studentekonomiska undersökningen 1968* (Student Finance Investigation 1968). Lund: Lunds Universitet, Sociologiska Institutionen.

Verry, D. (1977a). "Financial Incentives and Efficiency in Education," Open University Course ED 322, Economics and Education Policy, Block III, *The Internal Efficiency of Educational Institutions.* Milton Keynes: The Open University Press.

Verry, D. (1977b). "Some Distributional and Equity Aspects of the Student Loans Debate," Open University Course ED 322, Block V, *Education, Equity and Income Distribution.* Milton Keynes: The Open University Press.

Williams, G. (1974). "The Events of 1973–4 in a Long Term Planning Perspective," *Higher Education Bulletin* (Autumn).

Woodhall, M. (1970). *Student Loans: A Review of Experience in Scandinavia and Elsewhere.* London: Harrap Publishing Co.

Woodhall, M. (1978). *Review of Student Support Schemes in Selected OECD Countries.* Paris: OECD.

[8]

Can Independent Education be Suppressed?

I. MARK BLAUG

Private Schools, a Labour Party National Executive Committee Discussion Document, sets out the divisive social and educational effects of private schools and spells out a feasible policy of inte- grating them into the state system of education with a view to abolishing private schooling altogether, not today or tomorrow, but certainly the day after tomorrow. The recommendations of *Private Schools* were redrafted, with one or two alterations, in *A Plan for Private Schools*, published jointly by the TUC and the Labour Party in July 1981, with the aim of terminating all public support to private schools within one year of the election of a Labour government, and of abolishing fee-paying in private schools within a period of no more than ten years. These are hard-hitting documents: the case against private schools is pungently stated and the analysis of available policy options is informed by practical realism. Nevertheless, I am struck not so much by what is put into the argument but by what is left out, and in particular by the failure seriously to address the central philosophical question at issue in all

debates about private schooling: should individuals in a democratic society in which incomes are not equally distributed be allowed to employ their incomes to purchase privileges for themselves (or members of their families), such as yachts, Rolls Royces, large houses, private medical care, private pensions, and private education?

Let me declare my sentiments at the outset. This is a subject on which it is almost impossible to 'keep one's cool' and I feel as passionately about private schooling as the authors of the docu- ments. It happens that I dislike 'public' schools, not because they are private, but because they are typically boarding schools and typically single-sex board- ing schools in secluded rural areas. I believe that the hot-house, boarding atmosphere of the average public school has a lasting, disastrous psychological effect on children and I find this much more alarming than what I take to be the no less disastrous social effects of these schools. Having spent large parts of my youth in the Netherlands and the United States, I am amazed by the

30

apparent eagerness of Britain middle-class parents to send their children away at the earliest possible age. Other countries have private schools: all over Asia and Africa there are more private than public secondary schools and even in America, where in the past private schools were few and far between, recent years have seen a steady growth in private schooling even at the elementary level.

But outside Britain the debate about private schools is a debate about private day schools, and most foreigners are amazed to learn that many British parents think nothing of sending their 13, 11 and even 7 year old children away to a boarding school for nine months of the year. On the other hand, the boarding phenomenon is simply taken for granted in Britain and many of the enemies of public schools, like the authors of these documents seem almost unaware of the vast difference between buying *private* education and buying private *boarding* education.

Having declared my prejudices against public schools, I nevertheless resist any notion of legislating private schools out of existence. I am a libertarian and since we all believe in freedom when it comes to behaviour or activity we approve of, the litmuss-paper test of a libertarian is whether he will tolerate behaviour or activities he disapproves of. There is an alarming paragraph in *Private Schools* which illustrates the point in question: 'Freedom necessarily involves rights which can be exercised by *all*. Private education is not a freedom but a privilege confined to a tiny elite . . . Labour believes that the only real freedom are those available to all citizens.' If we pursue the logic of this proposition, it follows that we must put an end to private medical care, private medical insurance and private pensions. This might not worry the members of the Labour Party's National Executive Council. But why should wealthy parents be allowed to purchase large houses, thus providing their children with the undoubted advan-

tage of private study space, or houses near good state schools, which again confers an unequal advantage? Thus, private housing privilege must also be abolished, or at least severely circumscribed. Furthermore, wealthier parents must also be prevented from buying private tutoring for their children, or from taking them on continental holidays, because these too confer special advantages in the educational 'rat race'. Where indeed do we draw the line in ensuring that freedoms are available in equal amounts to all citizens?

Choice and state education

The authors of *Private Schools* mock the language of 'free choice' invoked by the advocates of private schooling. What is wrong with a state monopoly of education, they ask? All parents make use of maintained primary schools without worrying about 'freedom of choice' and why should a state monopoly of *secondary* education be considered any more threatening than a state monopoly of *primary* education? As a matter of fact, many parents opt out of the state system well before the age of secondary education, as witnessed by the large numbers of private preparatory schools admitting children after the age of seven. But apart from this debating point, it seems odd that the authors have forgotten about the entire history of 'progressive' primary education under largely private auspices. If British primary education is now something to be proud of, it is in part due to the influence of many educational iconoclasts who opened private schools to promote new ways of teaching young children. Similarly, 'alternative medicine' would have been doomed from the start if it had had to rely entirely on the National Health Service.

Paying twice?

So much then for the fundamental philosophical question. If we value freedom more than equality, we must tolerate private schools whether we like them or not. Yet I can see no reason to use public money to subsidise private schools as we do through such things as tax and rate relief, boarding allowances for military and diplomatic personnel and local authorities paying private school fees for bright pupils. Parents who purchase private education pay for education twice over: once for maintained education by their contribution to general tax revenues, and once for private education by the fees paid to private schools. There is a sense in which such parents are relieving the rest of the community of the expense of educating their children for which they may in justice demand a *quid pro quo*. This is an argument which (the reader will not be surprised to learn) is never mentioned in either document before us. It is an argument which must be taken seriously and yet I find it unconvincing, particularly as the subsidies in question are little understood by the general public and are deliberately played down by spokesmen for the public schools. By all means let us fight for a genuine alternative to state education but let us have the courage of our convictions by insisting that it be a choice between subsidised state education and unsubsidised private education.

I hope I have now said enough to reveal my own biases. Let us return to the content of *Private Schools*. It begins with some factual background and then proceeds to make the case against private schools. Taking all private schools together, including the remaining direct grant grammar schools, private enrolments amount to only 6% of the total school population but their share of pupils rises to 7% for children over the age of 13 and to 10% for sixth formers over the age of 16. Almost 40% of the students at the 150 most prestigious independent schools are boarders; in the remaining 220 independent schools most students are day-students. The authors rehearse the familiar facts about the

middle-class composition of students in these schools, emphasizing the extent to which the private school system is hereditary, the bulk of demand coming from parents who themselves attended private schools, whose parents in turn attended private schools. The ethos of independent schools, which derives principally from those which have boarders, claims to develop unique qualities of self-confidence and leadership in students — which claims seem to be largely justified by their results. As we all know, there are a disproportionate number of former public school pupils in positions of power and influence in the civil service, the judiciary, the armed forces, the Church of England, the banking community, and, of course, Parliament (60% of Conservative MPs and 8% of Labour MPs attended public schools and as many as 21 members of Mrs Thatcher's Cabinet are products of public schools). The authors might have added, but do not, that the products of public schools earn more than the products of maintained schools even when we hold constant the total years of schooling received, the level of qualifications attained, and their fathers' occupations. Evidence such as this is profoundly paradoxical. On the one hand, it can be used to show that public schools should be eliminated because they serve to create a tiny power élite. On the other hand, it can be employed to show that parents are perfectly rational in thinking that private education confers a real advantage on their children which is worth the cost of a £2–3,000 fee; surely, if we could show that the demand for private schooling is simply pure snobbery, having no real return in enhanced occupational income for their children, the case for public schools would long ago have collapsed under its own weight?

The authors struggle to disprove the widely held view that independent schools are more efficient in producing O-level and A-level results than maintained schools, or, to express it in popular language, that public schools are of superior 'academic quality'. They do not deny that private schools have smaller classes and superior teaching resources, but they argue that most of the superiority in examination results is due to the rigid selection of students in independent schools at the point of entry and to a tendency to hold on to students until the age of 18 or 19. In short, they argue that the available figures on the comparative educational attainments of private and maintained schools do not compare like with like, particularly as so many of the existing comprehensive schools are comprehensive in name only because neighbouring private schools cream off all the local pupils with high academic attainments.

Better results in private schools?

The evidence on this question is extremely mixed: it is perfectly true that we cannot say that students with similar IQs and similar family backgrounds have a better chance of ending up with higher educational achievements if they attend a private school rather than a comprehensive school. On the other hand, we also cannot assert the opposite with perfect confidence. *Private Schools* cites some irrelevant evidence from a longitudinal study by the National Children's Bureau, which reported that bright children do as well in comprehensive schools as in selective maintained schools, which is interesting news but neither here nor there as far as the question at issue is concerned. Other evidence suggests that private schools are more efficient examination-factories than maintained schools for pupils of identical characteristics (for example, G. Kalton, *The Public Schools: A Factual Survey*, Longmans, 1966). There is also little doubt that private schools corner the market for higher education places in general and Oxbridge places in particular — the maintained school applicant has only a one-in-three change of getting an Oxbridge place as

against an even chance for his or her private school counterpart — and this has less to do with their intrinsic academic excellence than with the single-mindedness with which they pursue the task of sitting examinations. We may deplore this mania for A-level results, which distorts the whole of upper secondary education and produces earlier specialisation in Britain than anywhere else in the world, and we may lay much of the blame for the situation at the doors of the public schools. The fact remains, however, that this is what British parents want and are willing to pay for — if they can afford it. Either we must persuade them to want something else, or we must remind them of how much more it would really cost if the rest of us refused to subsidise them.

In the meanwhile, and here I fully endorse the arguments of the Discussion Document, the more the Government encourages local authorities to buy places in private schools for children selected on grounds of their attainment, the more difficult it is for comprehensive schools ever to match the achievement records of private schools, which then justifies parents in the belief that schools ought to be judged exclusively in terms of paper qualifications, and that private schools are superior in this respect to state schools. The Government's Assisted Places Scheme, small as is its effect in total numbers of places in private schools, is nevertheless well designed to encourage some of the worst tendencies in British education; the scheme is means tested to help 'pupils of high academic ability from less well-off families' but the stipulation that students must be able to pass the common entrance examination of private schools at age 11 or 13 severely limits its potential for helping the disadvantaged.

Indirect subsidies

The heart of the problem is the large number of indirect subsidies going to private schools. As a result of their charitable status they are exempt from income tax, corporation tax, and capital gains tax, and they are entitled to reclaim income tax at source from dividends received on investments held by charitable trusts acting on their behalf, from interest received by parents on educational annuity insurance policies, and from payments received under deeds of covenants for, say, a school appeal. They are also entitled to a 50% reduction in rates on property occupied. The tax loss from the charity status of independent schools has been officially estimated at £25m in 1977 and the rate loss at something like £1m. In addition, the remaining direct grant schools continue to receive a direct per pupil grant, which was estimated at £15m in 1977. More important than all of these are the boarding school allowances paid by the Government to military and diplomatic personnel irrespective of whether they are stationed overseas or not. Over 20,000 private school places are thereby paid for wholly or in large part out of public funds, to the tune of £37m in 1978, three-quarters of which, by the way, goes to government personnel stationed in Britain. Next, there are a variety of schemes whereby parents receive tax relief on capital used to pay their children's school fees either now or in the future through trusts set up by specialist brokers or insurance companies; the costs to the Exchequer of these forms of tax avoidance have never been officially estimated but I would venture to say that they must amount to £1–2m. All these figures are dwarfed by the £80m paid by local education authorities for some 56,000 public places in private schools; even if we deduct from this the £44m paid in 1978 for handicapped pupils to independent special schools, we are still left with £36m paid by LEAs to the independent sector. Finally, there is the Assisted Places Scheme which will add £3m to the annual income of private schools in 1981–82, rising to as much as £55m in

1987–88 when the scheme is fully implemented.

Adding all these public subsidies together, we arrive, as *Private Schools* observes at a *minimum* sum of £121m in 1977–78 or £178m in 1980–81 prices. And all this says nothing about a peculiar and perhaps controversial subsidy: most of the 40,000 teachers in private schools have been trained at taxpayers' expense at a cost of £8–10,000 per teacher. It might be argued that this is no subsidy because the state should accept as much responsibility for teachers in independent as in maintained schools. Yet neither the private school nor the trained teacher ever compensates taxpayers for a training received at public expense. If the parents of students in private schools are to be subsidised because they pay twice over for education, they ought likewise to be taxed for imposing on the rest of the community a higher teacher-training bill than would otherwise be required. On the other hand, it would be an innovation to charge all charities the real cost of any publicly produced resources they may happen to employ (roads, ports, the National Health Service, etc.). On the whole, one is inclined to shrug off the notion of counting the training costs of teachers in private schools as one of the indirect public subsidies to private education.

Still, there is the figure of £178m for total current public subsidies to private schools, the withdrawal of which could only be offset by a rise of fees of 35–40 per cent from current levels of £2,500 for public boarding schools to about £3,500. At this point, however, hard-heeled realism finally breaks into the Discussion Document: 'It would be a mistake to think that a Labour Government could make net savings by ending all public support to private schools and at the same time embark on a policy of integrating all private pupils within the maintained sector. The net recurrent institutional cost of educating the half million private school pupils within the maintained sector would be almost £300m per year (at 1980 prices). The capital cost of providing places (including boarding places) in the maintained sector would have to be added to that cost.' It is not clear how this figure is arrived at but presumably it allows for the taking-over of buildings and equipment with financial compensation to the owners of schools, the loss of a certain proportion of teachers in private schools who would rather leave the profession than teach in maintained schools, and the cost of adapting specialised buildings to new uses. A more practical course of action, the Document goes on to say, would be to deprive independent schools of the fiscal privilege of £178m, while incurring the expense of shifting the 56,000 hitherto publicly supported students in private schools to the maintained sector at a cost of £33m, thus saving the Exchequer at least £146m. This is not a new policy recommendation: it echoes Labour's manifesto pledges of 1974 and 1979.

The closing pages of the Discussion Document canvass a range of policy options, repeated with minor alterations in *A Plan for Private Schools*, for implementing the long-run aim of eliminating private schools:

(1) Prohibiting attendance at private schools: this is rejected in principle and condemned as being unenforceable in practice.

(2) Prohibiting the continuance or establishment of private schools: this, too, is rejected on the same grounds of both principle and practice.

(3) Prohibiting private schools charging fees: the door is not closed to legislation along these lines in the future but it is granted that some wealthy public schools might nevertheless survive entirely on endowment income.

(4) Public ownership: unless the schools were confiscated, national-

isation would have to be accompanied by legislation prohibiting the owners from using their compensation payments to establish new private schools; the costs of re-allocating students and converting existing schools to new uses would be considerable, as noted above, and the main aim of ensuring that private schools are used to serve community purposes would not necessarily require public ownership.

(5) Withdrawal of public support: 'the most immediately practical option for a Labour Government to adopt is to withdraw all public support from private schools and thus isolate them'; this would not cause more than a certain fraction of private schools to 'wither away' but it would mark a first step and present few practical difficulties; the law on charity and the Finance Act would have to be amended but there is ample legal precedence for such amendments; private schools could be charged VAT on their fees in line with other private institutions charging fees; they could also be charged for being inspected by Her Majesty's Inspectorate, currently a free service rendered by the state; and, finally, they might be charged a surcharge for employing publicly trained teachers.

(6) Withdrawal of higher education grants for students educated in private schools: rejected in principle.

Withdrawal of public support is taken to be a first step towards the eventual integration of private schools into the maintained sector. The next step would be to persuade private schools to cater for children with special psychological or social needs for residential education, as well as for community needs in non-boarding education (sixth form colleges, retraining schemes for younger workers, etc.), and to do so without charging fees. Legislation to prohibit the charging of private fees after a given date and to enable the Secretary of State to take over particularly recalcitrant schools could be employed to give teeth to the use of persuasion. Private schools and LEAs could prepare development plans for the use of such schools for community purposes, leaving them in private ownership and retaining their charitable status, provided they charged no private fees, co-operated with the maintained comprehensive schools in the area, and abandoned selection on grounds of attainment or social background. They would thus enter the state system on more or less the same basis as voluntary schools in 1944. For all practical purposes that would be the end of private education.

I subscribe to the withdrawal of all forms of public finance for private schooling but I reject all the subsequent steps in the total operation. The 1980 Discussion Document and *A Plan for Private Schools*

both under-rate the importance of breaking the chain that runs from private schools to Oxbridge to the civil service. It is the special entrance examinations of Oxbridge that favour the products of public schools. Oxbridge is dependent on public money for 90 per cent of its income (only a little less than the 95 per cent ruling for other universities) and the public insistence that it should bring its admission policies into line with other universities would break the chain at its weakest point. The continued preponderance of Oxbridge graduates in civil service recruitments under both Labour and Tory governments is another link in the chain which could so easily be broken. Breaking the chain would significantly weaken demand for independent schools and a fee of £3,500 would make parents think again about the value of private schooling. It is the state that stimulates both the demand for and the supply of public school places. If it withdrew its stimulus, there would be little need for the draconian measures proposed in either *Private Schools* or the later document.

[9]

The Distributional Effects of Higher Education Subsidies

Mark Blaug

This article provides a review of the inconclusive debate between Hansen–Weisbrod and Pechman on the distributional
effects of subsidies to public higher education in California,
with particular reference to its significance for other American
states and for European countries. The cross-sectional effects
are distinguished from the longitudinal, lifetime effects, and an
effort is made to state the necessary and sufficient conditions
to infer lifetime redistributive effects from observations of current data. Some general conclusions are drawn for the case of
the United Kingdom.

More than ten years ago, Lee Hansen and Burton Weisbrod (1969a)
published an article on "The Distribution of Costs and Benefits of
Public Higher Education: The Case of California," which purported
to show that low-income families in the State of California gain less
in higher education subsidies than high-income families even after
allowing for the fact that they also contribute less in taxes to support
public colleges and universities. It followed, therefore, that the Californian system of subsidizing higher education out of public funds
redistributes income from the poor to the rich, the exact opposite of
the effect it was designed to achieve. This finding for California was
soon confirmed by similar findings for Wisconsin (Hansen 1970)
and Florida (Windham 1970), and all these studies have been widely
cited as demonstrating the regressive effects of the American system
of subsidizing public higher education.

Thus, in their recent best-seller, *Free to Choose*, Milton and Rose
Friedman (1980: 182–83, 320–22) reproduce the findings of Hansen and Weisbrod and Windham, concluding:

> The facts are not in dispute. Even the Carnegie Commission
> admits the perverse redistributive effects of government ex-

Mark Blaug is Professor of the Economics of Education at the University of London Institute of Education. He acknowledges the valuable comments received from W. Lee Hansen
and Joseph A. Pechman, neither of whom, however, are responsible for the views expressed
in the article. [Manuscript received December 16, 1980; revision accepted for publication
March 30, 1981.]

> penditures on higher education. . . . We know of no govern-
> ment program that seems to us so inequitable, in its effects . . .
> as the financing of higher education. In this area those of us
> who are in the middle and upper income classes have conned
> the poor into subsidizing us on the grand scale.[1]

Now, this is very odd because a year after the publication of the
original article by Hansen and Weisbrod, Pechman (1970) published
a rebuttal showing that Hansen and Weisbrod's data can be reworked
to stand their conclusion on its head: it is the lower income classes
in California who receive positive net transfers (subsidies minus
taxes), while the higher income classes receive negative net transfers;
thus public support for higher education does promote equity in
California. In short, contrary to what the Friedmans say, the facts
are in dispute. Moreover, Pechman criticized Hansen and Weisbrod
for drawing conclusions about income distribution solely on the basis
of annual, cross-sectional data: the benefits of higher education
accrue in the future and are not enjoyed by the same individuals that
now pay the taxes to subsidize it. Hence, an adequate appraisal of
the distributional effects of higher education subsidies must address
itself to lifetime incomes. Since then, Conlisk (1977) has constructed
a theoretical model of this life-cycle process of taxing parents in the
current period to subsidize an activity whose yields will accrue to
their children in a future period. Although the absence of matched
parent-child lifetime income data prevented him from testing the
model, Conlisk concluded that it lent support to the Pechman method of classifying the available cross-sectional evidence. In other
words, if the facts are indeed in dispute, it would appear that Pechman is more likely to be right than Hansen and Weisbrod.

This conclusion is not esoteric knowledge. One authoritative
American textbook in the economics of education—a veritable com-
pendium of findings and results—boldly announces the fact that
Pechman has reversed the Hansen–Weisbrod conclusions, adding a
list of references to the subsequent literature that includes the study
by Conlisk just cited and many more besides (Cohn 1979: 299). In
that case, however, how is it possible that so many commentators

---

1. Similarly, Psacharopoulos (1978: 364), listing the major results of recent research in the
economics of education, observes: "*It appears that poor families finance the education of
the children of more wealthy families.* This result first came about in a study of the California system of higher education, and it was repeated for other states. . . . This finding becomes plausible when one thinks that it is mainly the wealthier families who enroll more
children in higher education, yet these children receive a higher effective subsidy relative to
the taxes paid by their parents (relative to the corresponding position of poorer families)."

The Distributional Effects of Higher Education Subsidies

keep repeating the Hansen–Weisbrod results as if they were gospel truths?

There are at least two answers to that question. Hansen and Weisbrod were the first in the field, and their findings were congruent with the deeply held intuitions of many economists of education. Moreover, they chose the richest state in the union, and what was true of the richest, it was believed, must surely be true of poorer states. Finally, their results were almost immediately replicated in two other states, which served to bolster their claims. Thus, one reaction to Pechman was to doubt that a similar reworking of the data in states other than California would succeed in reversing what we might call the Hansen–Weisbrod thesis. Those of us who are concerned with higher education outside America—where age-group participation rates in higher education are one-half to one-quarter of the rates in America and where levels of subsidies are frequently large enough to finance both tuition costs and living expenses—no doubt choose this route as an excuse for ignoring Pechman's arguments.[2]

Secondly, even if it were a conceptual error to judge this issue in terms of annual, cross-sectional data, the fact remains that we are not likely to obtain clinching life-cycle data in the foreseeable future. In the meanwhile, however, it would be irresponsible to ignore the redistributive effects of higher education subsidies even if all one can do is to suggest probable rather than certain effects. After all, neither Pechman nor Conlisk has definitely reversed the Hansen–Weisbrod implication in a lifetime perspective: they have merely shown that it *may* be reversed.[3] We can indeed go on believing that Hansen and Weisbrod have put their fingers on an important truth, if not for all American states then at least for some, and perhaps for many higher education systems outside America.

To see why we might reach this latter conclusion, we need to look in somewhat greater detail at this furious and frustrating controversy.

2. There is no European study directly comparable in scope to the work of Hansen and Weisbrod. For suggestive evidence on France, see Eicher (1979), which supports the Hansen-Weisbrod thesis. There are a few studies dealing with the Third World, which likewise support the Hansen–Weisbrod thesis for *higher* education (see Fields 1975; Jallade 1974: 37–41; Psacharopoulos 1977b; and Selowsky 1979: 72–76).

3. Crean (1975) claims to have shown that Canadian higher education subsidies redistribute lifetime income from the rich to the poor, but his argument is not fully convincing because he merely extrapolates cross-sectional data.

Economics of Education Review

HANSEN AND WEISBROD VERSUS PECHMAN

The redistributive effects of higher education subsidies are the joint outcome of two entirely distinct distributions: the distribution of higher education subsidies among families and the distribution of taxes among families. We begin with the subsidy distribution because it is easier to deal with.

Every family pays taxes (although not necessarily income taxes), but not every family receives higher education subsidies. Even in California, the richest state in one of the richest countries of the world, 33 percent of all high school graduates did not go to college in 1964, and another 8 percent went to a private college or a college outside the state where they received no subsidy from the State of California. The remaining 59 percent of Californian high school grad- uage received a higher education subsidy from the state that might be as low as $750 or as high as $6,500 (in 1964), depending on whether they attended an inexpensive two-year junior college or the expen- sive four-year University of California. A third category of students attended one of the state colleges and received an intermediate level of subsidy (Hansen and Weisbrod 1969a: 181–82).

The pattern of college-going by levels of family incomes in Cali- fornia is representative of all advanced countries. The median income of families without any children in higher education is below the me- dian income of all California families; the median income of families with children in two-year junior colleges is just above the median family income; and the median income of families with children in state colleges and in the University of California is well above the median family income (Hansen and Weisbrod 1969a: 183). In other words, higher education subsidies in California, as everywhere else, are positively correlated with family income (Hansen and Weisbrod 1969a: 185).

On the other hand, it does appear that rich and poor in California are represented in each of the three types of colleges. Although there is a strong tendency for the most subsidized colleges to draw a higher income clientele, the overlap of the distributions of family income by the three types of colleges attended is nevertheless very substan- tial, and this constitutes the first doubt about the Hansen–Weisbrod thesis.

We turn now to the tax distribution. We have so far established that there is a tendency for higher education subsidies in California to rise with family incomes, but if the California tax system is in some measure progressive, it follows that there will also be a ten- dency for taxes to rise with family incomes. However, Hansen and

The Distributional Effects of Higher Education Subsidies

Weisbrod (1969a: 189) estimate the incidence of state and local taxes by family income levels and show that they are regressive below $8,000 (in 1965) and strictly proportional above $8,000, which completes their case: if the subsidy system is progressive and the tax system is either regressive or proportional, it follows that net transfers (subsidies minus taxes) will be regressive, being negative for the poor and positive for the rich.

Hansen and Weisbrod make no attempt to distinguish those taxes paid to support higher education from those paid to support other government services; they assume that this is a hopeless task in a system in which few taxes are earmarked for specific purposes. As a matter of fact, however, the yield of excise and license taxes in California, which are particularly regressive, cannot be employed to support colleges and universities, and the local funds which support higher education in California rely heavily on estate and gift taxes and on the state income tax, all of which are more progressive than the state tax system as a whole. Moreover, state and local taxes finance only 71 percent of expenditure on higher education in California, the rest (largely research and capital expenditure) coming from the federal government whose tax system is more progressive than the California state tax system (Cohn, Gifford, and Sharkansky 1970: 232).

Apparently, there is some advantage in attempting to allocate among Californian families those taxes paid to support higher education in that state. It is at this point that Pechman begins his argument. He allocates taxes among families in proportion to the costs of each type of tertiary institution in total California government expenditure on higher education, taking into account the fact that all the costs of state colleges and of the University of California are borne entirely by the state government, whereas 60 percent of the costs of junior colleges are borne by local governments in California. To give a single example of his method, consider his treatment of University of California students: subsidies to the University of California account for 7 percent of all state and local tax revenues in 1964; the average tax burden for a relatively poor Californian family with an income of $5,000 in 1964 was $135; 7 percent of $135 equals $9.45, and this sum is conceived as being paid by these families in support of the University of California; but 1.5 percent of these families had a child attending the University of California in receipt of a benefit worth $1,700, and 1.5 percent of $1,700 equals $25.50; since $25.50 minus $9.45 equals $16.05, it follows that there is a positive net transfer of subsidy over taxes paid in this income class (Pechman 1970: 365). Applying similar methods to each of the three types of institutions at every level of family income, Pechman concludes that very poor families (incomes under $4,000) and very rich families (incomes of $12,000 and over) subsidize the education of middle-income families. Once we include families with self-supporting students, however, there is a net redistribution from families with incomes above $12,000 to families with incomes below $12,000 (Pechman 1970: 367*n*); this last point should perhaps be ignored because Pechman assumes incorrectly that self-supporting students nevertheless report their parents' income rather than their own (Hansen and Weisbrod 1971a: 366-367). In one sense therefore, Pechman has *not* reversed the findings of Hansen and Weisbrod: he has severely qualified them and once again demonstrated "Director's Law" (Stigler 1970) of government expenditures: the very poor and the very rich always pay for the public services consumed by the middle classes.[4]

Hansen and Weisbrod, as we have said, compare the median subsidies for four groups of families with and without students in public higher education with the rate of progression of the entire state and local tax system in California. Pechman, on the other hand, calculates the subsidies received by each family income class and allocates the tax burden of higher education across families in proportion to the fraction of the total tax bill at each level of government going to each of the three types of institutions. In effect he assumes that if there were a given change in expenditure on public higher education, it would affect all families in the state equiproportionately. Thus, he weighs the distribution of tax payments by the relative mix of local versus state expenditure on public higher education, and this method applied to Florida at first supported the Hansen–Weisbrod and not the Pechman thesis (Windham 1970). However, this Florida result has been shown to depend on the particular data set employed in which subsidy benefits refer to 1967 but tax burdens to 1961; a recalculation of the data to bring taxes paid out into line with the year in which higher education subsidies are received reproduces the Pechman finding for Florida (Nelson 1981). Moreover, the Pechman

---

4. Hartman (1970: 521) sums up the Californian situation in these words: "(1) Poor people pay taxes and very few of them use public higher education. Those who do gain thereby; those who don't, don't. (2) Middle-income people are heavy users of the system. Their taxes don't cover the costs. (3) A few rich people use the system and gain handsomely thereby. The rest of the rich pay substantial taxes and get no direct return." Using fictitious but representative data from a nine-student world, he neatly constructs an example that generates both the Hansen–Weisbrod and the Pechman conclusions depending on how subsidies and taxes are allocated.

The Distributional Effects of Higher Education Subsidies

thesis has been further confirmed by a study for New York City (Machlis 1973). There is a third method for handling the incidence of net transfer by income classes in which we simply compare the percentage distribution of higher education students by family income classes with the percentage distribution of federal–state–local tax payments by family income classes; this approach sustains the Hansen–Weisbrod thesis in Florida and clearly refutes it in Hawaii, while leaving the California case undecided (Hight and Pollock 1973).

Be that as it may, we are not yet at the end of the story. So far the only kind of higher education subsidy we have considered are subsidies to undergraduate tuition costs. Both Hansen and Weisbrod and Pechman ignore direct financial aid to students in the form of state and federal scholarships and bursaries, which indeed were few and far between in the early 1960s.[5] They increased significantly, however, in the late 1960s, and by 1971 McGuire (1976: 348–349) showed that when we add financial aid to tuition subsidies and take account of both postgraduates and undergraduates, Californian students from wealthy families do *not* receive a greater total subsidy than do students from poor families in any of the three types of public higher education institutions, either on average or in the aggregate: 60 percent of subsidies go to the lower half and 40 percent to the upper half of Californian families by income size. In other words, the total subsidy system is mildly regressive (subsidies fall as a proportion of income as income rises). After this, it requires only a more regressive system of federal, state, and local taxes to produce the Hansen–Weisbrod conclusion. On balance, however, the combined effect of the three tax systems in California is proportional throughout the entire middle range of the distribution of family incomes, being regressive at the very lower end and steeply progressive at the very upper end. The final verdict for the case of California, therefore, is that Hansen and Weisbrod were wrong on almost every method of calculating subsidies and taxes, at least for 1971, if not for 1964 (Hansen and Weisbrod 1978).

Outside of California, most studies have employed some version of the Pechman approach and have invariably replicated his findings (Machovec 1972; Zimmerman 1973; Crean 1975; Moore 1978; Nelson 1981). Nevertheless, the Pechman principle of the equiproportional allocation of taxes remains an arbitrary one that seems to have little justification in either positive or normative maxims of public

---

5. Even the Carnegie Commission Study (CCHE 1973: 44–45) of the redistributive effects of higher education subsidies across all American states ignores financial aid to students.

Economics of Education Review

finance (Hansen and Weisbrod 1971a: 369–371, 1971b, 1972). We are left at the end of this discussion with a frustrated feeling of inconclusiveness: in terms of annual cross-sectional data, it seems possible to classify the data so as to produce more or less whatever conclusion one wishes to reach.

LIFETIME VERSUS ANNUAL INCOMES

The idea of a net transfer calculation is to break the population of households into income classes and then to check whether each class gains more or less in subsidy benefits than it pays out in taxes to support higher education; if the lower income classes receive negative net benefits, while the higher income classes receive positive net benefits, we conclude with Hansen and Weisbrod that higher education subsidies reduce equity.[6] The problem with this approach is essentially the inherent ambiguity of the classification by income classes. For a given generation, each observation consists of a household made up of parents paying taxes and children receiving higher education benefits. But whose income class is relevant — the parents' class or the children's future class? If nuclear families stayed together throughout the working lives of both parents and children, the ambiguity would disappear. But if the incomes of parents and children are only weakly correlated, or, worse still, statistically independent, there will be considerable ambiguity, and a net transfer calculation based on current incomes can then result in the wrong answers.

By focusing on families with children in higher education, we necessarily focus on parents aged thirty-five to sixty at or near the peak of their age-earnings profiles, while excluding the young and the old at or near the bottom of the cross-sectional age-earnings profiles who have no children who are currently being subsidized. Thus, even if the net transfer over the lifetime of all families were in fact zero, it might appear from a cross-sectional point of view that there was a redistribution of funds from the poor to the rich. In the same way, a cross-sectional analysis of old-age assistance programs will almost certainly show a transfer from rich to poor even if old-age pensions are entirely paid for by individuals out of their previous earnings.

---

6. This is what Fields (1975: 245–246) called "the ability-to-pay criterion" for assessing the equity effects of a fiscal program. He contrasts this criterion with two cruder criteria: (1) "the equal-opportunity criterion," according to which different groups in the population have access to a program in strict proportion to their numbers in the population; and (2) "the cost-benefit criterion," according to which the costs paid by different groups in the population are proportional to the benefits they each receive, even though they may have unequal access.

The Distributional Effects of Higher Education Subsidies

Quite apart from the positive merits of a life-cycle approach to higher education subsidies, there is the normative argument that the life-cycle approach alone accounts for the widespread support for programs of public aid to higher education: a large number of families without children or with young children hope some day to benefit from subsidized higher education and are hence willing to commute future costs into a present stream of tax payments.[7]

However, we are left with a positive question of fact: to be sure the benefits of higher education are not enjoyed by the same generation that pays taxes, but are higher education subsidies by family cohorts positively or negatively correlated with subsequent changes in the lifetime distribution of incomes?[8] The necessary and sufficient conditions to infer an income transfer over the lifetimes of family cohorts from a set of annual observations are so stringent as to preclude any categorical answer to the question. As Miklius (1975) has shown, they are that: (1) the lifetime income streams of the rich lie continuously above those of the poor; (2) the lifetime tax streams of the rich lie continuously below those of the poor, meaning that the poor do not only pay a larger proportion of their income as tax than the rich, as they do under any regressive tax system, but a larger absolute amount of tax in every year of their working life; and (3) the rich attend college in greater numbers than the poor and, moreover, their own tax payments are insufficient to finance the tuition costs of their own higher education. It is patently obvious that the second condition is always violated everywhere, from which it follows that it would be foolhardy to rush to conclusions about the lifetime income distributional effects of higher education subsidies simply on the basis of current cross-sectional data about the distribution of taxes and subsidies. It is one thing to establish the Hansen–Weisbrod thesis for one year and quite another to extrapolate it over the lifetimes of those concerned.

We can, however, establish probable lifetime effects in two different ways. The first way is to notice that the reason we find it so difficult to infer lifetime consequences from annual observations is that we lack knowledge of two of the main connecting links: namely, (1) the correlation between a parent's present income and the child's adult income, and (2) the correlation between the child's present

---

7. The case for studying lifetime income distribution from both a positive and a normative point of view is powerfully argued by Layard (1977).

8. Pechman (1970: 368) seems to deny the meaningfulness of this question, arguing, apparently, that parents' willingness to pay taxes that support higher education is unconnected in their minds with the income gains of higher education that their children will someday enjoy; this is at best a highly implausible assumption.

Economics of Education Review

schooling and his or her adult income.[9] If we can establish the Hansen–Weisbrod thesis from current observations, showing that children of higher income parents receive education subsidies that exceed their parents' education taxes, and if both the first and second correlations are significant and relatively large, it would follow as a matter of logic that the original subsidy is highly correlated with the child's adult income, which is to say that higher education subsidies are bound to increase income inequality over time. Conversely, if both correlations are insignificant or significant but relatively small, it would follow that higher education subsidies are dispersed to students in each generation largely at random relative to their later adult incomes; in that case even a system of higher education subsidies, heavily but not exclusively concentrated on wealthier families, might nevertheless have an equalizing effect over time (Conlisk 1977: 154). Now, the first issue is the same as asking whether there is little or much intergenerational social mobility, and the second issue is the same as asking whether the schooling coefficient in an earnings function is significant or insignificant and, if significant, whether it is large or small. It is perfectly true that both questions are difficult to answer decisively and that we lack longitudinal family data to clinch the matter. But that is not to say that we are totally ignorant about these problems and must therefore resign ourselves to agnosticism about the lifetime distributional effects of higher education subsidies.

If we consider the case of Britain, the fact that participation in full-time higher education is confined to 12 percent of the age group of eighteen to twenty-one (as against nearly 50 percent in the United States) and that it is known to be biased in favor of the professional classes even within this small nucleus of less than half a million families,[10] appears to establish the likelihood that the Hansen–Weisbrod cross-sectional thesis is upheld in the British case. But we cannot be sure even of this much. Almost all home students in British higher education have their entire tuition fees paid out of public grants, but in addition, they receive a "maintenance" grant toward their living expenses, which is "means tested" so as to vary inversely with paren-

---

9. We also lack knowledge of the externalities of higher education, in particular the spill-over effects of college graduates on the earned income of high school dropouts and graduates, now and in the future. However, this consideration is largely a red herring as no one has yet been able to demonstrate that the magnitude of these spill-over effects are positive (Blaug 1972: 108–114; Friedman 1980: 178–181).

10. Department of Education and Science (1980). A recent Universities Central Council of Admissions analysis report shows that the fraction of students entering British universities whose parents held manual rather than professional jobs has in recent years declined below the fifty-year-old figure of 25 percent (UCCA 1980).

The Distributional Effects of Higher Education Subsidies

tal incomes. If all British students received identical tuition subsidies, the means-tested system of maintenance grants would therefore guarantee that the Hansen–Weisbrod thesis does not apply to Britain.[11] As a matter of fact, actual costs of instruction and therefore implied tuition subsidies vary widely, partly between universities and polytechnics, but especially between fields of study. If there is any tendency for the children of high-income parents to favor the study of expensive laboratory-based subjects, such as medicine, physics, engineering, and so on, rather than low-cost subjects, such as the liberal arts, the Hansen–Weisbrod thesis might nevertheless be sustained for Britain despite the means-testing of maintenance grants. We lack information on the distribution of subsidies to tuition costs in Britain by levels and fields of study and must therefore remain agnostic about the question. Let us assume, however, for the sake of argument, that the Hansen–Weisbrod thesis applies to Britain. What then follows about the effects on lifetime income distribution?

British sociologists generally argue that there is little intergenerational mobility in Britain, but what little there is tends to be systematically upward (Goldthorpe 1980: 72–73, 250–251; Halsey, Heath, and Ridge 1980: 77, 88). Furthermore, intergenerational mobility in Britain is positively correlated with a child's schooling. The higher the child's level of schooling, the more likely he or she is to move far up the occupational hierarchy away from the position occupied by his or her father; similarly, schooling contributes the most and father's occupation the least in explaining occupational differences among fathers and children. All this is to say that there is nothing random about intergenerational mobility in Britain and that schooling does to some extent act as an avenue of social mobility (Psacharopoulos 1977: 330–331; Goldthorpe 1980; 54–57, 66).[12]

We are thus left in doubt as to our first question referring to the correlation between a parent's present income and the child's adult income. As we have said, to make safe inferences about lifetime income distributional effects from current observations of the incidence of taxes and subsidies, we require little or no intergenerational mobility and, above all, little or no intergenerational mobility which is systematically related to parental circumstances, including the schooling of children. Our findings for Britain suggest that higher education subsidies do act to promote intergenerational mobility,

---

11. See the Appendix for details.
12. The American findings are very similar to the British ones; see Treiman and Terrell (1975).

Economics of Education Review

however weakly, and to that extent they *may* work to equalize life-time incomes.

Turning to the second question, we note that correlation between present schooling and future income in Britain is positive and signifi-cant around 0.3, exceeding the correlation of 0.16 between family background and earnings (Psacharopoulos 1977: 323; also Psacharo-poulos and Tinbergen 1978: 510–511; Layard and Zabalza 1979: 141–142). Whether 0.3 is a large enough correlation to justify the conclusion that higher education subsidies are disequalizing in a life-cycle perspective remains an open question.

There is another way of attacking this problem of making life-cycle inferences about the distributional effects of higher education subsidies. In replying to Pechman, Hansen and Weisbrod (1971a: 364–365*n*) write:

> No one knows whether the rate of return on higher education varies systematically by income class of students. . . . until evi-dence is obtained, however, we see no justification for assum-ing, as Pechman seems to suggest, that the income distribution effects of subsidies is either uncorrelated or negatively corre-lated with subsequent changes in the lifetime distribution of earnings.

They go on to note that "if the price elasticity of college-going is greater (absolutely) for lower-income—as seems probable—then a shift of subsidies from the non-needy to the needy would narrow the distribution of lifetime income unless rates of return on higher edu-cation are correlated in a *strongly* negative manner with parental income." But the latter proviso is, surely, the wrong way round? If the private rate of return is negatively correlated with parental in-come, it is lower for students from wealthy families than for students from poor families, and this is just the situation in which a shift of subsidies toward poorer students will indeed tend to equalize the dis-tribution of lifetime income.

It is when private rates of return to higher education are positively correlated with parental income that subsidies to poorer students may nevertheless increase the degree of inequality in the lifetime dis-tribution of income. The same thought may be expressed in terms of the difference between private and social rates of return to higher education when these are cross-classified by levels of family income. This gap between the two rates across family incomes is *almost* a pre-cise measure of the size distribution of net subsidies, since the two rates differ on the cost side by public subsidies to different levels of education, and on the earnings side by the taxes paid out of higher

The Distributional Effects of Higher Education Subsidies

incomes. (If the latter were the only source of government revenues, the difference between the two rates of return by family income levels would be a *precise* measure of the redistributive effects of public subsidies to education.) However, if the gap between the two rates increases with rising family incomes, this does indeed suggest that net subsidies are positively related to income levels, and conversely for a decreasing gap between the two rates as we move up the income distribution.

Unfortunately, as Hansen and Weisbrod said, "No one knows whether the rate of return on higher education varies systematically by income class of students." Nevertheless, there is some suggestive evidence from France that the private rates of return to higher education are indeed greater for students whose fathers are in the professions than for those whose fathers are in blue-collar jobs (Eicher 1979: 127).[13] This is not a finding that is intuitively obvious: if an advantageous family background raises the future earnings of a graduate beyond those of the average graduate, it also raises the earnings he or she foregoes to obtain higher education, and these two tendencies may well cancel out, leaving the yield of a degree invariant to parental incomes. At any rate, if these findings for France were duplicated elsewhere, they would constitute the strongest grounds we have yet found for believing that any tendency to subsidize rich students at the expense of poor students affects lifetime incomes in the same way that it affects current incomes.

CONCLUSIONS

To determine the distributional effects of higher education subsidies in a country we must, first of all, determine the degree of progression of both taxes and subsidies. The Hansen-Weisbrod thesis is, in effect, that the tax system in California is regressive throughout all ranges of income, while the higher education subsidy system is progressive again throughout all ranges of income. The degree of regression (progression) of a tax system is traditionally expressed in terms of a falling (rising) ratio of tax to income levels, or, alternatively expressed, a falling (rising) ratio of the marginal to average tax rate with successively higher income levels; the degree of progression or regression of a subsidy system can be similarly expressed. Figure 1 shows the Hansen and Weisbrod argument: the rich fall to the right

---

13. There is also evidence for Brazil, showing that private rates of return to *primary* education rise with family income levels (Jallade 1977: 7).

Economics of Education Review

FIGURE 1.   DEGREE OF PROGRESSION OF THE TAX AND SUBSIDY
                          SYSTEMS OF CALIFORNIA.

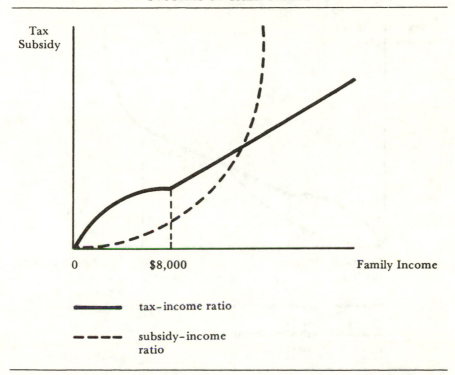

of the intersection of the two curves, and the poor to the left of the intersection.

If the tax system were proportional throughout all ranges of income, it would be shown as a straight line coming out of the origin. Hansen and Weisbrod argued that the California tax system is regressive at family income levels below $8,000 (in 1965) and proportional thereafter; but, provided that the subsidy system is progressive so that the subsidy-income curve cuts the tax-income line from below, the precise incidence of the tax system makes no difference to their argument. We have seen that the combined federal-state-local tax system in most American states is regressive in the first one or two deciles of the income distribution, then proportional right up to the eighth or ninth decile, and steeply progressive in the last two deciles. This trend is depicted in Figure 2.

Once again, this does not affect the Hansen-Weisbrod thesis, provided that the subsidy system is indeed more steeply progressive than the tax system in the last two deciles of the income distribution: if

The Distributional Effects of Higher Education Subsidies

FIGURE 2.   DEGREE OF PROGRESSION OF THE TAX AND SUBSIDY
SYSTEMS IN ALL AMERICAN STATES.

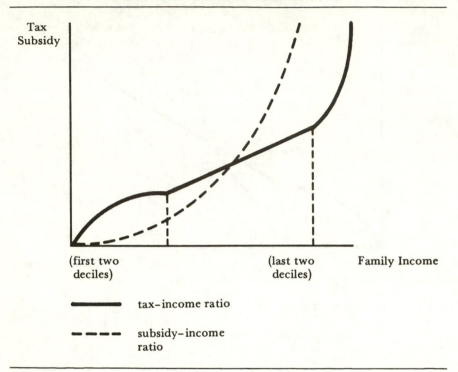

tax–income ratio

subsidy–income
ratio

the very rich receive a net transfer of subsidy over tax, the Hansen–
Weisbrod thesis is confirmed. It is clear from this analysis that the
Hansen–Weisbrod thesis may hold in one country but not necessarily
in another.

We switch now to the lifetime implications. Higher education
tends to raise lifetime incomes, and it is possible to imagine a tax system so steeply progressive that every graduate eventually repays the
costs of his own subsidized higher education out of the extra taxes
paid on his augmented income. In that kind of world, we can conceive of higher education subsidies as nothing more than society's
peculiar way of lending students the wherewithal to participate in
higher education, the costs of which will be fully recouped in the
course of the graduate's working life. But this is not the world in
which we live. No tax system is so progressive that graduates, whatever the income-raising power of higher education, ever pay back the
costs of their education to the community (Hansen and Weisbrod
1969b: 59). It follows that higher education subsidies always involve

223

some transfer of income from the less to the more educated, from those who fail to receive higher education to those who do. And since the unequal incidence of higher education subsidies necessarily results in unequal effects on future incomes, we can hardly escape a life-cycle approach to the distributional effects of higher education subsidies.

To gauge these life-cycle effects we need to form a judgment on (1) the magnitude of the tendency of schooling to raise future incomes, and (2) the degree to which opportunities to gain additional schooling are or are not related to parental incomes, that is, the degree to which schooling provides an avenue for upward social mobility. The more powerful the impact of schooling on income, and the lower the rate of intergenerational mobility, the greater is the chance that higher education subsidies will have perverse effects on lifetime income distribution. I have little doubt that, in a country like Britain, or for that matter most of Europe, the burden of proof is on those who would pretend that current subsidies to higher education work to equalize the distribution of lifetime incomes. I am less sure that the same burden-of-proof argument also applies to the United States. At any rate, there can be little doubt that if current subsidies were increasingly directed by income-related "means tests" exclusively toward low-income students, say, by full-cost fees and subsidized student loans repayable as a proportion of future income, the results would almost certainly be better in terms of equality than is the present system. Appraisals of the redistributive effects of current methods of subsidizing higher education are only a prelude to the task of devising a new and more equitable system of subsidies (see Hansen and Weisbrod 1971c; Hartman 1972; Pechman 1972; and Nelson 1981).

APPENDIX: BRITISH MAINTENANCE GRANTS

For reasons stated in the text, it is not possible to compare the distribution of total subsidies to higher education in the United Kingdom by family incomes with the distribution of direct and indirect taxes by family incomes. What is possible to compare is the distribution of maintenance grants with the distribution of total tax burdens, keeping in mind the fact that maintenance grants only constitute, on the average, about a quarter of total subsidies to higher education.

For the current year, 1980–81, the maintenance award to any full-time student on a first-degree course at a British university or

The Distributional Effects of Higher Education Subsidies

polytechnic varies from a minimum sum of £385 paid to everyone regardless of their parents' income to a maximum sum of £1,695 if the student lives in London, with amounts for students outside London varying between these two extremes, depending on whether they are living at home or away at college. For a student who is under twenty-five and unmarried, the means test takes account of his own income and that of his parents. In practice, however, because of a number of exclusions from a student's income, in the vast majority of cases it is only parental income that counts.

The precise level of the income-related supplement that is added to the minimum grant of £385 depends not on parents' income before or after tax, but on their "residual income" in the previous financial year after deducting a number of allowances from their gross income from all sources. The most common deductions are £65 for each additional child, mortgage interest payments, life insurance premiums, and pension payments. To this calculated residual income a scale is applied, which starts at £5,800 and then falls continuously with higher incomes up to £18,000, at which point the minimum level of award of £385 applies to all higher income levels. The effect of the scale is to create a system in which subsidies to living expenses are regressive, in the sense of falling continuously as a fraction of family incomes, at least up to gross family incomes of £20,000 (see Table 1, column 5).

Parents are legally obligated to make up what the student loses, so that the scale of parental contributions is the other side of the coin of the scale of student awards. The scale of parental contributions is progressive, again up to levels of gross family incomes of £20,000 (see Table 1, column 6).

Unfortunately, evidence on the proportion of students receiving grants of various magnitudes is not yet available for 1980–81, and without that it is difficult to draw any significant conclusions about the distributional effects of the means-tested grants system. The most recent information available is from 1976–77, which indicated that the fraction of students from very rich families receiving no more than the minimum award was only about 5 percent of all students; at the lower end of the distribution, some 25 percent of students receive the maximum award because their parents are poor (see Table 2). Evidently, the vast majority of British higher education students come from families with gross incomes below £20,000 (in 1980). Needless to say, the median income of families with children in higher education (£3,400 in 1977) exceeds that of the median income of all families (£2,600 in 1977).

Economics of Education Review

TABLE 1. MISCELLANEOUS DATA ON MAINTENANCE GRANTS, 1960–81.					
1	*2*	*3*	*4*	*5*	*6*
Assumed Residual Income	*Mainte-nance Grant*	*Parental Contribu-tions*	*Estimated Gross Parental Income*	*Ratio of Grant to Gross Income*	*Ratio of Parental Contribution to Gross Income*
(£)	(£)	(£)	(£)	(£)	(£)
0	1,520	0	0	—	—
1,000	1,520	0	1,000	1.52	0
2,000	1,520	0	2,000	0.76	0
3,000	1,520	0	3,000	0.51	0
3,900	1,520	0	4,000	0.38	0
4,800	1,520	0	5,000	0.30	0
5,700	1,520	0	6,000	0.25	0
6,600	1,451	69	7,000	0.21	1.0
7,500	1,326	194	8,000	0.17	2.4
8,400	1,213	307	9,000	0.13	3.4
9,300	1,101	419	10,000	0.11	4.2
10,200	988	532	11,000	0.09	4.8
11,100	876	644	12,000	0.07	5.4
12,000	782	738	13,000	0.06	5.7
12,900	713	807	14,000	0.05	5.8
13,800	644	876	15,000	0.04	5.8
15,900	482	1,037	17,500	0.03	5.9
18,000	385	1,135	20,000	0.02	5.7
20,500	385	1,135	22,500	0.02	5.0
23,000	385	1,135	25,500	0.02	4.3
25,500	385	1,135	28,000	0.01	4.0
28,000	385	1,135	31,100	0.01	3.7
30,500	385	1,135	33,500	0.01	3.4
33,000	385	1,135	36,000	0.01	3.1

Notes: The maintenance grant in column 2 is a weighted average of grants to students in London and elsewhere, living at or away from home. Gross parental contributions in column 4 are estimated by assuming that all parents are married, have one additional dependent child, and incur mortgage, life assurance and pension payments, which increase by ever larger amounts from zero on gross incomes of £3,000 or less to £2,000 on incomes of £20,000 and £3,000 on incomes of £31,000 or more.

Source: Data for the first three columns were supplied by the U.K. Department of Education and Science.

The Distributional Effects of Higher Education Subsidies

TABLE 2.   DISTRIBUTION OF STUDENTS IN 1976–77
BY PARENTS' RESIDUAL INCOME, 1975–76.

Assumed Residual Income (£)	Assessed Parental Contribution (£)	Percentage of Students		
		University	Further Education	Total
Under 2,700	0	21.1	29.5	25.4
2,700–2,804	30–50	1.8	2.5	2.2
2,805–3,054	51–100	3.8	5.1	4.5
3,055–3,304	101–150	4.4	5.4	5.0
3,305–3,554	151–200	5.3	6.0	5.7
3,555–3,804	201–250	5.5	5.9	5.7
3,805–4,054	251–300	5.4	5.7	5.6
4,055–4,409	301–350	6.3	6.4	6.3
4,410–4,909	351–400	7.2	7.3	7.3
4,910–5,909	401–500	11.4	9.9	10.7
5,910–6,909	501–600	7.7	5.7	6.7
6,910–7,909	601–700	5.3	3.3	4.3
7,910–8,909	701–800	3.5	1.9	2.7
8,910–9,909	801–900	2.2	1.0	1.6
9,910–10,909	901–1,000	1.3	0.6	0.9
10,910–11,909	1,001–1,100	0.5	0.2	0.4
11,910–12,909	1,101–1,200	0.2	0.1	0.1
12,910 or over	1,201 or more	0.3	0.1	0.2
Minimum awards	—	6.6	3.4	4.9
Total		100.0	100.0	100.0

Source: Department of Education and Science (1977: 34), Table 19.

In practice, the progressivity of parental contributions to the maintenance grant is lessened by the operation of covenanting schemes under which the parents of a higher education student undertake to give their offspring a certain amount of money per annum for a fixed period, during which the student remains in education. The student in question can then claim back the tax paid on the sum covenanted at the standard rate of 30 percent. This has the effect that parents pay only 70 percent of the assessed contribution toward maintenance grants. The significance of covenanting for the overall progressivity of the system is dependent on how widespread the practice is and on whether it is more common among rich than among poor parents. No information on either the level or the incidence of covenanting schemes is available in Britain.

Economics of Education Review

As for the tax system, the personal income tax is progressive over the entire range of income, but the rest of the tax system contains a number of extremely regressive taxes (Kay and Kay 1980: 215–216). One recent study (Pechman 1980: 218) concluded that if both incomes and taxes are comprehensively defined, the U.K. tax system is regressive for the bottom quarter of the income distribution; it becomes slightly progressive up to the median income of £2,900 (in 1978), then turns regressive again from the median to the ninety-sixth percentile, and becomes progressive once again in the top four percentiles.

Everything depends, therefore, on the precise distribution of total higher education subsidies, on which question, as we have explained in the text, it is impossible to arrive at an answer. Hence, we are unable either to verify or refute the Hansen–Weisbrod thesis for Britain.

REFERENCES

Blaug, Mark/1972
AN INTRODUCTION TO THE ECONOMICS OF EDUCATION. London: Penguin Books.

Carnegie Commission on Higher Education (CCHE)/1973
HIGHER EDUCATION: WHO PAYS? WHO BENEFITS? WHO SHOULD PAY? A REPORT AND RECOMMENDATIONS. New York: McGraw-Hill.

Cohn, Elchanan; Adam Gifford; and Ira Sharkansky/1970
BENEFITS AND COSTS OF HIGHER EDUCATION AND INCOME REDISTRIBUTION: THREE COMMENTS. *Journal of Human Resources* 5, no. 1 (Spring): 222–236.

Cohn, Elchanan/1979
THE ECONOMICS OF EDUCATION. 2nd ed. Cambridge, MA: Ballinger.

Conlisk, John/1977
A FURTHER LOOK AT THE HANSEN–WEISBROD–PECHMAN DEBATE. *Journal of Human Resources* 12, no. 2 (Spring): 147–163.

Crean, John F./1975
THE INCOME REDISTRIBUTIVE EFFECTS OF PUBLIC SPENDING ON HIGHER EDUCATION. *Journal of Human Resources* 10, no. 1 (Winter): 116–121.

Department of Education and Science/1980
TRENDS IN ENTRY TO FULL-TIME HIGHER EDUCATION, STATISTICAL BULLETIN 12. London: DES.

Department of Education and Science/1977
STATISTICS OF EDUCATION 1977, vol. 5. London: HMSO.

Eicher, Jean-Claude, and others/1979
ECONOMIQUE DE L'ÉDUCATION. Paris: Economica.

The Distributional Effects of Higher Education Subsidies

Fields, Gary S./1975
HIGHER EDUCATION AND INCOME DISTRIBUTION IN A LESS DEVELOPED COUNTRY. *Oxford Economic Papers* 27, no. 2 (July): 245-259.

Friedman, Milton and Rose/1980
FREE TO CHOOSE. A PERSONAL STATEMENT. London: Secker & Warburg.

Goldthorpe, John H./1980
SOCIAL MOBILITY AND CLASS STRUCTURE IN BRITAIN. Oxford: Clarendon Press.

Halsey, A.H.; Arthur F. Heath; and John M. Ridge/1980
ORIGINS AND DESTINATIONS: FAMILY, CLASS, AND EDUCATION IN MODERN BRITAIN. Oxford: Clarendon Press.

Hansen, W. Lee/1970
INCOME DISTRIBUTION EFFECTS OF HIGHER EDUCATION. *American Economic Review* 60, no. 2 (May): 335-340.

Hansen, W. Lee, and Burton A. Weisbrod/1969a
THE DISTRIBUTION OF THE COSTS AND BENEFITS OF PUBLIC HIGHER EDUCATION: THE CASE OF CALIFORNIA. *Journal of Human Resources* 4, no. 2 (Spring): 176-191.

Hanson, W. Lee, and Burton A. Weisbrod/1969b
BENEFITS, COSTS, AND FINANCE OF PUBLIC HIGHER EDUCATION. Chicago: Markham.

Hanson, W. Lee, and Burton A. Weisbrod/1971a
ON THE DISTRIBUTION OF COSTS AND BENEFITS OF PUBLIC HIGHER EDUCATION: REPLY. *Journal of Human Resources* 6, no. 3 (Summer): 363-376.

Hanson, W. Lee, and Burton A. Weisbrod/1971b
WHO PAYS FOR A PUBLIC EXPENDITURE PROGRAM? *National Tax Journal* 24, no. 2 (November): 515-517.

Hansen, W. Lee, and Burton A. Weisbrod/1971c
A NEW APPROACH TO HIGHER EDUCATION FINANCE. In *Financing Higher Education: Alternatives for the Federal Government*, edited by M.O. Orwig, pp. 206-236. Iowa City: American College Testing Program.

Hansen, W. Lee, and Burton A. Weisbrod/1972
DISTRIBUTIONAL EFFECTS OF PUBLIC EXPENDITURE PROGRAMS. *Public Finances* 27, no. 4: 414-420.

Hansen, W. Lee, and Burton A. Weisbrod/1978.
THE DISTRIBUTION OF SUBSIDIES TO STUDENTS IN CALIFORNIA PUBLIC HIGHER EDUCATION: REPLY. *Journal of Human Resources* 13, no. 1 (Winter): 137-141.

Hartman, Robert W./1970
A COMMENT ON THE PECHMAN-HANSEN-WEISBROD CONTROVERSY. *Journal of Human Resources* 5, no. 4 (Fall): 519-523.

Hartman, Robert W./1972
EQUITY IMPLICATIONS OF STATE TUITION POLICY AND STUDENT LOANS. *Journal of Political Economy* 80, no. 3, part 2 (May/June): S142-S71.

Economics of Education Review

Hight, Joseph E., and Richard Pollock/1973
INCOME DISTRIBUTION EFFECTS OF HIGHER EDUCATION EXPENDITURES IN CALIFORNIA, FLORIDA, AND HAWAII. *Journal of Human Resources* 8, no. 3 (Summer): 318–330.

Jallade, Jean-Paul/1974
PUBLIC EXPENDITURES ON EDUCATION AND INCOME DISTRIBUTION IN COLOMBIA, World Bank Staff Occasional Papers No. 18. Baltimore: John Hopkins.

Jallade, Jean-Paul/1977
BASIC EDUCATION AND INCOME INEQUALITY IN BRAZIL: THE LONG-TERM VIEW, World Bank Staff Working Paper No. 268. Washington, D.C.: World Bank.

Kay, John A., and Melvin A. King/1980
THE BRITISH TAX SYSTEM. 2nd ed. Oxford: Oxford University Press.

Layard, Richard/1977
ON MEASURING THE REDISTRIBUTION OF LIFETIME INCOME. In *Economics of Public Services*, edited by M.S. Feldstein and R. Inman, pp. 172–198. New York: Macmillan.

Layard, Richard, and Antoni Zabalza/1979
FAMILY INCOME DISTRIBUTION: EXPLANATION AND POLICY EVALUATION. *Journal of Political Economy* 87, no. 5, part 2 (October): S133–S162.

Machlis, Peter D./1973
THE DISTRIBUTION EFFECTS OF PUBLIC HIGHER EDUCATION IN NEW YORK CITY. *Public Finance Quarterly* 1, no. 1 (January): 35–57.

Machovec, Frank M./1972
PUBLIC HIGHER EDUCATION IN COLORADO: WHO PAYS THE COSTS? WHO RECEIVES THE BENEFITS? *Intermountain Economic Review* 3, no. 2 (Fall): 24–35.

McGuire, Joseph W./1976
THE DISTRIBUTION OF SUBSIDY TO STUDENTS IN CALIFORNIA PUBLIC HIGHER EDUCATION. *Journal of Human Resources* 11, no. 3 (Summer): 343–353.

Miklius, Walter/1975
THE DISTRIBUTIONAL EFFECTS OF PUBLIC HIGHER EDUCATION: A COMMENT. *Higher Education* 4: 351–355.

Moore, Gary A./1978
EQUITY EFFECTS OF HIGHER EDUCATION FINANCE AND TUITION GRANTS IN NEW YORK STATE. *Journal of Human Resources* 13, no. 4 (Fall): 482–501.

Pechman, Joseph A./1970
THE DISTRIBUTIONAL EFFECTS OF PUBLIC HIGHER EDUCATION IN CALIFORNIA. *Journal of Human Resources* 5, no. 3 (Summer): 361–370.

Pechman, Joseph A./1972
A NOTE ON THE INTERGENERATIONAL TRANSFER OF PUBLIC HIGHER-EDUCATION BENEFITS. *Journal of Political Economy* 80, no. 3, part 2 (May/June): S256–S59.

Pechman, Joseph A./1980
TAXATION. In *Britain's Economic Performance*, edited by R.E. Caves and L.B. Krause, pp. 183–216. Washington, D.C.: Brookings Institution.

The Distributional Effects of Higher Education Subsidies

Psacharopoulos, George/1977a
FAMILY BACKGROUND, EDUCATION AND ACHIEVEMENT. *British Journal of Sociology* 28, no. 3 (September): 321–335.

Psacharopoulos, George/1977b
THE PERVERSE EFFECTS OF PUBLIC SUBSIDIZATION OF EDUCATION OR HOW EQUITABLE IS FREE EDUCATION? *Comparative Education Review* 21, no. 1 (February): 69–90.

Psacharopoulos, George/1978
ECONOMICS OF EDUCATION: AN ASSESSMENT OF RECENT METHODOLOGICAL ADVANCES AND EMPIRICAL RESULTS. *Social Science Information* 16, no. 3/4: 351–371.

Psacharopoulos, George, and Jan Tinbergen/1978
ON THE EXPLANATION OF SCHOOLING, OCCUPATION AND EARNINGS: SOME ALTERNATIVE PATH ANALYSES. *De Economist* 126, no. 4: 505–520.

Selowsky, Marcel/1979
WHO BENEFITS FROM GOVERNMENT EXPENDITURE? A CASE STUDY OF COLOMBIA. New York: Oxford University Press.

Stigler, George J./1970
DIRECTOR'S LAW OF PUBLIC INCOME REDISTRIBUTION. *Journal of Law and Economics* 13, no. 1 (April): 1–10.

Treiman, David J., and Keith Terrell/1975
THE PROCESS OF STATUS ATTAINMENT IN THE UNITED STATES AND GREAT BRITAIN. *American Journal of Sociology* 81, no. 3 (November): 563–583.

Universities Central Council of Admissions/1980
STATISTICAL SUPPLEMENT TO THE 17TH REPORT 1972–79. Cheltenham: UCCA.

Windham, Douglas M./1970
EDUCATION, EQUALITY AND INCOME REDISTRIBUTION. Lexington, MA: Heath Lexington Books.

Zimmerman, Dennis/1973
EXPENDITURE-TAX INCIDENCE STUDIES, PUBLIC HIGHER EDUCATION, AND EQUITY. *National Tax Journal* 26, no. 1 (March): 65–70.

[10]

Mark Blaug

Declining Subsidies to Higher Education: An Economic Analysis

I. Introduction

As a result of the baby boom of the 1950s, most industrialised countries are now facing falling enrolments in primary schools, which is
soon to be followed by falling enrolments in secondary schools. At the
same time, and years before the decline in enrolments will have
reached the tertiary levels of the educational system, almost all industrialised countries have started to cut back on higher education
spending. Indeed, there is now a general consensus throughout the
Western World that the 1980s will be a decade in which the continual
expansion of higher education, which characterised the 1960s and
1970s, will be more or less brought to a halt, if not actually reversed.

Lower financial budgets will force higher education institutions to tap
alternative public and private sources of funding, to find new ways of
raising fees and to explore new systems of student aid. There will be
increased pressures to make colleges and universities more accountable to social and economic needs, meaning that the age-old cry for
vocational rather than academic higher education will be heard even
more frequently than before. In addition, the current trends towards
enrolling more adult students will generate pressures to lower admission standards and to alter traditional modes of study. A contracting
system soon discovers that job security for academic staff reduces
financial flexibility. No wonder then that tenure rules have already
come under fire and may be drastically revised in the years to come.
Likewise, contraction will almost certainly involve a new balance between teaching and research, accompanied by the call for problem-
oriented rather than basic research. These strains in the system
have made themselves felt just about everywhere in Europe and America. Possible exceptions are France and Norway, which have recently
announced plans for expanding higher education in the near future. But
elsewhere in Canada, the United States, Japan, the United Kingdom,
and the continent of Europe, the trend towards cutting back on public
expenditure on higher education and towards restricting the autonomy
of higher education institutions over courses, staffing, and student
numbers appears to be inexorable.

126

Can economics say anything about this current trend and, in particular, can we show on strictly economic grounds that reductions in the
level of spending on higher education are either deplorable or desirable? A brief answer to that question is: very little. Economics has
much to say about the form which subsidies to higher education ought
to take but almost nothing about the appropriate level of these subsidies: we can no more show that subsidy levels in the 1960s and 1970s
were too high than that they are now too low. Those who wish to defend colleges and universities against the New Philistinism will, I am
afraid, have to look outside economics for allies.

II. The Efficiency Case for Subsidising Higher Education

The economist's case for subsidising higher education is based on the
familiar argument that the production of certain goods and services
is subject to "market failures", which inhibit the attainment of Pareto
optimality. The list of these market failures usually includes (1) consumer ignorance, (2) technical economies of scale, (3) externalities
in production and/or consumption, (4) "public goods", and (5) inherent
imperfections in capital and insurance markets. The first two, consumer ignorance and economies of scale, have little relevance to education and certainly do not apply to higher education[1]. If we treat
"public goods", that is, non-rival and non-excludable goods, as an
extreme version of the case of unrecouped externalities, we are left
with two out of the five market failures, namely, externalities and
imperfections in capital and insurance markets, both of which appear
to be relevant to the production and consumption of higher education.

Let us take first the question of the externalities, spillovers, or
"neighbourhood effects" of higher education. An economist would begin by distinguishing real from pecuniary externalities, and marginal
from total externalities, concluding that the externalities of higher
education, whatever they are, must ultimately take the form of raising the productivity and/or psychic satisfaction of Smith in sole consequence of the higher education of Jones. This is not, however, how
the question of externalities of higher education is usually posed. Typically, the real, marginal externalities of higher education are con-

---

[1] I argue this at length in my "Introduction to the Economics of Education"
[1971, pp. 103 ff.].

127

fused with the much wider question of whether higher education produces "social" benefits over and above the private economic benefits
to university graduates. Thus, evidence that higher education changes
the attitudes and values of the average graduate, making him or her
more inclined to be politically "liberal" - meaning more inclined to
vote for politicians who favour government intervention in economic
affairs - has nothing whatever to do with the alleged "market failure" of privately financed higher education. No doubt, higher education has all sorts of consequences, some of which are even desirable,
but so has going to work at 18 and that is hardly a reason for subsidising wage employment. What we have to show is not that higher education has many unintended social consequences, because so does every
other human activity, but that these consequences have economic value
and are functionally related to the size of the higher education system. The literature on this question, even when it is written by economists, frequently ignores all such elementary considerations[1].

Having spelled out the nature of the real, marginal externalities of
higher education, the next problem is to quantify them, at least or-
dinally if not cardinally, if only to ensure that the positive externalities outweigh the negative ones. But as the Carnegie Commission on
Higher Education [1973, p. 180] in the United States admits: "no precise - or even imprecise - methods exist to assess the individual and
societal benefits of higher education as against the private and public
costs." The failure on the part of almost all investigators to measure
any of the externalities of higher education has produced a new scepticism about their magnitude: in the 1960s the standard view was that
the externalities were large in relation to the private benefits of higher education but the new consensus, at least for advanced countries,
is that they may well be negligibly small [Friedman, Friedman, 1980,
pp. 178 f.]. For one thing, the so-called "screening hypothesis", if
true, implies that higher education generates negative external effects
in the sense that every successful graduate blocks someone else from
a preferred position in the queue for high-paying jobs; in other words,
higher education is merely what Fred Hirsch [1977, pp. 41 ff.] has
called a "positional good". The "screening hypothesis" is clearly not
the whole story [Layard, Psacharopoulos, 1974], but it may be part
of the story, reminding us that the externalities of higher education

---

[1] See Davis [1970]; Hartman [1973]; Mundel [1973]; and, the most notorious example of all, Bowen [1977, especially Ch. 14]. For more careful expositions of the nature of the externalities of higher education, see
Blaug [1971, pp. 107 ff.] and the references cited there; Windham [1979];
and Friedman, Friedman [1980, pp. 178 ff.].

128

are by no means necessarily positive. But even if they were, the fact remains that we can ascribe no number to the externalities of higher education and hence cannot say how much to subidise higher education so as to reduce these externalities to zero.

That brings us to imperfections in capital and insurance markets. Because a non-slave society prohibits people from selling rights to their future labour services, individuals cannot offer a lien on their personal services as collateral against a loan to finance a personal investment in schooling. Even if the personal returns on that investment were expected with perfect certainty, there are no wholly effective legal mechanisms for extracting a repayment of that loan. In addition, however, the variance in private returns to post-compulsory education (education beyond the level required by law) is so large relative to the mean return that the inability to repay a study loan in some individual cases would be almost as large a problem as the unwillingness to repay it. It follows that a private capital market will require a large risk-premium in addition to the market rate of interest, such that student loans will only be available at, say, two to three times the average private rate of return to higher education; at such interest rates, the demand for student loans will be exceedingly small. The problem is one of launching a student loan scheme at a scale large enough to pool risks and so reduce the risk premium. It is in this sense, and only in this sense, that private capital markets for study loans are "imperfect". A student loans scheme, artificially created as a matter of deliberate public policy, may nevertheless be able to employ the funds of the commercial banking system to finance the scheme if the government guarantees all repayments. It is this guarantee which then constitutes the subsidy to higher education. If, in addition, it is argued that student loans must be available at rates below the market rate of interest, there is an additional element of subsidy to higher education in the form of a payment by the government to commercial banks to bridge the gap in the two rates. Notice, however, that the latter subsidy has nothing whatever to do with the inherent imperfections of capital markets but must rather derive from the prior judgement that higher education generates externalities. In either case, however, it is easy to see that economic analysis leads only to a qualitative judgement in favour of public subsidies to higher education but not to any quantitative judgement as to the magnitude of these subsidies.

III. Other Grounds for Subsidising Higher Education

So far, we have only examined what economists like to call "efficiency arguments" for subsidising higher education. In addition, however, there are equity arguments for subsidising higher education resting on the principle of equal educational opportunities, which undoubtedly weigh more heavily with governments and the general public than the efficiency arguments beloved by economists. Since subsidies to promote equity allow wealthy as well as poor students to obtain an inexpensive education, it remains an open question whether higher education subsidies in the United States and elsewhere have actually had the effect of promoting social mobility and greater equality of income distribution. Starting with the work of Lee Hansen and Burt Weisbrod in 1969 on public higher education in California, a long but confusing discussion, largely focussed on the United States but also covering France and one or two Third World countries, has more or less concluded on a note of general agnosticism: the net redistributive effects of higher education subsidies remain uncertain everywhere; at best, one may say that current patterns of subsidies nowhere achieve the dramatic improvements in income distribution that they were intended to achieve[1]. This is not to say, therefore, that a case for subsidising higher education cannot be constructed on equity grounds but merely that the form in which higher education is subsidised - tuition grants to institutions rather than to students, maintenance grants to students rather than loans, tax relief to parents rather than direct aid to students, etc. - matters more for equity than the total level of the subsidy. Once again, we find that economic analysis has little to contribute to the current controversy about the cutbacks in public expenditure on higher education.

This completes our discussion of valid economic arguments for subsidising higher education. But there are yet other invalid arguments which invoke the authority of economists. A principal example of such invalid arguments is the notion that education has been shown to contribute to economic growth and hence that any public policy designed to stimulate growth must include measures to step up participation rates in higher education. Obviously, this contention is a non sequitur:

---

[1] For a review of the literature, see Blaug [1982]. For evidence that the social class composition of the higher education student population has not significantly altered in America and Western Europe since 1965, see Cerych and Jallade [1981].

130

it may be granted that education contributes to growth but so do many
other activities and what must be shown is, not that education contributes to growth, but that more education would contribute more to
growth at the margin than more health, more housing, more roads,
etc.

All discussions of the question whether education contributes to economic growth sooner or later come back to Edward Denison's book
on "The Sources of Economic Growth in the United States" [1962], followed by his study of "Why Growth Rates Differ" [1967]. Much doubt
has been thrown on Denison's framework, involving as it does the implicit estimate of an aggregate production function of the Cobb-Douglas
type coupled with the arbitrary assumption of neutral technical progress[1]. But even if we waive all such objections, it is interesting to
note that even Denison himself concludes that intercountry differences
in educational levels of the workforce do not help to explain much of
the differences in postwar growth rates experienced by industrialised
countries [Denison, 1967, pp. 78, 113 f., 199].

Thus, Denison found that the United Kingdom in 1960 was ahead of the
rest of Europe and neck-to-neck with the United States in terms of the
number of years of schooling embodied in the labour force. If we update Denison's figures to 1978, the United Kingdom with its low growth
rate still stands ahead of every country in Europe, falling only slightly below the United States, whereas West Germany with its high growth
rate remains well behind both the United Kingdom and the United States
[Daly, 1981]. To be sure, such gross comparisons conceal important
differences in the distribution of education in the labour force. Thus,
the United Kingdom has a lower starting age for education than almost
any country in the world, which alone tends to raise the average
amount of education in the British labour force to about eleven years.
Similarly, the United States has a much larger proportion of the population with less than nine years of schooling and a much larger proportion with 14-15 years of education than either the United Kingdom or
West Germany. Moreover, Denison entirely omits part-time education, which differs more radically between countries than full-time education. Indeed, it has been argued that the German system of com-
pelling all those who are not in full-time schooling between the ages
of 15 and 18 to attend a vocational school one day a week, including
an elaborate network of vocational training schemes for shop floor
workers, is at least in part responsible for the higher productivity

---

[1] For this and other criticisms, see Nelson [1973].

rates of many German industries compared to British ones [Prais, 1981].

Be that as it may, all growth accounting of the Denison variety at best succeeds in showing what education contributes to earnings differentials between people, which leaves open the question whether such earnings differences reflect changes in the productivity of individuals brought about by schooling or the so-called "screening" or filtering function of the educational system, in effect redistributing a given growth capacity among the participants in the process. If education plays an important role in promoting economic growth, as is so often claimed, it has to be said that the models so far examined in the growth-accounting literature fail utterly to explain the mechanism by which this effect is produced.

We come back to the more fundamental objection that growth accounting ignores the costs of resources invested in the educational system and thus tells us nothing about the net returns of spending on education. This suggests yet another argument for subsidising post-compulsory schooling resting on the demonstration that the social rate of return on investment in, say, higher education exceeds the social rate of return on investment in physical capital or other types of social expenditure. This is not an invalid argument. It is merely one which is hopelessly inconclusive. We can calculate both the private and the social rate of return to education but the latter would be better labelled the "public" rate of return since it does not include any measure of the externalities of education. We can similarly measure rates of return to health, housing, transport, etc., but these will involve variables that do not enter the calculations of rates of return to education, and will also exclude quantified estimates of external effects. We thus end up with an array of rates of return which are incommensurable[1]. We seem to be doomed therefore to analysing allocative efficiency in education at a sub-optimal level. We can ask how to allocate a given budget for education among different levels and types of education, not to mention different clients for the educational process, but we cannot seriously answer the grander question about the overall size of the educational budget.

---

[1] In the case of health, we do not even end up with rates of return to national spending on health care: health economics has not posed this ambitious question [see Drummond, 1981].

132

Even so, it is interesting to note that recent rate-of-return figures for education suggest that the demand for higher education has by now been saturated all over the industrialised world. Earnings differentials by years of education have been drastically compressed in the 1970s, not just in the United States, but also in the United Kingdom, France, and West Germany. In consequence, social rates of return to educational investment have declined to the point where in many countries they now stand below the common 10 per cent yardstick for the opportunity cost of capital [Psacharopoulos, 1980, Table 5, p. 97]. For example, between 1966 and 1978 social rates of return on education in the United Kingdom declined for university degrees from 8 per cent to 4 per cent, for A-level secondary school qualifications from 8-9 per cent to 6-7 per cent, and for HNCs, an intermediate technical qualification, from 10 per cent to 7 per cent [Daly, 1981]. There has always been a good deal of scepticism about the notion that rate-of-return calculations provide suitable criteria for public investment choices in education, and I am not making any such claims for them, but they do serve to provide one sort of rationale for the present trend towards the contraction of higher education.

IV. Trends and Patterns in Higher Education Expenditures

Our argument has so far been almost entirely theoretical. By considering entirely general principles, we have come to the conclusion that economists can neither condemn nor praise the recent downturn in higher education expenditures. In point of fact, we could have arrived at the same answer by a different route. If we examine past trends and patterns in higher education expenditures around Europe over the last 10 or 20 years, it becomes perfectly obvious that there is little or no relationship between a country's economic performance and its commitment to higher education (or, indeed, to all forms of education taken together). Thus, between 1961 and 1975 the United Kingdom actually spent more in absolute terms on higher education than did West Germany and, I need hardly tell you, these two countries stand at either end of the spectrum of European growth rates over the post-war period.

Let us review the general pattern in more detail[1]. For the period

---

[1] All the figures in this section are derived from UNESCO data analysed by Jallade [1980]. Data for OECD member-states, which is separately

1965-1977, annual growth rates of public expenditure on higher education fall into four groups: (1) high rates of 20 per cent or more (Austria, Italy, Yugoslavia); (2) above-average rates of 15-20 per cent (Belgium, Denmark, Netherlands, Norway, Spain); (3) below-average rates of 10-15 per cent (France, West Germany, Sweden, the United Kingdom, Bulgaria); and (4) low rates of 10 per cent or less (Switzerland and the entire Eastern bloc except Bulgaria). The European average for annual growth rates in higher education expenditure over this period was 16 per cent as against 14 per cent in the United States. All these figures refer to current prices but even at constant prices, expenditure on higher education in Europe grew at almost 10 per cent per annum over the 15 years 1960-1975, which more or less matches the corresponding figure for the United States. Even after 1975, what slowed down was only the rate of increase in higher education expenditure; it continues to grow to this day at about 5 per cent per annum.

We may also compare European countries in terms of that notorious and rather misleading indicator, the proportion of Gross National Product (GNP) allocated to expenditure on higher education. In 1961, no European country spent more than 0.4 per cent of its GNP on higher education. By 1975, seven countries were spending as much as one per cent of GNP on higher education and four others were approaching the one per cent mark. The biggest spender of all in 1975 was the Netherlands, whose 2.2 per cent of GNP was more than twice as much as any other country devoted to higher education. The smallest spenders were Italy, France, and Spain, who consistently kept higher education spending at 0.4 - 0.6 per cent of GNP throughout the entire period 1960-1975. Again, the United Kingdom devoted a larger proportion of GNP to higher education (around 1.2 per cent) throughout the entire decade and a half than both West Germany and France. These increased expenditures on higher education all over Europe did not come at the expense of lower levels of education but in fact reflected a growing share of GNP everywhere for the educational sector as a whole.

These overall trends disguise vast differences in real expenditure per higher education student across Europe. There were countries with "expensive" higher education in 1975, such as Denmark, the Netherlands, and Switzerland. There were countries with "cheap" higher edu-

---

collected, is analysed by Psacharopoulos [1981]. The differences between UNESCO and OECD statistics are small and refer rather to what is collected and to the number of countries from which data is collected.

134

cation in 1975, such as Bulgaria, France, Italy, Poland, Spain, and Yugoslavia. In between these two extremes were countries like Austria, Belgium, West Germany, Norway, Sweden, Czechoslovakia, Hungary and the United Kingdom. If we contrast 1965 with 1975, there has been little change in real expenditure per student in most countries; but several, such as Austria, Belgium, the Netherlands, Norway, Denmark, Sweden, and Switzerland, have actually managed significantly to increase and in some cases to double the real resources devoted to each higher education student.

The vast differences in instructional costs per student unit in different countries begin to suggest why there is no correlation between growth rates in educational expenditure and levels or growth rates of economic performance. Within very wide limits, there is in fact no such thing as an objectively determined cost of higher education: higher education institutions raise all the money they can from public and private sources and spend all the money that they raise; unit costs are determined, not so much by standards of quality and certainly not by standards of efficiency, but by changes in revenue. No doubt, tuition costs are necessarily higher in very small and very large institutions (under 1,000 and over 50,000 students) but within these wide limits, costs per student depend more on total revenue available than on the imperatives of teaching and research[1]. Thus, if we compare the Netherlands with Italy, it is difficult to find any objective reason in terms of "manpower requirements" to account for the vast differences in the two systems of higher education. Dutch professorial salaries, measured in U.S. $ of constant purchasing power, are four times those of Italian professors; student-staff ratios in the Netherlands are 10:1 as against 24:1 in Italy; hence, it costs almost ten times as much to educate a Dutch student than an Italian student. Would anyone argue, however, that Dutch professors produce work that is ten times as good as that of Italian professors, or that the Dutch economy is more sophisticated than the Italian one and therefore warrants the much more expensive higher education system? The fact of the matter is that the relationship between higher education spending and economic activity is so loose that it can accommodate almost any size and standard of higher education which politicians decree.

Public expenditure on higher education depends not only on the costs of instruction but also on the volume of direct aid to students. This element in the total higher education bill seems to vary even more be-

---

[1] This is what Bowen [1980, Ch. 1] calls the "revenue theory of cost".

tween countries than the level of grants to educational institutions to cover the costs of tuition. Some countries, like the United Kingdom and Sweden, provide student aid to almost all higher education students whereas others, like France or the Netherlands, subsidise only one third or less of all students. There are also significant differences in the methods of aiding students, from the reliance on student loans in Sweden, to the exclusive reliance on maintenance grants in the United Kingdom, to the French emphasis on subsidised food, housing, travel, and health care, coupled with generous tax relief to parents [Blaug, Woodhall, 1978]. Whatever we may say about the instructional costs of higher education, levels of public spending on student aid can encourage or discourage the private demand for higher education but cannot directly affect levels of economic development or rates of growth of GNP per head. Here then is yet another reason why we should not expect to find any well-determined relationship between total subsidies to higher education and any measure of economic activity.

V. The Field of Research

I turn now, however briefly, to questions of research and particularly research performed in the higher education sector, which in most countries comprises one-sixth to one-third of the national R & D effort measured in money terms. I do so with some hesitation since I am not persuaded that economists have contributed much to our understanding of appropriate modes of conducting academic research or for that matter the determination of the desirable level of funding for higher education research.

In the United States, Canada, and most of Europe, the real resources devoted to research are bound up in fixed proportions with the instructional costs of higher education, such that an expansion of student numbers and the addition of academic staff inevitably represents an equiproportionate increase in the resources devoted to research, and vice versa for a contraction of student numbers. Outside the Latin countries, universities are subsidised so as to permit academic staff to devote something like half of their time to research; this 1:1 ratio between instruction and research time is arbitrarily regarded as optimal for each and every member of staff. In addition to this channel of support, there is a second channel of research councils, that is, semi-autonomous bodies which provide additional finance for both pure and applied research carried on in colleges and universities. The funds flowing through this channel do not vary systematically across countries in proportion to the size of higher education systems; moreover, there are few systematic international patterns in the allocation of these funds among specific disciplines or fields of research [Blume, 1980].

The level of direct support for higher education research through research councils represents a decision which is subject to an unusually high level of uncertainty: frequently, the outcome of the research can only be judged after a decade or more, and, moreover, there is little to guide the choice between one researcher and the next other than personal track-records established in the past. Since most research councils are largely made up of senior academics with impressive research achievements, there is an inevitable tendency to favour well-tried approaches building on previous work and to discourage innovatory research. Such tendencies are perhaps stronger in the Anglophone countries who generally prefer the "responsive" model of research councils in which the individual researcher takes the initiative in applying for project funds. France and Italy instead prefer the dirigiste model in which the council itself stipulates the priority projects which it wishes to finance, sometimes going so far as to operate its own laboratories and research units. Obviously, the dirigiste model does not automatically favour innovatory research: it all depends on who actually mans the councils in question and on the influence of relevant ministries on the research agenda of the councils. It is worth noting that both the United Kingdom and West Germany, which at one time were firmly within the "responsive" camp, have recently moved sharply towards the dirigiste model. Clearly, governments everywhere are trying to get a firmer grip on university research in the effort to steer it into applied rather than basic research.

As general university income has declined since 1975, or rather grown at a sharply reduced rate, so have the imputed costs of the time spent on research by academic staff. In addition, however, there has been an absolute decline of external finance for higher education research in almost all OECD countries since 1973, with the exception of Denmark, Norway, the Netherlands, and France; but even in these countries, external research funds have grown less rapidly since 1973 than before [Ferne, 1980; OECD, 1981, Graphs A.10, p. 24 and A.38, p. 84].

It is easy to describe the patterns and trends but it is difficult to say much about them which is not either banal or self-interested pleading. I believe, as you probably all do, that teaching and research are generally complements, not substitutes, and therefore reject the Soviet pattern of financing academic research in specialised research institutes, leaving universities to devote themselves exclusively to teaching. Yet I also believe that academics are not equally endowed with capacities in both teaching and research. This suggests that there would be great advantages in subsidising higher education institutions as if they were largely, although not exclusively, teaching factories; individual university teachers who wished to specialise in research would then have to apply to research councils for funds, not just to purchase equipment and to hire research assistants, but also to replace a fraction of their own teaching time. Rejecting the assumption that teaching and research must always be combined in fixed proportions, we would thus maximise the benefits of the principle of comparative advantage in different activities. If economics suggests anything about the way we conduct higher education, it creates the strong presumption that this would result in a more efficient university system. Needless to say, I know of no country that has ever seriously considered this proposal.

There remains the question of the desirable total level of outside finance for higher education research. Research contributes to the total stock of human knowledge and human knowledge is a "public good" par excellence. Now we know that consumers have no incentives to reveal their demand for public goods and the problem of non-revelation of demand for research findings points firmly in the direction of public support for research activities. Nevertheless, the social benefits of academic research are painfully difficult to assess and with all the monitoring and post-mortems in the world will remain impossible to predict with any degree of accuracy. In the light of these considerations, any level of research support, other than zero, is arbitrary. It is a feeble conclusion but I do not think that economic analysis justifies any firmer pronouncement.

My conclusions have been almost wholly negative and destructive. But that is because we have posed a super-optimality problem - the total level of subsidy to higher education and higher education research - and economics happens to be weak in answering such questions. Its strength lies rather in examining suboptimal problems - should higher education be geared to young people or to adults?; should higher education be full-time or part-time?; should we aid institutions or students?; etc. For example, we noted earlier that there is little evidence that current patterns of higher education subsidies in industrialised countries are effective equalisers of lifetime chances. This is not because the level of subsidies has been too low but because its pattern has been ill-conceived to achieve the objective of greater equality in the lifetime distribution of income. Instead of directing

140

subsidies exclusively towards low-income students, say, by full-cost fees, subsidised grants scaled to parental income, and loans repayable as a proportion of future student income, tuition costs have been largely or wholly subsidised indiscriminately to everyone and even maintenance costs have been partly subsidised on a non-selective basis. And yet, from the viewpoint of equity, there is a simply overwhelming case for "privatising" post-compulsory and particularly higher education, that is, shifting the entire costs from general taxpayers to students and their families, exceptions being made only when the poverty of the individual families has been clearly established. If there is to be any general subsidy to post-compulsory schooling, it should be confined to the completion of secondary education, ideally taking the form of an "entitlement" to two or three years of post-compulsory schooling to be "cashable" at any future date in the working life of an individual.

The case for the "privatisation" of post-compulsory education is easy to make on equity grounds. However, there are also good efficiency arguments for moving in the same direction. The present system of subsidising the whole of the tuition costs of higher education out of tax receipts, which is now universal in Europe but of course not in America or Japan, deprives institutions of higher education of any financial incentives to maximise educational outcomes per unit of student costs, while at the same time reducing the incentives of students to work at their maximum capacity. It has resulted in considerable overinvestment in producer-oriented higher education, lacking any halting mechanism other than the political will to resist the Malthusian pressure of growing numbers.

141

References

Blaug, Mark, Introduction to the Economics of Education. London
  1971.

--, "The Distributional Effects of Higher Education Subsidies". Economics of Education Review, Vol. 2, No. 3, 1982, pp. 123-148.

--, Maureen Woodhall, "Patterns of Subsidies to Higher Education in Europe". Higher Education, Vol. 7, Nov. 1978, pp. 331-361.

Blume, Stuart S., "The Finance of University Research in Western
  Europe". European Journal of Education, Vol. 15, No. 4, 1980,
  pp. 72-101.

Bowen, Howard R., with Peter Dlecak, Jacqueline Powers
  Doud, Gordon K. Douglass, Investment in Learning: The
  Individual and Social Value of American Higher Education. The
  Carnegie Council Series, San Francisco 1977.

--, The Costs of Higher Education. San Francisco 1980.

Carnegie Commission on Higher Education, Higher Education: Who Pays? Who Benefits? Who should Pay? A Report and
  Recommendations. New York 1973.

Cerych, Ladislav, Jean-Pierre Jallade, Student Flows and Expenditure in Higher Education, 1965-1979. Institute of Education,
  Paris 1981.

Daly, Ann, "The Contribution of Education to Economic Growth in
  Britain: A Note on the Evidence". National Institute of Economic
  and Social Research, Paris 1981, unpubl.

Davis, J. Ronnie, "The Social and Economic Externalities of Education". In: Roe L. Johns, Irving J. Goffman, Kern F. Alex-
  ander, Dewey H. Stollar (Eds.), Economic Factors Affecting the Financing of Education. National Educational Finance Project, Gainesville 1970, pp. 59-82.

Denison, Edward F., The Sources of Economic Growth in the United
  States and the Alternatives before Us. New York 1962.

--, assisted by Jean-Pierre Poullier, Why Growth Rates Differ:
  Postwar Experience in Nine Western Countries. The Brookings
  Institution, Washington 1967.

Drummond, Martin F., "Welfare Economics and Cost Benefits
  Analysis in Health Care". Scottish Journal of Political Economy,
  Vol. 28, No. 2, 1981, pp. 125-145.

142

F e r n é , Georges, "Is University Research on the Decline?", Euro-
    pean Journal of Education, Vol. 15, No. 4, 1980, pp. 102-121.

F r i e d m a n , Milton, Rose F r i e d m a n , Free to Choose: A Per-
    sonal Statement. London 1980.

G r i m m o n d , John (Ed.), Youth Unemployment and the Bridge from
    School to Work. Anglo-German Foundation for the Study of Indus-
    trial Society, London 1979.

H a r t m a n . Robert W., "The Rationale for Federal Support for
    Higher Education". In: Lewis C. S o l m o n , Paul J. T a u b m a n
    (Eds.), Does College Matter? New York 1973, pp. 271-292.

H i r s c h , Fred, Social Limits to Growth. London 1977.

J a l l a d e , Jean-Pierre, "Expenditure on Higher Education in Europe:
    Past Trends and Future Prospects". European Journal of Edu-
    cation, Vol. 14, No. 1, 1980, pp. 35-48.

L a y a r d , Richard, George P s a c h a r o p o u l o s , "The Screening
    Hypothesis and the Returns to Education". Journal of Political
    Economy, Vol. 82, 1974, pp. 985-998.

L i n d l e y , Robert, "Education, Training, and the Labour Market
    in Britain". European Journal of Education, Vol. 16, No. 1, 1981,
    pp. 11-21.

M u n d e l , David S., "Whose Education Should Society Support?". In:
    Lewis C. S o l m o n , Paul J. T a u b m a n (Eds.), Does College
    Matter? New York 1973, pp. 293-316.

N e l s o n , Richard R., "Recent Exercises in Growth Accounting: New
    Understanding or Dead End?". The American Economic Review,
    Vol. 63, 1973, pp. 462-468.

O r g a n i s a t i o n   f o r   E c o n o m i c   C o - o p e r a t i o n   a n d   D e v e l -
    o p m e n t (OECD), Science and Technology Indicators I. Trends
    in Science and Technology in the OECD Area during the 1970s.
    First Draft of Part A: Resources Devoted to R & D. OECD, Paris
    1981.

P r a i s , Sigbert J., "Vocational Qualifications of the Labour Force
    in Britain and Germany". National Institute Economic Review,
    Vol. 98, No. 4, 1981, pp. 47-59.

P s a c h a r o p o u l o s , George, Returns to Education: An Updated In-
    ternational Comparison. World Bank Staff Working Paper No. 402,
    Washington 1980.

143

Psacharopoulos, George, Higher Education Expenditure in OECD Countries. Organisation for Economic Co-operation and Development (OECD), Paris 1981.

Sorrentino, Constance, "Youth Unemployment: An International Perspective". Monthly Labor Review, Vol. 104, No. 7, 1981, pp. 3-15.

Windham, Douglas M., "Economic Analysis and the Public Support of Higher Education". In: Douglas M. Windham (Ed.), Economic Dimensions of Education. Washington 1979, pp. 117-140.

[11]

Education Vouchers – It All Depends on What You Mean

MARK BLAUG

INTRODUCTION

Despite considerable international differences in the pattern of educational finance, it is true to say that the bulk of educational expenditure the world over is financed out of general tax receipts, so that there is little if any connection for most families between the taxes they pay and the education their children receive. The idea of establishing a direct link between taxation and educational choice by giving all parents an education voucher – a coupon of prescribed purchasing power that can be 'cashed' at any school whatever and that can be topped up like a book token or a luncheon voucher – was put forward by a number of British and American economists in the 1960s. It was thought to have been invented by Milton Friedman (1962), but an earlier version is found in Wiseman (1959; Horobin and Smyth, 1960). Actually, the concept of education vouchers is a much older idea that goes back to Thomas Paine in the eighteenth century (West, 1967). Moreover, it was debated as a serious proposal in the French parliament in the 1870s (Van Fliet and Smyth, 1982).

The Institute of Economic Affairs in Britain published a number of books and pamphlets in the 1960s and 1970s advocating education vouchers in both compulsory and post-compulsory schooling (Peacock and Wiseman, 1964; West, 1967, 1968; Beales *et al.*, 1970; Maynard, 1975; Crew and Young, 1977); the notion nevertheless remained a taboo subject in Britain among both politicians and educators. Since the election of 1979, however, the question has been repeatedly mooted by Tory ministers, encouraged in part by the publication of a voucher feasibility study for the Ashford area of Kent by the Kent County Council (1978). The concept of education vouchers fits remarkably well into the Tory programme of 'privatisation' of the social services and one might have expected the Conservative Party to move quickly towards a practical scheme of education vouchers. It is not even clear that a voucher system would require a new act of Parliament since the 1980 Education Bill appears to give Local Edu-

Education Vouchers – It All Depends on What You Mean   161

cation Authorities (LEAs) the necessary legal powers to implement such a scheme. Nevertheless, the idea of education vouchers is, rightly or wrongly, regarded as so politically explosive that even the Tory government has moved very cautiously on the voucher front, constantly taking away with one hand what it has just promised to deliver with the other. Thus, nothing is said about education vouchers in the Tory manifesto of 1983 and Sir Keith Joseph, the Secretary of State for Education, claims that open enrolments, under which LEAs would be encouraged to expand and contract schools in response to parental demand, would raise fewer difficulties than a voucher scheme while reaping many of its advantages.

In point of fact, an open enrolment policy would fall far short of the objectives of a voucher scheme. But, of course, everything depends on what is meant by a voucher scheme. Although the possible advantages and disadvantages of vouchers have been thoroughly aired by both advocates and critics, the debate has been confused by a bewildering variety of interpretations of the concept of education vouchers. It is difficult enough to assess the possible effects of a new, untried method of financing education, but when its proponents differ among themselves about the precise details of the scheme, the task of evaluation becomes virtually impossible. I shall begin, therefore, by sorting out the types of voucher schemes that are possible, at least in principle, after which I shall return to the kind of education voucher that has been recently proposed for Britain.

A GLOSSARY OF VOUCHER TERMINOLOGY

Imagine a typical country with, say, ten years of compulsory education and a mixed system of public and private schools; state education is financed out of general taxes but parents may opt out of the state system by sending their children to private schools, thus paying 'twice', so to speak, for education. We now introduce a system of education vouchers, that is, we issue every parent with children of school-going ages with a 'coupon' whose value is just sufficient on average to 'buy' a place in a state primary or secondary school. If we have done our sums correctly, and if parents do not switch between public and private schools as a result of the issue of education vouchers, the tax bill for education will be exactly the same as before.

We can guarantee that parents will not switch between the public and private sector of education by confining our vouchers to state schools. I shall call such vouchers 'limited vouchers'. In that case, however, education vouchers have only a modest effect because they amount simply to the 'de-zoning' of schools, that is, the elimination of

162 Privatisation and the Welfare State

the legal provision that gives parents a right to send their children to state schools but only in the catchment area in which they reside. The 'zoning' of schools has been an emotive issue in the educational history of the United States. It has been considerably undermined in recent years by a series of Supreme Court decisions that have forced American schools to draw their pupils from distant neighbourhoods even if this entails 'bussing' children from home to school at public expense. Similarly, secondary schools have been effectively 'de-zoned' in Britain by the Education Act of 1981. Thus, if 'limited vouchers' are all we mean by education vouchers, they are virtually in operation under another name in both the United States and the United Kingdom.

Suppose, however, that such vouchers were made 'unlimited' by permitting parents to cash them at any school whatever, public or private. Most private schools, however, charge fees that exceed the current-plus-capital costs per place in a state school. It would be necessary, therefore, to allow parents who opt for private education to supplement the value of a voucher out of their own pocket. I shall call such vouchers 'supplementable vouchers' in contrast to 'fixed-value vouchers'. Thus, a system of 'unlimited vouchers' would have to include the notion of 'supplementable vouchers'.

So far, I have gone along with the cosy belief that all state schools at a given level of education have equal costs, being the simple quotient of total public education expenditure on a given level of education and the number of children enrolled at that level. This is clearly not the case. State schools differ in the age of their buildings, in the size of their plant, in the mix of their teachers in terms of sex, age and qualifications, and sometimes even in their course offerings. In short, there are cheap and expensive state primary and state secondary schools. Suppose we now allow state schools to charge cost-covering rather than uniform fees in a world of unlimited, supplementable vouchers. The value of the voucher is sufficient, or more than sufficient, to buy a place in a cheap state school, but parents can top up the voucher and thus choose expensive state schools as well as private schools. I label such a system one of 'cost-fees vouchers', taking it for granted that such vouchers are also unlimited and supplementable.

It is tempting to think that such an arrangement would maximise parental choice, but we have forgotten the major constraint on parental choice of schools, which is distance and the implied cost of transportation. To underwrite a system of cost-fees, unlimited and supplementable vouchers, we need to include transport costs (up to some limit) in the value of the vouchers. I label such vouchers 'transport-included vouchers'.

Nothing I have said so far has addressed itself to the issue of equity:

Education Vouchers – It All Depends on What You Mean   163

rich parents can normally afford to buy more expensive education for their children than poor parents and a system of cost-fees, unlimited, supplementable and transport-included vouchers merely increases the scope of their superior position in the education market. It is easy to deal with this problem, however, under a voucher scheme: we simply make the value of the voucher a declining function of parental income. The obvious way to do this is to make the voucher part of taxable income to the full extent of its value; the existence of the progressive income tax will then guarantee that the voucher will be worth less to rich than to poor parents. If this fails to reduce its nominal value sufficiently to the well-to-do, we can stipulate that it be taxed at twice or three times its value. In other words, we can scale down the value of a voucher in relation to income to any extent we like. If, on the other hand, the income tax base in a given country fails to reach down to all parents with children of school-going ages, we can reduce the value of the education voucher in direct proportion to declared income. Whichever of these two variants is adopted, I shall call any such voucher an 'income-related voucher'.

I have assumed that the government sets minimum educational standards that must be observed by all private and public schools. Some advocates of vouchers have gone further and argued that no school in receipt of vouchers ought to be permitted to deny access to pupils on racial or ethnic grounds. However, what is true of the racial or ethnic characteristics of students might also be held to be true of their religious characteristics. In other words, education vouchers could be used to break down the entry barriers of parochial schools. And to go still further, schools in receipt of vouchers might be required to practise an open door policy by having to admit all students who apply, regardless of their educational qualifications. Be that as it may, I shall label vouchers that deny schools the right to bar admission on grounds other than strictly educational ones as 'restricted vouchers' and vouchers that leave schools free to exclude potential students on any grounds whatsoever as 'unrestricted vouchers'.

To sum up, I have constructed a tree of possible vouchers, running from the most modest to the most ambitious versions of the concept (see Figure 11.1).

The reader is warned that the particular labels I have adopted have no general currency. The first practical scheme for vouchers was devised in America by Christopher Jencks and his associates (1970) and implemented in a pilot project in Northern California, the so-called Alum Rock experiment. Jencks called his vouchers 'regulated compensatory vouchers'. Other authors (for example, Maynard, 1975) proliferate yet another set of labels.

164   Privatisation and the Welfare State

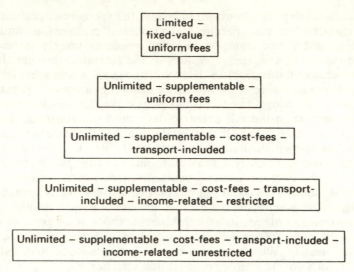

Figure 11.1   *The voucher tree*

Even my extensive glossary does not capture all the nuances that may be conveyed by a particular interpretation of the concept of education vouchers. A much-discussed question is what to do about popular, over-subscribed and unpopular, under-subscribed schools. In the case of over-subscribed schools, the usual notion is that parents should be given choice of second-preference schools, third-preference schools, etc. Should educational authorities, however, be required to provide mobile classrooms to supplement the places of an over-subscribed school? Similarly, should an under-subscribed school be given a period of grace before it is closed down, and how long should this period of grace last? These remain open questions to which various advocates of vouchers have, as we shall see, their own particular answers.

The voucher model that Friedman originally proposed was in my language an unlimited, supplementable, cost-fees, unrestricted voucher whose value did not vary with income. On the other hand, the Jencks voucher that was used in the Alum Rock experiment was a limited, fixed-value, uniform fees, transport-included, restricted voucher with an income-related feature in the form of a 'compensatory' voucher issued to low-income families. Income-related features are also built into the so-called 'effort voucher' of the influential American team of Clune, Coons and Sugarman (1971), in which the fees charged by schools, rather than the value of the voucher, are scaled inversely to income. Finally, Peacock and Wiseman (1964) and West

Education Vouchers – It All Depends on What You Mean   165

(1967, 1968) propose the exact equivalent for the United Kingdom of my most ambitious voucher model, the unlimited, supplementable, cost-fees, transport-included, income-related, unrestricted voucher.

The voucher scheme that the Department of Education and Science was said to be considering in 1982 for primary and lower secondary schools falls roughly halfway between the most modest and the most ambitious voucher model. Parents were to be given means-tested vouchers worth the annual cost of an average place in a maintained school (£800 for primary schools, £1,100 for secondary schools, and £1,600 for a sixth form college), which would then be cashable at any school, maintained or independent, provided they were used only to buy day places. Maintained schools would continue to charge uniform fees but would adopt an open enrolment policy: popular schools would be assisted with loans to expand and unpopular schools would be encouraged to contract and eventually to close. Maintained schools would have to admit all students applying to them, exactly as under the present system, and independent schools would presumably be allowed to refuse students as they do now. It is not clear whether transport costs to distant maintained schools would be paid for under public funds, as is now the case, but at any rate nothing was said about financing transport to private day schools. So, in my terminology, the DES scheme was one of unlimited, supplementable, uniform fees, partly transport-included, income-related, partly unrestricted vouchers.

THE EFFECTS OF VOUCHERS

I have already dismissed the limited, fixed-value voucher as being of little interest, since it amounts in effect to the de-zoning of schools, which is perfectly feasible without the introduction of voucher schemes. The moment a voucher is made unlimited, however, the total fiscal cost of the scheme must exceed the public costs of the present educational system by virtue of the vouchers issued to families with children in private schools. Such families are better off under an unlimited voucher scheme than they now are, despite the fact that they will have to share the higher tax burdens of the voucher scheme with all other families. The long-term effect of an unlimited voucher on total education expenditure is difficult to predict. A number of families might switch out of the state sector into the private sector, thus increasing private expenditure on education. Since the level of taxation would vary directly with the face value of the unlimited voucher, there might well be broader electoral support for increased public expenditure on education under a voucher scheme

166   Privatisation and the Welfare State

than exists at present: parents with children in private schools have little reason under the present system to press for increased public expenditure on education because they share the burden of increased taxation but receive none of its benefits.

Once we allow state schools to charge different fees in accordance with their different cost structures – unlimited, supplementable, cost-fees vouchers – we begin to get the efficiency effects so frequently invoked by the advocates of education vouchers: vouchers would be the principal source of income for schools, which would therefore have to compete for clientele, in the course of which waste and slack would be eliminated. Moreover, competition would generate a much greater diversity of educational services because parents have radically different tastes for schooling: some schools would specialise in expensive, academic-type education; others would specialise in cheap, vocational-type education; some schools would offer a narrow, carefully chosen curriculum; others would offer a broad, comprehensive curriculum; some schools would invest heavily in facilities; others would instead devote their resources to teachers and paraprofessional assistants; but whatever the choice, each school would be forced to provide the best possible service at the lowest possible resource cost. Competition would also generate the incentive to search for, and experiment with, new teaching methods. Private schools in Britain were among the first to introduce computer-based language laboratories and do-it-yourself computer workshops, and this is only a small indication of the stimulus to educational innovations that a voucher scheme would promote. The fact that the basic technology of education has altered little over the past two or three centuries is due, not to any inherent features of the learning process, but to the existing state monopoly of education.

Such are the claims of voucher enthusiasts: vouchers would increase efficiency, promote diversity and encourage technical dynamism (Blaug, 1970; Richter, 1976; Cohen and Farrar, 1977; Greenaway, 1979; Friedman, 1980). The critics of vouchers, however, point to the danger that competition would force schools to advertise themselves (Horobin and Smyth, 1960; Woodhall, 1977). In the effort to gain a particular brand image, much of the advertising might be misleading: schools would appeal to their opulent buildings, their fancy equipment and their examination results (even if these were obtained only by an extremely selective admission policy). Education being a difficult process to evaluate, parents might be forgiven if they judged quality by price. Thus, high-fee schools would attract the wealthier parents, while the higher fees would at the same time allow such schools to hire better teachers and to purchase the most up-to-date equipment. Poorer parents would be driven to choose

Education Vouchers – It All Depends on What You Mean   167

low-fee state schools, which would then become educational 'ghettos' for children with deprived backgrounds. The division into high-fee and low-fee schools would soon become a self-perpetuating vicious circle, thus exacerbating the segregation between public and private schools that already exists under the present system. In short, vouchers would be socially divisive.

Although such criticisms raise serious objections to a voucher scheme, they seem to be based on a number of implicit assumptions derived from the existing state monopoly of education. Even the friends of vouchers agree that the quantity and quality of information in the education market is critical to the operation of any voucher scheme. The great merit of educational vouchers is that they generate a demand for information that is irrelevant to parents under the present system of education finance. Because education vouchers will force parents to choose between schools, they will create a market for advisory services that will assist parents to interpret the information provided by schools. Moreover, the state may regulate school advertisements to, say, provide information about the activities of schools in a common format so as to facilitate comparisons between schools. The very existence of vouchers will constitute, as it were, an education in choice, and educational choices will naturally improve with practice. Finally, vouchers and the pressure to advertise will force schools to be clearer about their own objectives and more eager to determine the degree to which they succeed in achieving these objectives. In consequence, vouchers would almost certainly make schools more cost-effective and more willing to be seen to be cost-effective.

I say 'cost-effective' and not 'efficient' because the notion of efficiency makes little sense if we are talking about non-profit-maximising institutions. It is perfectly true, of course, that an ambitious voucher scheme would force all schools to operate like profit-maximising firms. Even in these circumstances, the inherited endowment income of certain private schools might allow them to escape the penalties of the market place, in effect operating schools at a loss for all sorts of paternal reasons. Furthermore, in order to capture all the classic efficiency effects of free competition by means of a voucher scheme, we would have to allow popular state schools to borrow in the private capital market to finance their expansion; this stretches the ambitious interpretation of education vouchers even further than most voucher advocates would allow. Finally, to the extent that vouchers stimulate greater diversity of educational offerings, it becomes increasingly difficult to define what is meant by more efficiency in education. Schools that pursue different objectives can be compared not in efficiency terms but only in terms of the costs that they incur to achieve identical objectives at lower or higher levels of effectiveness.

168   Privatisation and the Welfare State

Suffice it to say that 'cost-effectiveness' is a less question-begging term than 'efficiency' in educational matters.

The notion that vouchers would create a dual system of education, condemning the children of the poor to attend slum schools, presupposes that poor parents are indifferent about education and that only well-to-do parents are willing to make financial sacrifices to send their children to better, more expensive schools. There is little reason to believe that parental attitudes to education are so tightly linked to family income even under present circumstances, and, under the greater diversification of schooling promoted by a voucher system, parental attitudes would likewise become more heterogeneous. In other words, vouchers may promote the polarisation of schools into 'good' and 'bad' schools, but there is no necessity for them to have this effect.

In any case, any such tendency towards educational 'apartheid' can be offset by making vouchers income-related. Indeed, an extreme version of the income-related voucher reduces the after-tax value of the voucher to zero at a median family income level; in that case, only 'poor' families receive effective vouchers, which is to say that they are given an advantage over 'rich' families that they totally lack under the present system of financing education. It is difficult to imagine a better demonstration of the extraordinary flexibility of the voucher mechanism than this: educational vouchers can be adjusted to achieve almost any objective that is deemed desirable. However, perhaps this apparent strength of vouchers is actually its principal weakness: any government wishing to enact a voucher scheme is faced with almost endless controversy about the specific features of the scheme. As a consequence, a voucher scheme may never get off the ground.

Of all these specific features of vouchers, the most divisive are those pertaining to the admission criteria of schools eligible for vouchers. Some British advocates of vouchers (Peacock and Wiseman, 1964, p. 55) agree that a heterogeneous society like that of the United States, with a large immigrant population and sizeable coloured minority, would be justified in preventing voucher-approved schools from barring students on racial and ethnic grounds; what they deny, however, is that such considerations are applicable to a more homogeneous society like that of Great Britain. Milton Friedman (1962, p. 8), on the other hand, is convinced that forcible desegregation of schools increases rather than decreases political tensions and he is therefore in favour of unrestricted vouchers. The American ideal of the comprehensive high school was clearly based on the notion that immigrant populations are more easily assimilated if all children are made to go to the same kinds of schools. Nevertheless,

American educators were forced to tolerate private parochial schools in which children are segregated on religious grounds. Similarly, the British movement towards the comprehensive reorganisation of secondary schools was predicated on the theory that schools mixing children of different home backgrounds would work to break down traditional class barriers in Britain. We see, therefore, that the 'melting-pot' theory of schooling has had wide support in both countries. Moreover, the concept of the melting-pot has always been extended in the state sector to admission standards based on purely educational achievements: state schools have had to accept all children, regardless of their educability. There is an argument, therefore, for extending the same restriction to private schools that enter the voucher scheme. Why should public money be used to subsidise schools that claim the right to select children on any grounds other than financial ones?

However, restricted vouchers would have very different social effects from unrestricted vouchers and, moreover, they would also have different efficiency effects. It is one thing to talk about cost-effectiveness in a high-fee school that selects its children to be of outstanding quality and quite another to talk about it in a high-fee school with children of mixed abilities. A completely unrestricted voucher takes us into hitherto untried areas without any historical precedence. No wonder then that its consequences invite almost unlimited speculation.

PRACTICAL EXPERIENCE WITH VOUCHERS

As I noted earlier, there has been one practical experiment with education vouchers in Alum Rock, California, and a number of feasibility studies have been conducted in both America and Britain. What, if anything, do these have to teach us?

The Alum Rock experiment was based on the 'regulated compensatory voucher' model of Jencks and his associates (1970). Jencks' voucher sought to give parents a greater range of choice over educational alternatives without permitting increased segregation by race, ethnic origins, social class or educational ability, while at the same time providing low-income families with additional purchasing power over education. Its main features were:

- the creation of an Education Voucher Agency, which received all government funds for education and paid them to schools in return for vouchers;

170   Privatisation and the Welfare State

- the issue of a basic voucher to every family with a child of school-going age 6–14 equal in value to the average recurrent costs of schooling in the area; this voucher could not be supplemented, but low-income families were furnished with a second 'compensatory' voucher whose value varied inversely to their declared income;
- any school, public or private, was eligible to receive a voucher provided it charged the uniform fee equal to the face value of the voucher and accepted all students who applied to fill vacant places; if demand exceeded the supply of places, at least half of the available places had to be allocated randomly (in practice, these provisions limited the voucher scheme to state schools);
- all voucher-approved schools were required to cover their own expenses out of voucher income, to maintain an adequate accounting system, to provide standard information about themselves to parents, to conform to certain broad curricula and staffing standards, and to submit their advertising claims to the Education Voucher Agency; and
- free transport was provided for children enrolled at schools distant from their home within the entire area of jurisdiction of the local school board.

The Alum Rock School District in East San Jose, California, consists of nineteen elementary schools (age range 6–11) and six middle schools (age range 12–14), serving some 15,000 pupils. The area is relatively poor, urbanised, predominantly Mexican-American in ethnic composition (53 per cent of the population) and has a high rate of residential turnover. The voucher experiment started in September 1972 with the participation of six state schools serving 4,000 pupils; no private schools joined the experiment. The school district provided the basic voucher but the federal government provided the funds for transport and administration as well as all the finance for compensatory vouchers. During the five-year period of the experiment, the number of voluntarily participating schools rose from six to fourteen state schools and from 4,000 to 9,000 pupils.

The degree of parental choice that the Alum Rock experiment provided was, however, greater than these figures imply. In order to offer parents a wider range of educational alternatives, each voucher school had to provide two or more educational programmes within the same building. These 'mini-schools' were given autonomy over budgets, curricula and staff appointments under the overall authority of the school's principal. By the end of the experiment in 1977, there were fifty-one mini-schools in operation within the fourteen voucher-approved institutions, ranging from the traditional,

Education Vouchers – It All Depends on What You Mean   171

academic curriculum through various versions of informal, individual-ised learning programmes. At first, every effort was made to expand popular schools and mini-schools by means of mobile classrooms and the use of satellite space in less popular schools with empty places. However, teachers in voucher schools had been promised security of tenure and seniority rights at the outset of the experiment and this made it impossible effectively to contract unpopular schools. In time, mobile classrooms and satellite schools were abandoned as being unmanageable, maximum school and class sizes were reimposed, and thus mini-school programmes came to be fitted into the previous structure of local schools, including the previous distribution of teachers among schools.

The voucher experiment at Alum Rock came to an end in September 1977. What survived the experiment were not vouchers but a limited range of mini-school programmes in six schools, an increased volume of school information to parents, a network of parent advisory committees, and a system of open enrolment by parental choice backed up by the provision of free transport within the school district. The experiment proved that state schools can provide a greater range of alternative educational options than was thought practical hitherto. Apart from this result, however, the experiment demonstrated once again how difficult it is to take power away from teachers and administrators and to give it to parents. Counselling and information programmes for parents were slow to take effect and parents continued to think of the neighbourhood school as a unit rather than a bundle of mini-schools. Even if a particular set of mini-school programmes proved popular, they were only allowed to expand within definite limits. Contrariwise, if they were unpopular, they were only allowed to contract if this did not endanger the employment of teachers. In these circumstances, it is hardly surprising that vouchers at Alum Rock failed to produce the dramatic effects hailed by advocates of vouchers (Mecklenburger and Hostrop, 1972; Weiler *et al.*, 1974; Levinson, 1976; Cohen and Farrar, 1977).

One needs to keep in mind, however, the severely limited nature of the Alum Rock experiment, which involved what was in effect a limited, fixed-value, uniform fees, transport-included, partly income-related and restricted voucher. Even if it had proved successful, it would have told us nothing about the effects of a really ambitious unlimited, supplementable, cost-fees, transport-included, fully income-related, unrestricted voucher.

Six voucher feasibility studies have been conducted in various American cities, none of which however reached the stage of being implemented. In Seattle, the experiment was defeated by the attempt to include the participation of private schools (US Office of

172   Privatisation and the Welfare State

Economic Opportunity, 1971). In Gary, Indiana, teachers threatened to take strike action over the voucher issue, which killed off the proposal. In San Francisco, the community at large showed little interest in vouchers, their attention being taken up instead with the issue of bussing consequent on a court-ordered desegregation plan. In Rochester, New York, teacher opposition once again proved decisive (US Office of Economic Opportunity, 1973). In New Hampshire and in East Hartford, Connecticut, frequent changes in the proposed voucher model and the vexed issue of parochial schools proved to be the principal stumbling block (Milne, 1975; Esposito and Thomson, 1976). Although the education voucher as an instrument of parent power is no longer a vital political issue in the United States, some school districts have used the experience to develop systems of open enrolment, greater scope for parent–teacher associations, and methods of presenting comparable information about local schools to parents.

Britain has witnessed only one feasibility study, in the Ashford educational division of Kent County. The Kent study, carried out in 1977, surveyed parents, pupils, teachers and headmasters in an effort to discover their reactions to a hypothetical unlimited, supplementable, uniform fees, transport-included voucher with income-related features on Alum Rock lines, the value of the voucher being set equal to the average recurrent costs of state primary and state secondary education in the county (supplements only being required for private schools). Surprisingly enough, most parents, while dissatisfied with the amount of information about local schools they were currently receiving, asserted that they already obtained a place in their first-preference school. Thus a voucher scheme would cause only 10 per cent of Ashford parents with children in a maintained school to transfer their child to another maintained school and only 9 per cent to transfer their child from a maintained school to an independent school; needless to say, a large proportion of that 9 per cent turned out to be parents from social class I. Not so surprisingly, three-quarters of the surveyed teachers opposed the idea of vouchers and half went as far as to say that they would refuse to teach in a voucher-eligible school. Even headmasters of private schools were not particularly keen on vouchers, doubting apparently that the voucher subsidy (about one-quarter to one-third of private school fees) would greatly increase the demand for private schooling (Kent County Council, 1978, pp. 30–9).

There is some excess capacity in maintained schools in Kent, which meant that the costs of mobile classrooms to facilitate school transfer would have been small. If one adds transport and administration costs, however, and if furthermore one adds the costs of supplemen-

Education Vouchers – It All Depends on What You Mean 173

tary vouchers for disadvantaged children, sums of £0.9–1.3m. a year are reached in Ashford alone, one of fourteen divisions in a county whose total education budget is £172m. (in 1977). In other words, a voucher scheme such as the one contemplated by the Kent authorities might increase public expenditure on education in the county by 10 per cent, suggesting that it is a perfectly practical but by no means insignificant proposal.

After the submission of the report, the Kent authorities announced the introduction of a pilot voucher scheme in the county to be financed from funds outside the normal county budget. However, little more has been heard of this pilot scheme since then. More recently, they have been experimenting with a system of open enrolments in Tonbridge and Tunbridge Wells secondary schools.

The evidence from Alum Rock and the American and British feasibility studies cannot support or refute the extensive claims made for education vouchers. There has never been a full practical trial of unlimited, cost-fees, income-related, unrestricted vouchers and yet many of the arguments in the voucher debate are precisely about their effects on the size of the private sector, the fate of different state schools with different cost structures, the demand for schooling when poor parents are given an inherent advantage in the education market, and the proliferation of schools segregated by race, religion and ethnic origins. On all these controversial questions, one gains little insight from Alum Rock and the feasibility studies to date.

CONCLUSIONS

Let us recapitulate. Education vouchers have been assessed in terms of six criteria: parental freedom of choice, cost-effectiveness, diversity, innovation-mindedness, the level of total educational expenditure, and equality of educational opportunities. On all these criteria, the debate has failed to come down decisively on one side or the other. But that is the nature of the case. For one thing, the participants in the debate cannot even agree on what is meant by freedom of choice, efficiency, diversity, equity, etc. The criterion of parental freedom to choose, for example, is frequently trivialised to mean being able to choose any school within hailing distance. It is obvious, however, that one does not need education vouchers to secure wider access to schools. Provided there is surplus capacity in schools and provided the community is willing to be taxed to finance bussing across school boundaries, freedom to choose among available schools can be achieved by the simple expedient of abolishing 'zoning'. The de-zoning of schools and the provision of free transportation, how-

174   Privatisation and the Welfare State

ever, will not secure parental sovereignty in educational matters, which depends critically on a direct rather than an indirect connection between choosing a school and paying for education in that school. Similarly, there is much loose talk about vouchers promoting efficiency, diversity and educational innovation in schools, as if these were achievable at zero cost. Obviously, however, the disappearance of inefficient schools imposes definite resource costs on the educational system. Finally, equity questions have been similarly vulgarised to imply equality of access to a uniform pattern of educational provision, as if greater income were the only advantage that rich parents have over poor parents. The present state monopoly of education – subordinating parents to educational professionals, disguising the true cost of education, repressing the diversity of tastes for educational services – has had such a powerful hold on our minds that even the friends of vouchers, and certainly its critics, have been unable to think through the radical implications of an unlimited, supplementable, cost-fees, income-related, and possibly unrestricted voucher.

The educational system is a formalised, bureaucratic organisational structure and, like any bureaucratic organisational structure, it strives for maximum autonomy from external pressures as its cardinal principle of survival. While ostensibly devoted to the education of children, teachers, school administrators and local education officers must nevertheless regard parents acting on behalf of children as a force to be kept at bay because parental pressures in effect threaten the autonomy of the educational system. Education vouchers are therefore to be resisted, not because they might increase parental choice, promote efficiency, stimulate innovations, etc. but because they tend to undermine the locus of power in the educational system.

It is sometimes argued (Woodhall, 1977) that all the so-called advantages of vouchers could be achieved more effectively and cheaply by a piecemeal approach: if the chief aim is to encourage cost-effectiveness in schools, this might be accomplished under the present system by greater accountability and superior auditing; likewise, if the aim is to encourage diversity and innovation in schools, this might be achieved by the creation of mini-schools on the lines of Alum Rock; similarly, if equity is the ruling objective, schools in poor neighbourhoods might be provided with additional finance; and so on. In short, there is no need for a radical change of the financing mechanism for education because all our educational objectives can be achieved by a one-at-a-time approach. But this is, surely, an illusion of the first order. The present educational system is firmly in the hands of educational administrators, headmasters, principals and teachers and, if the Alum Rock experiment has anything to tell us, it is that no half-way measures have the least chance of giving real

Education Vouchers – It All Depends on What You Mean   175

power to parents. Of course, something could be done under the present system to reduce waste, to increase diversity, to promote innovation and to widen the range of choice of parents. In my view, however, this remains icing on a largely inedible cake. I would hold that the stupefying conservatism of the educational system and its utter disdain of non-professional opinion is such that nothing less than a radical shake-up of the financing mechanism will do much to promote parent power. And, in the final analysis, parent power is what the entire debate is all about.

However, the sort of voucher plan that has been under discussion in Britain – unlimited, supplementable, uniform fees, partly transport-included, income-related, partly unrestricted vouchers – is a far cry from the ambitious cost-fees vouchers that Friedman, Peacock and Wiseman, and West originally had in mind. It would do nothing as such to spur competition between maintained schools, and it amounts quite simply to an additional subsidy for independent schools. Independent schools already enjoy a subsidy of about £200m. per annum as a result of various tax exemptions, as well as school places purchased out of public funds (Blaug, 1981). These subsidies are usually regarded as a *quid pro quo* for the 'double' taxation imposed on parents who opt out of the state system. But most of the 40,000 teachers in private schools have been trained for a year at taxpayers' expense, which dilutes, at least to some extent, the force of the argument of 'double taxation'. At any rate, even if one defended more competition between maintained and independent schools on grounds of 'efficiency', one might have doubts about increased subsidies to independent schools on grounds of 'equity'. Besides, it is a little perverse to argue for 'privatisation' in education by means of greater subsidies to private schools, while leaving maintained schools largely as they are. An open enrolment policy was said to be an integral feature of the DES voucher scheme, so that maintained schools would not be left as they are; but an open enrolment policy is to be welcomed on its own merits and is not a necessary feature of a voucher plan. The fact remains that, so long as the fiction is upheld that the costs of education are the same in all maintained schools, many if not most of the acclaimed virtues of education vouchers fall to the ground.

It is not difficult to understand why the Tory government has, at least for the present, abandoned its plans to introduce vouchers in education. The biggest cost of any unlimited voucher would be the subsidy to children already going to independent schools, not to mention the subsidy to additional children switching from maintained to independent schools. Even if the full value of the voucher were added to taxable income, as Peacock (1983) has proposed, the additional

176   Privatisation and the Welfare State

cost to the Exchequer of a national voucher scheme might be as much as half a billion pounds. To a government committed to cutting public expenditure, this is clearly what took the steam out of the voucher movement in Britain.

REFERENCES

Beales, A.C.F., Blaug, M., West, E.G. and Veale, D. (1970), *Education – A Framework for Choice* (London: Institute of Economic Affairs).

Blaug, M. (1970), *Introduction to the Economics of Education* (London: Penguin Books).

Blaug, M. (1981), 'Can Independent Education Be Suppressed?', *Journal of Economic Affairs,* vol. 2, no. 1, pp. 30-37.

Clune, W., Coons, J., and Sugarman, S. (1971), *Private Wealth and Public Education* (Cambridge, Mass.: Harvard Education Press).

Cohen, D.K. and Farrar, E. (1977), 'Power to Parents – The Story of Education Vouchers', *The Public Interest,* no. 48, pp. 63-79.

Crew, M.A. and Young, A. (1977), *Paying By Degrees* (London: Institute of Economic Affairs).

Esposito, A. and Thomson, W. (1976), *Parents' Choice: A Report on Education Vouchers in East Hartford, CO* (East Hartford, CO: East Hartford School District).

Friedman, M. (1962), *Capitalism and Freedom* (Chicago: University of Chicago Press).

Friedman, M. (1980), *Free to Choose* (London: Secker & Warburg).

Greenway, D. (1979), 'Voucher Systems in Education. The Arguments For and Against', in P. Maunder (ed.), *Case Studies in the Economics of Social Issues* (London: Heinemann Educational Books).

Horobin, G.W. and Smyth, R.L. (1960), 'The Economics of Education: A Comment', *Scottish Journal of Political Economy,* vol. 7, no. 1, pp. 69-74. Reprinted in M. Blaug (ed.), *Economics of Education 2* (Harmondsworth, Middlesex: Penguin Books, 1969), pp. 373-81.

Jencks, C., *et al.* (1970), *Education Vouchers: A Report on Financing Elementary Education By Grants to Parents* (Cambridge, Mass.: Center for the Study of Public Policy).

Kent County Council Education Department (1978), *Education Vouchers in Kent: A Feasibility Study for the Educational Department of the Kent County Council* (Maidstone, Kent: Kent County Council).

Levinson, E. (1976), *The First Three Years at Alum Rock* (Santa Monica, CA: Rand Corporation).

Maynard, A.K. (1975), *Experiment with Choice in Education* (London: Institute of Economic Affairs).

Mecklenburger, A. and Hostop, R. (eds) (1972), *Education Vouchers – From Theory to Alum Rock* (Homewood Ill.: ETC Publication).

Milne, W.H. (1975), *New Hampshire Educational Voucher Project: Final Report – Feasibility Study* (New Hampshire: NH State Board).

Peacock, A.T. and Wiseman, J. (1964), *Education for Democrats* (London: Institute of Economic Affairs).

Peacock, A.T. (1983), 'Education Voucher Schemes – Strong or Weak?', *Journal of Economic Affairs,* vol. 2, no. 3, pp. 113-16.

Richter, P.C. (1976), *Education Vouchers – Bibliography* (Cambridge, Mass.: Center for the Study of Public Policy).

U.S. Office of Economic Opportunity (1971), *Feasibility Study for the Design and Implementation of an Education Voucher Scheme in Rochester, New York* (Washington, D.C.: OEO).

U.S. Office of Economic Opportunity (1973), *The Feasibility of Implementing a Voucher Plan in Seattle* (Washington, D.C.: OEO).

Van Fliet, W. and Smyth, J.A. (1982), 'A Nineteenth Century French Proposal to Use School Vouchers', *Comparative Education Review,* vol. 12, no. 3, pp. 95-103.

Weiler, D. *et al.* (1974), *A Public School Voucher Demonstration: The First Year at Alum Rock* (Santa Monica, CA: Rand Corporation).

West, E.G. (1967), 'Tom Raine's Voucher Scheme for Public Education', *Southern Economic Journal,* vol. 33, no. 3, pp. 378-82.

West, E.G. (1968), *Economics, Education and the Politician* (London: Institute of Economic Affairs).

Wiseman, J. (1959), 'The Economics of Education', *Scottish Journal of Political Economy,* vol. 6, no. 1, pp. 48-58. Reprinted in M. Blaug (ed.) *Economics of Education 2* (Harmondsworth, Middlesex: Penguin Books, 1969), pp. 360-72.

Woodhall, M. (1977), 'Alternatives in the Finance of Education Vouchers', *The Finance of Education: Open University Course, Economics and Education Policy IV* (Walton Hall, Milton Keynes: Open University Press), pp. 65-115.

Part III
The Third World

[12]

Education, Economic Situation and Prospects of India, 1971

by Marc Blaug*

Structural Trends.

The dominant characteristic of Indian education
since independence has been the tendency of higher education
to expand faster than and indeed at the expense of primary
and secondary education, a tendency which flies in the
face of 20 years of verbal commitments to the goal of
universal primary education. Consider, as a case in
point, the contrast since 1950 between the target and
the actual rates of growth of enrolments in various
levels of the Indian educational system (see TABLE 1).

As we can see, the first three Five Year Plans
laid down enrolment targets - a practice that has now
been abondoned - and in each Plan except the First,
the targets were either met or greatly exceeded, the
excess being greater the higher the level of education.
Furthermore, the targets themselves called for faster
expansion of secondary and higher education than of
primary and middle education, contradicting statements
in every one of the Plan documents that give top priority
to primary education in accordance with the provisions
of Article 45 of the Indian Constitution. This Article
directs the government "to provide, within a period
of ten years from the commencement of this constitution
(1950), for free and compulsory education for all children
until they complete the age of fourteen years". The
date has been postponed at various times to 1965, 1975
and 1985. Even by the end of the Fourth Five Year Plan
(1974), only 86% of children aged 6-11 and only 41%
of children aged 11-14 are expected to be enrolled in
primary and middle schools (see TABLE 2). The Fourth

---

* Professor Blaug is the Director of the Research Unit
in Economics of Education, the Institute of Education,
University of London.

Bulletin. Vol. 3, No. 3, June 1971
University of Sussex: IDS.

4

TABLE 1: Annual Growth Rates of Enrolments, Targeted & Actual, 1950/1 - 1973/4 (in %)

note: n.a. = not applicable   x = not available

| | First Plan 50/51 - 55/56 | | Second Plan 55/56 - 60/61 | | Third Plan 60/61 - 65/66 | | Annual Plans 65/66 - 68/69 | | Fourth Plan 68/69 - 73/74 |
	Target	Actual	Target	Actual	Target	Actual	Target	Actual	Target Proj.
Primary (ages 6-11)	8.2	5.6	5.5	6.8	7.6	7.8	n.a.	3.0	4.3
Middle (11-14)	n.a.	5.3	6.5	9.3	8.8	10.0	n.a.	5.4	8.0
Secondary (14-17)	n.a.	9.0	6.5	9.0	9.6	12.5	n.a.	7.6	8.0
University, except engineering (17-23)	n.a.	11.4	n.a.	9.6	9.2	10.8	n.a.	11.1	9.9
Post-graduates (23+)	n.a.	9.7	n.a.	12.7	n.a.	11.1	n.a.	13.8	x
Engineering, diploma	n.a.	x	14.4	19.7	7.7	13.1	n.a.	0.7	0.0
Engineering, degree	n.a.	x	13.6	18.3	6.7	12.4	n.a.	0.0	0.0

Source: *Report of the Education Commission 1964-66* (1966); Education Commission, Statistical Paper No.1, *Expansion of Educational Facilities in India 1946/47 to 1965/66* (1965); *Fourth Five Year Plan 1969-74* (1969), University Grants Comm. (unpublished).

TABLE 2: Enrolments (millions) and % of Age Groups Enrolled, 1968/9 & 1973/4

| | 1968/9 | | 1973/4 | |
	Actual Enrolments	% of Age Group	Proj. Enrolments % of Age Group / Enrolments	% of Age Group
Primary	55.5	77.3	68.6	85.6
Middle	12.3	32.3	18.1	41.3
Secondary	6.6	19.3	9.7	24.2
University	1.7	2.9	2.7	3.8

Source: *Fourth Five Year Plan 1969-74* (1969).

Five Year Plan once again announces that priority will
be given to primary education; nevertheless, primary
education is projected to grow at only 4.3% over the
Plan period, while university education is projected
to grow at 9.9%.

At this rate, India will be enrolling a higher
proportion of the relevant age group in colleges and
universities but a lower proportion in primary schools
by 1973/4 than Korea, Singapore and the Philippines,
Asian economies that have incomes per head eight to
ten times that of India. Similarly, India already
enrols a much higher proportion of her college-aged
population and a much lower proportion of her young
children in primary schools than did Japan in 1905,
a time when Japan's income level was just about that
of India today. Although *comparaison n'est pas raison*,
these figures begin to create the suspicion that India
is peculiar among underdeveloped countries in her extraordinary emphasis on higher education.

The fact that an educational plan gives priority
to primary education does not necessarily imply that
primary education must be made to grow faster than
higher education. It is conceivable that the expansion
of primary education requires the prior growth of teacher
training which is counted as part of secondary and
of higher education. Unfortunately, this argument
does not carry much weight in the Indian situation
where less than a quarter of the employed matriculates
and graduates are teachers: it would be perfectly
possible to increase the output of teachers without
requiring secondary and higher education to grow faster
than primary and middle schooling. Then again, if
higher education were cheaper than primary education,
there would be no contradiction between a stated objective
that accords priority to primary education and a policy
that permits the faster expansion of higher education.
But the average cost of educating an undergraduate
in arts and science for one year is 11 times that of
educating a primary school pupil and a post-graduate
student costs as much per year as 39 primary school
pupils. In consequence, the tendency of university
enrolments to grow faster than school enrolments has
led to a steady shift of expenditure towards the higher
levels. In 1950, India spent 1.2% of her national
income on education, of which primary education constituted
49% and higher education 23%; in 1965, India spent

6

almost 3% of her income on education but the share of primary
education had by then fallen to 43% while that of higher
education had risen to 29%. In short, although total
educational expenditures have grown faster than national
income, university expansion has steadily reduced the
share of expenditures going to school education.

It must be conceded that the goal of universal
primary education becomes more difficult to achieve
the nearer we approach it. In addition, certain stubborn
facts beyond the control of educational planners, such
as the lack of roads on which to travel to school and
the real economic value to parents of young children
at home, impede the achievement of 100% enrolment rates.
Nevertheless, other causes of the high wastage rates
in Indian primary education - over-crowded classes,
inadequately prepared teachers, out-dated curricula,
lack of textbooks and equipment, etcetera - can be
remedied by spending more money. For example, the education
of "scheduled castes" is already being stimulated by
means of free textbooks, free uniforms and free midday
meals, and no one doubts that the extension of such
subsidies to all students would have a significant impact
on wastage in primary schools.

It is clear, therefore, that if more resources
had been invested in primary education in the past,
universal primary education would not have had to be
postponed again and again. That this has not happened
must be attributed in large part to the resources pre-
empted by the pell-mell growth of higher education.

The truth is that India has never practiced educational
planning in any true sense of the term except in the
fields of technical and medical education. The targets
of the first three Five Year Plans were merely extrapolations
of past trends in enrolments and the fact that they
were frequently exceeded simply means that past trends
were misread. If educational planning is to be effective,
the authorities must be able to resist the private demand
for education. But the truth is that the educational
authorities of India have never been able to control
admission into secondary and higher education. This
is precisely why the Fourth Five Year Plan has abandoned
the notion of targets for enrolment. The fact that
the so-called "targets" of past plans were simply projections
of what was considered likely rather than what was considered
desirable is now public knowledge, at least among educators.

7

Educated Unemployment.

     The failure to control or to resist the private
demand for secondary and higher education and thus
to divert additional resources into primary education
takes on additional significance when we consider the
problem of "educated unemployment". The term "educated"
refers to members of the labour force who have at least
completed secondary education, that is, some 10 million
people in 1970 who are either matriculates or graduates.
In a country like India, any single figure for unemployment,
whether for educated or for uneducated people, is bound
to be misleading: the absence of unemployment compensation
forces an individual who cannot get a full-time job
to take whatever part-time work is available. Instead
of a sharp distinction between being employed and being
unemployed, there is a continuous distribution of people
in terms of days worked per week and even hours worked
per day. Thus, depending on how conservatively we
define unemployment, we can get estimates for the degree
of educated unemployment that range from 3 to 13% of
the stock of educated labor (see the Dantwala Committee
Report: *Report of the Committee of Experts on Unemployment
Estimates*, 1970). From what is known of casual employment among matriculates and graduates, a figure of
about 6-7% is probably as near to the truth as any
single figure can be. This implies a total number
of 650,000 educated people who work only a day a week
if at all, which is equivalent to more than one third
of the current out-turn of matriculates and graduates
from schools and colleges in a single year!

     It is worth noting that the rate of unemployment
appears to rise with additional education up to the
level of matriculation, after which it declines for
graduates and post-graduates: unemployment is worse
among arts and commerce graduates but it is not negligible
for science graduates and post-graduates. It is also
worth noting that educated unemployment in India constitutes,
as it were, a revolving queue: it is not that some
are permanently employed and others are unemployed
for life, but rather that large numbers have to wait
years before finding a job. The number of new jobs
is growing all the time but as soon as one cohort has
been absorbed, a new cohort comes along to take up
the vacant places in the queue. Indeed, on the best
available evidence the numbers of educated employed
appears to have remained an almost constant proportion

8

of the stock of educated people over the whole period
1950 to 1970. In other words, the longterm growth rate
of national output of 3.5% since 1950 has just managed
to absorb an out-turn of educated people at an annual
rate of about 6%. But it has not been able to make
any dent into the backlog of educated unemployment;
the explosive growth of secondary and higher education
always creates a new backlog as fast as the old one
is eliminated.

The persistent tendency of the supply of educated
people to run ahead of the demand for them has led to
a steady decline in the real earnings associated with
educational qualifications. That is to say, there has
been sidespread and continuous upgrading of minimum
hiring standards in Indian labor markets ever since
Independence: jobs that used to be filled by matriculates,
such as clerks, typists and bus conductors, now typically
call for graduate qualifications. In that sense, unemployment
among the educated in India has in fact led to a reduction
in their relative earnings, exactly as predicted by
economic theory. Nevertheless, earnings have never
declined fast enough to reduce the incentives to acquire
still more education. As a recent study has shown,(1)
secondary and higher education still pay off handsomely
to the individual in India, even after allowing for
the private costs of education and the possibility of
unemployment. Indian labour markets do respond to unemployment but only sluggishly and with very long time lags:
there are strong taboos about changing jobs and this
alone makes it rational for a new entrant into the labour
market to spend a long time finding the best possible
job available.

Searching for work is a lengthy process in India's
poorly organised labour markets. Despite the rapid
growth of labour exchanges around the country since
1950 and despite the increased use of newspapers as
a source of information about job vacancies, Indian
job seekers still rely to this day on personal contacts
as the principal source of job offers, which again tends
to lengthen the period of search; lastly, the institution
of the "joint family" reduces the incentive of job seekers
to cut down on the length of search: unemployed Indian
students can depend almost indefinitely on some financial

(1)   M. Blaug, R. Layard, M. Woodhall, *The Causes of
Graduate Unemployment in India.* (1969).

support from their families. All of which can be summed
up by saying that the persistence of educated unemployment
ever since Independence is essentially explained by
certain characteristic features of Indian labour markets
that slow down the rate of which the unemployed are
willing to lower their reservation price.

The fact that education is privately profitable
does not tell us whether it is socially profitable.
Since education is heavily subsidized in India and since
the government recovers little of the extra earnings
of the better educated through income taxes, one would
expect the social rate of return on educational investment
to fall below the private rate of return. Such is indeed
the case at all levels of education. More to the point,
that social rate of return falls steadily as we move
up the educational ladder: it is about 19% on primary
education but it is only 10% on university education
(the figures are adjusted for the probability of unemployment
and wastage at the various levels and for the proportion
of earnings which are due to better-than-average home
background). This fact alone argues for a re-allocation
of a given budget for education towards primary education.
Even if we drop the assumption of a given budget for
education and compare the rates of return on educational
investment with the yield of other public investment,
it is impossible to justify continued expansion of higher
education. The social rate of return on higher education
is distinctly less than the target rates of return of
12% which are required of public sector enterprises
in the Fourth Five Year Plan. Even the rate of return
on secondary education is only just on the border-line
of being acceptable. It is difficult to resist the
conclusion, therefore, that higher education in India
is badly overexpanded.

About three-quarters of all graduates and almost
three-quarters of matriculates work in the public sector,
whereas the bulk of primary-school leavers work in the
private sector. It is very likely that the public sector
"hoards" educated people, which is equivalent to saying
that it pays them more than their marginal productivity.
In that case, the true social rate of return on investment
in higher education is even less than 10%, which doubles
the force of our previous conclusion. Even if education
generates significant externalities which are not adequately
reflected in earnings and hence in rate-of-return calculations,
one has to believe that the magnitude of these externalities

10

are much greater at the higher than at the lower levels
of education to reverse the conclusion of over-investment
in higher education. In a country like India, which
has an average literacy rate of 30%, this does not strike
us as a tenable proportion.

The entire argument up to this point simply takes
for granted the idea that education is conducted to
serve the goal of maximizing the growth of national
income. But although this is one of the stated objectives
of Indian education, the authorities have never lost
sight of other objectives, such as equality of educational
opportunity, political stability and national integration.
There is very little solid evidence on the social class
origins of Indian students but the *Report on the Pattern
of Graduate Employment* (1963) and some data gathered
by the Education Commission 1964-66 suggest that the
bulk of undergraduates are members of families whose
incomes lie in the upper two deciles of the urban income
distribution and in the upper decile of the rural income
distribution. Thus, if the goal is equity rather than
efficiency, there is little doubt that too much of the
educational budget has gone to the higher levels and
too little to the lower levels of the educational system.
Likewise, it would strain credulity to argue that the
reduction of regional and communal strife is better
served by producing more matriculates and graduates,
many of whom will be unemployed, than by producing more
people with at least four or five years of schooling,
which seems to be the minimum amount required to achieve
functional literacy through life. In short, if equality,
political stability and social cohesion in India can
be promoted by education, the optimum strategy is once
again to divert resources from the higher to the lower
levels. It is perfectly true that to deny higher education
to a matriculate will not by itself cure the unemployment
problem; it only converts graduate unemployment into
matriculate unemployment. But it does release resources
for other uses and so long as resources are scarce,
to provide education for one more university student
means denying it to eleven primary school pupils.

There is a further problem about the growth of
higher education in India that we can only allude to
here, namely the problem of quality. Any educational
system which is growing at an accelerated rate will
experience shortages of good teachers and a system which
is growing faster at the top than at the bottom will

steadily deprive the lower schools of the best teachers.
After some time, however, the rot will pass up through
the system eventually contaminating the quality of
higher education. In the view of many Indian educators,
"a large segment of higher education in India has become
a caricature of what higher education is supposed to
be" (to quote K.N. Raj in his 1970 Patel Memorial
Lecture, "Crisis of Higher Education in India") and
the Indian Education Commission Report 1964-66 made
no bones about the fact that an Indian B.A. is generally
regarded outside India as barely equivalent to an American
high school diploma. The decline in standards is only
partly the result of accelerated growth, in addition,
there was the unwillingness to finance expansion at
the same accelerated rate. Thus, the real salaries
of university and college teachers actually fell between
1950 and 1965, a period when real income per head in
India rose by 21%. If the salary position of teachers
is to be improved in the future as an integral part
of the effort to raise quality, the pressures on resources
will multiply. The question takes on new significance
in view of the cut-backs in educational expenditure
in the present Fourth Five Year Plan to 5.8% of total
planned outlays, the smallest allocation ever given
to education. As the Ministry of Education frankly
concedes, "The axe has fallen very heavily on primary
education in particular and generally on all programmes
of qualitative improvement" (*Ministry of Education Report*
1969-70).

The case for cutting back the growth of secondary
and higher education in India is overwhelming but the
instruments for actually enforcing this policy are
few. In the practical circumstances of Indian politics,
it would be suicidal for State Governments to institute
a selective admissions policy. It might be possible,
however, to gradually raise tuition fees from the average
current level of Rs. 250 to the full costs of Rs. 750
(the figures refer to art and science colleges) in
an effort to reduce the private rate of return to higher
education; if this were accompanied by the more vigorous
use of scholarship programs for poor students, it is
likely that it could be made politically acceptable
to the Indian electorate, at least after a preliminary
propaganda campaign. Another .suggestion, which has
been mooted in Indian educational circles, is to select
people for public service jobs before they go to college,
while at the same time making their appointment conditional

12

on their getting a satisfactory degree. Be that as
it may, the problem is at least in principle capable
for solution in so far as the government is itself the
principal employer of highly-educated people. At any
rate, until it is solved, most of the other improvements
that are currently being put into effect in Indian education
are unlikely to make much difference.

Current Problems.

        The best way of reviewing current developments
in Indian education is to ask what has become of the
recommendations of the *Report of the Education Commission
1964-66* (1966). At the center of all their proposals,
is that of introducing a "policy of selective admissions"
in secondary and higher education; in their own words,
"to restrict the unplanned and uncontrolled expansion
of general secondary and higher education, if massive
educated unemployment is to be avoided; to make special
and intensive efforts to vocationalize secondary education
and to develop professional education at the university
stage".

        The Commission was driven to the conclusion that
the proportion of middle school leavers who go on to
secondary school, and matriculates who proceed to colleges
and universities, would have to fall.(1) They called
for an end to the open-door policy in higher education,
amounting in fact to a relative declaration of the rate
of growth of enrolments in higher education. However,
they did not spell out any measures by which this could
be achieved. In particular, they did not recommend
any upward revision of fees. On the contrary, after
recommending abolition of fees in all primary and middle
schools, they also proposed to abolish them for "needy
students" in secondary and higher education over the
next ten years to the point where 30% of students would
not be paying fees of any kind.

        But, the fundamental proposal of the Education
Commission to slow down the expansion of higher education
has fallen on deaf ears and the prevailing attitude
in India to educated unemployment continues to be a

(1)   Unless this happened, they predicted that there
would be 4 million unemployed matriculates and 1.5
million unemployed graduates by 1986.

complacent one. Thus the Fourth Five Year Plan document
has no qualms about the proposition that "there are
greater risks of loss when such available shortages
(of manpower) arise then when there is a marginal surplus
of trained manpower". This seems entirely to ignore
the real cost to society of producing educated people
who will be unemployed.

The major problems of Indian education remain
surely:
  (1) the heavy wastage in primary and middle education;
  (2) the uncontrolled expansion of secondary
  and higher education;
  (3) the massive illiteracy of the adult population;
  (4) the enormous inequalities in educational
  provision between different States and between
  different districts within States; and
  (5) the appallingly low quality of all education,
  accompanied by the failure of quality significantly
  to improve over time.
If these are the outstanding problems, it is difficult
to find any coherent plan for tackling them in the
current battery of educational policies. The Education
Commission Report may have had its weaknesses but its
recommendations did add up to some unified approach
to Indian education. It is this unified approach,
and not so much any specific recommendation, which
seems to have been largely abandoned since the Commission
reported in 1966.

14

[13]

EDUCATED UNEMPLOYMENT IN ASIA: A CONTRAST BETWEEN INDIA AND THE PHILIPPINES

Mark Blaug[*]

Educated unemployment in India was the subject of a study [3] published three years ago, to which I contributed. This book examined the evidence on educated unemployment, developed a dynamic labor surplus model to account for its persistence under conditions of continuous economic growth, calculated private and social rates of return to educational investment to check the predictions of the model and, lastly, canvassed some feasible solutions to the problem. The purpose of the present paper is to ask whether the arguments of that book can be extended to the Philippines. In brief, the answer is yes. Nevertheless, there are some striking differences in the nature of educated unemployment in the two countries; in particular, the major policy instruments that the Indian authorities can employ to deal with the problem are not available to the government of the Philippines.

I

I want to begin with some general comments on the measurement of educated unemployment in underdeveloped, labor surplus economies.

If we define the term "educated" to refer to all those who have at least completed secondary education, the number of educated unemployed men in India in 1967 was about half a million. Half a million is equal to 6-7 per cent of the total stock and 15-20 per cent of the economically active stock of Indian "educated manpower", the former figure being more firmly based than the

[*]Professor of the Economics of Education, University of London. This paper was originally written for the Presidential Commission, to Survey Philippine Education. Although my services were made available by the Ford Foundation, at the request of the Presidential Commission, the views expressed below are entirely my own.

276

latter owing to the difficulties of accurately estimating labor force participation rates by levels of education. In either case, we count only men who are out of work the entire week and make no allowance for almost an equal number doing casual or part-time work for a few days in the week; in ILO language, we neglect "visible underemployment" of educated labor.

The phenomenon of part-time work is precisely what makes it so difficult to measure the rate of unemployment in less developed countries (LDC's).[1] The absence of unemployment compensation induces the unemployed to accept some work in preference to none. Hence, the distribution of employment by hours or days worked per week, which in advanced countries is virtually a discontinuous function at 40-45 hours a week, is a remarkably smooth continuous function from zero to about 45 hours in LDC's. In consequence, the problem of defining the labor force and the unemployment rate in LDC's is very similar to committing Type I and Type II errors in the Fisher-Neymann theory of statistical inference: if one is made larger, the other is necessarily made smaller. If we define "employment" as working at least one day in the reference week, we get a large definition of "labor force" and therefore a small definition of "unemployment". If instead we define "employment" as working at least 30 hours a week, we get a small definition of "labor force" but a large definition of "unemployment". In that sense, a country can make its unemployment rate anything it likes by suitably defining the "labor force" as the denominator of the rate.

As if all that were not bad enough, we have the further problem of "the discouraged worker", a cyclical phenomenon in advanced countries which may well be a secular phenomenon in LDC's. In other words, if persistent unemployment discourages workers from actively seeking employment, they cease to be counted in the labor force; in this way, chronic unemployment in LDC's steadily reduces their labor force participation rates and hence imparts a constant downward bias to their reported unemployment rates.

To sum up. The population of any country may be divided into six groups: (1) full-time students; (2) those unable to work because they are sick, disabled, too young or too old, to which must be added

---

[1]The next few paragraphs are a succinct precis of Myrdal [11, pp. 2203-21].

BLAUG: EDUCATED UNEMPLOYMENT   35

those unwilling to work on any terms; (3) those wholly unemployed
who are not actively seeking work because they think there is none
available; (4) those partly unemployed who are not actively seeking
more work; (5) those wholly or partly unemployed who are actively
in search cf work; and (6) those who are employed full-time. It is
categories (4) and (5) that bedevil unemployment statistics in LDC's.
If we are talking about educated labor rather than labor in general,
there is the further difficulty that the labor force participation rate,
conventionally defined, is in most countries positively related to
levels of educational attainment. This factor alone, everything else
being the same, will always produce a tendency for the unemployment rate to decline with levels of education, simply because the
denominator of the unemployment rate rises with higher and higher
levels of education. But everything else is not the same: if the
educational system is growing very rapidly, students will constitute a
rising percentage of the labor force as time passes. If the upper
levels of the educational system are growing more rapidly than the
lower levels, as in most LDC's, this tends further to reduce the rate
of educated unemployment. But this is a small effect next to the
impact of population growth. A population growing at 3 per cent
or more may have an age distribution in which half of the population
is 15 years or younger (the case of the Philippines). If the labor
market is poorly organized, so that even in the best of circumstances
it takes a graduate weeks if not months to find suitable work, then
the rate of educated unemployment is almost bound to be higher
than that of unemployment in general, not because they are educated
but because they are young. It is clear from this that we need
evidence, not just on the rate of open unemployment, but also on
the waiting-period before entering a job, or the average duration of
unemployment. There is a world of difference between the situation
in which everybody takes 6 months to find a job and then holds on to
it until retirement, and one where 90 per cent find work the day they
leave school, while 10 per cent take 5 years to get a job, although
both situations actually yield identical unemployment rates. Thus, it
is more illuminating to be told, not that educated unemployment in
India is 6-7 per cent of the stock of educated labor, but rather that
the "average waiting time" in India of matriculates (high school
graduates) is 18 months, while that of college graduates is 6 months.

36   THE PHILIPPINE ECONOMIC JOURNAL

Enough has now been said to show why data on educated unemployment are worth little unless (1) they are cross-classified by
age, and (2) they are accompanied by the entire distribution of employment or unemployment by hours worked per week.

That a poor country with a high rate of population growth
should suffer from a chronic surplus of labor is hardly surprising. But
general unemployment is one thing and educated unemployment is
another. Many people in LDC's argue that educated unemployment
is really an economic problem and not an educational one: the blame
lies with economic planners for not making the economy grow faster.
But this view implies a profound misunderstanding of the nature of
educational planning. Even if the expansion of education did nothing
more than to convert the uneducated unemployed into the educated
unemployed – and we might have hoped that it could do more than
this – it would only do so at considerable costs in resources foregone
for other uses. So long as education is costly, the fact that many
people still remain unemployed despite completing secondary and
even higher education cannot be simply ignored by educational
planners. To be sure, if education were conducted entirely as an end
in itself, having no instrumental value whatsoever, the problem of
educated unemployment could be shrugged off and consigned to
economic planners. But so long as the objectives of education are
regarded as partly economic, partly social and partly political,
educated unemployment will remain a matter of abiding concern to
educational planners. The real question, however, is what are we
supposed to conclude from the existence of educated unemployment
in a country? Is it that there are too many high school and college
graduates relative to existing job opportunities, or rather that they
have received the wrong kind of education to match the demands
of the labor market? This is the $64 question to which the rest
of this paper is devoted.

II

If we examine Indian statistics on enrolments in higher education
by fields of study, we discover that over half of all Indian university
students are enrolled in Arts and Commerce degrees (law, literature,
book-keeping and accounting) and only about one-quarter are

BLAUG: EDUCATED UNEMPLOYMENT   37

enrolled in technical and vocational degrees, like Science, Engineering and Medicine. This has caused some observers of the Indian scene (e.g., Myrdal [11, pp. 1124-31]) to conclude that the blame for educated unemployment rests partly on the educational system for not encouraging practical subjects and partly on the students them- selves for preferring white-collar to blue-collar occupations, implying that educated unemployment would soon vanish if only education were "vocationalized" and if only educated people were willing "to get their hands dirty". Unfortunately, this ignores the fact that there is considerable unemployment even among those with master and doctoral degrees in Science and Engineering. Furthermore, it neglects the realities of admission procedures in Indian universities and colleges.

We know from attitude surveys and from application rates that Medicine and Engineering are in fact highly favored subjects with Indian students. Unfortunately, these are also the only fields of study in higher education to which admission is severely restricted. The rest of higher education and the whole of secondary education have always been allowed to grow in response to private demand. Therefore, the fact that so many Indian university students are enrolled in Arts and Commerce courses is not evidence that they are addicted to purely academic pursuits: it is simply that they lack the matriculation marks that are required to enter a science faculty, or a medical and engineering college.

This shifts the problem to explaining the pressure for admission into Arts and Commerce courses in the face of heavy unemployment among graduates with these qualifications. One answer is that a B.A. in Law or Literature does earn more than a matriculate, even after allowing for a 15-20 per cent probability of unemployment. There are costs attached to remaining in full-time education for another four years and therefore the more interesting question is: what is the private rate of return to a B.A. after adjusting for the possibility of unemployment? A glance at the fourth row and second column of Table 1 shows that the adjusted private rate of return to B.A.'s, although below that of a matriculate, still compares favorably with the rate which urban Indian parents could earn on their personal savings (about 7 per cent at any bank), or which they would have to pay if they borrowed funds to finance education. Thus, despite

38   THE PHILIPPINE ECONOMIC JOURNAL

educated unemployment, a B.A. is a profitable investment for an Indian student of average ability. Paradoxically, therefore, an Arts degree is actually a vocational degree in Indian circumstances.

TABLE 1

PRIVATE AND SOCIAL RATES OF RETURN
URBAN INDIA, MALES, 1960

Levels of Education	Social Rate	Private Rate
Primary over none	13.7	16.5
Middle over primary	12.4	14.0
Matriculation over middle	9.1	10.4
College over matriculation	7.4	8.7
Matriculation over none	12.2	14.7
College over none	10.3	12.3
Eng. degree over none	12.3	15.2

Source: Blaug, Layard and Woodhall [3, Tables 9-1 and 9-2].

Note: Only half of the observed earnings differentials associated with different levels of education are here attributed to the effect of education. These earnings differentials are then multiplied by the probability of employment at each level before being expressed as a proportion of the social or private costs of education; the costs are adjusted for wastage. A final adjustment is made for the expected growth of all earnings over a working life time. For further explanations, see Blaug [2, pp. 51-60, 227-28].

Economic theory predicts that the existence of educated unemployment will cause salary differentials associated with education to fall, thereby increasing employment in the short run and reducing the financial advantages of acquiring more education in the long run. In this way, the market mechanism will eventually eliminate educated unemployment. Yet in India, educated unemployment has been a problem ever since 1947, and perhaps ever since 1918, and this had led many commentators to scoff at the notion of competitive labor markets in a country like India. The fact is, however, that the market mechanism does work in India, but only slowly and imperfectly. Unemployment among the educated has produced a steady decline in their real earnings at a rate of about two to three per cent a year, largely via the device of upgrading the minimum hiring standards for jobs: jobs that used to be filled by matriculates now increasingly call for graduate qualifications, and so on for jobs lower down the occupational hierarchy. Nevertheless, upgrading has always failed to clear the market for educated manpower at any moment in time. Earnings have never declined fast enough to reduce the incentive to acquire still more education. Indeed, the supply of educated people has so persistently run ahead of demand that educated unemployment as a fraction of the total stock of educated manpower has remained virtually constant in India for at least twenty years.

The chronic character of Indian educated unemployment must be explained, therefore, by certain features of Indian labor markets that slow down the process of adjustment to an excess supply of labor. Most of the unemployed are young and have not yet found their first job. The number of jobs is growing all the time and everyone will eventually find employment at a more or less satisfactory rate of pay if only they search long enough. There are strong taboos in India about changing jobs to enhance one's prospects, and this alone tends to lengthen the search for a first job. In addition, there are few institutions in Indian labor markets devoted to speeding up the search process. Lastly, the institution of the "joint family", with its creed of pooling resources, reduces the incentive to cut down on the length of search: the unemployed Indian student can rely almost indefinitely on some support from his family.

When we put all these factors together, we get an "average waiting time" for matriculates and graduates that is much longer than anything experienced by educated job seekers in advanced countries; this is of course only the other side of the coin of the much higher rates of educated unemployment in India. Having said this much, however, it seems that we have successfully shifted responsibility for the problem of educated unemployment from the Ministry of Education to the Ministry of Labour. After all, the educational authorities might say, to cut down on college places would simply increase the number of unemployed matriculates; to cut down on secondary-school places would simply increase the number of unemployed primary-school leavers; and so on. Since the fault lies with the functioning of labor markets, we might as well expand educational facilities, thereby keeping people off the labor market as long as possible.

40   THE PHILIPPINE ECONOMIC JOURNAL

This intuitively appealing argument shows immediately that the fact of educated unemployment by itself can be used as easily to justify an expansionary policy in education as a contractionary one. The fallacy in the argument we have just heard is the omission of any mention of the resources used up in producing more educated people, a social cost which in India is only partly borne by students themselves. Indian secondary and higher education is heavily subsidized, not as heavily as in Great Britain but more heavily than in the United States. In fact, three-quarters of total educational expenditure in India comes from government funds but the government recovers little of the extra earnings of the better educated via the income tax. The result, as Table 1 shows, is that social rates of return on educational investment invariably fall below private rates. More to the point is the fact that social rates of return to secondary and higher education (except engineering) are considerably less than rates of return to primary and middle-school education. If the total educational budget is regarded as given, this argues for a reallocation of educational expenditure towards primary education, or, to put it bluntly, a reduction in the rate of growth of secondary and higher education. We arrive at this conclusion not because there is educated unemployment but because the social rate of return adjusted for the probability of unemployment indicates that secondary and higher education is overexpanded relative to primary education.

If we do not regard the educational budget as given we are faced with the necessity of comparing the rate of return on education with the yield of other public investments in India and indeed with the "social discount rate" of Indian economic planners. A variety of arguments all lead to the figure of 12.5 per cent as the best estimate of the Indian "composite social discount rate" [2, pp. 232-33] and the Fourth Five-Year Plan (1966-71) in fact lays down target rates of return of 11-12 per cent for public sector enterprises. If this much is accepted, it follows that there is social underinvestment in Indian primary and middle schooling and social overinvestment in secondary and higher education.

Have we left anything out of the comparison that might alter our conclusions? Rate-of-return calculations on educational investment generally take no account of the consumption benefits and the "externalities" of education. But provided the magnitude of these extra benefits are identical at all levels of education, they do not affect our central conclusion. Insofar as they are not identical, they probably strengthen our conclusion. In a country like India, where the literacy rate is still about 30 per cent and where half of all primary school children drop out before completing Grade IV, it is difficult to sustain the notion that it is higher and not primary education that generates a greater sense of personal enrichment, or greater indirect benefits for those with less education.

Next there is the possibility that relative earnings do not reflect the relative contributions of individuals to productive capacity. It is a striking fact that two-thirds of all graduates in India, and nearly two-thirds of all matriculates, work in the public sector (the army, the civil service, the nationalized industries and of course the educational system itself). It is undoubtedly true that the public sector in India tends to disguise unemployment by systematic over-manning of almost all of its activities, which is to say that the earnings of public sector employees exceed the value of their marginal private products [2, p. 207]. The bulk of primary and middle-school leavers, however, are employed in the private sector which is much more likely to pay labor its marginal product. This means that we have probably overestimated the social rate of return on secondary and higher education, which doubles the force of our central thesis: higher education is badly overexpanded relative to primary education.

This conclusion is entirely dependent on the assumption that we are striving to maximize the contribution of education to economic growth. Arguments derived from the noneconomic goals of education, however, go in the same direction as those drawn from economic goals. The "social distance" between an illiterate and someone who has completed primary education is much greater than that between a matriculate and a graduate. If the goal is equity rather than efficiency, therefore, there is hardly any doubt that too much of the educational budget has gone to the higher levels and too little to the lower levels of the educational system. Similarly, it is difficult to believe that political stability and the reduction of regional and religious strife in India is better served by producing more matriculates and graduates to compete for a limited pool of jobs than by increasing enrolment rates in primary education and thus making sure that everybody gets at least four years of schooling. Thus, if equality, political stability and national solidarity in India can be secured by educational policies (which I somehow doubt), the optimum policy is once again to divert resources from secondary and higher education to primary education, middle schooling and perhaps adult literacy.[2]

The case for cutting back the growth of secondary and higher education in India is overwhelming but the instruments for actually enforcing this policy are few. However, so long as the public sector itself is the principal employer of educated manpower, there are effective devices which could be used to discourage students from demanding more education, such as the policy of adopting maximum rather than minimum educational qualifications for a job. A still more effective general policy, which would be perfectly feasible if it were preceded by a well-managed publicity campaign, would be gradually to raise the level of fees in an effort to lower the private rate of return to secondary and higher education. Obviously, everything else being the same, a rise in fees will reduce the aggregate demand for education. There is nothing wrong with some of the curriculum changes that were proposed by the 1963 Indian Education Commission to discourage students from staying on at school but curriculum reform is a painfully slow method of dealing with the problem of educated unemployment. Besides, without a change in fees or without a change in the hiring practices of the government, curriculum reform will run counter to the grain of private rate-of-return calculations and will therefore fail.

III

We may now proceed to examine educated unemployment in the Philippines. Is it India all over again or is it something different?

We begin by noting that there is presumptive evidence to suggest that the Philippines is a relatively overeducated country. Whether the measure is the ratio of total educational expenditure to

---

[2]It is interesting that Myrdal [11, p. 1669, 1817-8], while rejecting rate-of-return analysis, reaches the same conclusions along the lines just indicated.

BLAUG: EDUCATED UNEMPLOYMENT   43

GNP (6.7 per cent), the share of educational expenditure in the budget of the national government (37 per cent), the proportion of people with bachelor degrees in the active population aged 14-65 (6.5 per cent), or the proportion of the relevant age groups 13-16 and 17-20 enrolled in secondary and higher education (62 and 25.5 per cent, respectively), the Philippines in 1971 ranks just below the United States, above most of the countries of Western Europe and above all of the countries of Asia and Southeast Asia.[3] But of course GNP per head in the Philippines is only $200, and more than half of the population is still engaged in agriculture. At a per capita growth rate of about 3 per cent, maintained over 25 years, she is a developing but still underdeveloped country. Still, she is richer than India and growing faster than India and, besides, *comparaison n'est pas raison:* international comparisons of the kind just made prove nothing since there is no reason to believe that there is a unique relationship between the provision of education in a country and either its level of economic development or its rate of economic growth [2, Ch. 3].

We turn next to data on educated unemployment. Generally speaking, the Philippine data show somewhat higher rates of educated unemployment than are found in India but, in point of fact, the data are not comparable: there are no reliable Filipino estimates of the total stock of educated manpower; there are no cohort studies which for India provide firm evidence of the "average waiting time" of the educated unemployed,[4] and there is practically no historical data before 1960. All the evidence for the Philippines applies to the "labor force", as conventionally defined, and hence involve those endlessly debatable distinctions between voluntary and involuntary idleness, and between part-time and full-time employment, mentioned earlier. The two major sources of information on educated unemploy-

---

[3]For a quick glance at an Asian comparison plus Sweden, see Myrdal [11, Fig. 33-6, pp. 1792-93]. In Asia and Southeast Asia, the Philippines is only exceeded by Ceylon and Malaysia with respect to the age group enrolled in primary schools; in secondary and higher education, it is exceeded by none. For wider comparisons, see Harbison, Maruhnic, and Resnick [7, App. VIII.A, pp. 192-204] and the graphs in OECD (1970) which regress educational indicators on economic ones for 53 countries around the world, the Philippines more often than not falling well to the left of the regression line.

[4]The only comparable Filipino study is by the Fund for Assistance to Private Education (FAPE) [1], which analyzes the employment records in 1969 of five cohorts of college graduates who had graduated in 1965, 1966, etc. Nevertheless, the findings of this study do not permit precise calculation of the "average waiting time".

44   THE PHILIPPINE ECONOMIC JOURNAL

ment, as distinct from general unemployment, are a joint ILO-Philippine Study for 1961 [10] and the Bureau of the Census and Statistics Survey of Households for 1965 [12]. The former is confined to high school and college graduates, and distinguishes unemployment by type of high school attended and by kind of first degree obtained, while the latter cross-tabulates the entire labor force by age, sex, employment status, educational attainment, urban/rural residence, and major industry and occupational category.

In general, as we would expect, unemployment is heavily concentrated among the young aged 25 years or less and among those looking for their first regular job; this category, which constitutes a mere 4 per cent of the total labor force, contains over half of all those who are totally unemployed; indeed, one-third of the unemployed are less than 20 years old. Obviously, they are also more educated than the average employed worker. Against the background of a general unemployment rate of 8 per cent in 1965, educated unemployment in the Philippines falls from 55 per cent for those with some or completed elementary education, to 26 per cent for those with high school, to 13 per cent for those with college education. Oddly enough, and contrary to general impression, unemployment for those with secondary and higher education is actually greater in cities than in rural areas and it is greater for urban males than for urban females. Furthermore, despite the considerable undercounting that is no doubt created by the conventional definition of the "labor force", the figures for higher-educated people are much more reliable than those for the rest of the population: since labor force participation rates rise with educational qualifications, only 6 per cent of males with college degrees are excluded from the labor force.

The 1961 study generally yields higher unemployment rates than the 1965 household census, largely it seems because of a narrower definition of the labor force. Among graduates, the average unemployment rate of 20 per cent ranges from 50 per cent among those with a degree from collegiate secretarial courses, to 36 per cent among those with degrees in Liberal Arts, to 30 per cent for those with degrees in agriculture and veterinary medicine, down to 7 per cent for medicine and dentistry, the lowest unemployment rates observed for any discipline. It is difficult to say how seriously we should take these figures because they are accompanied by large swings in the labor force participation rate by fields of study. Similar objections apply to the 1965 household survey which placed about one-quarter of all educated households in the work status category of "unaccounted".[5] It is worth adding, however, that both of these surveys suggest that, in addition to open educated unemployment, only about two-thirds of the educated work 40 hours a week.

Perhaps it is not so much the absolute level of educated unemployment that should worry us as the failure of educated unemployment, at least at the college level, to fall between 1961 and 1965. Over that five-year period, college graduate employment increased by 156,000 but 288,000 new college graduates were produced. Even allowing for the fact that some graduates will not enter the labor market, graduate unemployment must have increased in the first half of the decade. Since the rate of growth of employment in the Philippine economy accelerated somewhat in the last half of the decade, it is not certain whether graduate unemployment has become a more serious problem in 1971 than it was in 1961:

Another way of looking at the problem is to ask what the future portends as indicated by forecasts of "manpower requirements" as compared with projections of student numbers coming out of high schools and colleges. In recent years, two groups have made independent manpower forecasts up to 1974, the terminal year of the second National Development Plan. Neither of these used anything but the crudest of techniques. Nevertheless, the results are interesting. The first, prepared by the Presidential Commission to Survey Philippine Education, fitted linear regressions of employment on output for three sectors of economic activity and for four educational levels to data for the years 1965-68, and then extrapolated these trends up to 1974. Combining these with enrolment projections (extrapolated from linear and curvilinear trends fitted to 1956-69 enrolment data for each of ten types of schools and colleges in the system), they concluded that the unemployment rate for high school graduates would remain in 1974 what it was in 1965, while that for college graduates would actually worsen [8].

---

[5]If any of these were to be added both to the labor force and to that portion of the labor force that is unemployed, the unemployment rate would nevertheless decline as a simple arithmetical consequence of the fact that the unemployment ratio is a quotient.

46   THE PHILIPPINE ECONOMIC JOURNAL

The manpower forecasts that underlie the second Plan, on the other hand, represent alternative extrapolations of the rates of growth of employment over the years 1965-69 based on three assumptions: (1) that employment will grow at the same rate as it did throughout the first half of the decade 1960-70, namely, 1.6 per cent; (2) that it will grow at the average rate for the entire decade, namely, 2.6 per cent; and (3) that it will grow at a still higher targeted rate of 4.5 per cent. The educational distribution of the labor force by seven educational levels is known for 1961 and 1965. These percentages are now linearly extrapolated to 1974 and multiplied into the three aforementioned employment forecasts to yield estimates of future demand. On the supply side, the labor force is first projected to 1974 from demographic data and from past participation rates and then the educational distribution of the labor force in 1961 and 1965 is used again to yield the probable supply of educated labor in 1974 to compare with demand [13]. The results yield surpluses at all levels of education by 1974, whichever of the three employment-growth assumptions is used. Furthermore, the surpluses will grow larger for all levels up to high school completion even if the second Plan is fully realized; for high school and college graduates, however, employment growth as high as that experienced in the years 1965-70 will act to reduce the surplus and the fulfilment of the plan will reduce it still further. Nevertheless, even on the most optimistic assumptions there will still be 200,000 college graduates unemployed in 1974, or 13 per cent of the output of graduates projected for that year. Nor will the surplus consist entirely of graduates in Liberal Arts: in fields such as Natural Science, Social Science, Agriculture and Technology, there will be a surplus of 172,000 in 1974, as compared to 109,000 in 1969.[6]

Despite these ominous forebodings of chronic surpluses of all types of educated manpower, the belief that economic growth in the Philippines is somehow held back by manpower shortages is so firmly held that lip service is forever being paid to the notion of a "shortage"

---

[6]Similarly, using the rule of thumb that higher-level educated labor should grow two times and secondary-educated labor three times as fast as GNP, a rule that is known to give inflated estimates, Hunter [9] estimated the Philippines' annual manpower needs at the tertiary level by 1967-68 at only 5,600. Yet the annual output of college graduates in that year was well above 50,000.

BLAUG: EDUCATED UNEMPLOYMENT   47

of technicians. If what is meant is that there is a shortage of *good* technicians, in the sense that employers cannot find enough competent technicians at the rates of pay they are offering and frequently end up hiring graduate engineers to do the job, this could be said of almost any country. As the Education Survey Report (hereafter referred to as ESR) candidly admits: "There are no national statistics that would identify specific skills required by industry" [6, p. 84] and I would add, there cannot be in the nature of the case. To be sure, structural shortages of particular types of educated manpower may co-exist with general educated unemployment but, if so, manpower forecasting of the traditional variety cannot accurately identify them.

We may sum up by noting that there is ample evidence that the Philippines faces problems of educated unemployment, which are not likely to be eliminated by economic growth in the 1970's. But as in the case of India, what we must ask is: would it improve matters if we cut back on secondary and higher education, assuming that we could do so? If the cause of educated unemployment is largely the long delay between leaving school and finding a first job, a reduction in secondary and higher education might simply solve educated unemployment by increasing general unemployment more than proportionately. It might well be a better policy to improve vocational counselling and labor placement services.

IV

Let us now consider rates of return to educational investment in the Philippines to see whether educated unemployment has in fact eroded the economic value of education. In the case of India, the rates were calculated from a survey of personal earnings in the whole of urban India but the results were checked against special surveys conducted in four cities and in three manufacturing industries, not to mention evidence from several tracer or follow-up studies of the graduates of particular educational institutions. As against this wealth of data for India, we have one study in the Philippines of earnings by age and education for Imus, Cavite, a small town just south of Manila; the data is based on only 1,000 observations distributed across 80

48   THE PHILIPPINE ECONOMIC JOURNAL

cells (16 age categories by 5 educational levels) and mean earnings are reported without standard deviations (Williamson and DeVoretz [18, Table 4.1, pp. 148-49]).

The fact that the absolute level of earnings obviously differs throughout the Philippines does not necessarily invalidate this study because earnings differentials by stages of education may be fairly uniform throughout the country — this proved to be the case for India — and rates of return depend only on absolute differences in earnings, not on relative differences, or on the levels themselves.

TABLE 2

PRIVATE AND SOCIAL RATES OF RETURN TO
PUBLIC AND PRIVATE EDUCATION IN
IMUS, MALES, 1966

Levels of Education	Public Education		Private Education
	Social Rate	Private Rate	Private Rate
Elementary over none	8	9	8
High School over elementary	21	29	27
College and university over high school	11	12	13

Source: Williamson and DeVoretz [18, Table 5.3.1, p. 162].

Note: The adjustment for the impact of factors other than education is the same as for Table 1; no adjustment for unemployment was required as the unemployed appear in the data at zero earnings; earnings below the age of 18 were estimated by the application of a linear regression to the pre-peak phase of each age-earnings profile; earnings are not distinguished by type of institution attended and the differences between columns two and three are entirely due to costs; earnings before and after tax were assumed equal because of the minimal incidence of income tax; no allowance was made on the cost side for wastage and no adjustment was made for the secular growth of earnings, considerations which, to some extent, cancel each other out.

Furthermore, the fact that Imus is only an hour's ride from Manila suggests that it is probably representative of earnings differentials in the Manila Area where half of all educated labor in the Philippines is employed. Nevertheless, we must be wary of leaning too heavily on a single data source, which means that much of what follows is merely

BLAUG: EDUCATED UNEMPLOYMENT   49

illustrative of what might be revealed by rate-of-return calculations in the Philippines if better data were available.[7]

So for the sake of argument, let us treat Table 2 seriously. What does it tell us? It differs from Table 1 in two respects. Taking the total educational budget as given, it suggests that both elementary and higher education are overexpanded relative to secondary education and the differences are large and indeed much larger than they are in India; furthermore, except in secondary education, the social and private rates of return are virtually the same since a difference of 1 per cent is well within the margin of error that surrounds all these calculations. The latter effect is precisely what one would have predicted from certain facts about the costs of education and levels of government subsidies to education in the Philippines.

In terms of enrolments, elementary education is almost wholly public (96 per cent), secondary education is only one-third public (36 per cent), and higher education is almost wholly private (92 per cent) [6(ESR), Table 1.7b, p. 45]. In terms of public expenditure on education, the bulk of it, about 75 per cent, goes to elementary education; about 15-20 per cent goes to higher education, government finance in this area consisting principally of aid to 23 state-run colleges and universities [6, p. 45]. The fact that elementary education is heavily subsidized might be expected to produce a much lower social than private rate of return to investment in elementary education. The fact that the difference is only 1 per cent is largely due to the fact that elementary education is relatively cheap, with the level of subsidization amounting to only ₱113 in 1966 [6, Table 1-9, p. 49]. Contrariwise, higher education is relatively expensive (about 12 times that of elementary education); but as it is almost wholly privately financed, the social rate of return to higher education is virtually the same as the private rate. Of course, if the progressive income tax in the Philippines took a heavy bite out of

---

[7]DeVoretz [4, p. 110] reports additional rates of return for secondary vocational schools and for college degrees in education. These are derived in his doctoral dissertation [5] by imposing the pattern derived from the Imus study on the observed earnings of vocational graduates and teachers in a *single* year. It does not get much further, therefore, than the Imus data themselves. There is other evidence for the Philippines on the starting salaries of high school and college graduates, and on their mean earnings without reference to age, but there is no data to my knowledge that could be used as a check on the representativeness of the Imus survey.

50   THE PHILIPPINE ECONOMIC JOURNAL

earned income, which it does not,[8]   the social rate on higher education, calculated as it is on before-tax earnings, might actually exceed the private rate which is calculated on after-tax earnings. It is only at the secondary level, where per student costs are sufficiently high and government subsidies to public and private schools sufficiently important, that the social rate of return is driven well before the private rate.[9]

As in the Indian case, we now consider the consequence of regarding the scale of public expenditure on education as a variable rather than a parameter, which forces us to look outside education at alternative rates of return. Here, too, we have much less evidence in the Philippines than in India. There has been so far little discussion of target rates of return for regulated public utilities in the Philippines, and few examples of cost-benefit analysis that invoke a social discount rate. One study of average rates of return on capital in manufacturing in the Philippines produces figures well above 15 per cent and frequently above 20 per cent (Sicat [15]) and the market loan rate in the Philippines is about 12 per cent. Although a full assessment would require estimates of the incidence of government tax collections on investment and consumption decisions, the fact remains that the social rates of return on both elementary and higher education appear distinctly unfavorable. With respect to educated unemployment, we may conclude that higher education is, in fact, overexpanded and that the problem is not simply one of improving the operations of the labor market.

The usual objections to rate-of-return analysis do little to upset this conclusion. For one thing, public sector employment of educated people is much less of a difficulty in the Philippines than in India. Although no reliable estimates are available on public sector employ-

---

    [8]A Filipino who is married with two dependents is liable to an income tax only 2 per cent on a gross income of ₱10,000, only 10 per cent on a gross income of ₱20,000 and only 33 per cent on a gross income of ₱100,000.

    [9]It is worth noting that Williamson and DeVoretz have probably overestimated rates of return to secondary education because they allocate public expenditures on education to the different stages of the educational system by assuming that (1) national government expenditures on education go exclusively to elementary and higher education; and (2) all local government expenditures are entirely devoted to secondary education. Since then, evidence that has been made available by the Presidential Commission suggests that these assumptions lead to inflated estimates of public expenditures on secondary education.

ment by levels of education,[10] it appears that only about 10 per cent of high school and college graduates work for central or local governments. When we talk about earnings in the Philippines, therefore, we are talking largely about earnings determined by private employers. It is difficult to say anything concrete about externalities by levels of education, except to note that the Philippines is a leading exporter of higher-educated personnel to the United States, which must of course make the social rate of return on higher education, as calculated from observed costs and earnings in the Philippines, an overestimate of the true social rate. Lastly, if social objectives for education are in question, there is reason to believe that college students are drawn disproportionately from the professional, landed and business classes with annual incomes of between ₱5,000 and ₱10,000. This is a deduction which we may draw from household surveys, showing that few families spend more than 5 per cent of their income on education, that students depend for two-thirds of their finance on parents, and that tuition fees in colleges run at about ₱600 [6, pp. 50-51]. Although this is only indirect evidence, we are fairly safe in inferring that further expansion of higher education, which has long been the most rapidly growing stage of education in the Philippines, would do little to promote social equality. The conclusion that elementary education is overexpanded will not, I think, stand up in the light of social and political objectives for education; but the view that higher education is overexpanded is actually enforced by a wider view of the goals of education.

We have said nothing so far about the private rate of return, although it is crucial in explaining the pell-mell growth of higher education in a country where higher education is almost wholly privately financed. Table 2 tells us that, despite graduate unemployment, higher education is a lucrative investment for Filipino students. When time deposits earn 6.5 to 8 per cent, when money market bill rates run around 7-8 per cent, when private bond issues carry fixed interest returns of 10-12 per cent, a rate of return on educational investment of 12-13 per cent, while not stupendous, is hardly likely to discourage a high school graduate from going to college. However, 12-13 per cent is an average rate for all colleges and universities and

---

[10]There is a study, however, on the distribution of scientific and technical manpower in public and private employment [14].

52   THE PHILIPPINE ECONOMIC JOURNAL

there is a great deal of evidence in the Philippines to show (1) that tuition fees vary widely between institutions of higher education [6, Table 1.9, p. 49]; (2) that employers prefer the graduates of certain institutions and pay them higher starting salaries, if not higher lifetime salaries [8]; and (3) that starting salaries and "average waiting times" differ significantly among graduates from different institutions and among graduates with different degrees[1].[11] In short, there is a wide spectrum of private rates of return by type of college or university and by fields of study in the Philippines; at an *average* rate of 12-13 per cent, there must be some rates which are distinctly unprofitable. If we are going to assume that students are rational calculators, we will have to argue that students keep their eye on average earnings and then choose the best college they can afford, unaware that in this way they will not necessarily command the average earnings of college graduates [16]. This is a problem which we managed to evade in interpreting the Indian findings since virtually no Indian college charges cost-covering fees; the choice of college is rarely an important issue for the Indian student, although of course the type of degree is, but in either case the decision is unrelated to the costs of attendance. What creates difficulties in the case of the Philippines is that choice of college and choice of subject are necessarily bound up together with the fees a student can afford.

Medicine is the most expensive field of all and the non-laboratory teaching fields like Education, Liberal Arts and Business are the least expensive. But the last three are typically the only fields offered in cheap private schools, so that students who can only afford fees of ₱300 to ₱400 inevitably end up taking degrees in Education, Business, Commerce, etc. [17]. This raises the interesting question why so many private colleges find it profitable to offer cheap, low quality education. Is it simply the pressure to make money in a market where students are poorly informed of the quality of instruction? Is the demand actually price-elastic?

___

[11]They differ significantly among graduates from different institutions with certain degrees (Commerce, Architecture, Engineering, Liberal Arts, and Science) but not with others (Education and Agriculture). The same is true for the period of waiting before a suitable job is found. However, no simple inverse relationship between variations in earnings and variations in waiting periods can be deduced from the data.

BLAUG: EDUCATED UNEMPLOYMENT   53

It is fashionable in the Philippines as elsewhere to deny that students pay much attention to costs and prospective earnings in choosing fields of study, and the constant proportions enrolled in Medicine and Engineering throughout the 1950's, despite rising earnings for doctors and engineers, give support to this kind of skepticism. On the other hand, there have been massive shifts in the distribution of enrolment among most subjects since 1950 — away from Agriculture, Pharmacy, Law, Business and Medicine and towards Education, Engineering, Technology, Social work and Nursing [6, Table 1.5, pp. 35, 129], [17], which suggest a response, however imperfect and long delayed, to market forces. Nevertheless, students' choices, involving a complex interaction between individual aptitudes and interests, parental income, the differential fees that schools charge, the subjects they offer and the necessarily casual knowledge that students have acquired of job opportunities and earnings in different fields, may be subject to a variety of bandwagon and snob effects. All of which is simply to say that it is much easier to explain a generalised demand for higher education than to explain the pattern of demand for particular fields of study. The point is that if the latter is ever going to be investigated, the Philippines is a perfect laboratory for conducting such a study: higher education in the Philippines is virtually unique in the world for consisting almost of private profit-maximizing sellers facing privately self-financed buyers.

V

I want to close by returning to the planning issue of graduate unemployment. In India, the fact that there is considerable graduate unemployment has not persuaded the authorities that too much is spent on higher education. The Indian Education Commission Report of 1966 based its recommendations with respect to the future growth of higher education on a long-term manpower forecast, using methods rather similar to those employed in the Philippines for the purposes of the second plan; these forecasts implied a gentle decline in the current 8 per cent rate of growth of enrolments in higher education, which would nevertheless leave three million educated people un-employed by 1986. Although some of the Commission's suggestions have been put into practice, the recommendations to reduce the intake into higher education were immediately rejected by the Indian Parliament and there appears to be little prospect at the moment of any change in this climate of opinion. In the Philippines, on the other hand, the mere fact that there is graduate unemployment is frequently used, incorrectly I have been arguing, to infer that higher education is overexpanded.

The Education Survey Report cites evidence on the low rate of utilization of college-educated manpower, that is, the ratio of graduates fully employed to the total stock of graduates, and immediately concludes that "this low rate of utilization of educated manpower means a waste of resources spent on education. From the social viewpoint, investment in the education of the unemployed manpower earns no return" [6, pp. 39-40]. But what if the labor market functions so poorly that it is necessary to produce four graduates if three are going to be employed? What if firms will not hire applicants under 18 or 20, which is indeed the case with some large companies in Manila, so that the "diploma mills" in fact fulfill the useful social function of keeping youngsters off the street? Perhaps it is mass produced, low quality higher education but it seems to have a value in the labor market. Besides, since students virtually pay their own way, are we saying that they do not know what they want? These are not questions that can be answered without evidence on both the private and the social rates of return on investment in college education and yet no such evidence is presented in the Education Survey Report.

If the Imus study is representative of the general situation, we can however rationalize the view that there is an oversupply of graduates. The question is: what to do about it, given the fact that it is largely the outcome of spontaneous forces? In India, as we saw, raising fees, which simultaneously chokes off demand and reduces government subsidies to higher education, might do the trick but this avenue is not open to the Filipino government.

The practical proposals of the Education Survey Report are neatly summarized in one paragraph: "For higher education, there is an oversupply of sizeable number of college-trained manpower. This fact should encourage bold recommendations that would result in cutting down college enrolment, especially those involving raising quality through accreditation of schools, selective admission and

BLAUG: EDUCATED UNEMPLOYMENT   55

dissemination of information on the labor and education markets since there will be no danger of incurring a shortage" [6, p. 40]. In other words, the solution is to raise fees; but since this cannot be done directly, the idea is to achieve it indirectly on the notion that accredited colleges achieve their superior quality by high fees and that cheap, unaccredited colleges will raise their fees in an effort to meet the new standards. This policy would probably succeed if accreditation were imposed from above but, since this is politically unacceptable, the standards for accreditation will have to be developed by the colleges themselves. Some of them are already members of accreditation schemes but so far these include only a minority of universities and colleges. As they are expanded, the danger is that standards will be diluted, or what is even worse, that several non-comparable accreditation schemes will develop to confuse students even further.

The idea that markets for technically complex products will only yield socially desirable results if furnished with a legal framework, laying down minimum standards of quality is, of course, a central tenet of economic liberalism. The experience with markets where sellers provide their own quality and specifications, however, is not a happy one and it must be doubted that the private universities and colleges of the Philippines can be trusted to develop their own standards. Furthermore, the colleges must be given financial incentives to join accreditation schemes, which, at the same time, must not significantly increase government support of higher education. One idea that is mooted in the Philippines that would meet this double requirement is a Development Loan Fund, which would be available to all accredited colleges. In addition, FAPE, which now administers a College Entrance Test for about 100 out of the 600 colleges and universities in the Philippines, hopes to extend the scheme to more and more institutions, eventually encouraging Congress to make such a test mandatory for all colleges. If it works, it would of course leave many high school students who now go on to college with no other choice but to enter the labor market. Youth employment programs, therefore, are a necessary adjunct of the whole policy.

At any rate, the general lines of policy in this area are clear-cut; the object must be to reduce demand by raising fees while simul-

56   THE PHILIPPINE ECONOMIC JOURNAL

taneously improving the quality of vocational and educational counselling. Accreditation is a way of achieving this and, in the circumstances, it is probably the only way.[12] At the same time, there
can be little justification for indiscriminate government subsidies to
higher education, except to foster research in high-quality universities,
to encourage wider accreditation, to disseminate information, or to
achieve specific social goals by means of scholarship programs for
poor students. But unless such measures are carefully monitored as
they are put into practice, there is the danger that government
finance, instead of being used to raise the social rate above the private
rate of return, will in fact raise the private rate still further above the
social rate and thus aggravate the present malallocation of resources
invested in Filipino education.

REFERENCES

1. *Absorption Study*. Prepared by the Fund for Assistance to Private
    Education (FAPE), Manila, 1970, mimeo.
2. M. Blaug. *An Introduction to the Economics of Education*. London: Allen
    Lane, The Penguin Press, 1970.
3. M. Blaug, R. Layard and M. Woodhall. *Causes of Graduate Unemployment
    in India*. London: Allen Lane, The Penguin Press, 1969.
4. D. J. DeVoretz. "Alternative Planning Models for Philippine Educational
    Investments," *Philippine Economic Journal*, Vol. VIII, No. 2 (Second
    Semester 1969).
5. _____. "Investment in Philippine Educational Resources: 1966-
    1974." Unpublished doctoral dissertation, University of Wisconsin,
    Madison, Wisconsin, 1968.
6. ESR (Education Survey Report), *Education for National Development —
    New Patterns, New Directions*. Prepared by the Presidential Commission
    to Survey Philippine Education, Makati, Rizal, 1970.
7. F. H. Harbison, J. Maruhnic and J. R. Resnick. *Quantitative Analysis of
    Modernization and Development*, Industrial Relations Section,
    Princeton, New Jersey, 1970.
8. Human Resources, Presidential Commission (The Special Area Group for
    Human Resources and Manpower Development of the Presidential
    Commission to Survey Philippine Education), Makati, Rizal, 1970,
    mimeo.

---

[12]A tax on non-accredited colleges would ensure the success of accreditation. Oddly
enough, however, no one has suggested this idea perhaps because the idea of taxing
educational institutions flies in the face of conventional wisdom.

BLAUG: EDUCATED UNEMPLOYMENT   57

9.   G. Hunter. *Higher Education and Development in Southeast Asia,* Vol. III, Pt. 1, High-Level Manpower, IAU-UNESCO, Paris, 1967.

10. ILO-OMS (International Labour Organization — Office of Manpower Services, Department of Labor), *Summary Report on Inquiry into Employment and Unemployment Among Those With High School or Higher Education,* Department of Labor Office, Manila, 1961.

11. G. Myrdal. *Asian Drama,* 3 Vols. New York: Pantheon, 1968.

12. Republic of the Philippines, Bureau of the Census and Statistics, *Survey of Households Bulletin,* Series No. 19, Manila, October 1965.

13. _____ , Planning Division, Department of Education, DEP/13/71, Manila, 1971, mimeo.

14. _____ , National Science Development Board, *Survey of Scientific and Technological Manpower in the Philippines, 1965: Private Industry; National Governments Sector; Non-Profit Organizations,* Manila, 1967, mimeo.

15. G. P. Sicat, *Rates of Return in Philippine Manufacturing,* I.E.D.R. Discussion Paper No. 65-4, University of the Philippines, 1965, mimeo.

16. E. A. Tan. "Implications of Private Demand for Education on Manpower Planning," *Philippine Economic Journal,* Vol. VIII, No. 2 (Second Semester 1969).

17. _____ . *The Structure and Performance of Philippine Educational Institutions,* I.E.D.R. Discussion Paper No.   , University of the Philippines, 1970, mimeo.

18. J. G. Williamson and D. J. DeVoretz "Education as an Asset in the Philippine Economy," in *Philippine Population in the Seventies,* ed. Mercedes B. Concepcion. Manila: Community Publishers, 1969.

[14]

An Economic Analysis of Personal Earnings in Thailand*

Mark Blaug

University of London Institute of Education and London School of Economics

The theory of human capital rests fundamentally on the idea that people invest in themselves in a variety of ways in the sense that they incur present costs for the sake of future financial returns. An important manifestation of this phenomenon of self-investment is the act of choosing to stay on in school (and perhaps also the act of choosing one kind of school rather than another). To test the proposition that such decisions are in fact motivated by investment considerations, one has to show that the quantity and quality of schooling received by individuals has a significant effect on the structure of personal earnings. Since so much else besides formal schooling determines personal earnings, the test clearly calls for multivariate statistical analysis. And indeed the use of multiple-regression techniques to analyze the pattern of earnings in an economy has proved to be an important by-product of what has been aptly described as "the human investment revolution in economic thought." Most of these studies have been carried out on American data,[1] but a few brave souls have tried their hand on data

* What follows is a summary of parts of a larger study commissioned by the National Planning Committee on the Third Educational Development Plan of Thailand. Copies of the study, entitled *The Rate of Return to Investment in Education in Thailand* (1972), complete with the questionnaire form and the manual for interviewers, are available on application to the National Education Council, Sukothai Road, Bangkok, Thailand. Although I designed the study and must be held responsible in the final analysis for the results, virtually all the work was carried out by Thai nationals and in particular by Kwanjai Smith of Chulalongkorn University, Aporn Chawadee of the National Statistics Office, and Anuchin Kanistarat and Siviroj Piompiti of the National Education Council. Dr. N. Spoelstra of Indiana University and H. F. McCusker of the Ford Foundation gave valuable help at critical stages of the study. R. A. Shedden of the Asian Systems Development Company prepared the computer program.

[1] See J. N. Morgan, M. H. David, W. J. Cohen, and W. F. Brazer, *Income and Welfare in the United States* (New York: McGraw-Hill Book Co., 1962); J. N. Morgan and M. H. David, "Education and Income," *Quarterly Journal of Economics*, vol. 77 (August 1963); S. J. Hunt, "Income Determinants for College Graduates and the Returns to Educational Investment," *Yale Economic Essays*, vol. 3, no. 2 (1963); W. Z. Hirsch and E. W. Segelhorst, "Incremental Income Benefits of Public Education," *Review of Economics and Statistics*, vol. 47 (November 1965); G. Hanoch, "An

1

Economic Development and Cultural Change

for the less developed countries.[2] The present exercise is another such attempt which is worth recording if only because it contains some new features.

First of all, it was based on door-to-door interviews of a random sample of *households* in the leading metropolitan area of Thailand, supplemented by a quota sample of highly educated people. Second, the survey collected evidence on earnings from all jobs held, multiple-job holding being a pervasive phenomenon in many Asian and Southeast Asian countries. Third, the survey collected information on fringe benefits received; the monetary value of these earnings in kind were then imputed by rules of thumb and added to cash earnings. Last, the interview included questions on the social background of respondents, the type of school they had attended, occupation, hours of work, sector of employment, and even on income from self-employment as well as from property. This takes us well beyond the sort of information that is usually available for regression analysis of earnings functions in LDCs (less developed countries) and made it possible to test a large number of plausible hypotheses about the determinants of earnings in a country like Thailand.

Economic Analysis of Earnings and Schooling," *Journal of Human Resources*, vol. 2, no. 3 (1967); A. B. Carroll and L. A. Ihnen, "Costs and Returns for Two Years of Postsecondary Technical Schooling: A Pilot Study," *Journal of Political Economy*, vol. 75 (December 1967); O. Ashenfelter and J. D. Mooney, "Graduate Education, Ability, and Earnings," *Review of Economics and Statistics*, vol. 50 (February 1968); B. A. Weisbrod and P. Karpoff, "Monetary Returns to College Education, Student Ability, and College Quality," *Review of Economics and Statistics*, vol. 50 (November 1968); N. A. Tolles and E. Melichar, "Studies of the Structure of Economists' Salaries and Income," *American Economic Review*, vol. 58, suppl. (December 1968); D. C. Rogers, "Private Rates of Return to Education in the United States: A Case Study," *Yale Economic Essays*, vol. 9 (Spring 1968); R. D. Weiss, "The Effects of Education on the Earnings of Blacks and Whites," *Review of Economics and Statistics*, vol. 52 (May 1970); W. Lee Hansen, B. A. Weisbrod, and W. J. Scanlon, "Schooling and Earnings of Low Achievers," *American Economic Review*, vol. 60 (June 1970); R. H. Reed and H. P. Miller, "Some Determinants of Variations in Earnings for College Men," *Journal of Human Resources*, vol. 5 (Spring 1970); J. C. Hause, "Ability and Schooling as Determinants of Lifetime Earnings, or, If You're So Smart, Why Aren't You Rich?" *American Economic Review*, vol. 61 (May 1971); and "Earnings Profile: Ability and Schooling," *Journal of Political Economy*, vol. 80, pt. 2 (May/June 1972); Z. Griliches and W. M. Mason, "Education, Income and Ability," ibid.; S. Bowles, "Schooling and Inequality from Generation to Generation," ibid.; D. Metcalf and J. Bibby, "Salaries and Recruits to University Teaching in Britain," *Higher Education*, vol. 1 (August 1972). Even this long list is by no means exhaustive.

[2] The first was M. Carnoy, "Earnings and Schooling in Mexico," *Economic Development and Cultural Change*, vol. 15 (July 1967). See also H. H. Thias and M. Carnoy, *Cost-Benefit Analysis in Education: A Case Study on Kenya* (Washington, D.C.: IBRD, 1970); R. H. Stroup and M. B. Hargrove, "Earnings and Education in Rural South Vietnam," *Journal of Human Resources*, vol. 5 (Winter 1970); M. Carnoy, "The Quality of Education, Examination Performance, and Urban-Rural Income Differentials in Puerto Rico," *Comparative Education Review*, vol. 14 (October 1970); M. Carnoy and H. Thias, "Educational Planning with Flexible Wages: A Kenyan Example," *Economic Development and Cultural Change*, vol. 20 (April 1972).

Mark Blaug

I. The Sample Survey and the Regression Model

The only Thai social survey to ask individuals both their education and their earnings was the Household Expenditure Survey of 1962–63, repeated in 1969–70. This survey covered a random sample of about 4,600 households in the entire country, but it produced information on only 166 college graduates, which is slightly more than the figure of 2.5 percent of the population as revealed by the 1960 census. This number is clearly too small to permit statistical analysis of the earnings of higher-educated people, a topic which was one of our principal concerns.

We decided, therefore, to conduct a survey of our own, varying the sampling fractions so as to generate more information on older men and women and those with secondary and higher educations than would be produced by a purely random sample. Unfortunately, this procedure almost always introduces unknown biases into the sample values. In an attempt to guard against this danger, we divided the survey into two parts: approximately 2,000 men were interviewed on a purely random basis while another 3,000 men and women were interviewed "purposively," that is, they were selected to reach predetermined quotas defined in terms of age, sex, and education. We subjected each of the two samples to an identical regression analysis and only pooled them after demonstrating that, insofar as they partly overlapped, the purposive sample produced essentially the same statistical "explanation" of earnings as the random sample.[3] The result was, to give only one example, that we managed to collect apparently unbiased data on 1,485 college graduates with a sample as small as 5,000 individuals.

We planned initially to sample from the entire population of the kingdom, but it soon became evident that this task was out of all proportions to the resources placed at our disposal. We therefore limited ourselves to the Greater Bangkok area, and this means that our results refer only to urban Thailand. Since something like one-half of all high school and three-quarters of all college graduates in Thailand reside in Greater Bangkok, the findings with respect to highly qualified manpower are probably representative of the country as a whole.[4] When it comes to people with primary education or less, however, there is hardly any doubt that the level of earnings is lower in rural than in urban areas, and the structure of earnings by age, education, and other characteristics may well be quite different from that in the capital of Thailand. It needs to be kept in mind, therefore, that the findings tell us little about the distribution of earnings in the Thai countryside. The survey was conducted in February–March 1970. The results are summarized in figure 1 in terms of some

[3] The test we used was the well-known Chow test of equality between sets of coefficients in two linear regressions (G. C. Chow, "Tests of Equality between Sets of Coefficients in Two Linear Regressions," *Econometrica*, vol. 28 [July 1960]).

[4] See M. Blaug, "Manpower Forecasting in Thailand," *Journal of Development Studies* 8 (October 1971): 60, 65.

Economic Development and Cultural Change

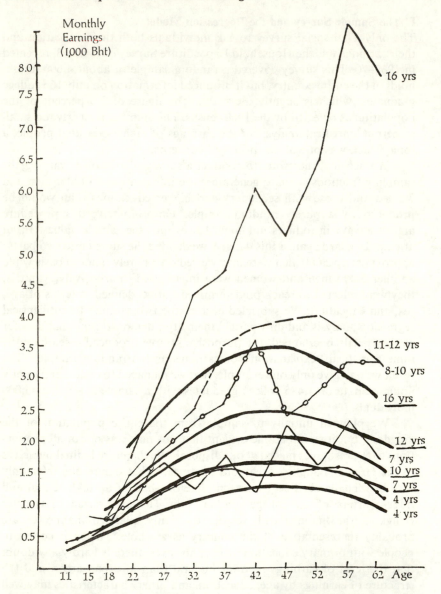

Fig. 1.—Crude and adjusted age-earnings profiles of men and women, before tax (Bangkok-Thornburi, 1970). Heavy lines indicate regression-adjusted profiles.

selected age-earnings profiles of men and women with different years of schooling (readers are asked to ignore the heavy lines for the time being).

So much for the sampling methods. Our model was classical least squares with both continuous and dummy regressors:

$$Y = b_0 + \sum_{i=1}^{n} b_i X_{ij} + u_j$$

Mark Blaug

where j stands for an individual, i for a variable, Y is the continuous dependent variable, X_i $(i = 1 \ldots n)$ are n independent variables, continuous or dummy, b_0 and b_i are parameters to be estimated, and u_j are random, unobserved disturbances with zero mean and constant, unknown variance.

The dependent variable, Y, is total monthly earnings before tax in all jobs held, plus the imputed monetary value of fringe benefits received. The enormous variety of fringe benefits provided to employees in Thailand is hard to credit,[5] and at the outset we shared the view of most of the experts that fringe benefits are more common in the public than in the private sector.[6] To our surprise, however, fringe benefits proved to be more common and more generous in the private sector, accounting on average for 25–35 percent of base salaries of public officials but for 40–80 percent of the base salaries of private-sector employees. Since age-specific salaries are also higher in the private than in the public sector, the effect of including the value of fringe benefits in total earnings is to further widen the differential in earnings between public- and private-sector employment. For fear that our methods of imputing a money value to fringe benefits biased our analysis of total earnings, we ran separate regressions for both cash earnings and total earnings. In fact, the coefficients on the independent variables in the two regressions proved to be very similar.

Some 697 individuals in our sample reported the receipt of property income (rent, dividends, royalties, winnings, fees, interest on loans, etc.). Property income proved to be unrelated to age, sex, education, and occupation. It must be remembered, however, that answers to questions about property income are inherently less reliable than questions about earnings from employment. In any case, we excluded property income from the final analysis. Hence, "total earnings" hereafter refer exclusively to earnings from employment, including self-employment (876 individuals

[5] They include: (1) annual bonuses; (2) annual vacations with pay; (3) overtime pay; (4) allowance for children's school fees; (5) income tax paid by the employer; (6) paid sick leave and maternity leave; (7) medical care and hospitalization; (8) provident funds; (9) pension funds; (10) formal training courses; (11) leave with pay for priesthood or education; (12) allowance for committee meetings; (13) meal allowance; (14) use of car or transportation allowance; (15) low-interest loans; (16) life insurance premiums; (17) housing allowance or free lodgings; (18) discount on company products; and (19) hardship post allowances. In cases (2), (6), (10), and (11), we asked for physical measures (number of days per year, number of weeks, etc.) and then used rules of thumb to translate the answer into a sum of money. In cases (7), (13), (14), (15), (17), and (18), we asked the respondent to impute a money value to the item in terms of outlays that otherwise would have been incurred. In the remainder of the cases, the answer was in fact a sum of money.

[6] See W. J. Siffin, *The Thai Bureaucracy: Institutional Change and Development* (Honolulu: East-West Center Press, 1966), pp. 233–35. Strictly speaking, the comparison is not between public and private employment but between people employed by central, municipal, and local governments, on the one hand, and people employed in state enterprises and private firms, on the other. Salaries in state enterprises are administered separately from the salaries of civil servants, teachers, police officials, members of the armed forces, etc., and for all practical purposes they are determined competitively by bidding against private firms in different local labor markets.

5

Economic Development and Cultural Change

in our sample of 5,000 respondents were found to be either self-employed or family workers).

We explain total earnings in terms of six "basic variables"—(1) age, (2) amount of education, (3) sex, (4) family background, (5) type of schooling, (6) employment status—but family background, type of schooling, and employment status were each measured in various ways, which expanded the six basic variables to 18 derived variables. The use of dummy variables further expanded the list of 18 to 69 derived variables. Let me explain how this happened.

First, there is "age" as a proxy for work experience, a relatively uncomplicated variable. If we had to do it all over again, I would have discarded age in favor of "actual years of work experience" as age itself is negatively correlated with length of education.[7] However, this is wisdom after the event. Second, there is "amount of education" measured in years of schooling attained. We will see subsequently that age and years of schooling appear as regressors in several different forms. It is apparent from figure 1 that the age-earnings profiles by years of schooling are typically concave downward, and so we experimented with a variety of nonlinear relationships between earnings, age, and education, such as the semilog, the double-log, and the quadratic forms; in addition, we used dummy variables to measure age and education as stepwise linear functions.

Third, there is "sex" measured dichotomously with the aid of dummy variables. Fourth, there is "family background" which we measured in four different ways. We asked both father's and mother's years of schooling received. We asked father's occupation and classified the answer in 10 categories, a slightly extended version of the first-digit categories in the official *Thailand Standard Classification of Occupations, 1969*. In an effort to distinguish the ethnic origin of the respondents, we also asked where parents were born and if a language other than Thai was spoken at home. We then coded an individual as "Chinese" if either of his parents was born in China or if a Chinese language was sometimes spoken at home. Since our sample included only those who were Thai citizens, all those who were not Chinese were almost certain to be ethnic Thais.[8]

The effects of education on earnings depend not only on the quantity of education received but also on its quality. We attempted, therefore, to incorporate "type-of-schooling" variables in our analysis, while admitting that the ones we did use are very imperfect measures of what is meant by differences in the quality of education. We asked individuals whether they

---

[7] J. Mincer, "Education, Age, and Earnings," mimeographed (New York: National Bureau of Economic Research, 1972), pt. 2, chap. 1.

[8] It must be explained that the history of the Chinese minority in Thailand makes it impossible to ask people directly whether they are Chinese or not (see W. Blanchard, *Thailand, Its People, Its Society, Its Culture* [New Haven, Conn.: Human Relations Area Files, 1958], pp. 66–69).

6

Mark Blaug

had attended a private or a public primary school and whether it was an urban or a rural school. If the individual received secondary education, we distinguished those who attended academic schools from those who attended vocational schools. We also asked them what score they obtained in their final high school examination. Last, if an individual went to college, we asked him (or her) where he had received his degree, whether he had received an ordinary or an honors degree (Thai universities, like British universities, issue two types of degrees), and in which of six fields he had majored.

This brings us to "employment status," which again is measured in a number of ways. There is the question of whether the individual is a wage earner, or is self-employed, or is a family worker. There is the matter of hours worked per week on all jobs held. There is the question of whether he is employed in the public or in the private sector, and if in the latter, whether he is employed by a small or by a large firm. Last, there is his occupational category, measured in the same way as his father's occupation.

What is missing from the list in independent variables is any indication of native ability or endowed intelligence. Thai children do not take IQ tests in school, nor indeed any centrally administered test of aptitude or achievement, until the secondary leaving examination at the age of 17 or 18. We have nothing to go on, therefore, in assessing their inborn abilities. This is a serious deficiency because studies in other countries have shown that native ability, even if crudely measured by an IQ score taken at an early age, does make an independent contribution to the explanation of earnings differentials. Those who believe, however, that all is nurture in the field of education will worry less than we do about the omission of ability variables.[9]

Table 1 sets forth a list of all the independent variables which we ran in one or more of our regressions. Some of these variables were subsequently dropped or combined into single variables. For example, the small-firm variable was tried along with the large-firm variable in the first two regressions, and then the former was dropped in favor of the latter in all subsequent regressions. Also, the number of years of father's and mother's education were combined after the first two regressions. Notice, too, that something like "father's occupation," while measured in 10 categories, is expressed in only nine variables. This is a simple consequence of the use of dummy variables in multiple regression: we always get rid of at least one subcategory, and its effect is then captured in the constant term of the regression equation.[10] Some examples of excluded categories are "female"

[9] See M. Blaug, *An Introduction to the Economics of Education* (London: Penguin Press, 1970), pp. 32–46.

[10] This is because the number of people in the *n*th category is already determined when the numbers in the $n - 1$ subcategories have been determined. In technical jargon, we must drop one of the subcategories in each dummy group to avoid "singularity" of the moment-matrix of independent variables. There is another way of

Economic Development and Cultural Change

from the dichotomous sex variables, "unclassified workers" from father's and from respondent's occupation, "self-employed and family workers" from the work-status variable, and so on.

TABLE 1

DEFINITIONS OF VARIABLES

Original	Derived (Regressors)
	Basic
Age (years)*	X_1 = actual
	X_2 = actual, squared
	X_3 = common logarithm
	X_4 = 1 if 17–19, 0 if otherwise
	X_5 = 1 if 20–24, 0 if otherwise
	X_6 = 1 if 25–29, 0 if otherwise
	X_7 = 1 if 30–34, 0 if otherwise
	X_8 = 1 if 35–39, 0 if otherwise
	X_9 = 1 if 40–44, 0 if otherwise
	X_{10} = 1 if 45–49, 0 if otherwise
	X_{11} = 1 if 50–54, 0 if otherwise
	X_{12} = 1 if 55–59, 0 if otherwise
	X_{13} = 1 if 60–64, 0 if otherwise
Education (years)	X_{14} = actual, of schooling
	X_{15} = actual, of schooling, squared
	X_{16} = log of actual, of schooling
Education (dummies)†	X_{17} = 1 if 1–3 years, 0 if otherwise
	X_{18} = 1 if 4 years (lower primary), 0 if otherwise
	X_{19} = 1 if 5–6 years, 0 if otherwise
	X_{20} = 1 if 7 years (upper primary), 0 if otherwise
	X_{21} = 1 if 8–10 years (lower secondary), 0 if otherwise
	X_{22} = 1 if 11–12 years (upper secondary), 0 if otherwise
	X_{23} = 1 if 13–14 years, 0 if otherwise
	X_{24} = 1 if 15 years, 0 if otherwise
	X_{25} = 1 if 16 years (college or university), 0 if otherwise
	X_{26} = 1 if 17 years, 0 if otherwise
	X_{27} = 1 if 18–20 years, 0 if otherwise
Sex	X_{28} = 1 if male, 0 if female
	Family Background
Parents' education	X_{29} = years of schooling of father
	X_{30} = years of schooling of mother
	X_{31} = sum of years of schooling of father and mother

dealing with the problem, which is to constrain the constant term to equal zero by allowing every subcategory of each independent variable to be represented by a dummy variable. In the case of sex, we would work with two pairs, one measuring the effects of being male, the other the effects of being female. If we do this for all the subcategories of each independent variable, the constant term will necessarily be zero. In some senses, this is the best method, but it does have the disadvantage of multiplying the number of coefficients that must be inspected. We have chosen the method of *not* constraining the constant to equal zero since we already have quite enough coefficients to think about.

Mark Blaug

TABLE 1 (*Continued*)

Original	Derived (Regressors)
	Family Background

Ethnic origin .... $X_{32} = 1$ if Chinese (at least one parent born in China or Chinese spoken in the home), 0 if otherwise

Father's occupation‡ ...
- $X_{33} = 1$ if professional, technical, or related, 0 if otherwise
- $X_{34} = 1$ if executive or managerial, 0 if otherwise
- $X_{35} = 1$ if clerical worker, 0 if otherwise
- $X_{36} = 1$ if sales worker, 0 if otherwise
- $X_{37} = 1$ if service worker, 0 if otherwise
- $X_{38} = 1$ if farmer, hunter, forester, etc., 0 if otherwise
- $X_{39} = 1$ if transport and communications worker, 0 if otherwise
- $X_{40} = 1$ if laborer or craftsman, 0 if otherwise
- $X_{41} = 1$ if military or police worker, 0 if otherwise

| | **Type of Schooling** |

Private vs. public schooling $X_{42} = 1$ if private schooling (at least one-half of total years of primary and secondary school in a private school), 0 if otherwise (public school, or not applicable)

Rural vs. urban schooling
- $X_{43} = 1$ if rural primary (at least one-half of grades 1–7 in a rural school), 0 if otherwise (urban primary, or not applicable)
- $X_{44} = 1$ if rural secondary (at least one-half of grades 8–12 in a rural school), 0 if otherwise (urban secondary, or not applicable)
- $X_{45} = 1$ if rural primary and secondary school (i.e., X_{43} and X_{44} both equal "1"), 0 if otherwise (urban primary and secondary, or not applicable)

Vocational vs. academic schooling .... $X_{46} = 1$ if vocational schooling (highest level completed in vocational secondary school, or college, or teacher training, excluding 4 years' university graduates), 0 if otherwise (academic secondary school, or higher education, or not applicable)

Secondary leaving-examination score ..... $X_{47} =$ actual percentage at mid points of ranges $50\%-59\% = 55\%$, $60\%-69\% = 65\%$, $70\%-79\% = 75\%$, $80\%-89\% = 85\%$, $90\%-100\% = 50\%$; don't remember $= 95\%$; not applicable $= 0.0\%$

Foreign vs. home degree . $X_{48} = 1$ if foreign degree (in 3- or 4-year program, higher education), 0 if home degree, or not applicable

Honors vs. ordinary degree $X_{49} = 1$ if honors degree (4-year program higher education), 0 if ordinary degree, or not applicable

Field of study (higher education)§ ....
- $X_{50} = 1$ if humanities or fine arts, 0 if otherwise
- $X_{51} = 1$ if education (university degree only), 0 if otherwise
- $X_{52} = 1$ if social sciences, 0 if otherwise
- $X_{53} = 1$ if medicine, 0 if otherwise
- $X_{54} = 1$ if natural science, engineering or agriculture, 0 if otherwise
- $X_{55} = 1$ if military, or police, 0 if otherwise

9

Economic Development and Cultural Change

TABLE 1 (*Continued*)

Original	Derived (Regressors)
	Employment

Work status . . . . X_{56} = 1 if employee (works for regular wage or salary), 0 if self-employed, or family worker

Hours of work . . . . X_{57} = total number of hours per week in all jobs

Sector of employment‖ . . . $\begin{cases} X_{58} = 1 \text{ if government employee, 0 if otherwise} \\ X_{59} = 1 \text{ if private sector employee, 0 if otherwise} \end{cases}$

Size of firm# . . . . $\begin{cases} X_{60} = 1 \text{ if large firm (100 or more workers), 0 if otherwise} \\ X_{61} = 1 \text{ if small firm (less than 100 workers), 0 if otherwise} \end{cases}$

Respondent's occupation** $\begin{cases} X_{62} = 1 \text{ if professional, technical and related, 0 if otherwise} \\ X_{63} = 1 \text{ if executive and managerial, 0 if otherwise} \\ X_{64} = 1 \text{ if clerical worker, 0 if otherwise} \\ X_{65} = 1 \text{ if sales worker, 0 if otherwise} \\ X_{66} = 1 \text{ if service worker, 0 if otherwise} \\ X_{67} = 1 \text{ if transport or communications worker, 0 if otherwise} \\ X_{68} = 1 \text{ if farmer or laborer, 0 if otherwise} \\ X_{69} = 1 \text{ if military or police worker, 0 if otherwise} \end{cases}$

* If 14–16 years, X_4–X_{13} = 0.
† If zero years, X_{17}–X_{27} = 0.
‡ If unclassified, X_{33}–X_{41} = 0.
§ If not applicable, X_{50}–X_{55} = 0.
‖ If state enterprise, or international organization employee, or no information, X_{58} and X_{59} = 0.
If not applicable, X_{60} and X_{61} = 0.
** If unclassified, X_{62}–X_{69} = 0.

II. Some Findings

We ran 11 regressions in an attempt to find the best statistical explanation of the variation in earnings between individuals. We select regressions 4 and 5 (table 2) as our "best fits," and the discussion of the findings will focus on them. However, we present all our regression results because much can be learned from the attempt to compare alternative forms, and, in any case, the selection of a best fit is by no means a mechanical exercise and depends in large measure on what questions one is trying to answer.

In each case, we estimated the equations by a stepwise regression procedure. The stepwise technique may be unfamiliar, and a word of explanation is therefore in order.[11] Our computer program begins by

[11] What we call "stepwise regression" some authors call "stagewise regression" (see A. S. Goldberger, *Econometric Theory* [New York: John Wiley & Sons, 1964], pp. 154–56; and *Topics in Regression Analysis* [London: Collier-Macmillan, 1969], p. 37). Stepwise regression is sometimes described as a method of entering variables successively in all possible orders (see N. R. Draper and H. Smith, *Applied Regression Analysis* [New York: John Wiley & Sons, 1966], pp. 171–72). In that case, our computer program falls short of that ideal: it enters variables successively but in definite order.

Mark Blaug

printing out the arithmetic mean and standard deviation of all variables and then calculates the simple correlation coefficient between all pairs of variables, including the dependent variable. It then enters into the regression equation the independent variable most highly correlated with the dependent variable and computes the regression equation. Next, it enters the independent variable with the next highest partial correlation coefficient, and in so doing recomputes the regression equation. It repeats this pattern for each independent variable until the list is exhausted and, at every step, it accepts or rejects an independent variable on the basis of a partial F-test with 95 percent confidence limits. The final equation may or may not include all the independent variables and usually does not.

Let us consider the 11 regressions of tables 2 and 3 in three groups. The first three are designed to test the question whether our quota sample of households provides biased evidence; that is, results which are significantly different from our random sample of households. Are we justified in merging the random sample (regression 1) with the quota sample (regression 2) in order to calculate regression 3 for the total sample? A precise statistical test of this statement is furnished, as we have said, by the Chow test: when applied to our data, it confirms the hypothesis that the quota sample observations come from the same "population" as the set of random sample observations. However, even a casual inspection of the first two regressions suggests as much.

We begin by noting the average earnings of the quota sample is $\mathcal{B}$. (baht) 3,315, whereas that of the random sample is only $\mathcal{B}$. 1,910. This is just what we would expect because the quota sample was specifically designed to produce a greater proportion of better-educated men and women. None of the three regressions "explains" more than 33 percent of the variance of personal earnings, which we shall see in a moment is due to the fact that we have regressed earnings in natural numbers. Be that as it may, let us now consider the coefficients for certain strategic variables, such as age, sex, and education. In each case, age enters at a very early stage in the stepwise regression procedure, and the coefficient on age for regression 3 is almost the arithmetic mean of the age coefficients for regressions 1 and 2: being a year older would on average add $\mathcal{B}$. 101 to one's earnings. It seems odd that age appears to be linearly related to earnings (the age^2 coefficient is insignificant) and even more peculiar that education, too, is linearly related to earnings. Notice that the education coefficients are practically the same for all three regressions and that even the standard errors of the three coefficients do not differ very much. Our random sample of 1,807 individuals unfortunately included no women so that little can be said for present purposes about the sex variable.

The evidence with respect to family-background variables is somewhat inconclusive. Practically all these variables dropped out in regression 1, but they do not figure significantly even in regression 3, except for fathers in executive and sales occupations. Similarly, none of the type-of-schooling

Economic Development and Cultural Change

TABLE

COEFFICIENTS FOR ALTERNATIVE

		REGRESSION					
VARIABLE	MEAN IN SAMPLE OR PROPORTION OF SAMPLE	1. Earnings, Random Sample	Step in (out)	2. Earnings, Quota Sample	Step in (out)	3. Earnings, Total Sample	Step in (out)
Basic:							
1. Age (yrs)	36.2	5.112 (0.555) a	2 a	16.390 (3.677)	2	10.111 (2.397) a	2
2. Age²	...			−0.128 (0.047)	11	−0.051* (0.031)	24
3. Log age	...	a	a	...		...	...
4. Age, 17–19	0.07	b	...	b	...	b	...
5. Age, 20–24	0.14	b	...	b	...	b	...
6. Age, 25–29	0.14	b	...	b	...	b	...
7. Age, 30–34	0.14	b	...	b	...	b	...
8. Age, 35–39	0.10	b	...	b	...	b	...
9. Age, 40–44	0.13	b	...	b	...	b	...
10. Age, 45–49	0.08	b	...	b	...	b	...
11. Age, 50–54	0.10	b	...	b	...	b	...
12. Age, 55–59	0.06	b	...	b	...	b	...
13. Age, 60–64	0.03	b	...	b	...	b	...
14. Education (yrs).......	10.47	11.033 (1.988) a	15 1 (16)	14.748 (2.839)	29 1 (30)	13.810 (1.741)	1
15. Education²	...						...
16. Log education	...	b	...	b	...	a	a
17. Education, 1–3	0.03	b	...	b	...	b	...
18. Education, 4	0.16	b	...	b	...	b	...
19. Education, 5–6	0.04	b	...	b	...	b	...
20. Education, 7	0.07	b	...	b	...	b	...
21. Education, 8–10	0.25	b	...	b	...	b	...
22. Education, 11–12	0.15	b	...	b	...	b	...
23. Education, 13–14	0.03	b	...	b	...	b	...
24. Education, 15	0.05	b	...	b	...	b	...
25. Education, 16	0.12	b	...	b	...	b	...
26. Education, 17	0.04	b	...	b	...	b	...
27. Education, 18–20	0.04	b	...	b	...	b	...
28. Sex (male)	0.79	b	...	80.054 (16.056)	8	70.805 (12.570)	7
Family background:							
29. Father's education (yrs)	5.54	a	a	5.431 (1.357)	10	b	...
30. Mother's education (yrs)	3.80	2.190* (1.526)	19	−3.905 (1.724)	19	b	...

Mark Blaug

2

STEPWISE REGRESSIONS

				REGRESSION					
4. Log Earnings	Step in (out)	5. Log Earnings, Omitting Employment	Step in (out)	6. Log Earnings, Age Dummies	Step in (out)	7. Log Earnings, Minus Fringe Benefits, Age Dummies	Step in (out)	8. Log Earnings, Age and Education Dummies	Step in (out)
a	a	a	a	b	...	b	...	b	...
−0.0001 (0.0000)	6	−0.0002 (0.0000)	4	b	...	b	...	b	...
1.7695 (0.0738)	2	1.8014 (0.0783)	2	b	...	b	...	b	...
b	...	b	...	0.1895 (0.0380)	3	0.2069 (0.0373)	2	0.1893 (0.0379)	3
b	...	b	...	0.3266 (0.0367)	4	0.3817 (0.0361)	3	0.3205 (0.0368)	5
b	...	b	...	0.4411 (0.0368)	8	0.5044 (0.0362)	6	0.4340 (0.0369)	11
b	...	b	...	0.5118 (0.0368)	11	0.5703 (0.0363)	9	0.5058 (0.0369)	17
b	...	b	...	0.5888 (0.0374)	23	0.6497 (0.0368)	18	0.5860 (0.0375)	30
b	...	b	...	0.6307 (0.0371)	21	0.7017 (0.0365)	16	0.6273 (0.0372)	28
b	...	b	...	0.6380 (0.0382)	22	0.6995 (0.0376)	17	0.6352 (0.0382)	29
b	...	b	...	0.6799 (0.0376)	18	0.7491 (0.0371)	14	0.6774 (0.0377)	23
b	...	b	...	0.6914 (0.0394)	20	0.7672 (0.0388)	15	0.6893 (0.0395)	27
b	...	b	...	0.5880 (0.0432)	24	0.6539 (0.0426)	19	0.5846 (0.0433)	14
0.0316 (0.0037)	1	0.0363 (0.0040)	1	0.0263 (0.0016)	1	0.0328 (0.0037)	1	b	...
b	...	b	...	b	...	b	...	b	...
−0.0820* (0.0514)	24	−0.0766* (0.0582)	14	a	...	−0.0952* (0.0514)	...	b	...
b	...	b	...	b	...	b	...	b	a
b	...	b	...	b	...	b	...	0.0724 (0.0232)	1
b	...	b	...	b	...	b	...	0.0638 (0.0298)	13
b	...	b	...	b	...	b	...	0.1307 (0.0265)	16
b	...	b	...	b	...	b	...	0.2190 (0.0235)	20
b	...	b	...	b	...	b	...	0.3067 (0.0260)	22
b	...	b	...	b	...	b	...	0.3143 (0.0335)	31
b	...	b	...	b	...	b	...	0.3727 (0.0314)	33
b	...	b	...	b	...	b	...	0.4017 (0.0308)	40
b	...	b	...	b	...	b	...	0.4508 (0.0378)	34
b	...	b	...	b	...	b	...	0.4681 (0.0401)	41
0.1248 (0.0110)	4	0.1597 (0.0113)	3	0.1277 (0.0112)	2	0.1135 (0.0110)	5	0.1243 (0.0114)	9
b	...	b	...	b	...	b	...	b	...
b	...	b	...	b	...	b	...	b	...

13

Economic Development and Cultural Change

TABLE

COEFFICIENTS FOR ALTERNATIVE

REGRESSION

VARIABLE	MEAN IN SAMPLE OR PROPORTION OF SAMPLE	1. Earnings, Random Sample	Step in (out)	2. Earnings, Quota Sample	Step in (out)	3. Earnings, Total Sample	Step in (out)
31. Parents' education (sum total in yrs) ...	9.34	b	...	b	...	1.218 (0.585)	17
32. Chinese	0.21	a	...	a	...	a	a
33. Father's occupation, professional	0.12	a	...	−24.579* (21.335)	33	a	a
34. Father's occupation, executive	0.08	a	...	43.398* (24.417)	15	46.630 (18.719)	19
35. Father's occupation, clerical	0.05	73.464 (31.083)	10	−60.124 (29.728)	21	a	a
36. Father's occupation, sales	0.26	a	a	47.115 (17.083)	12	35.402 (11.602)	18
37. Father's occupation, service	0.02	a	a	a	a	a	a
38/40. Father's occupation, farmer/laborer	0.30	a	a	a	a	a	a
39. Father's occupation, transport	0.02	a	a	72.109* (50.742)	23	44.087* (35.884)	27
41. Father's occupation, military	0.09	a	a	a	a	25.720* (17.256)	25
Type of schooling:							
42. Private	0.30	25.263* (13.609)	11	a	...	16.393* (10.612)	23
43. Rural primary	0.05	b	b	b	...	b	...
44. Rural secondary	0.01	b	b	b	...	b	...
45. Rural primary and secondary	0.06	−39.115* (26.499)	18	a	...	a	a
46. Vocational secondary	0.18	−23.535* (17.372)	21	28.331* (18.154)	30	a	a
47. Secondary leaving-exam score	20.13	a	a	0.400* (0.293)	20	0.360* (0.227)	10
48. Honors degree (4 yrs)	0.02	a	a	48.484* (41.912)	32	a	a
49. Foreign degree (3–4 yrs)	0.08	203.046 (45.840)	5	228.376 (25.091)	4	238.109 (20.724)	3
Higher education field:							
50. Humanities	0.01	249.818 (99.776)	12	119.147 (51.896)	27	142.762 (43.416)	15
51. Education	0.02	a	a	a	18 (28)	a	a
52. Social science	0.11	93.702 (32.964)	14	78.627 (25.454)	26	82.343 (19.847)	14
53. Medicine	0.03	229.389 (88.130)	13	140.944 (39.550)	22	158.586 (33.136)	13
54. Science/engineering/agric.	0.04	98.539 (51.027)	17	190.717 (35.765)	9	180.296 (28.725)	9
55. Military	0.02	a	a	114.883 (44.347)	25	105.912 (35.549)	16
Employment:							
56. Work status	0.82	a	a	72.030 (26.772)	17	56.485 (20.936)	21

Mark Blaug

2 (*Continued*)

S**TEPWISE** R**EGRESSIONS**

				REGRESSION					
4. Log Earnings	Step in (out)	5. Log Earnings, Omitting Employment	Step in (out)	6. Log Earnings, Age Dummies	Step in (out)	7. Log Earnings, Minus Fringe Benefits, Age Dummies	Step in (out)	8. Log Earnings, Age and Education Dummies	Step in (out)
0.0021 (0.0005)	16	0.0027 (0.0005)	8	0.0023 (0.0005)	19	0.0020 (0.0005)	22	0.0022 (0.0005)	24
0.0515 (0.0121)	13	0.0404 (0.0124)	9	0.0526 (0.0123	16	0.0512 (0.0121)	13	0.0537 (0.0123)	35
a	a	a	a	a	a	a	a	a	a
0.0531 (0.0162)	21	0.0502 (0.0171)	13	0.0530 (0.0165)	29	0.0607 (0.0162)	26	0.0519 (0.0164)	38
a	a	a	a	a	a	a	a	a	a
0.0329 (0.0105)	22	0.0380 (0.0110)	12	0.0333 (0.0106)	30	0.0338 (0.0107)	30	0.0333 (0.0106)	25
a	a	a	a	a	a	a	a	a	a
a	a	a	a	a	a	a	a	a	a
−0.0208* (0.0150)	28	a	a	0.0230* (0.0152)	35	0.241* (0.0150)	36	0.0230* (0.0152)	39
0.0333 (0.0094)	17	0.0419 (0.0100)	7	0.0331 (0.0095)	25	0.0364 (0.0094)	23	0.0338 (0.0096)	21
b	...	b	...	b	...	b	...	b	...
b	...	b	...	b	...	b	...	b	...
−0.0432 (0.0178)	23	−0.0458 (0.0190)	11	−0.0430 (0.0180)	31	−0.0595 (0.0177)	24	−0.0395 (0.0181)	42
a	a	a	a	a	a	a	a	a	a
0.0007 (0.0002) a	10	0.0008 (0.0002) a	6	0.0007 (0.0002) a	12	0.0005 (0.0002) a	12	0.0004 (0.0002) a	1
				0.0349* (0.0309)	40			0.0389* (0.0312)	19
0.1509 (0.0182)	5	0.1493 (0.0195)	5	0.1489 (0.0187)	7	0.1308 (0.0181)	8	0.1438 (0.0203)	4
0.1007 (0.0381) a	25	0.0914 (0.0407) a	18	0.1052 (0.0385) a	33	0.1184 (0.0380) a	33	0.1019 (0.0402) a	32 ...
0.0456 (0.0178)	26	0.0592 (0.0191)	16	0.0541 (0.0175)	32	0.0520 (0.0178)	34	0.0564 (0.0209)	37
0.1196 (0.0293)	19	0.0859 (0.0311)	17	0.1296 (0.0293)	27	0.1405 (0.0293)	25	0.1279 (0.0318)	43
0.0995 (0.0254)	2	0.1230 (0.0272)	10	0.1088 (0.0254)	28	0.0962 (0.0253)	28	0.1090 (0.0279)	44
0.1462 (0.0314)	15	0.1078 (0.0322)	15	0.1572 (0.0314)	17	0.1600 (0.0313)	21	0.1453 (0.0340)	12
0.2462 (0.0185)	8	b	...	0.2638 (0.0190)	9	0.0662 (0.0184)	29	0.2348 (0.0190)	6

15

Economic Development and Cultural Change

TABLE

COEFFICIENTS FOR ALTERNATIVE

REGRESSION

VARIABLE	MEAN IN SAMPLE OR PROPOR- TION OF SAMPLE	1. Earnings, Random Sample	Step in (out)	2. Earnings, Quota Sample	Step in (out)	3. Earnings, Total Sample	Step in (out)
57. Hours of work	47.68	1.017 (0.359)	8	2.736 (0.488)	7	1.815 (0.322)	8
58. Civil service	0.32	−113.149 (20.937) a	4 a	−194.404 (22.943) a	3	−171.082 (18.170)	4
59. Private sector	0.40				...	−53.909 (18.189)	20
60. Large firm	0.11	88.291 (20.177) a	6 a	93.048 (27.346)	5	136.545 (17.078) b	6
61. Small firm	0.07			−81.155 (24.579)	16		...
Occupation:							
62. Professional	0.25	108.622 (22.146)	7	56.496 (19.004)	14	70.807 (14.718)	11
63. Executive	0.12	228.306 (28.042) a	3 a	155.059 (22.831) a	6 a	177.440 (17.977) a	5 a
64. Clerical	0.14						
65. Sales	0.12	24.076* (17.681) a	20 a	a	a	22.669* (17.968) a	26 a
66. Service	0.07			a	a		
67. Transport	0.03	a	...	−68.412* (48.763) a	24 a	−46.319* (27.990) a	22 a
68. Farmer/laborer	0.17	a	a				
69. Military	0.08	82.164 (27.812)	9	87.034 (30.543)	13	83.721 (21.496)	12
Intercept	...	−165.446	...	−573.405	...	−413.081	...
Mean of dependent variable (in tens of Baht)...............	...	191.025	...	331.493	...	279.136	...
R^2	...	.248	...	.330	...	.321	...
R^2 (corrected)	...	...	...	...	...	...	...
F-value	...	...	...	...	...	...	...

variables below the level of higher education survived the screening process, whichever of the three regressions we consider. For those with completed higher education, the possession of a foreign degree emerges as a critical variable in all three regressions: it enters early in the stepwise process and comes in with a relatively large coefficient that is stable over all three regressions. In short, 4 years of education beyond high school add ฿. 552 to monthly earnings, but a foreign degree instead of one from a Thai university adds ฿. 2,381.

Last, in the list of employment variables, the most striking finding is the relatively large negative coefficient on civil service employment (public-sector employees in state enterprises are in the intercept term), which shows up whether we look at the random sample, the quota sample, or the two taken together in regression 3. Work status, that is, whether the employee works for a regular wage or salary (the self-employed and family workers are relegated to the intercept term) and working for a large firm enter with

Mark Blaug

2 (*Continued*)

STEPWISE REGRESSIONS

				REGRESSION					
4. Log Earnings	Step in (out)	5. Log Earnings, Omitting Employment	Step in (out)	6. Log Earnings, Age Dummies	Step in (out)	7. Log Earnings, Minus Fringe Benefits, Age Dummies	Step in (out)	8. Log Earnings, Age and Education Dummies	Step in (out)
0.0018	11	b	...	0.0019	13	0.0016	20	0.0019	45
(0.0003)				(0.0003)		(0.0003)		(0.0003)	
−0.1876	9	b	...	−0.1787	10	−0.1293	10	−0.1797	15
(0.0157)				(0.0160)		(0.0156)		(0.0161)	
−0.0815	14	b	...	−0.0703	15	−0.0371	52	−0.0700	18
(0.0158)				(0.0162)		(0.0158)		(0.0162)	
0.1481	3	b	...	0.1491	6	0.1405	7	0.1467	7
(0.0149)				(0.0152)		(0.0149)		(0.0152)	
b	...	b	...	b	...	b	...	b	...
0.0970	12	b	...	0.2407	14	0.1104	11	0.2339	8
(0.0156)				(0.0431)		(0.0147)		(0.0431)	
0.1967	7	b	...	0.3377	5	0.2015	4	0.3329	2
(0.0178)				(0.0440)		(0.0169)		(0.0439)	
0.0200*	30	b	...	0.1607	37	0.0265*	35	0.1582	46
(0.0153)				(0.0432)		(0.0145)		(0.0431)	
0.0351	27	b	...	0.1765	34	0.0199*	37	0.1715	36
(0.0167)				(0.0438)		(0.0159)		(0.0437)	
0.0260*	29	b	...	0.1678	36	a	a	0.1674	47
(0.0177)				(0.0443)				(0.0441)	
a	a	b	...	0.1372	39	a	a	0.1378	49
				(0.0480)				(0.0478)	
a	a	b	...	0.1447	38	a	a	0.4457	48
				(0.0428)				(0.0427)	
0.0847	18	b	...	0.2233	26	0.0674	27	0.2233	26
(0.0205)				(0.0451)		(0.0198)		(0.0450)	
−0.9940	...	−0.8402	...	0.8168	...	0.9618	...	0.8624	...
2.2225	...	2.2225	...	2.2225	...	2.1190	...	2.2225	...
.578	...	.512	...	.568	...	.573	...	.571	...
.575	...	.510	...	...	...	...	...	...	...
219.88	...	...	...	281.36	...	...	...	...	...

NOTE.—Figures in parentheses = standard errors of the regression coefficients; step column shows step at which the variable enters or leaves the stepwise regression procedure.
[a] Variable tried but rejected in stepwise regression on the basis of a partial F-test with 95% confidence limits.
[b] Variable not tried in that particular regression.
* Coefficient statistically significant at 95% level of confidence (t-test).

significant and relatively large coefficients. Again this statement does not depend on which of the three regressions we consider. Likewise, the important occupation variables, namely, professional, executive, and military occupations, stand out in all three regressions.

Enough has now been said to vindicate the addition of the quota sample to the random sample. Of course, the coefficients are not identical for the two samples. Nevertheless, they are all of the same sign and of the same relative orders of magnitude. If we lacked the quota sample and were furnished only with the random sample, we could say much less about personal earnings in Thailand, but what we did say would not be misleading.

17

Economic Development and Cultural Change

We turn now to regressions 4 and 5 in table 2 which regress the log of earnings on the same independent variables as before. These regressions produce a much better fit (R^2 is raised from .321 to .578 and .512, respectively)[12] but also a somewhat different one from regression 3. This is hardly surprising because regression 3 assumes that all independent variables are additive in their effect on earnings, whereas regressions 4 and 5 assume, by virtue of their log-linear form, that all independent variables are multiplicative in their effect on earnings. Since they are in log form, they must be read as giving, for a unit increase in an independent variable, the *percentage* change in personal earnings. Since we have not constrained the constant term to equal zero, the regression coefficients associated with dummy variables must be interpreted as giving the *percentage* difference in the earnings of an individual belonging to a particular category rather than to the excluded category, after holding all other variables constant. For example, in regard of regression 4, the education coefficient of 0.0136 means that an additional year of education raises earnings by 1.4 percent. On the other hand, being a salaried worker rather than a self-employed or family worker raises earnings by 24.6 percent; working for the government as a civil servant rather than for private industry depresses earnings by 10.6 percent (0.1876–0.0815); having a military occupation rather than a professional or technical occupation raises earnings by almost the same amount over an unclassified occupation (8.5 as against 9.7 percent); having Thai-Chinese instead of Thai parents raises earnings by 5.1 percent; and so on.

The only negative coefficients in regression 4 are, apart from age[2], the civil service, the private sector (relative of course to workers in state enterprises and those working for international organizations), and rural primary and secondary schooling. In terms of the size of coefficients, measuring the extent to which a change in earnings is associated with a change in a particular variable, the coefficients on sex (male), employee status, employment in the civil service, employment in large firms, executive occupations, foreign degree, and military fields of study (relative to, say, medicine) are all surprisingly high. By way of contrast, the coefficients on parental education, parental occupation, hours of work, and secondary leaving-examination score are all surprisingly low.

---

[12] Our R^2 of .512 may be compared with the best R^2s achieved by other investigators of earnings functions: Hansen, Weisbrod, and Scanlon, .15; Bowles, .15; Weiss, .16; Reed and Miller, .18; Stroup and Hargrove, .24; Ashenfelter and Mooney, .29; Griliches and Mason, .31; Hause, .34; Morgan and others, .35; Rogers, .40; Hanoch, .40; Hunt, .41; Hirsch and Segelhorst, .41; Hause, .46; Carroll and Ihnen, .55; Tolles and Melichar, .58; Carnoy, .79; Metcalf and Bibby, .80; and Thias and Carnoy, .89. Most of the sample sizes in these studies are smaller than ours, but some (like Tolles and Melichar) are much larger. Ashenfelter and Mooney examined an extremely homogeneous group of recent Woodrow Wilson Fellows, obtained an R^2 of only .29, and observed "our equations do a very good job of explaining income differentials."

Mark Blaug

Let us now look in somewhat more detail at the employment variables in regression 4. Four of the nine significant ones enter the equation at relatively early stages and with relatively large coefficients. The size of the coefficients for employee work status is particularly striking, suggesting that the variance in earnings among the self-employed and family workers (a category which is included in the constant term of the equation) must be relatively large.

Regression 4 also furnishes evidence of the earnings differentials between public- and private-sector employees. The variable "sector of employment" was divided into three dummy variables, with employees of state enterprises and international organizations being relegated to the constant term. The fact that the estimated coefficients for civil service and private-sector employees both take a minus sign means then that the average income in the excluded group is actually the highest of the three. But the coefficient for civil service is a larger negative number than the one for the private sector, and this implies that private-sector employment is associated with higher average earnings than public-sector employment. Since the dependent variable, earnings, here includes the monetary value of fringe benefits, we confirm our earlier conclusion that the inclusion of fringe benefits actually tends to widen the earnings gap between the two sectors.

Within the private sector, the size of firm seems to make a considerable difference to an individual's earnings. Persons employed in "large" firms with more than 100 workers may expect to earn considerably more than those who work for "small" firms. This suggestion of "wage dualism" in Thailand deserves further investigation.

In view of the prevalence of multiple-job holding in Thailand, the small coefficient for hours of work is revealing. While a person may expect to earn more if he works more hours, the payoff appears to be small. Note, however, that the average number of hours worked is 48 for the entire sample. Since government workers are only obligated to work 35 hours per week, it is possible that additional job holding is an important source of earnings for employees in the public sector.

We come finally to the respondent's occupation, of which only four out of eight regressors proved to be statistically significant. Not surprisingly, of the four significant ones, the largest coefficient is attached to an executive occupation. Perhaps this reflects the superior productivity of executives. It is fascinating to observe, however, that professional and military occupations are the second and third most important occupational categories. Coupled with the statistical importance of military field of study noted earlier, this suggests the striking generalization that the pattern of personal earnings in a country will reflect the social and political prestige of the military in society. It is no secret that military officials are prominent in all walks of life in Thailand. One reason that earnings in Thailand are positively related to military occupation is the size and frequency of official fringe

Economic Development and Cultural Change

benefits for, say, upcountry travel, but another is the superior access of the military to business ventures.[13]

The effects on earnings of family background and type of school make themselves felt before taking up employment. But the kind of occupation a person takes up, or the number of hours that he works, are part and parcel of the effects of education on earnings. If we are trying to predict the effect of more education on earnings, rather than to provide the best overall statistical explanation of earnings, there may be an argument therefore for excluding what we have called "employment variables."[14] Regression 5 shows what happens when we do this.

The first point to note is that R^2 falls from .587 to .512; in other words, employment variables do contribute some 6.6 percent to the explanation of the variation of earnings. Looking now at the basic variables, we see that the same variables enter in both regressions and, although the coefficients are always somewhat smaller in regression 4 than in regression 5, they have very nearly the same-size coefficients and stardard errors. The smaller size is to be expected because of some interaction between basic variables and employment variables. Nevertheless, it is reassuring to see that the coefficients on our basic variables are relatively stable and afford reliable estimates of the impact of age, education, and sex on earnings, given the effects of other variables.

Among the family-background variables, again essentially the same variables enter both equations, namely, parents' education, Chinese ethnic origin, and father's occupation (executive and sales). In general, these variables only enter the regression at later stages, and they account for only a moderate amount of the variation in an individual's earnings. Nevertheless, all these coefficients are statistically significant and positive, meaning that an individual's earnings are higher, the higher the educational attainment of his parents; and likewise, if they are Chinese and the father is engaged in an executive or sales occupation.

Of the 14 possible type-of-schooling variables, all but two enter both regressions 4 and 5. Considering them in order, private primary and secondary schooling takes a positive sign, meaning that a person may expect to earn more because schooling was private rather than public. Rural primary and secondary schooling, however, has the expected negative coefficient, meaning that other things being equal, rural education will reduce a person's earnings. Of the two variables that apply only to secondary education, the secondary leaving-examination score enters fairly early with a positive coefficient; however, the absolute size of the coefficient is small. A finding of major interest is that the dummy variable for secondary vocational education is not significant at all. It is so insignificant

[13] See F. W. Riggs, *Thailand: The Modernization of a Bureaucratic Polity* (Honolulu: East-West Center Press, 1966), pp. 249 ff.

[14] See G. S. Becker, *Human Capital* (Princeton, N.J.: Princeton University Press, 1964), p. 86.

20

Mark Blaug

that it does not even enter this regression, nor indeed any of the other regression equations we tried. In other words, there is no significant difference in the earning of a person who has gone through the vocational rather than the academic stream of secondary education.

At the level of higher education, the effect on earnings from possessing a foreign rather than a Thai degree, while not unexpected, is nonetheless striking in its magnitude (the coefficient being almost as large as that of male sex). Possessing an honors degree does not matter, according to our equation. This result is a little surprising, since the awarding of honors in a Thai university is usually thought to be a much better indicator of performance than, say, grade average.

For field of study in higher education, the differences between the coefficients in the regressions 4 and 5 are relatively large and, in fact, they change their relative ranking. In regression 4, military is largest, followed by medicine, humanities, engineering, and then social science. For regression 5, the coefficients for humanities, medical, and military fields are smaller than in regression 4, but the social science and science-engineering coefficients are larger. A plausible explanation here is that, in the first case, the occupation actually followed has a larger effect on earnings than does formal preparation for the occupation. It is more important in terms of earnings to follow a military occupation than to be a military graduate, similarly with medicine, and possibly with humanities. The reason is perhaps to be found in the relationship between access to an occupation and formal educational requirements. The medical profession is subject to restricted entry, and formal educational qualifications are the main method of enforcing the restriction. A more general scientific or social science preparation has less precise relevance to subsequent occupation: it opens up a wider variety of job opportunities, and much depends on the actual job that is eventually taken up.

On the whole, however, we may conclude that the coefficients estimated by the two regression equations are not very different. For the purpose of estimating average earnings by age, sex, and education, holding constant other differences between individuals, we seem to have arrived at statistically reliable results.

Regression 6 takes the argument a step further by allowing age to enter nonlinearly, or at any rate, in a stepwise linear fashion. Regression 7 alters the dependent variable and looks only at monetary earnings, just in case the addition of fringe benefits has biased all our findings. Regression 8 returns to total earnings as the dependent variable and extends the non-linear treatment to years of schooling.

We noted earlier that both age and education appear to be linearly related to earnings. We now observe that both age and education also appear to be *almost* linearly related to percentage changes in earnings. That is to say, the negative age^2 term in regression 4, combined with a significant log-age term, tells us that a graph of earnings on age would

21

Economic Development and Cultural Change

produce a very shallow curve, almost but not quite identical with a straight line. Similar remarks pertain to the education variable. Regression 8, which treats both age and education as dummy variables, shows us where the trouble lies. The relationship between age and percentage changes in earnings is practically constant between the ages of 35–39 and 60–64, rising rapidly between 17 and 29 and then rising very gently up to 55–59, after which they gently decline again. The graph of earnings on age has little curvature after the age of 35, and if age acts as a proxy for work experience, the evidence seems to show that the capacity to learn by doing is more or less exhausted by the age of 35.

Similarly, if we consider the education dummies in regression 8, we see that education is not really a linear function either of earnings or of the log of earnings. The power of a year of schooling to raise earnings in percentage terms rises with additional education acquired, despite the fact that these are percentage changes of an amount that is itself getting absolutely larger, equal additions to which would imply declining percentages. On the other hand, the steepness of the education-earnings curve does not change very radically after completion of secondary education (11–12 years of schooling); a straight line is only a bad fit for the first 10 years of education, after which it is really quite a good fit. And this explains why education^2 in regressions 1 and 2 enters first of all significantly and then drops out at later stages of the stepwise procedure. The fact is that earnings are a parabolic function of education, but the parabola is so shallow that the effect hardly comes through.

III. Additional Findings

The final regression equations produced above throw away the information that is provided along the way by the stepwise procedure itself. To illustrate the point, we consider for regression 4 the 30 steps that led up to the final equation. The table is too long to reproduce here, but what it shows is that the final R^2 of .578 in regression 4 is almost entirely achieved by seven variables, the other 23 out of 69 possible variables contributing only an additional .048 to the total explanation of the variance of earnings. In one sense, therefore, our model is much too complicated: sex, age, education, employment in a large firm, foreign degree, and executive occupation carry most of the final explanatory value, and indeed sex, age, education, and large-firm together already account for 47 percent of the variance.

It is well known that the size of a regression coefficient is no measure of the importance of a particular independent variable, that is, no measure of its contribution to the final estimated value of the dependent variable. After all, the size of a regression coefficient can be changed at will by measuring the variable in different units. There are essentially three objective measures of the importance of an independent variable of which we have chosen one, the so-called β-coefficients.[15] Beta coefficients are

[15] See Goldberger, *Econometric Theory*, pp. 197–200.

Mark Blaug

simply regression coefficients multiplied by the ratio of the standard deviation of an independent variable to the standard deviation of the dependent variable. When all variables are standardized in terms of their standard deviation, the β-coefficients are simply the regression coefficients of the standardized variables.

Table 3 lists the β-coefficients of three of our regressions and then ranks these in order from high to low, yielding a ready guide to which variables contribute most to the explanation of the variance of earnings. In all three regressions, age, sex, and education head the list. Thereafter, we get foreign degree, work status, civil service, executive occupation, and so on. In general, it is striking how little family-background variables and type-of-schooling variables contribute to the total explanation and how the overwhelming importance of what we have called basic variables is confirmed, whichever regression we consider.

It is clear, however, that many of the employment variables come close on the heels of the basic variables in order of importance. This is bound to raise the uncomfortable question whether the effects of education are not in fact being underestimated, some of the credit that is due to education going instead to a variable like occupation. Regression 5, leaving out the employment variables, is one way of dealing with this problem of interaction between variables, but another way is to split the sample into subgroups in terms of some leading classifying factor.[16] In the case before us, why not consider primary-educated, secondary-educated, and higher-educated individuals separately? In this way, we can get an indication of the degree to which different variables interact with education. If the coefficients of certain independent variables are the same for each of the subgroups, this is evidence of no interaction between years of schooling and other explanatory variables. In the light of these remarks, consider now regressions 9, 10, and 11 in table 4, which analyze the earnings of primary-, secondary- and higher-educated people, respectively.

The first point that strikes us is the decline in R^2 as we consider successively lower levels of education. It is apparent that much of the power of regressions 4–8 to explain the variance of personal earnings is due to the presence of secondary- and higher-educated individuals. Even the coefficients on education in regressions 9–11, depicting the effect of additional schooling *within* levels of education, are significantly higher in regressions 10 and 11 than in regression 9. Additional years of primary education contribute little to additional earnings unless they pave the way to secondary education.

It is also obvious that education does interact with occupation. Now that we have divided the sample by educational levels, some of the occupation variables prove to be insignificant, and all of them are shown to have

[16] This is not the only way to test for interaction. Another way is to include cross-products of variables. This would multiply the number of coefficients that we must consider, which explains why we have rejected this solution to the interaction problem.

Economic Development and Cultural Change

TABLE 3

β-COEFFICIENTS OF FINAL EQUATION FOR SELECTED REGRESSIONS

	REGRESSION					
VARIABLE	3. Earnings, Total Sample	Rank	4. Log Earnings	Rank	8. Log Earnings, Age and Education Dummies	Rank
1. Age (yrs)	0.3173	1	a	a	b	...
2. Age²	−0.1224	6	0.3130	3	b	...
3. Log age	a	a	0.6491	1	b	...
4. Age, 17–19	b	...	b	...	0.1093	26
5. Age, 20–24	b	...	b	...	0.2540	9
6. Age, 25–29	b	...	b	...	0.3498	7
7. Age, 30–34	b	...	b	...	0.4027	4
8. Age, 35–39	b	...	b	...	0.4133	3
9. Age, 40–44	b	...	b	...	0.4828	1
10. Age, 45–49	b	...	b	...	0.3927	5
11. Age, 50–54	b	...	b	...	0.4736	2
12. Age, 55–59	b	...	b	...	0.3697	6
13. Age, 60–64	b	...	b	...	0.2207	12
14. Education (yrs) .	0.1646	3	0.3419	2	b	...
15. Log education .	a	a	−0.0517	14	b	...
16. Education, 1–3 ..	b	...	b	...	a	...
17. Education, 4	b	...	b	...	0.0600	41
18. Education, 5–6 ..	b	...	b	...	0.0284	33
19. Education, 7	b	...	b	...	0.0756	31
20. Education, 8–10 .	b	...	b	...	0.2160	25
21. Education, 11–12	b	...	b	...	0.2527	21
22. Education, 13–14	b	...	b	...	0.1313	16
23. Education, 15 ...	b	...	b	...	0.1958	17
24. Education, 16 ...	b	...	b	...	0.3172	10
25. Education, 17 ...	b	...	b	...	0.2035	13
26. Education, 18–20	b	...	b	...	0.2139	14
27. Sex (male)	0.0730	11	0.1169	7	0.1164	8
28. Parent's education	0.0279	20	0.0440	20	0.0467	39
29. Chinese	a	a	0.0480	16	0.0501	35
30. Father's occupation, professional	a	a	a	a	a	a
31. Father's occupation, executive	0.0315	18	0.0326	24	0.0319	44
32. Father's occupation, clerical	a	a	a	a	a	a
33. Father's occupation, sales.	0.0396	17	0.0335	22	0.0338	42
34. Father's occupation, service	a	a	a	a	a	a
35/37. Father's occupation, farmer/laborer	a	a	a	a	a	a
36. Father's occupation, transport	0.0147	25	a	a	a	a

Mark Blaug

TABLE 3 (*Continued*)

	REGRESSION					
VARIABLE	3. Earnings, Total Sample	Rank	4. Log Earnings	Rank	8. Log Earnings, Age and Education Dummies	Rank
38. Father's occupation, military	0.0189	23	0.0139	29	0.0153	47
39. Private school ...	0.0190	22	0.0350	21	0.0356	46
40. Rural primary/ secondary.......	a	a	−0.0232	...	0.0212	46
41. Vocational secondary.......	a	a	a	a	a	a
42. Secondary leaving-examination score	0.0283	19	0.0475	17	0.0320	43
43. Honors degree .	a	a	a	a	0.0128	48
44. Foreign degree ..	0.1592	4	0.0917	11	0.874	29
45. Field, humanities.	0.0419	16	0.0269	25	0.0272	45
46. Field, education .	a	a	a	a	a	...
47. Field, social science	0.0663	13	0.0333	23	0.0413	40
48. Field, medicine ..	0.0654	14	0.0448	18	0.0479	38
49. Field, science/ engineering	0.0893	9	0.0448	19	0.0491	37
50. Field, military ...	0.0400	15	0.0501	15	0.0498	36
51. Work status.....	0.0549	14	0.2177	4	0.2076	15
52. Hours of work ..	0.0758	10	0.0677	12	0.0732	32
53. Civil service	−0.2027	2	−0.2020	5	−0.1936	18
54. Private sector ...	−0.0669	12	−0.0919	10	−0.0789	30
55. Large firm	0.1101	7	0.1086	8	0.1075	27
56. Small firm	b	...	b	...	b	...
57. Occupation, professional	0.0780	9	0.0971	...	0.2342	11
58. Occupation, executive	0.1444	5	0.1455	6	0.1461	19
59. Occupation, clerical	a	a	0.0160	27	0.1272	23
60. Occupation, sales	0.0185	24	0.0261	26	0.1295	22
61. Occupation, service	a	a	0.0155	28	0.0999	28
62. Occupation, transport	−0.0205	21	a	a	0.0555	34
63. Occupation, farmer/laborer ..	a	a	a	a	0.1270	24
64. Occupation, military	0.0586	13	0.0539	13	0.1421	20

NOTE.—See table 2 for explanation of symbols.

different effects at different levels. Professional and executive occupations only have a substantial independent effect on earnings at the primary level; at the secondary level, only executive occupation makes a positive contribution to earnings; and the effect of being a member of armed forces is

Economic Development and Cultural Change

TABLE 4

COEFFICIENTS FOR STEPWISE SUBREGRESSIONS

	REGRESSION		
VARIABLE	9. Log Earnings, Primary Education, Age Dummies	10. Log Earnings, Secondary Education, Age Dummies	11. Log Earnings, Higher Education, Age Dummies
Basic:			
1. Age, 17–19	0.1614	0.4717	0.6114
	(0.0427)	(0.0280)	(0.1200)
2. Age, 20–24	0.2905	0.3251	0.3726
	(0.0431)	(0.0194)	(0.0295)
3. Age, 25–29	0.4062	0.1925	0.2640
	(0.0446)	(0.0202)	(0.0210)
4. Age, 30–34	0.4674	0.1120	0.1844
	(0.0443)	(0.0229)	(0.0187)
5. Age, 35–39	0.4751	a	0.0819
	(0.0465)		(0.0210)
6. Age, 40–44	0.4693	a	a
	(0.0460)		
7. Age, 45–49	0.5026	a	a
	(0.0485)		
8. Age, 50–54	0.5036	a	0.0961
	(0.0479)		(0.0214)
9. Age, 55–59	0.4885	0.0584*	0.0903
	(0.0536)	(0.0327)	(0.0265)
10. Age, 60–64	0.3536	a	a
	(0.0594)		
11. Education (yrs)	a	0.0463	0.1708
		(0.0072)	(0.0872)
12. Education²	0.0014	a	−0.0042*
	(0.006)		(0.0027)
13. Sex (male)	0.1432	0.1201	0.0811
	(0.0258)	(0.0160)	(0.0171)
Family background:			
14. Parent's education	a	0.0033	a
		(0.0008)	
15. Chinese	0.0768	0.0506	a
	(0.0215)	(0.0198)	
16. Father's occupation, professional	0.1195	a	. . .
	(0.0512)		
17. Father's occupation, executive.	0.0906*	0.0627	0.0318*
	(0.0807)	(0.0259)	(0.0181)
18. Father's occupation, clerical	a	a	−0.0617
19. Father's occupation, sales	0.0662	0.0406	(0.0268) a
	(0.0279)	(0.0170)	
20. Father's occupation, service	a	a	a
21/23. Father's occupation, farmer/laborer	0.0509*	a	a
	(0.0261)		

Mark Blaug

TABLE 4 *(Continued)*

	REGRESSION		
VARIABLE	9. Log Earnings, Primary Education, Age Dummies	10. Log Earnings, Secondary Education, Age Dummies	11. Log Earnings, Higher Education, Age Dummies
22. Father's occupation, transport	a	a	a
24. Father's occupation, military	0.1407 (0.0476)	a	0.0286* (0.0201)
Type of schooling:			
25. Private	a	0.0611 (0.0141)	−0.0171* (0.0148)
26. Rural primary	−0.0337* (0.0183)	a	−0.0350 (0.0162)
27. Rural secondary	a	−0.0561 (0.0239)	a
28. Vocational secondary ...	b	b	−0.0501 (0.0226)
29. Secondary leaving-exam. score	b	a	0.0005 (0.0002)
30. Honors degree	b	b	0.0506* (0.0261)
31. Foreign degree	...	...	0.1465 (0.0166)
32. Higher educ. field, humanities	b	b	0.0884 (0.0342)
33. Field, social science	b	b	0.0322* (0.0184)
34. Field, medicine	b	b	0.0980 (0.0275)
35. Field, science/engineering ...	b	b	0.1040 (0.0241)
36. Field, military	b	b	0.1145 (0.0307)
Employment:			
37. Work status	0.2648 (0.0368)	0.2674 (0.0283)	0.2184 (0.0309)
38. Hours of work	0.0009* (0.0005)	0.0015 (0.0005)	0.0034 (0.0006)
39. Civil service	−0.1422 (0.0417)	−0.1784 (0.0239)	−0.2165 (0.0216)
40. Private sector..........	−0.1231 (0.0361)	−0.0965 (0.0243)	−0.0515 (0.0253)
41. Large firm	0.0632* (0.0339)	0.1987 (0.0223)	0.1279 (0.0241)
42. Small firm	b	b	b
43. Occupation, professional .	0.1777 (0.0479)	a	0.0838 (0.0219)
44. Occupation, executive ...	0.2517 (0.0595)	0.1617 (0.0239)	0.1273 (0.0239)

Economic Development and Cultural Change

TABLE 4 (*Continued*)

	REGRESSION		
VARIABLE	9. Log Earnings, Primary Education, Age Dummies	10. Log Earnings, Secondary Education, Age Dummies	11. Log Earnings, Higher Education, Age Dummies
45. Occupation, clerical	a	−0.0431 (0.0174)	a
46. Occupation, sales	a	a	a
47. Occupation, service	a	a	a
48. Occupation, transport ...	a	−0.1006 (0.0400)	−0.1109* (0.0990)
49. Occupation, farmer/laborer	a	−0.0782 (0.0221)	−0.0820* (0.0494)
50. Occupation, military ...	0.0741* (0.0451)	a	0.0806 (0.0320)
Intercept	1.1752	1.4376	0.5220
Mean of dependent variable (in tens of Baht)	1.9124	2.1778	2.5541
R^2	.23	.411	.542

NOTE.—See table 2 for explanation of symbols.

now shown to be confined to the higher educated. All the coefficients on civil service employment are still negative, but it is immediately evident that the spread in pay between the civil service and private industry widens as one climbs up the educational ladder. Similarly, the spread in pay between large and small firms widens with successively higher educational attainments.

Consider now family-background variables. Parental education disappears as a significant variable except for secondary-educated individuals. On the other hand, the effect of ethnic origin is stronger for those with primary than for those with secondary education and, in general, the coefficients on father's occupation for primary-educated individuals is large relative to the education coefficient at that level. In other words, the high earners among the primary-educated cohort came largely from Thai-Chinese parents or from fathers in professional, sales, and military occupations.

Among the type-of-schooling variables, we notice that the earnings of primary-educated individuals do not seem to be affected by rural rather than urban schooling. The negative coefficients on rural schooling are only significant for those with secondary and higher education. Similarly, vocational secondary education appears to hurt those who use it to gain admission to higher education, but it has no effect one way or the other for those who only complete secondary education.

The set of coefficients which relate to the quality or character of higher education take on quite different values in regression 11 than in

Mark Blaug

regressions 4–8. This is hardly surprising, given the ubiquitous presence of multicollinearity among variables. On balance, however, it is comforting to see how little the regression coefficients change when we consider the higher educated separately.

We may conclude that our main results—the importance, first of all, of age, sex, and education, and, second of civil service employment, foreign degree, large firm, employee status, and executive and military occupations —are *not* due to the interaction of schooling with other measured variables.

IV. Conclusion

The classical linear-regression model is perfectly capable of generating spuriously high R^2s and even spuriously low standard errors when the error terms of the equation are (1) not distributed with zero mean and constant, unknown variance; and when (2) they are not distributed independently of each other and independently of the explanatory variables. It is true that least squares is a robust method in that it yields unbiased, efficient, and consistent estimates even under wide departures from the two standard assumptions of (1) homoscedasticity and (2) independence. Nevertheless, we checked these assumptions by plotting the error terms of our final equation against the dependent variable for each of the 11 regressions we ran. For our best, regressions 4 and 5, a plot of the error terms, expressed in standardized form, against the estimated value of earnings, again in standardized form, yielded a spherical, symmetrical pattern of the residuals, thus vindicating the use of least squares.[17] The actual pattern of 5,000 dots is too cumbersome to reproduce here, but figure 2 gives a fair picture of it.

Multicollinearity among the independent variables is a further danger. Since it is a property of the sample data and not of the population, one cannot, strictly speaking, test for its existence. Nevertheless, the correlation matrix of our best regression and some other standard checks do not suggest that multicollinearity destroys our results.[18] Besides, we were basically interested in using the regressions to predict earnings in the short run for purposes of calculating the rate of return on educational investment in Thailand and not to estimate the parameters of what is in fact the reduced form of a simultaneous-equation system.[19] As is frequently

[17] On suspicious patterns of residuals, see Draper and Smith, chap. 3.

[18] D. E. Farrar and R. R. Glauber ("Multicollinearity in Regression Analysis: The Problem Revisited," *Review of Economics and Statistics* 49 [February 1967]: 104) present a set of measures, involving such statistics as the determinant of the correlation matrix of independent variables and the diagonal elements of the inverse correlation matrix, that are generated routinely in standard regression computations. However, they do not address themselves to the multicollinearity in the presence of dummy variables. Ashenfelter and Mooney suggest finding a linear combination of variables in each set of dummy variables that have maximum correlation and inspecting these. This we have not done.

[19] This is a fine point. Our regressions in fact represent the interaction of a demand-for-education and a supply-of-education equation. These two equations are equal to each other in equilibrium, allowing us to derive earnings as a function of the

Economic Development and Cultural Change

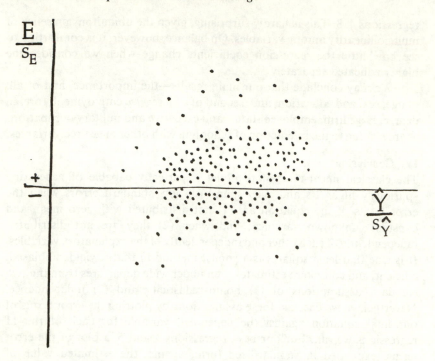

FIG. 2.—Normal deviates of errors and earnings for fourth equation

asserted,[20] multicollinearity is much less of a problem when prediction rather than fundamental explanation is the primary objective.

So what have we proved, or rather disproved? First of all, we have demonstrated the overwhelming importance of age, sex, and education in explaining the variance of personal earnings in urban Thailand, irrespective of family origins and of the type of school attended. Of course, it may be that an income measure of family background would give different results. If what matters is the level of aspiration of children, then parental education and father's occupation may be poor proxies of what we ought to be measuring. Likewise, there is more to the question of type of school attended than whether it is rural or urban, academic or vocational. However, even accepting our, no doubt, imperfect measures, I venture to say that our results are far from what might have been predicted a priori.[21]

---

quantity of education demanded and supplied. We have estimated this function, and one might ask whether estimating this reduced-form equation is tantamount to estimating the parameters of the demand and supply equations. This is the so-called identification problem. Suffice it to say that we do not claim to have "identified" a reduced-form equation.

[20] J. Johnston, *Econometric Methods* (New York: McGraw-Hill Book Co., 1963), pp. 207, 277–78.

[21] It might be argued that our results are due to the use of the wrong model: a regression of earnings on age, education, etc., instead of a recursive model in which we

Mark Blaug

Second, we have shown that secondary and, particularly, tertiary education results in significantly higher earnings at least in part because it increases the probability of being employed in a large firm in the private sector, or better still an international organization; even military employment is only really lucrative for the higher educated.

The point is illustrated by figure 1 above, which superimposes a set of regression-adjusted age-earnings profiles on the crude profiles obtained directly from our tabulated results. The regression we have selected for the purpose is regression 5, namely, one which excludes the employment variables. We set all statistically significant variables at their mean except age and education, and then for a given number of years of education we vary age a unit at a time. It is clear that every one of the regression-adjusted profiles lies below the crude profiles, and this difference provides an exact graphic description of the combined effects on earnings of all variables other than age and education. If we now consider the earnings differentials *attributable* to a certain level of education, that is, the difference between the adjusted profile for that level and the adjusted profile for the level below it, and compare it with the crude earnings differentials *associated* with that level, we will find that the former is usually smaller, especially at the higher ages and higher levels of schooling. This is still another way of demonstrating that education alone contributes more to the explanation of age-specific earnings than any other variable.

Are the better educated paid more because they are more productive? because they are more able? or because they are being deliberately recruited into the ruling elite of society? Results such as ours do shed light on these questions, but they are not capable of discriminating between these three types of explanations.[22] In part this is because of measurement problems. Few societies provide evidence of "native ability" in the form of IQ scores, and it is not even obvious that IQ scores measure the sort of achievement motivation that employers prize; even family background is only imperfectly measured by parental education, occupation, and income. But in part, I suspect, it is because these are actually not three different explanations but simply different ways of looking at exactly the same phenomenon. In any case, multivariate analysis of personal earnings, conducted in country after country with increasing sophistication, holds out some hope of eventually resolving the debate.

---

first regress length of schooling on family background and then earnings on schooling. The point is easily met: the regression of schooling on family background yielded a R^2 of .11.

[22] I have argued this at greater length elsewhere (M. Blaug, "The Correlation between Education and Earnings: What Does It Signify?" *Higher Education*, vol. 1 [February 1972]).

[15]

The Rate of Return on Investment in Education in Thailand

by Mark Blaug *

This paper summarizes the findings of a study carried out in 1970 by a small team of Thai and foreign research workers under the auspices of the National Education Council of Thailand. The study consisted essentially of (1) a statistical analysis of the structure of personal earnings in Greater Bangkok as revealed by a household survey specially conducted for the purpose; (2) an analysis of the costs of education in the entire country from data gathered by a mailed questionnaire to public and private schools; and (3) a calculation of private and social rates of return on educational investment in Thailand, making use of (1) and (2). [1] An earlier paper reported on the statistical analysis of earnings (Blaug 1974). The present paper concentrates on the rate-of-return calculations, with a passing glance at the cost figures.

1. EARNINGS BY AGE AND EDUCATION

We shall say little about the earnings side in this paper but we ought to explain that the rate-of-return calculations that follow are not based on crude tabulations of earnings by age and years of schooling, nor on these multiplied across-the-board by a Denison-type coefficient, but rather on a regression analysis of earnings, holding constant such factors as family background and type of school attended (but alas not native ability!).

Chart 1 depicts some crude age-earnings profiles for different years of education in Thailand: they are 'well-behaved' [*Blaug, 1970, pp. 26-7*] except those associated with 7 rather than 4 years of elementary education. Superimposed on these heavy, jagged lines are the corresponding regression-adjusted profiles, depicted as light, smooth lines: they always lie below the crude profiles, providing a graphic description of the combined effects on personal earnings of variables other than age and education.

Denison showed that about 65 per cent of earnings *differentials* associated with high school and college education in the United States is due to the effects of extra education, the other 35 per cent being due to better-than-average ability and favourable home background [*Denison, 1962, ch. 7*]. I once dubbed this 65 per cent figure the 'alpha coefficient' [*Blaug, 1965, p. 225*] and the term seems to have caught on. In the absence of adequate data, previous rate-of-return studies in less developed countries have sometimes applied the Denison alpha-coefficient to all the observed earn-

---

*University of London, Institute of Education and London School of Economics.

INVESTMENT IN EDUCATION IN THAILAND   271

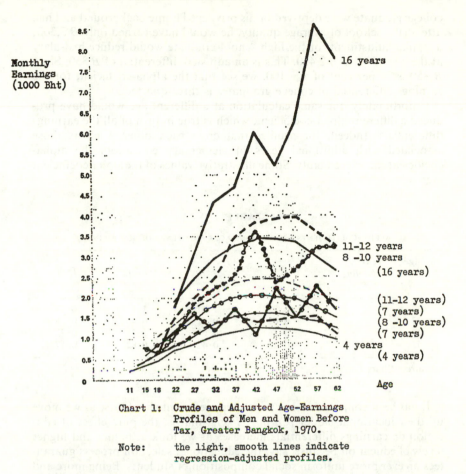

Chart 1:   Crude and Adjusted Age-Earnings
            Profiles of Men and Women Before
            Tax, Greater Bangkok, 1970.

Note: the light, smooth lines indicate
            regression-adjusted profiles.

ings differentials by years of schooling, in effect calculating the rate of
return on two-thirds and sometimes on one-half of the earnings differentials associated with additional years of schooling [see e.g., *Blaug and
others, 1969; Nalla Gounden, 1967;* and *Williamson and De Voretz, 1969*].
Although this adjustment is undoubtedly in the right direction, the present
analysis suggests that any uniform adjustment applied across-the-board to
all the earnings differentials is a gross oversimplification.

    If we consider, for example, the observed earnings differential in Thai-
land between a college and a high school graduate (16 years versus 12
years of schooling) and the regression-adjusted earnings differential between
these two cohorts, the latter divided by the former is indeed the so-called
alpha-coefficient. That is to say, a college graduate aged 37 earned *B* (baht)
4,600 per month in 1970; a high school graduate of that age earned
B 3,500 per month. This is a differential of *B* 1,100. But if a 37-year old

college graduate were deprived of his privileged home background and had attended a school of average quality, he would have earned only *B* 3,300; a similar adjustment for the high school graduate would reduce his salary at the age of 37 to *B* 2,450. This is an adjusted differential of *B* 850. Since *B* 850 is 78 per cent of *B* 1,100, we see that the alpha-coefficient for the earnings differential of college graduates is three-quarters.

Unfortunately, the same calculation at a different age would have produced a different alpha-coefficient, which is true in turn of all the earnings differentials. Indeed, for profiles that cross each other, such as those associated with additional years of elementary education, the alpha-coefficient can exceed unity. Some illustrative values of the alpha-coefficient are:

TABLE 1

ALPHA-COEFFICIENTS FOR VARIOUS AGES AND YEARS OF SCHOOLING

Age	Years of Schooling	4–7	7–10	10–12	12–16
27		0·57	1·61	1·64	0·77
37		0·02	0·52	0·40	0·78
47		0·46	0·69	0·25	0·72
57		0·42	0·42	0·82	0·17

Source: Chart 1.

It has been conjectured that the alpha-coefficient should rise as we move up the educational ladder [*Carnoy, 1971*], that is, the pure effect of education on earnings differentials increases as we look at higher and higher levels of education because, say, the educational selection process guarantees an ever more uniform social composition of students. Being more and more alike in ability and in family background, graduates eventually come to differ only in the length of educational attainment, in consequence of which the alpha-coefficient approaches unity. It sounds plausible but the evidence for Thailand is against it.

Be that as it may, the analysis that follows ignores the crude earnings differentials and has regard only to the regression-adjusted differentials between earnings.

2. COSTS OF EDUCATION

In so far as elementary and secondary education are concerned, the cost figures we collected derive from a mailed questionnaire sent to a random stratified sample of 1,200 schools throughout Thailand. We estimated both private and social costs as the sum in each case of certain direct and indirect costs:

INVESTMENT IN EDUCATION IN THAILAND 273

TABLE 1A

	Private Costs	Social Costs
Direct costs	Fees Books Extra travel (—) Scholarships	Teachers' salaries Administrative salaries Imputed rent on buildings Imputed rent on equipment Materials used up Books, extra travel
Indirect costs	Earnings foregone	Output lost as estimated by earnings foregone

The list itself and the methods used to calculate certain difficult items, such as rent on buildings and equipment, are well-known to educational planners and we will therefore spend no time to justify them. Our results for direct cost per student per year for five types of schools are as follows:

TABLE 2

PRIVATE AND SOCIAL DIRECT COSTS PER STUDENT PER YEAR, BY LEVELS AND TYPES OF EDUCATION, 1969 (BAHTS)

Levels	Private Direct Costs			Social Private Costs		
	Fees	Books, Travel	Total	Current Costs	Capital Charges	Total
Elementary	0	300	300	532	142	674
Public and Private Academic Secondary	450	750	1,200	915	522	1,437
Private Vocational Secondary	2,200	750	2,950	1,893	658	2,551
Public Vocational Secondary	220	750	970	2,768	1,584	4,352
Teacher Training	220	1,200	1,420	2,253	1,410	3,663

These are the direct costs per student per year but they are not the direct costs per successful student completing a cycle because they make no allowance for drop-outs and repeaters. No reliable data are in fact available on wastage and repetition but, given the flow rates between grades in successive years and the number of 7-year-old children in the population in 1960, both of which are known, it is possible to estimate these by an iterative procedure. The following table gives these estimates as well as their effects on direct costs:

TABLE 3

RIVATE AND SOCIAL DIRECT COSTS PER SUCCESSFUL STUDENT PER YEAR, BY LEVELS AND
TYPES OF EDUCATION, 1969

Levels	Average years to complete	Drop-out rates (percentage)	Direct Costs (Baht)	
			Private	Social
Elementary	7·81	22·7	440	960
Public and Private Academic Secondary	5·94	25·7	1,935	2,321
Private Vocational Secondary	3·42	22·3	4,526	3,777
Public Vocational Secondary	3·42	22·3	1,488	6,443
Teacher Training	2·12	0·08	1,601	4,239

Apart from teacher training, the effects of wastage and repetition is broadly to raise direct costs per successful student by 50 per cent over direct costs per student enrolled.

We did not conduct a new survey of universities to calculate direct costs but instead worked with the university accounts, supplemented by official estimates of capital costs per place. Our estimate of the private direct costs of attending a Thai university is B 1,400 per year, which when adjusted for drop-outs (23 per cent) and repetition (average length 4·3 years) increases to B 1,945. The corresponding figures for social direct costs are B 7,920 and B 11,114; these are an average for all nine universities in Thailand, which hides a considerable spread of low costs for the old and high costs for the new universities.

We have said nothing so far about indirect costs, which both from the private and from the social point of view consist of earnings foregone, after tax in the first case and before tax in the second case. We obtain these of course from our regression-adjusted age-earnings profiles; that is, the earnings foregone by a university graduate are simply the average earnings of a high school graduate; the earnings foregone of a high school graduate are simply the average earnings of elementary school leavers; and so on. Adding these indirect costs to the direct costs previously calculated, we obtain total private and social costs of education.

It is worth noting that of all the three levels of education, it is higher education that is most heavily subsidized by the State; nevertheless, because of earnings foregone, even university students do in fact pay most of the total costs of tertiary education. Compare, for example, the ratio of private to social direct costs as against the ratio of private to social direct plus indirect costs (Table 4).

The first column of Table 4 tells us that no Thai student pays the full *budgetary* costs of his education but academic secondary students do pay

83 per cent of the direct costs. The second column tells us that earnings foregone are negligible for elementary school students but a major source of the costs of higher education for individuals. Furthermore, while both elementary and higher education are heavily subsidized, academic secondary education is hardly subsidized at all.

TABLE 4

RATIOS OF PRIVATE TO SOCIAL COSTS OF EDUCATION, BY LEVELS OF EDUCATION, 1969

Levels	Ratio of Direct Private to Direct Social Costs	Ratio of Total Private to Total Social Costs
Elementary	0·46	0·46
Secondary (Academic)	0·83	0·95
Higher	0·18	0·70

3. THE RATES OF RETURN

We have now collected all the pieces that are required to calculate rates of return. The method of calculation is simple enough [*Blaug, 1970, pp. 54-60*]: we form an age-specific lifetime income stream for each additional year of education, which is negative when costs are incurred in the early years and positive when earnings accrue in the later years; we then compute its present value at various arbitrary discount rates; the discount rate which sets the present value equal to zero is the internal rate of return on investment in that extra year of schooling. The social rate of return is calculated on the social costs of education and the before-tax earnings differentials. The private rate of return, on the other hand, is calculated on the private costs of education and after-tax earnings differentials.

Borrowing a tabulation invented by Lee Hansen (1963), we set out our basic results as follows in Table 5.

Table 5 presents both marginal and average rates of return. We read it as follows: the first box on the 'staircase' in the upper left-hand corner gives us, first, the social and then the private rate of return on one year of schooling compared to no years of schooling, together with the typical age of students in these two cohorts; the second box on the 'staircase' gives us the rate of return on 2-3 years of schooling compared to one year of schooling; and so on. On the edge of our half-pyramid, we always have the *marginal* rate of return on additional years of schooling for the average student in a cohort. We also present a few *average* rates of return as a small sample of the ones that could have been calculated and these always appear inside the pyramid, for example, the rates of return on seven years of elementary education, considered as a block, compared to no education at all is to be found in the first column and the fifth row, being 17 per cent and 24 per cent.

In interpreting this table, the reader must accept a certain asymmetry of presentation. The earnings are for Greater Bangkok but the costs are for

TABLE 5

SOCIAL AND PRIVATE RATES OF RETURN TO EDUCATION, MEN AND WOMEN, 1970 (PER CENT)

Each column heading gives the "To" Age over the "To" Grade; each row gives the "From" Age over the "From" Grade. Values shown as Social / Private.

From (Age / Grade)	S/P	6/0	7/1	8-9/2-3	10/4	11-12/5-6	13/7	14-16/8-10	17-18/11-12	19-20/13 14	21/15	22/16	23/17	24/18
7 / 1	Social	17												
	Private	26												
8-9 / 2-3	Social		20											
	Private		34											
10 / 4	Social	20	22	27										
	Private	38	44	49										
11-12 / 5-6	Social				14									
	Private				18									
13 / 7	Social	17	17		14	14								
	Private	24	23		16	15								
14-16 / 8-10	Social						10							
	Private						11							
17-18 / 11-12 (Academic)	Social	14	13		11		10	10						
	Private	16	15		13		11	11						
19-20 / 13-14 (Teacher Training)	Social								8					
	Private								9					
19-20 / 13-14	Social								7					
	Private								12					
21 / 15 (Academic)	Social									7				
	Private									9				
22 / 16	Social	11	11		10		9		7	7	7			
	Private	13	14		12		11		11	9	11			
23 / 17	Social											8		
	Private											11		
24 / 18	Social												8	
	Private												11	
25-26 / 19-20	Social								7					7
	Private								11					11

INVESTMENT IN EDUCATION IN THAILAND   **277**

the whole of Thailand. I doubt that costs are higher in urban than in rural areas but undoubtedly earnings in Greater Bangkok exceed those prevailing in the countryside. All our rates are therefore somewhat on the high side but the upward bias is only serious at the elementary level as most secondary and higher-educated individuals in Thailand in fact reside in the capital [see *Blaug, 1973*]. Furthermore, we have not adjusted the earnings figures for the probability of death before retirement, or for the probability of unemployment. Our sample produced an unemployment rate of only 2·0 per cent and, according to the Labour Force Survey of 1969, unemployment rates in Greater Bangkok do not exceed 1–2 per cent of the labour force. If we had adjusted the rates for mortality and unemployment, the effect would have been to lower them uniformly by a fraction of 1 per cent. This did not seem worth the effort as all the rates in the tables must be read in any case as carrying a penumbra of doubt of ±2 per cent.

With these provisos, what can we learn from the figures? Beginning with the marginal social rates of return, we see that the first years of elementary schooling generally yield the highest returns, additional years of education yielding progressively lower rates of return. With one or two exceptions, these results are borne out by rate-of-return calculations in other countries [*Psacharopoulos, 1973, ch. 4*].

The highest social rate in the entire table, 27 per cent, is associated with completing grade 4, which until recently has been the minimum statutory school requirement in Thailand (most of the persons in our sample would have come under this law). The marginal social rate on obtaining at least some elementary schooling (2–3 years) comes second at 20 per cent, and the first year of elementary education yields the third highest rate, 17 per cent. The same pattern is repeated in the case of the marginal private rate, suggesting that while considerable benefits accrue to individuals who enter elementary education, the real pay-off comes to those who complete the level by finishing grade four.

After grade four, the marginal social rate of return falls by nearly one-half, so that completing either all or even a part of senior elementary education (grades 5–7) yields only 14 per cent. Both junior secondary (grades 8–10) and senior secondary education (grades 11–12) show social rates of return of 10 per cent. Finally, the rates of return on higher education are a uniform 7–8 per cent for all additional years, which is only one-half of the rate for the last years of elementary education and one quarter of the rate for finishing the first four grades.

We would expect *private* rates of return to exceed *social* rates, because in Thailand as in most other countries, the private costs of schooling represent only a fraction of the total resource cost of education (see Table 4). Because this difference in costs comes early in life and is ordinarily considerably greater than any difference in benefits arising from personal income taxation, the private rate of return will usually be greater than the social rate.

We see in Table 5 that indeed the marginal private rates are invariably higher, often considerably higher, than the corresponding social rates.

The private rates retain approximately the same rank-order as the social rates, except that there is virtually no difference between the private rates to secondary and to higher education. Thus, at the elementary level, the private rate for completing grade 4, 49 per cent, is very nearly double the social rate, 27 per cent. Staying on to complete grades 5-7, however, shows a sharp decrease in the private rate to 18 and then to 15 per cent, which for all practical purposes is the same as the social rate of return of 14 per cent. Similarly at the secondary level, the private and social rates are essentially the same. It is difficult to imagine that the equality just noted is the outcome of a deliberate policy; it is simply that at the secondary stage of education, the proportion of educational costs borne by the State (95 per cent) just about match the taxation of higher earnings.

Finally, private rates of return for higher education are of about the same magnitude as for secondary level education; once again, however, the private rates are considerably higher than the social rates, reflecting the drastic decline in the proportion of private costs to total costs as we move up the educational ladder (see Table 4).

The *average* rates of return refer to the yield of investment into blocks of education taken as a whole. Thus, while moving from zero to one year of education yields a *marginal* social rate of 17 per cent, completing grade 4 yields an *average* rate over the four years of 20 per cent; completing seven years of elementary education as a block yields 17 per cent; completing elementary plus secondary education in 12 years yields 14 per cent; and the entire cycle up to and including higher education yields 11 per cent. Since an average rate obviously carries with it the influence of the various marginal rates, we should not be surprised to find that junior elementary schooling is the most profitable social as well as private investment (20 and 38 per cent respectively), followed by senior elementary (14 and 16 per cent), secondary (10 and 11 per cent) and finally higher education (4 and 11 per cent).

4. INTERPRETATION OF THE RATES OF RETURN

Analytically, the data in Table 5 can be used and of course misused in several ways. Remembering that our model captures only the investment aspects of education, we are interested in the relationships between the various internal rates of return to schooling, on the one hand, and between those and the rates of return on alternative investment outlets on the other. Both of these comparisons can be considered from the social and from the private point of view. Let us first consider the private calculus, involving a student (or his parents) contemplating a given educational investment decision.

The decision to take four years of elementary education is a good investment at an interest rate as high as 37 per cent; continuing through grade 7 is also profitable if capital can be borrowed at anything less than 24 per cent; indeed, because of the high returns during the early years, finishing 16 years of school through university would be profitable at an interest rate as high as 12 per cent. While the reader may construct other comparisons from the table, we may confidently conclude that Thai students have an enormous financial incentive to get through at least four years of schooling and possibly as much as seven years. It is true of course that formal capital markets ordinarily do not function well enough to enable an individual to be able to borrow directly on his future earning capacity, in Thailand or anywhere else. Nevertheless, primary education in Thailand appears to pay well enough to justify resorting to the unorganized money market that is known to prevail throughout the country, even though high interest rates are common in this market.[2] One certainly knows of cases where Thai parents are actually borrowing privately to finance their children's education, although it is impossible to know how widespread the practice is.

Turning now to the social calculus, what guidance can Table 5 provide for the educational authorities in Thailand? We may look at this problem under two assumptions. If the education budget is more or less fixed, or determined exogenously by, say, political considerations, then the problem is to optimally allocate given resources among various levels and types of schooling *within* the educational sector. Alternatively, we may consider the broader question of the allocation of resources between education and other investment sectors.

Within the educational system, Table 5 clearly suggests that resources ought to be shifted towards primary education and away from higher education. In other words, a government faced with the problem of allocating a given budget for education among the different levels of the system, so as to maximize the contribution of education to national income, should in Thai circumstances divert expenditure from the higher to the lower stages of education. This conclusion refers to numbers of students enrolled at the various levels, given the existing quality of education; it does not of course tell us what the returns would be to specific measures to improve quality. Anything which tends to increase enrolments at the elementary level and to decrease them at the secondary and higher level is a move in the right direction.

So much for investment decisions *within* the educational sector. The problem of using rate-of-return analysis as a guide to the appropriate size of the entire educational budget is much more difficult. The task of comparing rates of return among alternative social investments is fraught with difficulty, not the least of which is that rates of return are simply not available for a large variety of social investments. If the Thai government laid down minimum target rates of return for nationalized industries, which it does not, these might serve as single indicators of best alternative opportunities outside of education. If the educational system could be entirely financed by foreign loans, which is out of the question, the rates of interest that would have to be paid on such loans might again serve as indicators of alternative yields. Suffice it to say that no single rate is available to serve as a bench-mark against which to compare social rates of return on investment in education. All we can say tentatively is that, according to the figures in Table 5, an across-the-board expansion of the educational system would be justified at a cut-off rate of 11 per cent. An expansion of the first 12 grades would be justified even if the cost of capital were 14 per cent, and so forth. Since the private rate of return before tax in Thai manufacturing is almost certainly 12 to 15 per cent, it is doubtful whether an increase in the budget for education can be justified on investment grounds. Of course, education is more than an investment good, including as it does elements of consumption, sometimes serving as a cohesive force for a country as a whole and sometimes as a disintegrating force, generating social unrest. Adding in the non-pecuniary benefits of education and subtracting the non-pecuniary costs might take the argument either way. On balance, the only firm case we are left with is that concerning the reallocation of the existing educational budget.

5. OTHER COMPARISONS

Table 5 does not exhaust the information that we collected. On both the costs side and the earnings side, we distinguished between public and private schooling and between the academic and vocational streams at the secondary level. As Table 1 implies, the data were inadequate to separate private academic from public academic costs in secondary education, and thus we show only an average figure for both sectors. However, we do have separate cost figures for private vocational and public vocational schools. Similarly, with respect to earnings, our regression estimates took account of whether the respondent had attended private rather than public schools and vocational rather than academic secondary schools.

To compute the rate of return for these various combinations of school types, we match the relevant costs with the appropriate regression-adjusted earnings profiles. Table 6 compares the rate of return for private and public *academic* secondary schooling, already reported in Table 5, with the rates of return for private and public *vocational* schooling.

TABLE 6

SOCIAL AND PRIVATE RATES OF RETURN, BY TYPE OF SECONDARY EDUCATION, MEN AND WOMEN, 1970 (PER CENT)

Type and Level of Schooling	Social	Private
Public and Private Academic Secondary		
Grade 7 to 10	10	11
Grade 10 to 12	10	11
Private Vocational Secondary		
Grade 7 to 10	8	10
Grade 10 to 12	8	10
Public Vocational Secondary		
Grade 7 to 10	8	13
Grade 10 to 12	8	12

In terms of the social rate, we see that vocational schooling, whether public or private, yields a lower rate of return than does academic schooling due, in the main, to the higher costs of vocational schooling, as there is no statistically significant difference in our sample between the earnings of an academic and a vocational school graduate. This is a striking finding as vocational secondary education is now the most rapidly growing part of the Thai educational system. A whole series of manpower forecasts that were done in Thailand between 1963 and 1968 led to the conclusion that there were serious shortages of middle-level manpower in the Thai economy and hence that the priority area was secondary education [see *Blaug, 1971*]. None of these forecasts actually had much to say on the question of the appropriate mix of academic and vocational schools but somehow they were translated at the policy level into a prescription for expanding vocational rather than academic schooling. We have already seen that secondary education is not a priority area in terms of economic objectives; now we see that there is even less justification for pouring extra funds into vocational rather than academic secondary schools.

With respect to the private rates, graduates of public vocational schools may expect to earn somewhat higher rates than graduates of private vocational schools; the reason for this is simply that costs in private schools are three times as great as costs in public vocational schools (see Table 1). Private vocational schools in Thailand are second-option schools, attractive only to those who have failed to gain admission to public vocational schools. Indeed it is interesting to ask why students seek admission to vocational rather than academic schools, since it is well known that employers are generally indifferent as to the type of secondary school a worker has attended. One explanation is simply that public vocational schools are cheap for students (see Table 1). Many other comparisons could be constructed from the earnings data we have gathered. For example, if it were possible to collect more reliable data on the costs of university education in Thailand, a comparison of rates of return on higher education by fields of study and by foreign versus home degree would appear to be highly rewarding, in view of the relative magnitudes of the coefficients for these variables in our regressions. However, we shall leave this exercise for another time.

Instead, we conclude with one more illustration of what can be done with rate-of-return analysis. Let us ask whether there is any difference in the rates of return on educational investment for men for women. The crude tabulations of earnings by age and education show that women in Thailand earn much less than men at every age and at every level of education. Our regressions equations show that this is not due to any difference between men and women in family background, in type of school attended, in work status, in occupation, or in sector of employment. Nevertheless, these differences in age-earnings profiles are *not* translated into substantial rate-of-return differences. While women show somewhat lower rates (see Table 7), the differences are well within our range of measurement error (± 2 per cent). The reason for this is almost obvious: since earnings foregone as a measure of output lost constitute a major proportion of the social costs of education, particularly at the higher levels, the fact that women earn less

TABLE 7
SELECTED SOCIAL RATES OF RETURN, MEN VERSUS WOMEN, 1970 (PER CENT)

Level of Schooling	Men	Women
From 1 to 4 years	23	*
From 4 to 7 years	14	13
From 7 to 10 years	11	9
From 10 to 12 years	10	11
From 12 to 16 years	7	6
From 16 to 20 years	8	7

Note: *—not computed because sample excludes women with less than five years of schooling.

than men also means that it is cheaper in terms of resources foregone to keep a girl in school than a boy in school. It only demonstrates once again how important it is to keep in mind both costs and benefits.

6. CONCLUSIONS

All our conclusions are naturally subject to a dozen 'ifs' and 'buts'. First of all, our earnings figures are only for Greater Bangkok and not for the whole Kingdom; while this creates little bias for the secondary and higher educated categories, since most of these live and work in Greater Bangkok, it is extremely doubtful that elementary-educated farmers earn as much from cash and subsistence crops as do elementary-educated workers from employment in Greater Bangkok. This throws some doubt on our principal result, namely, the higher rates of return to elementary as against secondary and tertiary education. Secondly, our cost data with respect to higher education were derived from an analysis of budgetary accounts and not, as in the case of elementary schools, from an independent survey; it is difficult to say, however, in which direction this biases our results. Thirdly, and lastly, our regression analysis of earnings failed to provide any measure of native ability or achievement drive and it is perfectly conceivable that the inclusion of such a variable in our model would have generated quite different age-earnings profiles and hence different rates of return. Nevertheless, we do not think that all these qualifications add up to a convincing denial of our results.

Our basic conclusion is that too much is being spent on higher education and too little on elementary education; at the secondary level, too much is being spent on vocational schools and too little on academic schools. All this would not matter if there were indications that the system is now changing in such a way as to shortly redress these imbalances. But as a matter of fact, all the momentum at the present time is in the wrong direction. Constant rates of growth of elementary enrolments have characterized Thai education ever since 1960 [*Blaug, 1971*], and there are absolutely no signs to suggest that this trend will shortly be broken. Likewise, the rate of growth of higher education, although it has been strictly controlled over the last 20 years, has long exceeded that of elementary education and the recent creation of Ramkamhaeng as an open-admissions

INVESTMENT IN EDUCATION IN THAILAND 283

university suggests still higher rates of growth in the future. And again, enrolments in vocational secondary schools have recently been growing much faster than enrolments in academic secondary schools. None of these tendencies can be justified in economic terms if our rates of return are to be believed.

NOTES

1. For details, see the enlarged study, *The Rate of Return on Investment in Education in Thailand*, copies of which are available on application to the National Education Council, Sukothai Road, Bangkok, Thailand.

2. The basic source on urban and rural interest rates in Thailand is Rozental (1969). The variance in the distribution of interest rates is much larger in poor than in rich countries and all we do here is to suggest the range in which the figures lie. Commercial banks in Thailand pay a maximum of 7 per cent on deposits but charge 15 per cent to ordinary borrowers. Even the rate of 15 per cent is well below much higher rates prevailing in the unorganized money market. The ultimate financing of capital formation in Thailand is done chiefly via the formal capital market but about a fifth of aggregate capital formation is in fact financed through the unorganized sector. Many firms that borrow from family or friends pay an annual rate of interest in excess of 24 per cent, the rate which is considered to be the 'prime unorganized market rate' for secured business loans. For personal loans, rates range from 2 per cent per month on loans from friends to 10 per cent per month from pawn-shops, goldshops, and rotating credit societies (Phia Huey), that is from 35-240 per cent per annum if the load is paid off on a monthly basis and from 18-120 per cent if the repayments are made once a year. It is easy to see, therefore, that one can make literally no general statement about the rate at which parents can borrow.

REFERENCES

Blaug, M., 1965, 'The Rate of Return on Investment in Education in Great Britain', *The Manchester School*, September, reprinted in M. Blaug, ed., *The Economics of Education, 1*, London, Penguin Books, 1969.

Blaug, M., R. Layard, and M. Woodhall, 1969, *The Causes of Graduate Unemployment in India*, London, Allen Lane, The Penguin Press.

Blaug, M., 1970, *An Introduction to the Economics of Education*, London, Penguin Books.

Blaug, M., 1971, 'Manpower Forecasting in Thailand', *Journal of Development Studies*, October.

Blaug, M., 1974, 'An Economic Analysis of Personal Earnings in Thailand', *Economic Development and Cultural Change*, October.

Carnoy, M., 1971, 'Class Analysis and Investment in Human Resources: A Dynamic Model', *Review of Radical Political Economy*, Fall/Winter.

Denison, E. F., 1962, *The Sources of Economic Growth in the U.S. and The Alternatives Before Us*, New York, CED.

Lee Hansen, W., 1963, 'Total and Private Rates of Return to Investment in Schooling', *Journal of Political Economy*, reprinted in M. Blaug, ed., *The Economics of Education, 1*, London, Penguin Books, 1969.

Nalla Gounden, A. M., 1967, 'Investment in Education in India', *Journal of Human Resources*, Summer.

Psacharopoulos, G., K. Hinchliffe, 1973, *Returns to Education*, Amsterdam, Elsevier Publishing Company.

Rozenthal, A. A., 1969, *Finance and Development in Thailand*, New York, Frederick A. Praeger.

Williamson, J. G., De Voretz, D. J., 1969, 'Education as an Asset in the Philippines', *Philippine Population in the Seventies*, ed., M.B. Concepcion, Manila, Community Publishers.

[16]

ECONOMICS OF EDUCATION IN DEVELOPING
COUNTRIES:
CURRENT TRENDS AND NEW PRIORITIES

Mark Blaug

The golden days of the economics of education in developing countries are over. In the 1950s and 1960s, economists were thick on the ground in every ministry of education in every capital city of Asia, Africa and Latin America. Those were the days when all the indicators pointed towards the rapid expansion of educational systems at all levels and when economists were welcomed for producing new arguments to support an educational inflation that was, anyway, desired on political grounds. What did it matter that manpower forecasting was crude and that cost-benefit analysis was based on rather implausible assumptions when, in fact, they led to answers that called for still more education? No one likes to look a gift horse in the mouth and politicians are always thankful for all the help they can get. Economists who still remember those days have reason to look back at them with nostalgia.

To be an economist interested in education in the 1970s is not quite so easy. The streets of Calcutta, Karachi, Cairo, Accra, Bogota and Buenos Aires are filled with unemployed university graduates, even as the civil services in these countries are overstocked with graduates. In Africa, the so-called 'school leaver problem', which only ten years ago referred exclusively to unemployed leavers from 'primary' schools, now designates the unemployed products of secondary as well as primary schools. In the famous Addis Ababa Conference of 1961, African Ministers of Education looked forward confidently to universal primary education by 1980. 1980 is only one year away and yet in more than half of the forty six countries in tropical Africa it is now perfectly obvious that universal primary education will not be achieved even by the year 2000. Everywhere there is deep dissatisfaction with the quality of education; the curriculum, the examination system, the standards of teacher training, *et cetera*. There must be something wrong with an educational system that encourages students to gear all their efforts to the passing of examinations, leading to the next cycle of education and still more examinations, for the sole purpose of gaining entry into

Lecture given by the author at the Max-Planck-Institut für Bildungsforschung, Berlin, 14 September 1977, on the occasion of Professor Friedrich Edding's Emeritierung.

wage employment in the modern sector of the economy, particularly as so many of them will never in fact achieve this goal. Ivan Illich's books appear to be addressed to audiences in advanced countries and yet his thoroughly subversive ideas of 'de-schooling' have not fallen entirely on deaf ears in developing countries. The new American theories of screening, namely, that educational certificates serve no other function than to discriminate between individuals in terms of achievement drive, adds strength to the impact of Illich's writings. The 'diploma disease' may be a world-wide phenomenon[1] but, surely, it is Third World countries that are really obsessed by 'credentialism'?

New Priorities

The new circumstances of the 1970s have produced new priorities in educational planning. No longer are ministries of education solely preoccupied with the building of more schools to accommodate ever larger enrolments and with the expansion of teacher-training facilities to equip the new schools with more teachers. Nowadays educational plans in the Third World consist largely of ambitious schemes:

a) to introduce work experience into the primary school curriculum;

b) to integrate adults with children in a more flexible system of first-stage education;

c) to vocationalise the curriculum of secondary schools;

d) to introduce a mandatory period of labour market experience between secondary and higher education;

e) to recruit the dropouts of the educational system into a national youth employment service.

Everywhere there is an interest in reforming the examination system so as to minimise the testing of academic achievement and to maximise the testing of natural aptitudes that cannot be acquired by rote learning. Some countries have begun to introduce geographical quotas as a basis for educational selection and there is even talk of imitating the Chinese by using social quotas in terms of family background. If the slogans of the 1960s were 'universal primary education', 'manpower planning' and 'investment in human capital', the slogans of the 1970s are 'basic education', 'earning while learning', 'lifelong education' and 'aptitude testing instead of examinations'.

In such an atmosphere, the arguments of economists appear to be both unnecessary and irrelevant. Must we conclude, therefore, that it is time for economists to quit the field of educational planning, leaving it instead to sociologists, political scientists, and even educationists? My answer to that question is no. I do believe that economists still have valuable lessons to impart to educational planners around the world. However, it is true that many of these lessons will be harder to teach than the old ones, more easily resisted than the lessons of yesterday, more politically dangerous to implement than the re-

[1] R Dore, *The Diploma Disease: Education, Qualification and Development*. London: Allen & Unwin. 1976.

commendations of ten years ago. I hope to make my point by a few illustrations. I have selected three illustrations of the power of economic reasoning to illuminate the issues of educational planning in the 1970s. The first harks back to the concerns of the 1960s; it is the way education in Third World countries is still financed so as to produce relative over-subsidisation of higher education and relative under-subsidisation of primary education. The second relates to the slogan of 'earning while learning' in the context of the new World Bank-sponsored promotion of the concept of 'basic education'. The third is the issue of educational reform when it is unaccompanied, as it almost always is, by reform of the labour market. It is not difficult to show that economists have valuable things to say about all three issues and, moreover, that the insights they bring to bear on these issues are easily missed by non-economists. In that sense, economists still have a contribution to make to educational planning in poor countries.

Higher Education vs. Primary Education

If you take a very broad historical look at some of the most prominent advanced countries that fifty or sixty years ago were underdeveloped, say, Japan and the Soviet Union, you will discern the following pattern: the typical picture of the expansion of education (in the case of Japan since about 1890, in the case of the Soviet Union since the Revolution) reveals a policy of first reaching universal primary education and holding back secondary and higher education. Then, having almost reached universal primary education (in Japan around 1912, in Russia around 1930) a more generous attitude was taken towards secondary education, while higher education was still kept tightly under control. Only when secondary education had become almost universal in these countries (in the case of Japan about 1930, in the case of the Soviet Union about 1950) was higher education allowed to expand. This classic pattern of allowing the educational pyramid to grow at the base and, only when the base has expanded substantially, to allow it to grow in the middle and at the apex, has been completely reversed in the Third World since the Second World War. Ever since 1950, in practically every one of the one hundred or so developing countries in the world, secondary education and higher education have grown faster than primary education both in terms of enrolments and in terms of educational expenditures. Or, to express the same thought in other words: secondary and particularly higher educated manpower have been over-produced in most of African, Asian and Latin American countries beyond all possible hopes of absorbing them in gainful employment, whatever the feasible rates of future economic growth in these countries. Therefore, the first priority in educational planning in the Third World is somehow to reduce the rates of growth of secondary and higher education, shifting resources from the upper to the lower levels of the educational system.

What is the evidence for such a bold assertion? It is evidence of three kinds. Firstly, there is fairly clear evidence of growing open unemployment of secondary and higher educated individuals throughout Africa and Asia.[2] Secondly, there is the fact that recent forecasts of manpower requirements in Third World countries are increasingly yielding predictions of middle level and higher level manpower surpluses rather than shortages in the decade to come. Thirdly, there is evidence that the social rate of return on investment in education is almost always lower in secondary and higher education than in primary education.

Enrolment Dilemma

One may quarrel about the reliability of unemployment statistics in developing countries. One may dismiss the technique of manpower forecasting as little more than guesswork dressed up in numbers. One may likewise throw doubt on rate of return analysis for relying too much on monetary earnings as a measure of the economic contribution of education. One may also point to certain countries, such as Burma, Mali, Botswana, Bolivia and Ecuador that continue to face serious shortages of middle level and particularly higher level manpower. But, by and large, in these three continents as a whole, it is true to say that all the indicators point towards the past over-expansion of the upper levels of the educational system and a concomitant under-investment in the lower levels. Even if we went no further than to take the planning targets of these countries themselves, the point would still remain valid. For example, primary enrolments in Africa in 1977 were well below the Addis Ababa targets set in 1962, whereas enrolments in secondary and tertiary education are now well above the original planned targets. Most of the over-expansion in higher education in Africa has so far been disguised by underemployment of university graduates in the public sector, in consequence of which over-expansion of education in Africa has only shown up dramatically to date in the form of open unemployment among secondary school leavers. But now that many African government are beginning to be unwilling to absorb university graduates in the civil service, owing to increasing fiscal pressures, we can expect to see Africa following Asia in massive open unemployment of university graduates alongside continuously increasing open unemployment of secondary school leavers.

Many countries are now agreed that current rates of growth of secondary and higher education cannot be allowed to continue, although very few have gone so far as the Philippines in asserting that these rates of growth will *not* be allowed to continue. Some countries, such as Tanzania, Zambia and Egypt, even agree that primary education should be expanded at the expense of the growth of secondary and higher education; that is that resources are to be reallocated from the top to the bottom of the educational system. But all this is easier said than done. Public opinion throughout the Third World is firmly opposed to enrolment ceilings and, in these circumstances, it would be suicidal for a politician to

[2] For these and other similar assertions in the text that follows, see UN-ECAFE, *Economic Survey of Asia and the Far East 1973, Part 1 Education and Employment*. Bangkok: UN-ECAFE, 1974, and UN-ECA, *Economic Survey of Africa 1977, Part 1 Education and Employment*. Addis Ababa: UN-ECA, 1978.

ECONOMICS OF EDUCATION IN DEVELOPING COUNTRIES   77

demand quantitative restrictions on secondary and higher education. Moreover, most Third World governments are deeply committed to the principle of higher education as a right and not a privilege for all those who are properly qualified, and this commitment militates against the attempt to clamp down on the growth of higher education. Moreover, there is an equally firm commitment to *free* higher education, including the cost of residence and out-of-pocket expenses of attendance, even if some governments have not yet been able to fully implement that commitment. This commitment to free higher education in fact denies a government the lever of increased tuition fees as a device for discouraging youngsters from going on to higher education.

Pressures on Governments

Although governments may seek to curtail the growth of enrolments simply by setting ceilings on admissions or expenditure limits on new buildings, experience has shown how easily such government plans may be abandoned in the face of strong public demand for more places. To achieve success, therefore, it is necessary to supplement direct with indirect measures. One such indirect measure is higher tuition fees combined with a limited number of scholarships for poor students from the backward regions and a student loans scheme for all students, to be financed by a special graduate tax on future incomes. Some African countries, such as Tanzania and Ethiopia, and some Asian countries, such as Sri Lanka, have begun to draw the attention of the public to the fact that university students are frequently a privileged elite, who ought not to demand higher education at state expense as a right; to have survived long enough in the educational system to qualify for entry into higher education, their parents are very likely to have been well-to-do and so might be expected to make some financial contribution to their children's higher education. Indeed, a survey of the social composition of students in higher education in Third World countries would reveal in most countries that the average university student is, to put it mildly, much better off than the average taxpayer, not to mention the average peasant or urban worker. So long as this is true, *free* higher education is a form of regressive taxation which makes a mockery of the policy of egalitarianism to which most Third World governments are dedicated.[3]

We can control secondary and higher education directly by admission ceilings, or indirectly by higher private costs. But there are still subtler indirect means of making secondary and higher education less attractive to students. For example, the ILO Kenya Report recommended postponement of entry into university courses by two or three years, with eventual admission being conditioned on evidence of work experience and community service. Since then, the idea of postponed entry into higher education has been taken up elsewhere, as in Tanzania, Zambia, Ethiopia, and Sri Lanka. There is hardly any doubt that

[3] G Psacharopoulos, 'The Perverse Effects of Public Subsidization of Education or How Equitable is Free Education?'. *Comparative Education Review 1977*, a development of this theme.

postponed entry, particularly for a period as long as two or three years, would serve to discourage some students from taking up higher education who otherwise would have done so, not to mention its effect in strengthening the motivation of students who did re-enter the educational system.

Narrowing Skill Differentials

A more potent indirect means of reducing the attractiveness of upper secondary and higher education is that of squeezing earnings differentials in labour markets. The ILO, Sri Lanka, and Kenya Mission Reports made a number of suggestions for reducing the private returns to education as, for example, the proposal in the Kenya Report that entry points on public pay scales should be reduced by 25 per cent for a five year period, after which entry points should no longer be defined in terms of formal education; however, this suggestion was not accepted by the Government of Kenya. Nevertheless, the Kenyan Government did accept the principle of working towards a narrowing of skill differentials in the years ahead. Incomes policies, to use a widely accepted shorthand, are now a regular feature of economic policy in a number of Third World countries and, although they are rarely designed to deal expressly with the problem of depressing the relative earnings of university graduates, they all have the effect of doing so. Nevertheless, even a general incomes policy that narrows earnings differentials in labour markets, and thus effectively saps the private incentive to acquire higher education, is not enough unless accompanied by specific changes in public sector hiring practices. As a principal employer of the bulk of educated people, Asian and African governments in particular share a heavy responsibility for the excessive growth of the upper levels of the educational system. Throughout the two continents, they tie salary scales rigidly to educational qualifications, they promote by age almost automatically, with little resort to performance rating; they fail to prove job titles and fail to practise scientific job evaluations; and they invariably provide generous fringe benefits and absolute tenure of employment. Even if they paid graduates no more than secondary school leavers, this would be enough to create a large demand for university education. In short, the recruitment and promotion policies of the public sector in Asia and Africa have done much to foster diploma disease. Large salary differentials and free, or almost free, university education have done the rest.

The case for expanding primary education at the maximum possible rate is as strong on economic grounds as it is on social and political grounds. There is some scope for cost-saving measures in primary education itself but these could finance only a small part of the expansion required to achieve universal primary education. The bulk of the resources will have to come from the contraction of secondary and higher education. And as long as a year of higher education costs a hundred times as much as a year of primary education, a median figure for Africa and Asia, even a marginal shift of resources from tertiary to primary education could work wonders in increasing enrolments in first level education. It has been calculated that in six African countries, primary enrolment ratios

ECONOMICS OF EDUCATION IN DEVELOPING COUNTRIES   79

could be raised to 100 per cent overnight merely by shifting 20 per cent of current educational expenditure on secondary or higher education to primary education. To achieve such a shifting of resources throughout the Third World remains a primary objective of educational planning.

Educational Reforms and Basic Education

I contend that universal primary education in Asia, Africa and Latin America cannot be achieved unless the locomotive of higher education can somehow be slowed down. There are some, however, who hold out an alternative course of action. The World Bank has recently been arguing that universal primary education in developing countries can only be achieved by providing a new flexible, low cost education called 'basic education' as a supplement to standard primary schooling, so that those children and adults who have failed to gain access to the existing system will nevertheless be provided with the 3Rs plus some minimum functional skills. Some, if not all, of the elements of 'basic education' are already taught in many developing countries in a wide variety of non-formal education programmes. Education that is provided in farmers' training centres, community education centres, rural education centres, literacy programmes, and even settlement schemes, includes important elements of 'basic education' as described above.

The growing disillusionment with the quality of primary and secondary schooling, together with the impossibility in many countries of ever absorbing all their products in the modern sector, have increased the appeal of basic education programmes. Basic education has the advantage of being designable to fit the specific needs of rural communites. It can be shorter, more functional and, it is argued, cheaper than the education that is provided within the orthodox school system. Since basic education courses generally do not involve certification of students, it is widely believed that they represent a means whereby useful attitudes and skills can be developed without at the same time encouraging aspirations for gainful employment in the modern sector.

But there are real dangers in the basic education approach. The establishment of a dual education system, comprising standard schools and colleges for a minority of the population and basic education programmes for the rest, would run directly counter to the aim of equality of educational opportunity. Governments following such a strategy are open to the charge that their policies are institutionalising existing inequalities between social groups in the community. This is indeed the major reason why, historically, approaches very similar to basic education have generally failed in Africa and elsewhere. Though the basic education programme may be popular in its early stages, students and parents quickly come to regard such schemes as a temporary expedient that should be replaced by primary schooling at a later date. If this does not happen, basic education soon becomes a symbol of discrimination against rural people and the programme begins to collapse.

Besides, it is very doubtful that basic education would in fact be cheaper than the rock bottom costs of an ordinary primary school. A teacher facing a mixed class of children and adults would have to be more experienced or better trained than the average primary schoolteacher, and would therefore be more expensive. Most primary schools in Africa do not in fact succeed in teaching children more than reading, writing, and arithmetic, yet basic schools are supposed to achieve that, in addition to knowledge required for running a household and bringing up a family, not to mention functional rural skills. This suggests a fairly diversified programme of a terminal nature and it is difficult to believe that such a programme could be organised, staffed and housed in rural areas at a cost below that of a modest primary school. Even if this were possible, it strains credulity to believe that it would be an equally effective education.

Basic Education Drive

Despite all these arguments against basic education, many governments in Asia and Africa are undoubtedly attracted by the general thinking that lies behind the drive for basic education. Algeria, Tanzania, Zambia and India are all reforming their educational systems to include large elements of the basic education philosophy. On a less comprehensive scale Upper Volta, Senegal, Ethiopia and Sri Lanka have instituted experimental basic education programmes for out-of-school youths which emphasise vocational subjects. Community schools, that is, self-sufficient rural schools that are closely linked to their local communities, are being developed in a range of countries, including Ghana, Zaire and Tanzania. A theme that recurs again and again in all these reforms is the view that education and production ought to be closely linked and indeed that the school should become a productive unit. This is generally seen as having two advantages. On the one hand, the integration of education and production, and particularly the possibility that schools can begin to market products for sale, means that some of the costs of running the schools can be subsidised by this production and hence that the total costs of expanding the school system can be greatly reduced. On the other hand, the integration of education and production is expected to discourage the attitude of students which leads them away from rural areas in search of wage employment in the cities. In short, it is hoped these new type of schools will minimise the alienation of students from their home community and will encourage aspirations for self-help and community work.

Within the more traditional schools, curricula are being reformed to reflect the environment of the home country rather than the culture and society of the metropolitan countries. Textbook and teaching materials are to be produced locally, and indeed in some countries it is envisaged, perhaps somewhat unrealistically, that the content of the curriculum will vary from region to region to reflect local social and economic circumstances. There are also significant moves away from traditional methods of selection in many Third World countries. In order to minimise the examination orientation of students and in order to get them to take the vocational aspects of the curriculum more seriously, there is increasing experimentation with aptitude testing, with continuous assessment, and in some countries with peer group selection methods for continuation within the formal educational systems. It is expected that these or similar changes will result in a significant change in student attitudes and behaviour.

Welcome Reforms

Many of these reforms are to be welcomed on strictly educational grounds. Nevertheless, it may be doubted whether they will succeed in having a dramatic impact on the school-leaver problem and, in particular, whether they will succeed in halting the pressures for expanding upper-secondary and higher education. The trouble with all these reforms is that every one of them increases the demand made upon teachers in Third World countries. The strength of the orthodox system, at least as far as the teachers were concerned, was that it laid down very strictly the specific information that had to be mastered by students if they were to be successful, both in terms of promotion within the education system and more generally in society at large. The vocationalisation of the curricula, the decentralisation of syllabuses, the integration of production and education, the move away from examinations, all require teachers who are enthusiastic, innovative and highly trained. When we consider the typical rural teacher in an African primary school who has himself had no more than primary education, it is difficult to believe that he will prove equal to the task that will be imposed upon him by the new educational reforms. Even the in-service teacher training courses that are currently planned by Third World governments about to engage on major educational reforms may fail to equip the teaching cadre with the skills and confidence it needs to implement the reforms in question. It is this which may prove to be the Achilles' heel of this new wave of educational reform in Asia and Africa.

A further critical variable concerns the earnings that regularly accrue to persons with advanced levels of schooling in developing countries. The appeal of standard examinations, for example, stems not merely from the wish of students to achieve entrance to higher education. Rather, it derives from the very high earnings and status associated with jobs to which higher levels of education give access. While changes in examination and in systems of selection may be expected to bring educational benefits, it is unrealistic to suppose that such changes will make people content to accept work at very low incomes in rural areas if they believe themselves to be eligible for highly paid urban jobs. In short, as long as employers continue to use the level of education attained as the main criterion for hiring recruits into first jobs, and as long as the existing income differentials between the highest and worst paid jobs in the occupational hierarchy remain what they are, the phenomena of educated unemployment and underemployment in Asia, Africa and Latin America is unlikely to be more than marginally affected by even major changes in the qualitative aspects of education.

Labour Market Reforms

When an economist examines the comprehensive educational reforms that are now under way in a large number of Asian and African countries, he gains the overwhelming impression that the direct links between the educational system and the labour market are still not adequately appreciated in developing countries. Again and again, he will witness countries overhauling their entire educational system without taking steps to alter the prevailing salary differentials by levels of schooling. Even when such countries pursue an incomes policy designed to restrain the upward movement of wages and salaries, no effort is made to monitor and publicise the squeezing of differentials that such a policy frequently entails, as if levels were everything and differentials nothing. There may be circumstances in which governments are powerless to affect the general pattern of rewards in the labour market, at least in the short run, but any government in, say, Africa can in fact make significant inroads on the rewards of educated people merely by altering its own hiring and promotion practices for the simple reason that African governments are generally the principal employers of the products of secondary and tertiary educational institutions.

The neglect of the intimate connection between educational developments and labour market trends is seen once again in the failure in country after country to couple curriculum reform with examination reform. Examinations perform many functions: they provide students with psychological incentives to study; they furnish teachers with an implicit curriculum; they rank students for purposes of admission to the next stage of education; and they certify the competence of students for purposes of selection by employers. To reform a curriculum without simultaneously reforming the examinations that test knowledge and understanding of the curriculum is not only to doom that reform; it is to doom all later attempts at reform because it creates cynicism among both teachers and students about the pronouncements of the educational authorities.

Teachers' Difficulties

The tendency to regard curriculum matters in isolation of examination problems betrays a curious disregard of the real difficulties of teachers in Third World classrooms: the students frequently come from homes in which the parents are illiterate; if the classroom is in rural areas, the students are likely to stay away during the peak periods of the agricultural cycle; many students come from far away and are kept home during the rainy season; few students will have textbooks and even stationery is scarce; the teachers themselves are inadequately prepared, and if all this were not enough, the curriculum is being constantly changed and is frequently so top-heavy that it cannot be taught in the available hours. If, in addition, large portions of the curriculum are not examined, teachers can only survive by ignoring the explicit curriculum, teaching instead merely to pass examinations. No doubt, all this is well known to every Ministry of Education in Asia, Africa, and Latin America. Nevertheless, it is depressing

ECONOMICS OF EDUCATION IN DEVELOPING COUNTRIES   83

to see how frequently one finds instances of examination reform trailing years behind curriculum reform, while in others the entire educational system is overturned without hardly a reference to changes in teacher training. I would suggest that qualitative reform of the educational system should begin and not end with the teacher problem, and it should start with examination reform and only thereafter should it consider reform of the curriculum.

Throughout the world, the school system performs the function of selecting people for occupations. This is of course only one of its functions but there is no doubt that it is everywhere one of its principal functions. But the relationship between schooling and jobs is more explicit and direct in the Third World than in the First or Second. Why this is so is a question for another article, but that it is so is not to be doubted. For that reason the solution of the so-called employment problem of educated people in Third World countries requires the effective loosening of the much too close ties between educational certificates and paid jobs. I doubt that these ties can be entirely broken because they exist, as I have said, the world over. But if earning capacities could be made to depend more on individual initiative and ability than on educational qualifications, and if general culture could become a product of schooling that is almost as important as vocationally useful skills, the school leaver problem in Africa and the graduate unemployment problem in Asia and Latin America would virtually disappear. In other words, the question is not how to gear education to employment opportunities, which is the way the problem is usually expressed, but how to stop education being geared willy-nilly to employment opportunities of the type that is represented by white collar jobs in the formal sector.

No Single Panacea

I know of no single panacea that will bring this about but it is clear that what is needed is a comprehensive strategy that simultaneously attacks the quantitative structure of the educational pyramid, the sharing of costs between students and the state, the qualitative content of schooling, the recruitment and promotion practices of the labour market, and the structure of wages and salaries of educated people. Elements of this strategy exist here and there in the Third World, and many of them can be found in certain innovative countries like Tanzania and Cuba. But I know of no developing country that has marched on all fronts in attacking these problems, and which can therefore serve as a model for the rest of the Third World. In short, there is still something left for economists to say on educational planning in poor countries, and some of the lessons that economists can teach are absolutely fundamental in their implications for government policy.

Name Index

Abramovitz, Moses, 29
Adams, W., 18
Adkin, Douglas, 109
Ahamad, Bashir, 132
Anderson, C. Arnold, 61
Arrow, Kenneth, J., 58, 85, 119
Ashenfelter, Orley, 302, 318, 329

Bakke Edward W., 66
Baldwin, George B., 67
Balogh, Thomas, 11, 21, 24
Beales, A.C.F., 260
Becker, Gary S., 8, 12, 13, 15, 16,
  20, 21, 23, 33, 35, 36, 41, 78, 100,
  102, 104, 105, 106, 109, 110, 112,
  114, 118, 119, 129, 320
Bengston, J., 145, 147
Ben-Porath, Yoram, 113
Benson, Charles S., 100
Berg, Ivar, 87-9
Bibby, John, 302, 318
Billings, B.B., 156
Blanehard, William, 306
Blau, Peter M., 116
Blaug, Mark, x, 56, 60, 62, 69, 70,
  77, 85, 87, 91, 94, 100, 101, 104,
  105, 109, 111, 115, 119, 129, 132,
  213, 214, 228, 229, 231, 237, 250,
  259, 270, 276, 281, 283, 284, 303,
  307, 331, 332, 333, 339, 343, 344
Bloom, Benjamin S., 132
Blume, Stuart S., 238
Bombach, Gustav, 58
Bos, H.C., 74
Bowen, Howard R., 229, 236
Bowen, William, G., 4, 16, 19, 62
Bowles, Samuel S., 75, 116, 130-32,
  302, 318
Bowman, Mary Jean, 4, 23, 31,
  32, 61, 72, 102, 113
Brazer, Herman F., 6, 301, 318
Bridge, R.G., 132
Burkhead, Jesse, 24
Burton Jr., John. F., 86

Cain, Glen C., 135
Campbell, John M., 113
Campbell, Robert, 106
Capron, W.M., 58, 85
Carnegie Commission, 113, 154, 210
Carnoy, Martin, 114, 130, 136, 302,
  318, 334
Carroll, A.B., 302, 318
Cartter, Alan, M., 72
Cerych, Ladislav, 231
Charnsuphrindr, Pichai, x
Chiswick, Barry R., 118, 119
Chow, G.C., 303
Clune, W., 260
Cohen, D.K., 260
Cohen, W.J., 6, 318
Cohn, Elchanan, 132, 205, 208, 229
Colclough, Christopher, x
Cole, Charles C., 6
Conlisk, John, 116, 188, 205, 206,
  213
Coons, J., 260
Cooper, Michael M., 105
Correa, Hector, 74
Council of Europe, 174, 175
Crean, John F., 206, 210
Crew, Michael, 190, 244
Crossley, J.R., 86
Crowther, George, 6
Crowther-Hunt, Lord, 178
Culyer, Anthony, 105
Curtis, Thomas D., 113

Daly, Ann, 232, 234
David, Martin H., 6, 12, 301
Davis, J. Ronnie, 229
De Haven, J.C., 28
Denison, Edward, vii, 13, 29, 30, 35,
  36, 91, 92, 104, 115, 129, 232, 332
Department of Education and
  Science, U.K., 152, 153, 179, 181,
  182, 213, 221, 222, 249
De Voretz, D.J., 291, 292, 293, 333
DeWitt, Nicholas, 67

Subject Index

Ability, measures of, 116-17
Active manpower policy, 66
Adult education, 153, 156

Basic education, 352-54

Capital market imperfections, 230
Consumption, of education, 16-18
Costs, of higher education, 236-37, 267; of elementary and secondary education, 334-37
Cost-benefit analysis, 24
Credentialism, *see* Screening hypothesis

Demand, for education, 102-3, 106-9, 296; for labour, 119, 133, 137
Diploma disease, 347
Discounted cash flow approach, 7

Earnings, current versus lifetime, 19-23
Earnings differentials, 351-52
Earnings foregone, 23-5, 103, 171, 343-44
Earnings function, 105, 115-18
Economic growth, and education, 29-31, 119, 138, 231-32
Economics of education, as a subject, 129-30, 346-48
Education, in India, 265-75
Educational planning, vii, 50-75, 268, 279, 347
Educational production functions, 132
Equity arguments, 231, 240, 246-47, 252, 272
External benefits of education, 32-9, 185-86, 213, 228-30, 271-72, 284, 293

Fringe benefits, 305, 319
Forecasts versus projections, 52-3, 68

Health economics, 105, 233
Higher education, definition of, 7
Human capital theory, vii, 3-49, 101-23, 301; *see* Rate-of-return analysis

Income distribution, and education, 130, 188-90, 204-23
Incomplete employment contract, 135-36

Job design, 112

Labour market segmentation, 106, 136-37
Labour markets, competitive or not, 25-8, 78-86, 96-7; internal, 120, 133-34; reforms of, 355
Longitudinal data, 117

Maintenance grants, in UK, 219-23
Manpower forecasting, 47-8, 50, 51-2, 54, 55, 56, 58, 59-60, 62, 64, 66-75, 130, 132, 288-90, 343, 350
Market failures, 228-30
Methodological individualism, 103
Methodology of economics, 101, 106, 122
Migration, of labour, 105

Nonpecuniary benefits, of education, 18-9, 111

Occupational choice, 112
Occupational classifications, 69-70, 80, 119
Open University, 153, 160-61
Overexpansion, of higher education, ix, 240, 294, 297, 348-52
Overseas student fees, 179

Paid educational leave, 154-55, 159-60
Private versus public education, ix, 197-203

362